MANAGING
GERIATRIC
HEALTH
SERVICES

Edited by:

Alice E. McDonnell, DrPH, MPA, RN

Professor of Gerontology and Health Services Administration
Director of Administrative Studies
Public Administration, Health Services Administration, and Gerontology Program
School of Social Work and Administrative Studies
College of Health and Human Services
Marywood University
Scranton, Pennsylvania
Consultant, Interim Healthcare, Northeastern Pennsylvania

JONES & BARTLETT
LEARNING

World Headquarters
Jones & Bartlett Learning
5 Wall Street
Burlington, MA 01803
978-443-5000
info@jblearning.com
www.jblearning.com

Jones & Bartlett Learning books and products are available through most bookstores and online booksellers. To contact Jones & Bartlett Learning directly, call 800-832-0034, fax 978-443-8000, or visit our website, www.jblearning.com.

Production Credits
Publisher: Michael Brown
Editorial Assistant: Chloe Falivene
Production Assistant: Leia Poritz
Senior Marketing Manager: Sophie Fleck
   Teague
Manufacturing and Inventory Control
   Supervisor: Amy Bacus

Composition: Abella Publishing Services
Cover Design: Kristin E. Parker
Cover Image: © silver-john/ShutterStock, Inc.
Printing and Binding: Edwards Brothers Malloy
Cover Printing: Edwards Brothers Malloy

Library of Congress Cataloging-in-Publication Data
McDonnell, Alice.
  Managing geriatric health services / Alice McDonnell.
    p. ; cm.
  Includes bibliographical references and index.
  ISBN 978-1-4496-0460-8 (pbk.) -- ISBN 1-4496-0460-9 (pbk.)
  I. Title.
  [DNLM: 1. Health Services for the Aged. 2. Aged. 3. Long-Term Care--organization & administration. 4. Quality of Health Care--standards. WT 31]

  618.97'023--dc23
                2012009502

6048

Printed in the United States of America
16 15 14 13 12   10 9 8 7 6 5 4 3 2 1

Contents

PART II   SPECIAL TOPICS 145

Chapter 7   **Financing Long-Term Care** 147
James Pettinato, MHSA, RN

Chapter 8   **Meeting Spiritual and Religious Needs in Long-Term Care** 173
Sr. Gail Cabral, IHM, PhD

Chapter 9   **Meeting Psychological Needs in Long-Term Care** . . . 191
Sr. Gail Cabral, IHM, PhD

Preface

For several years, we have needed a textbook for our course, Gerontological Health Services Administration. This textbook is a timely answer, covering multiple aspects of administration in long-term care and community settings. As a growing field of study due to our ongoing number of older individuals requiring services, leadership is essential in the provision and coordination of care. In addition, the role of disciplines/professionals is important to understand our interdisciplinary team requirements to meet all regulations. This text is presented in three parts. Part I is six chapters covering the roles of key professionals. Part II includes eight chapters covering special topics identified as being critical in understanding the implications of gerontology and geriatrics health services administration. Finally, Part III presents interdisciplinary case studies, giving readers the opportunity for application. The material in this book is valuable to practicing professionals, including administrators and students.

In the first chapter, "Administration Within Long-Term Care," I discuss the role of administrators in the field and introduce a new model. Based on a survey of administrators, responses are summarized allowing students to see how administrators respond to their organizational culture. Chapter 2, written by a professor in nursing and gerontology, covers the standards required for nurse administrators in the field. In Chapter 3, with assistance from Sneh Akruvala, graduate student, I review the role of physical, speech, and occupational therapists including credentialing requirements. A professor of social work has written Chapter 4, summarizing all aspects of social work in the field. Chapter 5 discusses the importance of nutrition and dietetics in care of the older population from experiences of two professors in nutrition and dietetics. In Chapter 6, Dr. Parker-Bell and her colleague, Sister Mariam Pfeifer, have looked at creative art therapies and music therapy and their value as services in gerontology, including requirements for practice by their professional organizations.

Part II: Special Topics starts with Chapter 7 discussing all aspects of financing, a complex process understood by the author, an instructor and administrator. Chapters 8 and 9 are written by Sister Gail Cabral, a professor in psychology and a spiritual leader in the field. Dr. Cabral discusses aspects of spirituality in working with the aged in Chapter 8. Chapter 9 further discusses psychological needs in long-term care. Her experience as a professor and her own personal experiences with the aged will engage the students in learning about these critical aspects of caring for our patients/clients. Chapter 10 is a most interesting chapter covering Dr. Parker-Bell's research in caring for our dementia population. She has conducted research in how nurses feel about caring for our demented residents based on her interviews with nurses and administrators. Dr. Parker-Bell further addresses the human resource concerns regarding staffing, recruitment, and turnover. Chapter 11 covers a very important aspect of care, quality, written by Joe Lyons, a Health Services Administration professor, assisted by Dr. Kathleen Healy-Karabell, a nursing professor. Students and administrators will better understand quality with an enhanced awareness after reading this chapter. Chapter 12 on oral histories brings an important perspective for both students and administrators. Dr. Munley has worked with our program participants to understand both the purpose and process of oral histories. As part of our gerontology curriculum she teaches a class on oral histories, and as a historian her enthusiasm is demonstrated in this chapter. Chapter 13 covers a very important aspect of care, ethics. Dr. Hasemann has contributed widely to this special topic based on her experience as a consultant in long-term care and her membership on ethics committees. She offers some very thoughtful points related to the issue. Chapter 14 discusses end-of-life concerns, issues, and programs. This important aspect of the aging population is based on my professional and personal experiences, including authoring a hospice book. Mr. William Miller, a doctoral candidate and graduate assistant, has assisted in the writing.

Finally, this publication concludes with Part III, providing interdisciplinary case studies, discussion questions, and responses from healthcare professionals. This model of presentation has been very effective for interprofessional education. Dr. Arscott, a physician, developed this section based on her experiences working with the interdisciplinary model, which includes a holistic approach as well as administrative issues.

The case studies are intended to be utilized by faculty to create a discussion by applying the material from the text. Information for answering each question is included in the chapters. Each chapter is a resource for case study discussion. Dr. Arscott interviewed all contributors for feedback relative to the case studies. It is our hope that the case studies will be helpful to faculty and students and administrators in an analytical approach to geriatric health services administration.

By providing learning objectives, key terms with definitions, summaries, and discussion questions, each chapter has a wealth of content to assist students, professionals, and administrators in understanding the field of geriatrics and gerontology. The interdisciplinary case studies are examples of how the best possible care can be provided to our older population.

This publication will stimulate critical thinking based on the underlying values and attitudes of old age. Perhaps this content will stimulate changes in our knowledge about old age. Scholarly attention is needed in our provision of services to our aging population. I feel this publication will accomplish needed learning objectives.

—Alice McDonnell, DrPH, MPA, RN, editor

Foreword

Managing Geriatric Health Services is a timely and accessible resource for any-one, whether you are a gerontologist, healthcare educator, board member for a long-term care facility, a health professions student, or a family mem-ber. I found this book relevant and pertinent to the many facets of long-term care and daily life of those who work with or encounter the long-term care system. Long-term care is coming of age. It emerged as a significant issue both in terms of quality and financing during the 1990s and has reached the spotlight in recent years as we fuss (definitely an academic word!) with payment systems, services, and how best to provide long-term care. The demand for long-term care is expected to skyrocket as the Baby Boomers age. This cohort will not go softly into that good night! Although studies indicate that medicine has increased life expectancy, it has not changed the onset of illness. Therefore, as our population ages, people who use the long-term care system will be diverse in age and in the level of needs and services required.

Having structural and functional knowledge of the long-term care system is imperative as we work attentively to create practical systems for older adults, their families, and the staff and administrators who serve them. Although on average, approximately 5% of those who are 65 years of age or older are living in nursing homes, it is expected that between 39–49% of older adults will use nursing homes at some point, either for rehabilitation or extended stays. Most people who make the nursing home their final resi-dence tend to live there for 1 to 2 years on average. Older adults who are able to access homecare services receive an average of 200 visits, hardly enough to remain at home if they experience challenges with activities of daily living.

The chapters in *Managing Geriatric Health Services* provide an excellent overview for those wanting to learn about long-term care or delve into specific areas within this field. This book addresses big issues in long-term care in comprehensive yet accessible ways. As I read this text, the image that kept surfacing was that of a weaving loom with each of the chapters representing the various threads woven into the creation of fabric—a tapestry composed of interlaced threads.

The reader may find it helpful to think about Part I: Role of Disciplines/ Professionals as one dimension of the tapestry that forms the foundation of function within long-term care. This section is particularly useful in orienting administrators, health professionals, and others so that they may realize the various nuances regarding scope of practice and interprofessionalism possibilities for long-term care. Part II: Special Topics weaves the threads of purpose, proficiency, and meaning into the fabric for those who work with or utilize long-term care services. The scope of long-term care services is intense, whether it involves its financial challenges, psychosocial needs, spirituality, ethics, or contributions to a good death. Part III: Case Studies provides an approach for handling the threads of knowledge and understanding gained from the first two parts of the book and weaving them into a serviceable pattern.

Managing Geriatric Health Services addresses long-term care in its broadest sense—the management of both facilities and community programs/organizations providing services to older adults (Chapter 1). Each chapter provides objectives, definition of terms, introductory statements, topic content, summary statements, and review questions. This approach guides and educates the reader as to the foundation and scope of the issues addressed in each chapter. Of note, the definition of terms that each author provides aids in alleviating confusion about how the terms are applied. In the field of aging we often find that terms may have a variety of definitions, all appropriate and some creatively applied, depending on the person using the term. It is helpful for the authors to define up front those terms that are significant in the chapter, making it explicitly clear how the terms are applied within the scope of their content area.

The threads woven through the chapters are congruent throughout and allow for a coalescence of concepts with care practice. For example, the thread of quality of care is interwoven into many of the chapters allowing the reader to consider the concept and its application within different professions/disciplines, among specialty topics, and in case studies. The authors have accomplished conveying information so that utilization and applicability can be improved. For example, in my opinion, the lifeblood of any organization is its people, and how appropriate to have a chapter dedicated to oral history projects within the long-term care setting. Additionally, to include nurse satisfaction, relationship building, spirituality, and psychosocial needs as topics for discussion and edification speaks to the inclusion of healthcare humanity.

Financing long-term care services is a patchwork of public (federal, state, and local) funds and private dollars. I have dealt with the system in professional and personal realms. However, it wasn't until I read Chapter 7: Financing Long-Term Care that the pieces came together. This chapter provides a clearly marked path to follow and presents concepts and controversies in bite-sized pieces that augment understanding. As stated, the aging population faces significant challenges in how care will be accessed due to the lack of funding related to the nation's healthcare programs, limiting reimbursement for long-term care. Financing long-term care is a critical issue to understand and become familiar with. Without a strong financial base, programs are and will continue to be compromised—possibly jeopardizing the humanity and quality that we so dearly want to ensure is part of the long-term care system.

The culture of long-term care is diverse and complex—valuing the professions that provide long-term care, nurturing interprofessional relationships, attending to staff and resident health and well-being, and maintaining safe and caring environments for all who work in and utilize these services requires mindfulness and skills not always easily acquired. This book provides the reader with it all. The informed experts (authors) have delivered a well balanced and useful guide that can help you navigate through the world of long-term care.

Marilyn R. Gugliucci

Marilyn R. Gugliucci, MA, PhD, AGSF, GSAF, AGHEF
Director, Geriatrics Education and Research
Department of Geriatric Medicine
University of New England College of Osteopathic Medicine,
    Biddeford, ME
President, Maine Gerontological Society
Chair, Gerontological Society of America Health Science Section,
    Washington, DC
Past-President, Association for Gerontology in Higher Education,
    Washington, DC

Acknowledgments

Many individuals have contributed to this text. The list of chapter contributors demonstrates the complexity of Gerontology and Geriatric Health Services Administration. Thank you to all for your dedication.

My gratitude of thanks goes to those working in the field of gerontology who served as participants in conducted surveys. Special thanks to Ilise Rubinow, The Jewish Home of Eastern Pennsylvania; Linda Steier, Meals on Wheels; Amy Minnich, LIFE Geisinger; Paco Peters, Allied Assisted Living; Janine Starinsky, Oakwood Terrace; Dr. Janet Melnick, Penn State University; Dr. Brooke Cannon, Marywood University; Maryann Rubino, Mountain View Care Center; and Amy Frantz, Allied Rehabilitation.

Many, many thanks go to Colleen Bennett, Sneh Akruvala, and William Miller, my graduate assistants, who gave tirelessly to the coordination of this text.

Maro Gartside and Chloe Falivene of Jones & Bartlett Learning have been most supportive; I appreciate their encouragement.

My heartfelt thanks go out to *everyone* contributing to the success of this publication. Special thanks to Judy Smeltzer, my administrative assistant, for completing details.

Contributors

Barbara Parker-Bell, PsyD, ATR-BC, LPC
Director, Graduate Art Therapy Program
Assistant Professor
Marywood University
Scranton, PA

Christina A. Hasemann, PhD, RD, L/CDN, CNSD
President/CEO
NY-Penn Nutrition Services, Inc.
Binghamton, NY

Doris Chechotka-McQuade, PhD, ACSW, LCSW
Assistant Professor, Pro-Rata Faculty
School of Social Work
Marywood University
Scranton, PA

James Pettinato, MHSA, RN
Director of Patient Care Services
Wayne Memorial Hospital
Instructor
Marywood University
Honesdale, PA

Jessica Rae Bodzio, MS, RD, LDN
Instructor
Department of Nutrition and Dietetics
Marywood University
Scranton, PA

Joseph P. Lyons, ScD
Tenure Track Faculty
Department of Health Professions
Bitonte College of Health and Human Services
Youngstown State University
Youngstown, OH

Karen E. Arscott, DO, MSc, AOBNMM
Clinical Associate Professor and Program Director
Physician Assistant Program
Marywood University
Scranton, PA

Kathleen Healy-Karabell, DNP, MSN, CNS, RN
Assistant Professor
Nursing Department
Marywood University
Scranton, PA

Kathleen P. Munley, PhD
Professor of History
Social Sciences Department
Marywood University
Scranton, PA

Lee Harrison, PhD, RD
Professor
Department of Nutrition and Dietetics
Marywood University
Scranton, PA

Marilyn R. Gugliucci, PhD, AGHEF, GSAF, AGSF
Past President, Association for Gerontology in Higher Education
Director, Geriatric Education and Research
Department of Geriatric Medicine
University of New England
Biddeford, ME

Mary Alice Golden McCormick, PhD, MSN, RN
Associate Professor
Nursing Department
Marywood University
Scranton, PA

Sneh Divyakant Akruvala, MS, RN
Graduate Assistant
Marywood University
Scranton, PA

Sr. Gail Cabral, IHM, PhD
Professor
Psychology Department
Marywood University
Scranton, PA

Sr. Mariam Pfeifer, IHM, MA, LCAT, MT-BC
Director of Music Therapy
Department of Music, Theater, and Dance
Marywood University
Scranton, PA

William F. Miller, MHA
Graduate Program Coordinator
School of Nursing
Wilkes University
Wilkes-Barre, PA

Part

I

ROLE OF DISCIPLINES/PROFESSIONALS

Chapter 1

Administration Within Long-Term Care

Alice McDonnell, DrPH, MPA, RN

LEARNING OBJECTIVES

1. To increase the understanding of the scope of gerontology and geriatric health services administration
2. To provide the importance of the role of management in quality of gerontology health services administration
3. To heighten the awareness of the continuum of care concept as a requirement for a successful healthcare system
4. To understand the importance of organizational culture in providing quality care
5. To create an awareness of the importance of a model in management application

KEY TERMS

Geriatric Health Services Administration/Long-Term Care (LTC) Administration: Refers to management of facilities and community programs/organizations providing services to the elderly

Continuum of Care: Refers to following individuals throughout all phases of their disease processes

Gerontology: The study of the aging process among administrators and professionals

Geriatrics: Medical care of the aging population

Organizational Culture: The unseen assumptions, values, beliefs, and ideas shared by staff

Organizational Climate: How staff members feel within the organization

Coordinated Care Retirement Community (CCRC): A campus providing multiple settings, typically including independent living, assisted living, skilled care, hospice care, and memory (dementia) care

INTRODUCTION

Face of Aging

Today, the Baby Boomers (born between 1946 and 1964) account for 41 million persons in the U.S. population aged 65 and older (Vincent & Velkoff, 2010). This means they stand on the edge of retirement. Even though this generation tends to age in place, many will encounter declining health and functional status. Wright (2010) verbalizes certainty that caregiving for older adults with declining health and functional status will become one of America's greatest challenges of the 21st century. When the last group of Baby Boomers turns 65 in 2029, that same population group will have grown to just over 70 million persons (Vincent & Velkoff, 2010). By 2020, 81 million persons will be managing more than one chronic condition (Bodenheimer, Chen, & Bennett, 2009).

> Older adults use many health care services, have complex conditions, and require professional expertise that meets their needs. Most providers receive some type of training on aging, but the percentage of those who actually specialize in this area is small. . . . Most older adults want to remain in their communities as long as possible. Unfortunately, when they acquire disabilities, there is often not enough support available to help them (Healthy People 2020, 2012).

As the Baby Boomers begin to lose their independence, they may be less accepting of the limited options offered by the system to deliver the care they most need and desire (Wright, 2010).

Community providers must assume the responsibility for services necessary to meet the needs of their older population. The expectations of our older consumers include a multitude of quality services available to them. Thomas (2010) uses the term "Eldertopia" to define a community that improves the quality of life for people of all ages by strengthening and improving the means by which the community protects, sustains, and nurtures its elders, and by which the elders contribute to the well-being and foresight of the community.

Gerontology and Geriatric Health Services Administration

Gerontology and Geriatric Health Services Administration is an area of health services administration that requires a focus on older adults. The administrative role dictates competencies in management and, equally as important, sensitivity for the elderly. One must develop a management style that warrants compassion and empathy for people, both the staff and consumer.

In order to acquire this background, the role of administrator is critical with an understanding of the theoretical base and application of management principals. Research on administrative experiences and the impact of management relative to quality is a part of the discussion.

Gerontology and Geriatric Health Services Administration occurs in all settings, from home to acute care, which could include adult day care, assisted living, skilled nursing, and community programs. There are different models of adult day care, such as the Medical Model and the Social Model. An example of the Medical Model is the Program for All-Inclusive Care for the Elderly (PACE), which is an expanded and enhanced comprehensive model of care offering services at a licensed adult day center by an interdisciplinary team. PACE blends the roles of healthcare provider and insurance payer. In Pennsylvania it is called the LIFE program, standing for Living Independently for Elders, since there is a PACE program for drugs. The LIFE program is licensed by Pennsylvania's Office of Long-Term Living for compliance with state aging regulations. The program is also under the jurisdiction of several other regulatory bodies, including Pennsylvania's Department of Public Welfare, as well as the Centers for Medicare & Medicaid Services. This model is a very innovative way to manage seniors who are nursing-home eligible in the community.

A Coordinated Care Retirement Community (CCRC) is a unique setting, providing care depending on needs of the elderly person. The CCRC campus may provide independent living, personal care/assisted living, skilled care, and hospice services. The resident ordinarily pays an entrance fee and periodic adjustable payments, which, in turn, gives the resident a package of residential and healthcare services that the CCRC is obligated to provide at the time these residential and healthcare services are required.

There are exceptions to some of the federal and state government's licensing requirements. For example, a licensed personal care home may take care of residents with dementias, including Alzheimer's disease, as long as a waiver is in place to accept this kind of resident. The facility must also have certain protections in place to prevent injury to its demented residents.

Role of Administration in Gerontology and Geriatrics

The reality of a broken system for providing long-term care is apparent, according to Wright (2010). Looming over the next 2 decades is the even harsher reality of major workforce shortages in long-term care, which may guarantee that high quality care cannot be delivered even if system reforms are implemented (Wright, 2010). Hence, the critical role of administration in long-term care is a component of the geriatric imperative. An understanding of the skills and competencies required for positive and effective administration determines successful outcomes of evidence-based care.

Administration in this field may occur in numerous settings; however, the concept of administration does not change, even though the job description will read differently in terms of specific activities. For example, an administrator for a community agency may need to focus more on planning for services and how to finance programs through grants, while the administrator in a long-term care facility may find application of governmental regulations a priority. Nevertheless, leadership skills, team organization, and coordination are imperative to a successful administrator.

The author visualizes the first step in becoming an administrator as exceptional training, both academically and on the job. Prerequisites include compassion and commitment. Commitment to improving the health of the older adult may come from experiences with a family member. Many times a passion for gerontology comes from an experience of living with a beloved grandparent. Firsthand, the vulnerability and excessive needs of the elderly person become apparent. Secondly, an understanding of the aging process itself brings forth this required commitment. A number of the administrators have had life experiences that dictate their love for the field of gerontology.

Nursing home administrators are required to have a license. This process is a lengthy exposure, which includes practicum/administrator in training, professional education, and state board examinations. Personal care administrators must also be licensed through an educational process. Middle management also requires initial and ongoing education. In June 2008, the American Geriatrics Society convened a meeting that led to the development of the Partnership for Health in Aging. Their first step was the development of a set of core competencies in the care of older adults that pertain to all health professional disciplines. Middle management also must acquire leadership skills with a culture of accountability. In a culture of accountability:

- The goal is continuous learning and improvement.
- Decisions regarding care and direction are guided by evidence-based protocols and clinical guidelines.
- Performance measurement is essential for assessing outcomes and guiding improvement initiatives.
- Reporting errors is encouraged, not punished.
- There is collaboration and coordination among and between all levels of the organization.

O'Hagan and Persaud (2010) suggest six steps to achieve accountability:[1]

1. *Provide leadership.* Strong leadership enhances employee responsibility, morale, cooperation, and trust, as well as reduces turnover, helping to maintain accountability within the organization. Leadership that exemplifies accountability should be pervasive at all levels of the organization.
2. *Emphasize quality.* It is important to reinforce that not only the quality of patient care will improve, but also the quality of work will improve.
3. *Make customer service a priority.* An environment that provides exceptional quality care not only improves the patient's experience, but also leads to more satisfied staff, fewer preventable medical errors, fewer malpractice lawsuits, and improved revenues.
4. *Performance management.* Performance measurement is important because measurement informs on quality, and you cannot manage what you do not measure. The measurement of outcomes includes monitoring the performance of the organization against service standards and organizational goals, as well as collecting feedback from patients and other stakeholders.
5. *Support the human dimension.* This begins by increasing the self-efficacy of employees, which positively enhances their beliefs about their capabilities. Ensure that employees are rewarded by using a recognition program that celebrates both small and large successes.
6. *Provide a supportive infrastructure.* It is important to provide people with the means and competencies necessary to be successful. Effective communication systems are needed that allow the distribution of information and knowledge to everyone.

Administrators also see their role changing due to the environment of uncertainty, greater stringency, and intensified public scrutiny.

---

1. Used with permission from O'Hagan, J., & Persaud, D. (2010). *Create a culture of accountability.* Hatboro, PA: Nurses Service Organization Risk Advisor.

LEADERSHIP

Leadership skills are an important component of success in geriatric health services administration, as shown at the end of this chapter as part of a model for administrators in the field. Effective leadership skills include numerous assets, such as:

- Be a model and lead by example
- Be a profound communicator as well as a good listener
- Must demand teamwork
- Must focus on decision-making solutions, not problems
- Must have the ability to influence behavior
- Must have integrity and stimulation
- Must respect high standards of dignity
- Must understand the politics within the community
- Understand success factors in the Six Sigma model for management
- Must have emotional and intellectual maturity

There is a direct relationship between a supportive environment for staff and asking them to take good care of their elderly consumers.

In order to meet the leadership challenges in long-term care, change is evident. Farrell, Brady, and Frank (2011) discuss their roadmap for successful change, focusing on people first, and then on systems that support people to work well together. A successful leader models genuine caring through good interpersonal skills. Stress reduction allows utilization of positive staff energy (Farrell, Brady, & Frank, 2011). Channeling energy into a positive framework brings about improved clinical outcomes with staff and patient satisfaction.

Leadership competencies must include team building, since a team model is essential to accomplishing excellent clinical outcomes and satisfaction. Pratt (2010) advocates that the team leader must provide direction to the team and facilitate its activities toward common goals. Team members will collectively share the challenges facing the team and celebrate its successes as a group with the leader, fulfilling dual roles, both as leader of the team and as a team member (Pratt, 2010). The interdisciplinary team functions within long-term care settings as collaborators and coordinators to execute superior care planning.

Time management is imperative for an administrator in that lack of coordination, organization, empowerment, and poor communication skills could result in concerns/issues. The ability to focus and set priorities becomes essential. The application of a tactical and strategic planning process allows a focus on needs and outcomes. Measurable goals and objectives must lead to successful outcomes utilizing evidence-based practice guidelines. Unmet timelines can result in failure.

ORGANIZATIONAL CULTURE

A good leader can cultivate the culture of an organization by reinforcing behavioral norms and expectations that lead to effectiveness. Research has shown that organizational culture can be characterized by 12 cultural styles, organized in 3 general cultural norm clusters that guide the way people interact with one another and approach their work (Human Synergistics International, 2012). **Table 1.1** details these cultural norms.

Changes in the external environment make the role of management ever evolving. Change may take place every day with new situations and new regulations/requirements from regional, state, and federal levels.

CONTINUUM OF CARE

In the field of gerontology, a continuum of care is most imperative. For the elderly person, an integrated system of care that guides and tracks the individual over time through a comprehensive array of health, mental health, and social services must span all levels of intensity of care (as cited in Evashwick, 2005). Hence, the CCRC model is effective in care of the elderly as both services and integrating mechanisms are provided. A continuum of care embraces a person-oriented system of care. A return to the basic principles of health care treats the whole person and ongoing needs, from wellness to illness to recovery, fostering the natural birth–natural death process. This can occur through informal arrangements, a network of affiliations, a team of professionals, or contracts for services. Services must be dependable, consistent, and traceable—a true system. A care coordinator may act as the case manager, facilitating services through collaboration of programs and facilities throughout the community.

In order to develop a continuum of care, an administrator must have vision with defined goals and objectives and a strategic business plan requiring energy, resources, and leadership (Evashwick, 2005). Levels along the continuum range from acute hospital care to home and community care. Once an individual requires some assistance with activities of daily living and cannot live alone, an assisted living facility would be an appropriate level of care. Long Term Care Education.com (LTCE) (2011) uses the United States Department of Health and Human Services' definition of assisted living—"a residential setting that provides either routine general protective oversight or assistance with activities necessary for independent living

Table 1.1 Descriptions of the 12 Styles Measured by the Organizational Culture Inventory® (and Sample Items)

Constructive Norms

[Cultural Styles Promoting Satisfaction Behaviors]

Achievement

An *achievement* culture characterizes organizations that do things well and value members who set and accomplish their own goals. Members are expected to set challenging but realistic goals, establish plans to reach these goals, and pursue them with enthusiasm. *(Pursue a standard of excellence; openly show enthusiasm)*

Self-Actualizing

A *self-actualizing* culture characterizes organizations that value creativity, quality over quantity, and both task accomplishment and individual growth. Members are encouraged to gain enjoyment from their work, develop themselves, and take on new and interesting activities. *(Think in unique and independent ways; do even simple tasks well)*

Humanistic/Encouraging

A *humanistic/encouraging* culture characterizes organizations that are managed in a participative and person-centered way. Members are expected to be supportive, constructive, and open to influence in their dealings with one another. *(Help others to grow and develop; take time with people)*

Affiliative

An *affiliative* culture characterizes organizations that place a high priority on constructive interpersonal relationships. Members are expected to be friendly, open, and sensitive to the satisfaction of their work group. *(Deal with others in a friendly, pleasant way; share feelings and thoughts)*

Passive/Defensive Norms

[Cultural Styles Promoting People/Security Behaviors]

Approval

An *approval* culture describes organizations in which conflicts are avoided and interpersonal relationships are pleasant—at least superficially. Members feel that they should agree with, gain the approval of, and be liked by others. *("Go along" with others; be liked by everyone)*

Conventional

A *conventional* culture is descriptive of organizations that are conservative, traditional, and bureaucratically controlled. Members are expected to conform, follow the rules, and make a good impression. *(Always follow policies and practices; fit into the "mold")*

Dependent

An *dependent* culture is descriptive of organizations that are hierarchically controlled and do not empower their members. Centralized decision making in such organizations leads members to do only what they are told and to clear all decisions with superiors. *(Please those in positions of authority; do what is expected)*

Avoidance

An *avoidance* culture characterizes organizations that fail to reward success, but nevertheless punish mistakes. This negative reward system leads members to shift responsibilities to others and avoid any possibility of being blamed for a mistake. *(Wait for others to act first; take few chances)*

(Continued)

Aggressive/Defensive Norms
[Cultural Styles Promoting Task/Security Behaviors]

Oppositional

An *oppositional* culture describes organizations in which confrontation and negativism are rewarded. Members gain status and influence by being critical and thus are reinforced to oppose the ideas of others. *(Point out flaws; be hard to impress)*

Power

A *power* culture is descriptive of nonparticipative organizations structured on the basis of the authority inherent in members' positions. Members believe they will be rewarded for taking charge, controlling subordinates and, at the same time, being responsive to the demands of superiors. *(Build up one's power base; demand loyalty)*

Competitive

A *competitive* culture is one in which winning is valued and members are rewarded for outperforming one another. Members operate in a "win-lose" framework and believe they must work against (rather than with) their peers to be noticed. *(Turn the job into a contest; never appear to lose)*

Perfectionistic

A *perfectionistic* culture characterizes organizations in which perfectionism, persistence, and hard work are valued. Members feel they must avoid any mistakes, keep track of everything, and work long hours to attain narrowly defined objectives. *(Do things perfectly; keep on top of everything)*

to mentally or physically limited persons" (para 6). Assisted living may be thought of as a bridge between active retirement living and care in a skilled nursing facility (Long Term Care Education.com [LTCE], 2011).

When an individual's medical status changes and continuous 24-hour nursing care is required, a skilled nursing facility is appropriate. The statutory definition of a skilled nursing facility from the Social Security Act is an institution primarily engaged in providing skilled nursing care and related services for residents who require medical or nursing care, or rehabilitation services for the rehabilitation of injured, disabled, or sick persons. This type of facility offers the highest intensity level of long-term care (LTCE, 2011).

Ownership varies among long-term care facilities. The types of ownership include nonprofit, for-profit, state-owned, investment-based, and religious-based organizations. A nonprofit owner uses surplus revenues to achieve organizational goals rather than distributing them as profit or dividends; whereas, a for-profit organization as a corporation operates as a business which will return a profit to owners. Nevertheless, each facility along the continuum must uphold the conditions of participations for regulation.

The SERVICE Model of Care[2]

The first leadership model for long-term care (LTC) administrators was discussed by Glister and Dalessandro (2009) using SERVICE as the acronym for seven domains—service, education, respect, vision, inclusion, communication, enrichment. In health care and long-term care, it is assumed that the primary job is to care for and serve others. Many focus their healthcare careers on a desire to do this. Yet, a service-oriented culture is not what many people experience in today's healthcare environment.

Service

Service involves providing for and caring for others. Service has several facets: the desire to serve, fulfillment of an obligation, and, for some, a duty or "calling." In leadership, the desire to serve is recognized as an important component for success. Service-oriented leadership involves putting the needs of others before one's own, finding ways to meet those needs, and recognizing other individuals' worth and value.

In this model, service is achieved when leaders and staff use their talents to serve and fulfill an obligation to others and to the organization's vision and mission. The driving force is to have them work for something more important than themselves, something that will make a difference in the lives of others. The leader in this service model wears many hats, including colleague, guide, helper, teacher, coach, mentor, facilitator, role model, and cheerleader.

Education and New Learning

From administrator to housekeeper, individuals are often asked to accept a position with little educational training and no specific expectation communicated. Still, they are expected to work "successfully." When employees do not work up to these "standards," although expectations are rarely communicated clearly, they shoulder the blame. They are considered lazy, negligent, or not very bright. The fault, however, lies with the system, facility, and leadership.

---

2. Reproduced with permission from Glister, S., & Dalessandro, J. (2009). Introducing the first leadership model for LTC administrators. *Long-Term Living: For the Continuing Care Professional*, 58(8), 32–35.

Supporting education begins with leadership valuing education and knowledge for themselves and others. Education is beneficial to staff performance. Education is more than training and skill development. It is a means of encouraging growth and development for staff in work and in life. It is a commitment to teaching and to continued learning as individuals and as an organization.

Ongoing training and educational support programs are essential to ensuring staff effectiveness. Educational needs do not end with the completion of orientation. Issues, questions, and problems surface continually, as does new information. Consistent and routine education and support meetings should serve to fulfill the educational needs of employees. Such programs also enhance communication, and demonstrate to staff that they are valued.

Respect

It is sad that the issue of respect must even be discussed—but it remains on the top of the list of what staff suggest is missing to ensure their workplace satisfaction. Employees in long-term care deserve more respect than they traditionally receive. Employees are to be treated with respect at all times, by all people. Staff is expected to respect one another; anything less is unacceptable and not to be tolerated. The message is: Respect others—or leave.

Vision

An exemplary organization begins with a clear vision and mission, guided by established principles and values, including respect, dignity, trust, honesty, and integrity. The vision is central to hiring, decision making, and problem solving, as it is the ultimate guide for the leader and all those who follow. The vision created or interpreted by all in the organization unites employees as they, in turn, share in the dream. A vision serves to move a group of individuals in an organization toward a common destination and provides meaning to their work.

Creating a vision that is shared by the staff takes time and effort; it does not happen on its own. The vision must be discussed and examined routinely as long as the organization is operational.

Inclusion

Involve staff in as much problem solving, decision making, and operational implementation as possible. This enhances staff interest and participation in the work and allows the organization to tap into their particular knowledge and experience. When staff members are part of the plan and solution, it becomes a reality to them. Because they are a part of it, they own it, and will work hard to see that it is successful.

To facilitate an inclusive philosophy, routine meetings with all staff should be held to relay information, and to offer the opportunity to discuss issues, plan, and problem solve. Specific department meetings are an added vehicle in which employees can offer input and communicate with their coworkers.

Staff members will be open to change and innovation, and accept it willingly, if involved in the planning and implementation process. Many staff members are creative—they can have wonderful ideas and be innovative in their solutions to problems. Employees are willing to try just about anything if it improves the care and outcome for residents. Therefore, their inclusion overall ensures a more effective organization.

Communication

When employees are asked to name what contributes to job satisfaction, the presence or absence of an effective communication system consistently ranks high. While no communication system is perfect, a variety of means for relaying and receiving information is essential to effectively leading the organization in a strategic direction. Such mechanisms must communicate not only the vision and direction of the organization, but how staff members are expected to work, interact, and care for residents and families. The purpose is to tap into all of the resources, knowledge, and talent at the disposal of the organization and thus design and implement the best possible mechanisms, programs, and solutions to realize the vision.

Enrichment

Enrichment as a domain teaches the leaders how to effect change collaboratively (Glister & Dallessandro, 2009).

ADMINISTRATORS' RESPONSES ABOUT THEIR ROLES

In order to understand and compare the experiences of administrators, this author conducted a hybrid qualitative survey with administrators of various facilities and programs for older adults in Northeastern Pennsylvania. Facilities from which administrators were interviewed included a CCRC, private and public skilled nursing settings, Area Agency on Aging subsidiaries, as well as private service industry management. Approximately hour-long interviews were completed with seven available administrators; the administrators were asked open-ended questions related to their views on the role of an administrator, as well as definitions of organizational culture and the concept of continuum of care. The responses to these semi-structured interviews were transcribed and analyzed for key themes and meaningful insights. The interviewer mailed a four-page structured survey to the four unavailable administrators, which was returned with handwritten or typed responses. Similarly, these direct responses were analyzed for meaningful insights, the results of which are included here.

Based on this mixed-methods approach, the discussion on administrative perception is as follows: Administrators were asked, what is the role of (or how would you define) an administrator in long-term care? Administrators verbalized their role as a combination of a lot of different areas. The role was described as:

- Orchestrator of the delivery of services by combining collective efforts to ensure service
- Enforcement of corrective actions
- Negotiator, such as peacemaker
- Overall oversight, including human resources, contract-management compliance, budget, and liaison to state and federal regulations
- Management of delegated staff
- Presence of middle management
- Corporate expectations
- Increased accountability demanded by consumer families and citizen groups, and increased political visibility of long-term care

Organizational culture was described by one administrator as a 12-year concept with a conscientious effort to create an environment conducive to having individuals thrive in an independent setting. The genuine goal of administrators is to try to provide as much continuity to their lifestyle as possible without cutting the umbilical cord to their community. Thus, the culture can be described as very relaxed and very familial, but never sacrificing the delivery of service or the educational component that is necessary for anybody to survive in this type of environment.

Other administrators described their organizational culture as:

- Innovative, nontraditional path
- Out-of-the-box solutions
- Always thinking, "What can we do to maintain an individual in the community?"
- Organizational structure with hands down from the administrative level through middle management and down to all direct care givers, governed by a board of directors
- When individuals of the "team" establish agreements among themselves to achieve a common goal
- Goals are defined as positive attributes or characteristics which individuals strive to achieve

· A centralized management approach providing for the needs of individuals, hence the organization develops from the top to the bottom

When administrators were asked about their continuum of care, their responses varied depending on their setting:

· "We are a CCRC with assisted living as the gatekeeper of the continuum of care. From assisted living the individual can be transferred to the appropriate level of care reflecting their needs. Our CCRC has the entire concept—independent apartments, assisted living, the nursing home, the rehabilitation hospital. This is the hub, this is where it begins; people come in, and, of course, if they get better and more independent, then we try to place them in a less restrictive environment, such as independent apartments; or, if they are medically deteriorating or cognitively deteriorating, then we look for appropriate level of care such as a nursing home. We also try to bring in home health prior to transferring the individual, so there are services out in the community and through sister divisions that we try to take advantage of in order to retard the discharge of an individual to another level of care."

· "Increased role in the continuum, day care, services in home, respite."

· "Generally, assisted living is the bridge between living independently and needing skilled nursing care. Specifically we are affiliated with a senior high rise and a skilled nursing facility."

· A dementia facility stated that its mission in continuum of care is to ensure continuing development and delivery of appropriate care to those diagnosed with dementia and their families whose needs are not being adequately met by existing services and programs. In order to carry out this mission, the continuum is supplemented with existing services available to this population to promote, support, and encourage family strength and self-sufficiency by providing or procuring services to complete the range of services needed in the least restrictive, most appropriate setting. Further, the continuum ensures that the delivery of those services represented in its array of services (treatment programs, education services, counseling services, outreach services, volunteer and community services) are in compliance with appropriate state laws.

The mission of a community organization, Meals on Wheels, is to help participants remain at home with a nutritious meal.

A management style for geriatric administrators is discussed in the following section of this chapter. Long-term care administrators gave some very thoughtful responses to questions about their management style:

- Democracy involves believing that your staff members are your resources, since these caregivers know the residents best. Therefore, maximization of staff as a resource is important for an environment within a facility.
- Allow all staff to express their opinions, then as a magnet, make a hybrid out of all the input from all staff.
- Engage everyone in the process.
- Using a very hands-on style leads to being aware of happenings of staff and the elderly persons for whom they care.

The author's experience and anecdotal research has shown that management style has an impact on quality of care. Administrative responses support that observation:

- If you invest in employees as human beings and cultivate them into the staff members you want, then you will reap the benefits of that cultivation. A manager must recognize issues with employees and create an environment that alleviates concerns/issues as much as possible. The work environment creates maximum outcomes.
- A management style that insures responsibility impacts quality of care.
- Being aware means being able to act on a timely basis whenever necessary.
- Management style involves "walking the walk and talking the talk."
- Management style "totally and dramatically" affects quality of care.

When addressing the impact of state and federal regulations, administrators find that a large percentage of time is spent on meeting regulatory requirements and keeping their organization viable. Administrators responded with earnest as follows:

- Regulations have a tremendous impact, primarily financial. Health care is a business; the bottom line cannot be divorced from the mission statement. We must adhere to regulations even though we may not agree with them.
- Closures indicate a definite impact.
- Adherence to state regulations is ever present, even when they don't have much to do with the reality of managing the facility.
- The state (Pennsylvania) continues to look at regulations.

Administrators were asked: To what extent is management (style and model) driven by ownership? This question is important here in that programs within the field of gerontology have varied types of ownership within profit and nonprofit organizations. A nonprofit organization administrator responded: We are a nonprofit organization, and depending on what type of facility you are licensed as, it certainly does have an impact on the administrator. I work to meet the goals of the delivery of service under the board. We have flexibility as a CCRC; I can implement services as long as the goal is beneficial to the consumer and fits within the goals of the organization (condensed answer).

Other nonprofit administrators stated that their organizations have regulations for quality, care, and organization as a whole. Under a board of directors, administration is given a great deal of responsibility and subsequently impacts management.

Administrators were asked, "Does management style impact organizational behavior, from your perspective?" Typical responses were:

· "My management style reflects the organization via the consumer's opinion of services. Satisfied customers generalize their opinions to the entire organization."
· "Yes, particularly so in a very hands-on type of environment."

Administrators have concerns on a daily basis that may challenge their strategic planning. When asked about these concerns, administrators responded with the following pressing issues:

· Appropriate staffing to meet regulations
· Meeting goals and needs of the organization
· Census
· Well-being of people you care for (alertness to their needs)
· Adequate services to prevent decline of the elderly
· Healthcare reform and financial implications
· Changing role of the caregiver
· Complexity of multiple regulatory bodies
· Competition
· Employee issues
· Financial issues
· Quality of care
· Resident and family concerns

Since quality of care is a major concern, administrators were asked about the frequency of quality assessment; responses varied, including four times per year assessments, formal annual assessments, everyday assessments, or ongoing assessments depending on areas of concern. Quality of care is foremost on any administrator's agenda and affects all of that administrator's decision-making solutions on a daily basis.

Staffing as a major concern to administrators dictates a discussion of approaches to staffing as a primary resource. When asked, "Does management style influence interactions with staff/residents/family members, and how do you address staff/resident/family concerns?" Administrators' responses were helpful in sharing insights into the value of the premier workforce:

- Staff members are the bloodline of this industry; the dynamics of their relationship with the elderly person is unlike any other in the healthcare system.
- Administrators must become involved personally/individually with family or we lose the person in our program. Families are under tremendous stress and appreciate administrative involvement and respect the administrator's knowledge.
- Families appreciate education and knowing their loved one is under the care of a sincere leader.
- Approachable open-door policy.
- Many concerns are handed to middle management.
- Importance of a belief system to decrease turnover, fostering staff who work well together.

Staff recruitment/retention is an ongoing challenge for any administrator. Administrators find difficulty in recruiting for therapies such as physical therapy, speech therapy, and occupational therapy. Generally, recruitment is competitive; however, a positive and attractive work environment is key to recruitment. Staff retention is an ongoing challenge that is handled through charge management effectively. Specific responses included luncheons, desserts, rewards, recognition, opportunities for advancement, ongoing performance evaluations, and intimate work environment. In-house training and ongoing continuing education incentives are imperative, especially since most professionals are required to have continued education for licensure renewal. An annual retreat for all administrative/management is beneficial and appreciated. Allowing staff to be involved in the decision process dictates that everyone's opinion is respected. Staff can then take ownership with flexibility. Management of staff concerns through monthly staff leadership meetings filters down to all levels of the organization. Constant communication is expected for a successful organization. One leads by example, setting the culture of the organization. Passion-driven staff are most valuable assets. If a staff member is genuine, longevity will flourish. One administrator looks for maturity, a certain personality, and a good work ethic when hiring staff.

When asked about stress, administrators responded that stress is inevitable from the elderly person to the handling of families, and is very difficult to keep in perspective. Administrators recommended direct involvement with stressful issues relative to staff, as they consider themselves as part of the team. They discussed their management style as being conducive to stress management and prevention of stress.

Administrators responded to ethical issues by stating that the organization's ethics committee handles ethical questions and assists in resolving issues as a qualified team with the required knowledge and background.

As administrators provide daily leadership within a continuum-of-care environment, each one must decide which management style is most effective in his or her own setting. The next section introduces a model developed by the author.

MODEL FOR GERIATRIC HEALTH SERVICES ADMINISTRATION

After years of experience and observation in this field, the author has developed a model that focuses on the patient/resident/client as a focus of care. If administrators focus on an elderly person and his/her family, they must be careful not to go wrong in service delivery. Due to the complexities of health care, one's attention is often diverted away from the elderly person, and that must not happen.

In this model, the elderly person/family heads up the team; see **Figure 1.1**. In order for an administrator to deliver quality services, leadership skills as described earlier are paramount. In addition to basic leadership skills, there are 12 requirements for effectiveness:

- *Knowledge.* Competencies for administrative practice are essential; therefore, a profound knowledge base must exist. The author has been told by administrators that they do not understand Alzheimer's disease, yet they administer discrete Alzheimer's units.
- *Commitment to excellence.* Centers of excellence do exist with clear mission statements, value determinations, and measurable goals and objectives. Commitment must be part of an administrator's driving force to work with the elderly.
- *Effective communicator.* Communication is key to a successful organization. Lack of communication creates a barrier to existence. The author has observed lack of communication leading to confusion and error. Errors are not acceptable in this field. Administrators must be viewed as approachable, and their words and actions must support the mission. Relationship building will result from effective communication and enhance team building at the same time. Appreciative inquiry may be used as a mechanism for team communication and effectiveness.

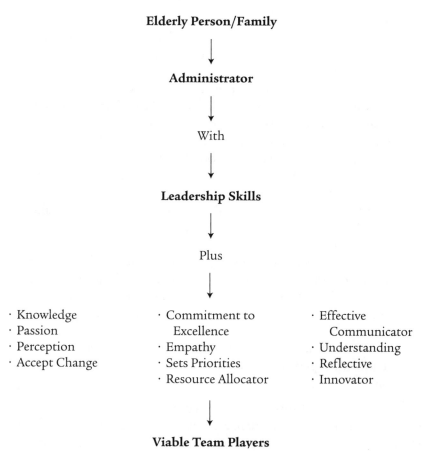

Figure 1.1 Model for Successful Administration of Geriatric Health Services

- *Passion.* If one has a passion for his/her position, this permeates the team. The team must live compassionate care and be passionate about service and serving.
- *Empathy.* With empathy, an administrator can better coordinate the team in delivering services. Empathy assists in creating, promoting, and fostering community.
- *Understanding.* As simple as this seems, administrators must understand the healthcare delivery system in order to foster partnerships within the community to achieve seamless service delivery, as discussed under continuum of care.
- *Perception.* One must be able to perceive both the internal and external environment. Vision must be a part of strategic planning. With vision one can perceive future outcomes of care.

- *Sets priorities*. Time-management skills are imperative with the ability to set priorities that are realistic and pertinent to each situation. Flexibility is a component needed to manage change and move the organization forward. At the same time, timelines must be identified. Administrators sometimes tend to set priorities based on their likes and dislikes of tasks, which could be troublesome without an awareness of one's own strengths and limitations.
- *Reflective*. Many times decisions are made without thought and reflection, as well as without facts. Reflective moments can yield better decisions. Reflection can also put issues and problems into perspective.
- *Accept change*. Change is inevitable and always present, especially for the administrator of tomorrow (and today). Managing change then becomes a key function.
- *Resource allocator*. Effective and efficient utilization of all resources is a challenge of every administrator, especially with the financial constraints of today. Creativity in programming is often indicated. For example, a well coordinated and administered volunteer program can be invaluable.
- *Innovator*. An administrator must embrace innovation and be able to provide supportive services and security to enrich the journey of aging.

Once leadership skills plus these 12 requirements are mastered, viable teamwork will enhance care management with excellent transition of care. Hence, quality of care will result and be recognized by consumers of care.

Long-term care facilities also require a medical director, many of whom are on contract. However, larger, skilled nursing facilities have a full-time medical director. The medical director must balance the clinical world with strong administrative leadership. The medical director works with the facility administrators to create medical policies, determine quality of care standards, and establish educational courses for the facility staff. Most medical directors hold the position as part-time employees.

The medical director may or may not be a Certified Medical Director. Almost 20 years ago the organization AMDA—Dedicated to Long Term Care Medicine (formerly the American Medical Directors Association) designed a certification program for medical directors. This certification program assists physicians with the balance required between clinical care and administrative management. In addition to the AMDA—Dedicated to Long Term Care Medicine certification, there are many other educational routes for medical directors. A physician desiring to gain a better understanding of facility administration—and therefore the medical director position—can opt to earn a degree in hospital administration, business administration, or medical management (to name a few).

The report *Improving the Quality of Long Term Care,* published in 2001 by the Institute of Medicine, encouraged facilities to grant medical directors an increased role in medical care policies, but also increased responsibility. The increased responsibility has been mandated more and more by state legislators and regulators. States may begin to set requirements for education of medical directors.

In addition, there has been an emergence of geriatric care managers who are health and human specialists trained and experienced in fields such as nursing, gerontology, social work, or psychology, with a specialized focus on issues related to aging and elder care. Geriatric care managers are members of the National Association of Professional Geriatric Care Managers (NAPGCM), committed to the NAPGCM Code of Ethics and Standards of Practice.

Geriatric care managers add to quality of care among elders and their families by providing counseling, support, coordination of resources, and assistance in solutions to problems encountered by our older populations. The NAPGCM website (www.caremanager.org) provides information such as how to find a geriatric care manager, as well as the benefits of their services (National Association of Professional Geriatric Care Manager, 2012).

SUMMARY

The role of the administrator in working in long-term care settings is imperative to successful programs. Leadership skills are essential in the enhancement of an organizational culture conducive to effective outcomes in the care of our elderly population. This chapter emphasizes varied models that can be applied in successful administration in a variety of settings and programs. The author introduces a new model, bringing together all aspects discussed. Responses from administrators can be most helpful in understanding the administrative process required.

Discussion Questions

1. What would you include in an ideal management model?
2. How can a continuum-of-care concept result in quality?
3. How do you see the role of a geriatric care manager as imperative in healthcare reform?

4. What do you see as qualities for leadership?
5. What is unique regarding management of long-term care?

References

Bodenheimer, T., Chen, E., & Bennett, H. D. (2009). Confronting the growing burden of chronic disease: Can the U.S. healthcare workforce do the job? *Health Affairs, 28*(1), 64–74. doi: 10.1377/hlthaff.28.1.64.

Evashwick, C. (2005). *The continuum of long-term care* (3rd ed.). Clifton Park, NY: Thomson Delmar Learning.

Farrell, D., Brady, C., & Frank, B. (2011). *Meeting the leadership challenge in long-term care, what you do matters.* Baltimore, MD: Health Professions Press.

Glister, S., & Dalessandro, J. (2009). Introducing the first leadership model for LTC administrators. *Long-Term Living: For the Continuing Care Professional, 58*(8), 32–35.

Healthy People 2020. (2012). *Older adults.* U.S. Department of Health and Human Services. Retrieved March 12, 2012, from http://www.healthypeople.gov/2020/topicsobjectives2020/overview.aspx?topicid=31.

Institute of Medicine. (2001). *Improving the quality of long term care.* Washington, DC: National Academies Press.

Long Term Care Education.com. (2011). What is assisted living? Retrieved March 22, 2012, from http://www.ltce.com/learn/assistedliving.php.

National Association of Professional Geriatric Care Managers. (2012). What is a geriatric care manager? Retrieved April 23, 2012, from http://www.caremanager.org/why-care-management/what-you-should-know/#section2.

O'Hagan, J., & Persaud, D. (2010). *Create a culture of accountability.* Hatboro, PA: Nurses Service Organization Risk Advisor.

Pratt, J. R. (2010). *Long-term care managing across the continuum.* Sudbury, MA: Jones & Bartlett Learning.

Thomas, W. H. (2010). Eldertopia. In S. Greenbaum (Ed.), *Longevity rules: How to age well into the future.* Stuart, CA: Eskaton.

Vincent, G. K., & Velkoff, V. A. (2010). U.S. Census Bureau, U.S. Department of Commerce, *The next four decades—The older population in the United States: 2010–2050* (P25-1138). Retrieved March 12, 2012, from http://www.census.gov/prod/2010pubs/p25-1138.pdf.

Wright, L. D. (2010). Caregiving's transformative influence on an aging America. In S. Greenbaum (Ed.), *Longevity rules: How to age well into the future.* Stuart, CA: Eskaton.

Chapter 2

The Nurse Administrator in Long-Term Care

Mary Alice Golden McCormick, PhD, MSN, RN

LEARNING OBJECTIVES

1. To understand the role and responsibility of the nurse administrator in long-term care (LTC)
2. To differentiate between the concepts of culture and climate in healthcare organizations
3. To analyze the competencies expected of the nurse administrator in long-term care
4. To evaluate one's own nurse administrator competencies using the AONE "self-assessment" checklist
5. To recognize the role that technology plays in long-term care administration

KEY TERMS

Lead: To direct on a course or direction

Manager: The person who handles or directs with a degree of skill

Culture: The set of shared attitudes, values, goals, and practices that characterize the institution or organization

Climate: The prevailing influence or environmental conditions characterizing a group

Competencies: Having requisite or adequate ability or qualities

Informatics: The collection, classification, storage, retrieval, and dissemination of recorded knowledge treated as a pure science and as an applied science

INTRODUCTION

Older adults consume 50% of all hospital care, both as consumers of healthcare services and as recipients of nursing care. Older adults also use more than 80% of home care services and occupy 90% of all nursing home beds in the United States (National Center for Health Statistics [NCHS], 2004). Because of this, nurses and nurse executives in long-term care are integral to the delivery of quality care to geriatric patients. The executive role of nurse administrators in long-term care places them in a unique and challenging position to manage, coordinate, and facilitate decision making in collaboration with allied healthcare professionals in providing long-term care.

THE NURSE LEADER IN LONG-TERM CARE

The Role of Nursing as a Profession

The authority for the practice of nursing is based upon a social contract that delineates professional rights and responsibilities, as well as measures for public accountability. In almost all countries, nursing practice is defined and governed by law on entrance into the profession and is regulated at the national or state level.

The aim of the nursing community worldwide is for its professionals to ensure quality care for all, while maintaining their credentials, code of ethics, standards, and competencies, and continuing their educations (Leader, 2011).

Nurses care for individuals of all ages and cultural backgrounds who are healthy or ill in a way based on the person's physical, social, psychological, emotional, and spiritual needs. The professional role combines physical science, social science, nursing theory, and technology in order to care for individuals.

The Role of the Assistant Director of Nursing

In many long-term care settings, an assistant director of nursing (ADON) is in place to back up the director of nursing (DON) and assist with administrative duties. The ADON may have specific responsibilities separate from, but complementary to, the DON. These may include the management of clinical operations, staff education or scheduling liaison among other faculty disciplines (i.e., nutrition, pharmacy), customer service, recruitment and retention, and quality assurance. The ADON is expected to work closely with the DON to determine his or her essential duties and responsibilities.

Additional Nursing Roles in Long-Term Care

Many long-term care facilities employ nurses who are certified in wound care and/or infectious diseases. Wound care nurses—sometimes referred to as wound, ostomy, and continence nurses (WOC)—specialize in wound management and the monitoring and treatment of wounds due to injury, disease, or medical treatment. WOC nurses work with patients' family and staff to educate them on wound care and prevention. For example, in long-term care, nurses' aids would be taught the proper way to avoid bed sores in the older adult population.

Infectious disease nurses are clinical nurse specialists who focus on infectious disease control work, primarily in major healthcare facilities such as hospitals and nursing homes. Their main goal is to monitor and prevent the spread of infections. These nurses may be referred to as "infectious disease nurses" or "infection control nurses;" however, there is a difference. An infectious disease nurse works primarily in an environment where physicians treat patients suffering from an infectious disease. The infection control nurse may be the administrative nurse who deals with policy making, surveillance of healthcare–acquired infections, and so on. In many facilities, the terms might be used interchangeably (Short, 2007).

Role and Scope

Nurse executives in long-term care lead with integrity, knowledge, and compassion in order to enhance an environment of quality care. They establish department directions and strategies, plan programs, and administer budgets to overall meet their institutions' or agencies' goals.

Nurse administrators are reliable human resources and facility resource managers. By setting and interpreting policy and developing structures for operating units, they assume a broad organizational perspective and represent the organization for their constituents, including the community.

The nurse leader in long-term care models, advocates, communicates, and leads in the development of programs and practice within the focus of the mission and goal of the organization (American Health Care Association, 2012). To be an effective leader, the nurse administrator must also be a good manager. Bennis (2003) draws several distinctions between managers and leaders. These differences essentially claim that managers are concerned with those issues focusing on system, short-term perspectives, maintenance, and watching the bottom line, for example. Leaders, on the other hand, are focused on people, inspiring trust, doing the right thing, looking at long-term perspective, and challenging the status quo (Bennis, 2003).

Siegel, Mueller, Anderson, and Dellefield (2010) discussed the pivotal role of the director of nursing in nursing homes. Their study found that a long history of inattention to the DON position, coupled with low expectation for the competencies and requisite educational preparation, has potentially compromised the capacity of DONs to promote and sustain high quality, cost-effective nursing home care.

Kotter (1999), in his book *What Leaders Really Do*, supports Bennis and suggests that the differences between management and leadership are real. He purports that management is about coping with complexity, whereas leadership, by contrast, is about coping with change. Both would agree that to be a success at management or leadership, a certain degree of competence is needed.

COMPETENCIES

What does it take for a nurse executive to be effective in long-term care? Is being considered a good leader or a good manager "enough"? What behaviors and competencies are necessary for the nurse executive in long-term care?

The "need to have" versus "nice to have" model can be applied to the competencies excellent nurse leaders should demonstrate. It is certainly not realistic to expect that a nurse leader would be equally competent in all areas. It is reasonable, however, to expect that the nurse executive would reach, at minimum, standard, if not above standard, competence in several areas, and be outstanding in others. These competencies include (but are not limited to): health communication promoter, quality performance overseer, developer of human resources, finance manager, compliance ensurer, and public relations cheerleader. **Figure 2.1** follows these interrelated roles of the nurse executive in long-term care.

The American Organization of Nurse Executives (AONE) published the AONE Nurse Executives Competencies in February 2005. In that document, skills common to nurses in executive practice in various organizations, regardless of their educational level or title, are described. These competencies

Figure 2.1 Healthcare Leadership Alliance (HLA) Model

The competencies are captured in a model developed by the Healthcare Leadership Alliance (HLA) in 2004. HLA members include AONE, the American College of Healthcare Executives, American College of Physician Executives, Healthcare Financial Management Association, Healthcare Information and Management Systems Society, and the Medical Group Management Association. This graphic model was used in work to identify a common core set of competencies for leadership executives in health care.

Source: Used with permission from American Organization of Nurse Executives (AONE)/The Healthcare Leadership Alliance (HLA).

can be used as a self-assessment tool, useful for the identification of areas needing growth. Additionally, aspiring nurse leaders can use them in personal planning preparation for their careers (AONE, 2005). Organizations may see them as a guideline for job descriptions, expectations, and evaluation of nurse leaders.

Basically, AONE believes that nurse leaders must be competent in:

- Communication and relationship management
- Knowledge of the healthcare environment
- Leadership
- Professionalism
- Business skills and principles

Table 2.1 AONE Competencies and Specific Behaviors (2005)

While all nursing leaders share these competency domains, the emphasis on particular competencies will be different depending on the leader's specific position in the organization.

Communication and relationship management competencies include:

1. Effective communication
2. Relationship management
3. Influence of behaviors
4. Ability to work with diversity
5. Shared decision making
6. Community involvement
7. Medical staff relationships
8. Academic relationships

Knowledge of the healthcare environment includes:

1. Clinical practice knowledge
2. Patient care–delivery models and work-design knowledge
3. Healthcare economics knowledge
4. Healthcare policy knowledge
5. Understanding of governance
6. Understanding of evidence-based practice
7. Outcome measurement
8. Knowledge of and dedication to patient safety
9. Understanding/utilization of case management
10. Knowledge of quality improvement and metrics
11. Knowledge of risk management

Leadership includes:

1. Foundational thinking skills
2. Personal journey disciplines
3. The ability to use systems thinking
4. Succession planning
5. Change management

Professionalism includes:

1. Personal and professional accountability
2. Career planning
3. Ethics
4. Evidence-based clinical and management practice
5. Advocacy for the clinical enterprise and for nursing practice
6. Active membership in a professional organization

(Continued)

Business skills and principles include:

1. Understanding of healthcare financing
2. Human resources management and development
3. Strategic management
4. Marketing
5. Information management and technology

This assessment tool is designed to assist you in assessing your level of preparation on each of the competencies.

For each competency, use a 5-pont scale to rate your level of competency from novice (1) to expert (5).

Identify the strategy(ies) you plan on implementing to raise your competency level. This will give you a good picture of how much preparation you will need to become a well rounded nurse executive.

Source: Used with permission from American Organization of Nurse Executives (AONE).

Recognizing that different types of organizations may emphasize particular competencies, all nurse leaders share the competency domains. **Table 2.1** depicts these competencies and the specific nursing leadership skills within each one.

The following discussion provides an in-depth description of the skills needed for competency in the five AONE leadership domains.[1]

Communication and Relationship Management

Effective Communication
- Make oral presentations to diverse audiences on nursing, health care, and organizational issues.
- Produce cogent and persuasive written materials to address nursing, health care, and organizational issues appropriate to the audience.
- Resolve and manage conflict.

Relationship Management
- Build trusting, collaborative relationships with:
  - Staff
  - Peers
  - Other disciplines and ancillary services

---

1. This section is printed with permission from American Organization of Nurse Executives (AONE).

- Physicians
- Vendors
- Community leaders
- Legislators
- Nursing and other educational programs
- Deliver "bad news" in such a way to maintain credibility.
- Follow through on promises and concerns.
- Provide service recovery to dissatisfied customers.
- Care about people as individuals and demonstrate empathy and concern while ensuring that organizational goals and objectives are met.
- Accomplish objectives through persuasion, celebrate successes and accomplishments, and communicate a shared vision.
- Assert views in nonthreatening, nonjudgmental ways.

Influencing Behaviors

- Create and communicate a shared vision.
- Reward appropriate behaviors and confront and manage inappropriate behaviors.
- Develop, communicate, and monitor behavior expectations.

Diversity

- Create an environment that recognizes and values differences in staff, physicians, patients, and communities.
- Assess current environment and establish indicators of progress toward cultural competency.
- Define diversity in terms of gender, race, religion, ethnicity, sexual orientation, age, etc.
- Analyze population data to identify cultural clusters.
- Define cultural competency and permeate principles throughout the organization.
- Confront inappropriate behaviors and attitudes toward diverse groups.
- Develop processes to incorporate cultural beliefs into care.

Shared Decision Making

- Engage staff and others in decision making.
- Promote decisions that are patient centered.
- Provide an environment conducive to opinion sharing.

Community Involvement

- Represent the organization to non-healthcare constituents within the community.
- Provide consultation to community and business leaders regarding nursing and health care.
- Be an effective board member for community and/or professional organizations.

Medical Staff Relationships

- Build credibility with physicians as a champion for patient care, quality, and nursing professionalism.
- Confront and address inappropriate behavior toward patients and staff.
- Represent nursing at the medical executive committee and other medical staff committees.
- Collaborate with medical staff leaders in determining needed patient-care services.
- Collaborate with physicians to develop patient-care protocols, policies, and procedures.
- Collaborate with physicians to determine patient-care equipment and facility needs.
- Utilize medical staff mechanisms to address physician clinical performance issues.
- Facilitate disputes involving physicians and nurses or other disciplines.

Academic Relationships

- Determine current and future supply and demand for nursing.
- Identify educational needs of existing and potential nursing staff.
- Collaborate with nursing programs to provide required resources.
- Collaborate with nursing programs in evaluating quality of graduating clinicians and develop mechanisms to enhance this quality.
- Serve on academic advisory councils.
- Collaborate with nursing faculty in nursing research and incorporate nursing research into practice nurse executive competencies.

Knowledge of the Healthcare Environment

Clinical Practice Knowledge

- Maintain knowledge of current nursing practice and the roles and functions of patient-care team members.

- Articulate patient-care standard as published by the Joint Commission, the Centers for Medicare & Medicaid Services, and professional nursing literature.
- Understand, articulate, and ensure compliance with the State Nurse Practice Act, State Board of Nursing regulations, regulatory agency standards, and policies of the organization.
- Ensure that written organization clinical policies and procedures are reviewed and updated in accordance with evidence-based practice.
- Role model lifelong learning, including clinical subjects such as disease processes, pharmaceuticals, and clinical technology.

Delivery Models/Work Design

- Maintain current knowledge of patient-care delivery systems and innovations.
- Articulate various delivery systems and patient-care models and the advantages/disadvantages of each.
- Serve as change agent when patient-care work/workflow is redesigned.
- Determine when new delivery systems are appropriate, and then envision and develop them.

Healthcare Economics

- Articulate federal and state payment systems and regulations, as well as private insurance issues, which affect organization's finances.
- Understand and articulate an individual organization's payer mix, case mix index (CMI), and benchmark database.

Healthcare Policy

- Provision of patient care (e.g., tort reform, malpractice/negligence, reimbursement).
- Participate in the legislative process concerning health care through membership in professional organizations and personal contact with public officials.
- Educate patient-care team members on the legislative and regulatory processes and methods for influencing both.
- Interpret impact of state and federal legislation on nursing and healthcare organizations.

Governance

- Articulate the role of the governing body of the organization in the following areas:

- Fiduciary responsibilities
- Credentialing
- Performance management
- Represent patient-care issues to the governing body.
- Participate in strategic planning and quality initiatives with the governing body.
- Interact with and educate the organization's board members regarding health care and the value of nursing care.
- Represent nursing at the organization's board meetings.

Evidence-Based Practice/Outcome Measurement

- Interpret information from research.
- Utilize research findings for the establishment of standards, practices, and patient-care models in the organization.
- Disseminate research findings to patient-care team members.
- Participate in studies that provide outcome measurements.
- Allocate nursing resources based on measurement of patient acuity/care needed.

Patient Safety

- Support the development and implementation of an organization-wide patient safety program.
- Design safe clinical systems, processes, policies, and procedures.
- Monitor clinical activities to identify both expected and unexpected risks.
- Support a nonpunitive reporting environment and a reward system for reporting unsafe practices.
- Support safety surveys, responding to and acting on safety recommendations.
- Ensure staff members are clinically competent and trained on their role in patient safety.
- Articulate and take action to support the Joint Commission National Patient Safety Goals.

Utilization/Case Management

- Articulate organization decision making for the criteria model adopted by the organization.
- Communicate key points of the model to a variety of audiences (nursing, financial, medical staff).
- Involve physicians in ongoing utilization management practices.

- Design continuum-of-care options for managing patient through-put (long-term care units, urgent-care centers, admission/discharge units, etc.).

Quality Improvement/Metrics

- Articulate the organization's quality improvement program and goals.
- Determine patient-care quality improvement goals and objectives.
- Define metrics as related to process improvement.
- Explain and utilize metrics as a unit of measure for any process.
- Articulate the link between metrics and goals.
- Articulate the link between organization metrics and national quality initiative/metrics.
- Target outcomes that are evidence based (comparison data benchmarking).
- Define quality metrics by:
  - Identifying the problem/process
  - Measuring success at improving specific areas of patient care
  - Analyzing the root causes or variation from quality standards
  - Improving the process with the evidence
  - Controlling solutions and sustaining success

Risk Management

- Identify areas of risk/liability.
- Ensure staff is educated on risk management and compliance issues.
- Develop systems that encourage/require prompt reporting of potential liability by staff at all levels.
- Envision and take action to correct identified areas of potential liability.

Leadership

Foundational Thinking Skills

- Address ideas, beliefs, or viewpoints that should be given serious consideration.
- Recognize one's own method of decision making and the role or beliefs, values, and inferences.
- Critically analyze organizational issues after a review of the evidence.
- Maintain curiosity and an eagerness to explore new knowledge and ideas.
- Promote nursing leadership as both a science and an art.

- Demonstrate reflective leadership and an understanding that all leadership begins from within.
- Provide visionary thinking on issues that impact the healthcare organization.

Personal Journey Disciplines

- Value and act on feedback that is provided about one's own strengths and weaknesses.
- Demonstrate the value of lifelong learning through one's own example.
- Learn from setbacks and failures as well as successes.
- Assess one's personal, professional, and career goals and undertake career planning.
- Seek mentorship from respected colleagues.

Systems Thinking

- Promote systems thinking as a value in the nursing organization.
- Consider the impact of nursing decisions on the healthcare organization as a whole.
- Provide leadership in building loyalty and commitment throughout the organization.
- Synthesize and integrate divergent viewpoints for the good of the organization.

Success Planning

- Promote nursing management as a desirable specialty.
- Conduct periodic organizational assessments to identify succession planning issues and establish action plans.
- Serve as a professional role model and mentor to future nursing leaders.
- Establish mechanisms that provide for early identification and mentoring of staff with leadership potential.
- Develop a succession plan for one's own position.

Change Management

- Utilize change theory to plan for the implementation of organizational changes.
- Serve as a change agent, assisting others in understanding the importance, necessity, impact, and process of change.
- Support staff during times of difficult transitions.

- Recognize one's own reaction to change and strive to remain open to new ideas and approaches.
- Adapt leadership style to situational needs.

Professionalism

Personal and Professional Accountability

- Create an environment that facilitates the team to initiate actions that produce results.
- Hold self and others accountable for actions and outcomes.
- Create an environment in which others are setting expectations and holding each other accountable.
- Answer for the results of one's own behaviors and actions.

Career Planning

- Develop own career plan and measure progress according to that plan.
- Coach others in developing their own career plans.
- Create an environment in which professional and personal growth is an expectation.

Ethics

- Articulate the application of the ethical principles to operations.
- Integrate high ethical standards and core values into everyday work activities.
- Create an environment that has a reputation for high ethical standards.

Evidence-Based Clinical and Management Practices

- Advocate use of documented best practices.
- Teach and mentor others to routinely utilize evidence-based data and research.

Advocacy

- Role model the perspective that patient care is the core of the organization's work.
- Assure that the clinical perspective is included in organizational decisions.
- Ensure that nurses are actively involved in decisions that affect their practice.

Active Membership in Professional Organizations
- Participate in at least one professional organization.
- Support and encourage others to participate in a professional organization.

Business Skills and Principles

Financial Management
- Articulate business models for healthcare organizations and fundamental concepts of economics.
- Describe general accounting principles and define basic accounting terms.
- Analyze financial statements.
- Manage financial resources by developing business plans.
- Establish procedures to assure accurate charging mechanisms.
- Educate patient-care team members on financial implications of patient-care decisions.

Human Resource Management
- Participate in workforce planning and employment decisions.
- Champion a diverse workforce.
- Use corrective discipline to mitigate workplace behavior problems.
- Interpret and evaluate employee satisfaction/quality of work surveys.
- Create opportunities for employees to be involved in decision making.
- Reward and recognize exemplary performance.
- Formulate programs to enhance work-life balance.
- Interpret legal and regulatory guidelines.
- Manage collective bargaining environments or implement programs to avoid the need.
- Identify and eliminate sexual harassment, workplace violence, and verbal and physical abuse.
- Implement ergonomically sound work environments to prevent worker injury and fatigue.
- Develop and implement bioterrorism-, biohazard-, and disaster-readiness plans.
- Identify clinical and leadership skills necessary for performing job-related tasks.
- Select top talent, matching organizational needs with appropriate skill sets (assess job candidate skill sets).

- Manage performance through rewards, recognition, counseling, and disciplinary action.
- Provide mentorship and career counseling to aspiring clinicians and leaders so they may develop required skill sets (succession planning).
- Identify future skill sets needed to remain competitive.
- Analyze market data in relation to supply and demand and manage resources to ensure appropriate compensation.
- Develop and implement recruitment and retention strategies.

Strategic Management

- Analyze the situation and identify strategic direction.
- Conduct SWOT (strengths, weaknesses, opportunities, and threats) and gap analyses.
- Formulate objectives, goals, and specific strategies related to mission and vision.
- Understand what organizations should measure in order to "balance" the financial perspective.
- Measure and analyze performance from the learning and growth, business process, customer, and financial perspectives.

Marketing

- Analyze marketing opportunities.
- Develop marketing strategies.
- Integrate marking and communications strategies.
- Use public relations and media outlets to promote your organization.

Information Management and Technology

- Demonstrate basic competency in email and common word processing, spreadsheet, and Internet programs.
- Recognize the relevance of nursing data for improving practice.
- Recognize limitations of computer applications.
- Use telecommunication devices.
- Utilize hospital database management, decision support, and expert system programs to access information and analyze data from disparate sources for use in planning for patient-care processes and systems.
- Participate in system change processes and utility analysis.
- Participate in the evaluation of information systems in practice settings.
- Evaluate and revise patient-care processes and utility analysis.

- Participate in the evaluation of information systems in practice settings.
- Evaluate and revise patient-care processes and systems.
- Use computerized management systems to record administrative data (billing data, quality assurance data, workload data, etc.).
- Use applications for structured data entry (classification systems, acuity level, etc.).
- Recognize the utility of nursing involvement in the planning, design, choice, and implementation of information systems in the practice environment.
- Demonstrate awareness of societal and technological trends, issues, and new developments as they apply to nursing.
- Demonstrate proficient awareness of legal and ethical issues related to client data, information, and confidentiality.
- Read and interpret benchmarking, financial, and occupancy data.

This is not intended to be an exhaustive list of all areas of expertise for individual nurses in executive practice. It does, however, illustrate how complex and important their roles have become. Nursing leadership/management is as much a specialty as any other clinical nursing specialty. As such, it requires proficiency and competent practice specific to the executive role. The AONE Nurse Executive Competencies sets the standard for that practice.

ORGANIZATIONAL CULTURE AND CLIMATE

Nurse executives in long-term care can be found in a variety of settings. These include assisted living, skilled nursing, rehabilitation, home care, and of more recent development, continuous care retirement communities (CCRC).

Wherever nurse executives are found in long-term care, there is one constant; the culture and climate of an organization leave an imprint on that organization. Nurse leaders must recognize the difference, especially in situations of change.

Culture is divided into five components: values, beliefs, myths, tradition, and norms. Although these components are different (yet impossible) to measure and even harder to articulate, they are real and have to be acknowledged by nurse administrators as part of their role and responsibilities (The Kennedy Group, 2007).

Climate is the label used to describe the dimension of the work environment, and can be measured with relative precision. Factors that can determine the climate of any organization include: leadership, organizational structure, historical forces, accountability standards, behavior standards, communication, rewards, trust, commitment, vision, and organizational connectedness (The Kennedy Group).

In 1990, Schneider edited a book that attempted to distinguish culture from climate. None of the contributors came to any clear conclusions (Ashkanasy, Wilderom, & Peterson, 2000). Regardless of the inability to find consensus among experts, the fact remains, nurse leaders in long-term care must recognize the impact that culture and climate have on their organizations.

NURSING INFORMATICS IN LONG-TERM CARE

Nursing informatics, as defined by the American Nurses Association (2001), is a specialty that integrates nursing science to manage and communicate data, information, and knowledge in nursing practice. All nurse leaders in long-term care can use information management concepts to help them identify, collect, and record data pertinent to nursing care. Technology should be used to support the organization's direct and indirect care services.

Nurse executives can manage department finances by using software that provides for budgeting and cost accounting. Staffing, scheduling, and resources can be managed with computer programs. Office automation that incorporates word processing, email, spreadsheets, presentation graphics, and data makes the work easier for the nurse executive.

Effective nursing leadership in long-term care demands knowledge of the field of healthcare informatics. These are the processes that help to smooth the interface between clinical and administrative systems to improve diagnoses and treatments and ultimately quality of life for the elderly individual.

SUMMARY

The impact that the "graying of America" has and will have on the current and future state of long-term care is unprecedented. Nursing executives will play a critical role in meeting the multiple healthcare needs of this burgeoning population. Nurse executives must have the distinct ability to merge nursing and management skills.

As the healthcare arena changes, due to bureaucratic and/or economic demands, the nurse leader is challenged to keep pace with this dramatically changing healthcare environment.

As the nursing leader in long-term care, it is solely up to you to ensure that the organization's mission becomes a reality and to be keenly aware of the current political, social, legal, economic, ethical, and spiritual developments that impact your organization.

So how do you do this? How do you ensure that your knowledge base is sound and that you are carrying out your role as nurse executive with all of the current information at hand? One way is to partner with graduate education programs at colleges and universities to work together to design graduate nursing administration programs and continuing education offerings to accommodate nurse executives. Additionally, it will be good practice to seek out Magnet long-term care nursing facilities (LTCNF) in order to identify excellent preceptors who can guide you and work with you to promote quality care for the aging population.

The complex role of nurses in administrative and executive practice in long-term care has certainly evolved over time. The focus on nursing services has moved to a much broader one of responsibility and accountability for patient services. This has, without a doubt, changed forever the perception of the nurse executive. Nurse leaders are now seen as integral members of senior management teams.

The complex role of the nurse leader in long-term care is demonstrated in her ability to possess strong management and leadership skills; to be a confident decision maker, utilizing critical thinking skills; to possess a strong knowledge base in accounting, finance, business, and computer technology; and to have solid communication, human relations, and organizational skills. When nurse executives in long-term care utilize these skills effectively, only positive organizational outcomes will emerge.

Discussion Questions

1. How does the Health Care Reform Act impact strategic planning by nurse executives in long-term care?

2. What actions by the nurse executive will contribute to the professional growth of the patient-care staff (nurses, certified nurse aides)?

3. Since the nurse executive is constantly involved in the decision-making process, the ability for her to make good decisions is an extremely important part of leadership. Discuss several decision-making models and explain their usefulness in making decisions in long-term care.

4. How can nurse leaders in long-term care deal with unplanned change?

REFERENCES

American Health Care Association. (2012). About AHCA. Retrieved March 13, 2012, from http://www.ahcancal.org/about_ahca.

American Nurses Association. (2001). *Scope and standard of nursing informatics practice.* Washington, DC: Author.

American Organization of Nurse Executives. (2005). AONE Nurse Executive Competencies. Retrieved March 13, 2012, from http://www.aone.org/resources/leadership%20tools/PDFs/AONE_NEC.pdf.

Ashkanasy, N., Wilderom, C., & Peterson, M. (2000). *Handbook of organizational culture and climate.* Thousand Oaks, CA: Sage.

Bennis, W. (2003). *On becoming a leader.* Cambridge, MA: Perseus.

Kotter, J. (1999). *What leaders really do.* Cambridge, MA: Harvard Business Review Press.

Leader, C. (2011, November 4). *Becoming a nurse: The journey.* Retrieved January 9, 2012, from http://www.castrocolonies.org/featured/becoming-a-nurse-the-journey/.

National Center for Health Statistics. (2004). *Nursing home care.* Retrieved January 12, 2012, from http://www.cdc.gov/nchs/fastats/nursingh.htm.

Schneider, B. (Ed.). (1990). *Organizational climate and culture.* San Francisco: Jossey-Bass.

Short, B. (2007, October). *Infectious disease vs. infection control nurses.* Nursing Forum. Retrieved January 9, 2012, from http://allnurses.com/infectious-disease-nursing/infectious-disease-vs-254775.html.

Siegel, E. O., Mueller, C., Anderson, K., & Dellefield, M. E. (2010). The pivotal role of the director of nursing in nursing homes. *Nursing Administration Quarterly, 34*(2), 110–121.

The Kennedy Group. (2007). *Culture vs. climate.* Retrieved October 10, 2011, from http://thekennedygroup.com/_pdfs/culture_vs_climate.pdf.

Chapter 3

Rehabilitative Therapists in Geriatric Health Services

Alice McDonnell, DrPH, MPA, RN, and Sneh D. Akruvala, MS, RN

This chapter introduces the role of therapists in a geriatric/gerontological environment. The following three healthcare professionals are discussed:

1. Physical therapy
2. Occupational therapy
3. Speech-language pathology

This chapter also explains how these services are integrated with the care of the aging population.

LEARNING OBJECTIVES

1. To understand the role of therapists (physical, occupational, and speech) in geriatric and gerontological administration
2. To heighten awareness about the role of therapist (physical, occupational, and speech) assistants and aides in long-term care
3. To gain knowledge about basic regulations needed for therapists to specialize in the field of gerontology
4. To identify the different environments in which therapists would treat the older adults
5. To gain knowledge about the implications involved for therapists in administration

KEY TERMS

Physical Therapy: Specialty involving diagnosis and treatment of disorders of the musculoskeletal system

Occupational Therapy: Specialty involving therapeutic use of self-care to increase independent function, enhance development, and prevent disability

Speech-Language Pathology: Rehabilitative treatment of physical and/or cognitive deficits/disorders resulting in difficulty with verbal communication

INTRODUCTION

"Health is defined as a state of complete physical, mental, social, and spiritual well-being of an individual and not merely an absence of disease or infirmity."

—World Health Organization

Various factors affect the health of an individual, amongst which "aging" plays an important role (see **Exhibit 3.1**). Aging is a natural and irreversible process. As we age, the function of the body organs and systems start to decline, and as a result, our bodies undergo many changes. Of all the age groups, it is the elderly population that has the highest number of diseases and disorders that reduce its functional abilities. Some of the most common problems of older adults are arthritis, osteoporosis, poor nutrition, cardiac diseases, stroke, dysphagia, hip fractures, joint replacements, atherosclerosis, and neurological diseases that lead to the rise in demand of healthcare professionals. Advances in the medical technologies are enabling more individuals suffering from critical problems to survive and live longer.

Exhibit 3.1   An Outlook on Aging

The elderly population in America is increasing at an unprecedented rate. The number of people aged 65 and older constitute the fastest growing segment of the population. When the Baby Boom generation enters its senior years, between 2010 and 2030, it is projected that one in five Americans will be over the age of 65. With this "graying of America" comes not only the demand for physicians and other healthcare professionals with expertise in gerontology and geriatrics, but also a huge growth in the number of caregivers who can help the aged live longer and healthier lives.

Source: Reprinted with permission from The AGS Foundation for Health in Aging. (2009). *What is Geriatrics?* Retrieved March 4, 2011, from http://www.healthinaging.org/public_education/what_is_geriatrics.php.

Older adults are particularly vulnerable to chronic, debilitating conditions such as heart attack and stroke. They also suffer from limited function or disabilities and may have neurological disorders that result in speech, language, and/or swallowing impairments. Thus, in the long run, the demand for therapists is going to increase, as the number of people opting for their services is on the rise (U.S. Bureau of Labor Statistics [BLS], 2009b; BLS, 2009d; BLS, 2009f).

PHYSICAL THERAPY

Physical therapy is a healthcare specialty that identifies and treats the diseases of the musculoskeletal system.

> It provides services to individuals for developing, maintaining/restoring maximum movement with functional ability throughout their lifespan. It is concerned with identifying and maximizing quality of life and movement potential within the spheres of promotion, prevention, treatment/intervention, habilitation, and rehabilitation. This therapy encompasses the physical, psychological, emotional, and social wellbeing of an individual (World Confederation for Physical Therapy, 2011).

Physical therapists, also referred to as PTs, are licensed healthcare professionals who diagnose and treat individuals of all ages having medical problems or other health-related conditions that limit their abilities to move and perform functional activities in their daily lives (BLS, 2009d).

Physical therapist assistants (PTAs) work as a part of the therapy team. They assist the PTs in rendering physical therapy services to the individuals suffering from conditions that limit clients' abilities to perform activities of daily living and their ability to move. They work under the direction and supervision of the therapists, who are responsible for the care provided by the assistants (American Physical Therapy Association, 2011). Physical therapist aides work under the direction and direct supervision of the physical therapist and/or physical therapist assistant and help to make the therapy sessions productive (BLS, 2009e).

The ultimate goal of physical therapy is to restore maximal functional independence to each individual. The therapy process includes examination/assessment, evaluation, diagnosis, prognosis, plan of care/intervention, and reexamination (World Confederation for Physical Therapy, 2011):

· *Assessment.* The examination or assessment is done by taking a history, screening, and using specific tests and measures to identify actual or potential impairments, activity limitations, participation restrictions, or disabilities.

- *Evaluation.* The evaluation of the results of the examination of the individual and environment is done through analysis and synthesis within a process of clinical reasoning to determine facilitators and barriers to optimal human functioning.
- *Diagnosis and prognosis.* Diagnosis and prognosis represent the outcome of the process of clinical reasoning and the incorporation of additional information from other professionals, as needed. A plan of care is developed with measurable goals.
- *Intervention.* Intervention/treatment is implemented to reach desired goals. It may aim at prevention of impairments, activity limitations, restrictions, disability, or injury, including promotion and maintenance of health, quality of life, workability, and fitness at all ages.
- *Reexamination.* Reexamination necessitates determining the outcomes.

The basic requirements for licensure as a physical therapist include graduation from an accredited physical therapy education program, passing the National Physical Therapy Examination, and fulfilling state requirements, such as jurisprudence exams. Some states require continuing education for maintaining licensure. In order to specialize in geriatrics, the therapist needs to:

1. Complete 2,000 hours of direct patient care in Geriatrics within a span of 10 years, with 25% or 500 hours having occurred within the last 3 years. Direct patient care must include activities in each of the following elements of patient/client management applicable to gerontology: examination, evaluation, diagnosis, prognosis, and intervention.
2. Submit evidence of successful completion of an American Physical Therapy Association (APTA)–credentialed post-professional clinical residency (American Board of Physical Therapy Specialists, 2011).

Physical therapist assistants must graduate from a Commission on Accreditation in Physical Therapy Education (CAPTE)–accredited, 2-year associate degree program and pass the national licensure or certification examination. Licensure or certification is required in most states to work as a PTA. The length of the PTA education program is usually 2 years (5 semesters). The education consists of general education, physical therapy courses, and clinical education (American Physical Therapy Association, 2011).

Physical therapist aides are typically required at minimum to have high school diploma. They are usually trained on the job, and the employers provide clinical on-the-job training. Licensing is not needed to practice as a PT aide. Moreover, after gaining experience and completing an accredited education program, a PT aide may advance to become a PT assistant (BLS, 2009e).

OCCUPATIONAL THERAPY

Occupational Therapy is a healthcare specialty that involves therapeutic use of self-care and work and play activities to increase independent function, enhance development, and prevent disability. It focuses on activities of daily living (ADLs), because they are the cornerstone of independent living.

The term *occupation* refers to the tasks and activities that one does in everyday life. Examples of ADLs are eating, dressing, bathing, preparing meals, doing laundry, shopping, driving, and using public transportation (Merck Manual for Health Care Professionals, 2009).

Occupational therapists, also referred to as OTs, are licensed healthcare professionals who help patients improve their ability to perform tasks in living and working environments. They work with individuals who suffer from mentally, physically, developmentally, or emotionally disabling conditions. They assist individuals to develop, recover, or maintain daily living and working skills (BLS, 2009b).

Occupational therapist assistants (OTAs) and aides work under the supervision of the OTs to provide rehabilitative services to individuals with mental, physical, emotional, or developmental impairments (BLS, 2009c).

The goal of an occupational therapist is not only to help clients improve basic motor functions and cognitive and emotional abilities, but also to compensate for loss of function. Their goal is to help clients have independent, productive, and satisfying lives (BLS, 2009b).

The occupational therapy process consists of three main steps of assessment, planning, and intervention:

- *Assessment.* The OT process is mainly based on initial and repeated assessments. The occupational therapist, together with the person seeking help, will focus on individual and environmental abilities and problems related to activities in the person's daily life. Assessment includes the use of standardized procedures, interviews, observations in a variety of settings, and consultation with significant people in the person's life.
- *Planning.* The results of the assessment are the basis of the plan, which includes short- and long-term aims of treatment. The plan should be relevant to the person's development stage, habits, roles, lifestyle preferences, and the environment.

· *Intervention.* This focuses on programs that are person oriented and environmental. These programs are designed to facilitate performance of everyday tasks and adaptation of settings in which the person works, lives, and socializes. Examples of intervention include teaching new techniques and providing equipment—which facilitate being independent in personal care, reducing environmental barriers, and providing resources to lessen stress (World Federation of Occupational Therapists, 2011).

The basic requirements for licensure as an occupational therapist include graduation from an accredited educational program and passing a national certification examination. Those who pass the exam are awarded the title "Occupational Therapist Registered." Almost all the states require continuing education for maintaining licensure. In order to specialize in gerontology, the therapist needs to:

1. Be certified or licensed by and in good standing with an American Occupational Therapist Association (AOTA)-recognized credentialing or regulatory body.
2. Have a minimum of 5 years of practice as an occupational therapist.
3. Have a minimum of 5,000 hours of experience as an occupational therapist in the certification area in the last 5 calendar years.
4. Have a minimum of 500 hours of experience delivering occupational therapy services in the specializing area to clients (individuals, groups, or populations) in the last 5 calendar years. Service delivery may be paid or voluntary (American Occupational Therapy Association, 2009a, 2009b).

To become an occupational therapist assistant, one must graduate from an Accreditation Council for Occupational Therapy Education (ACOTE)-accredited 2-year associate degree program, pass the national certification exam administered by the National Board for Certification in Occupational Therapy, and attain licensure as required by the state. Many states regulate the practice by licensing, certification, or registration. The courses to be studied to become an OTA include:

1. First year—an introduction to health care, anatomy, physiology, and basic medical terminology
2. Second year—rigorous occupational therapy courses in areas such as mental health, adult physical disabilities, gerontology, and pediatrics

3. The occupational therapist aides are typically required to have at minimum a high school diploma. They are usually trained on the job, and the employers provide clinical on-the-job training. Licensing is not needed to practice as an OT aide. Moreover, after gaining experience and completing an accredited education program, an OT aide may advance to become an OT assistant (BLS, 2009c).

SPEECH-LANGUAGE PATHOLOGY (SPEECH THERAPY)

Speech-language pathology (speech therapy) is the corrective or rehabilitative treatment of physical and/or cognitive deficits/disorders resulting in difficulty with verbal communication. This includes both speech (articulation, intonation, rate, intensity) and language (phonology, morphology, syntax, semantics, pragmatics, both receptive and expressive language, including reading and writing). Depending on the nature and severity of the disorder, common treatments may range from physical strengthening exercises and instructive or repetitive practice and drilling to the use of audiovisual aids (WordIQ.com, 2010).

Speech-language pathologists (sometimes called the speech therapists) assess, diagnose, treat, and help to prevent disorders related to speech, language, cognitive communication, voice, swallowing, and fluency. They work with clients of all ages. Speech, language, and swallowing difficulties can result from a variety of causes, including stroke, brain injury or deterioration, developmental delays or disorders, learning disabilities, cerebral palsy, cleft palate, voice pathology, intellectual disabilities, hearing loss, or emotional problems. These problems may be congenital, developmental, or acquired. The ultimate goal of speech-language pathologists is to help patients develop or recover reliable communication and swallowing skills so that they can fulfill their educational, vocational, and social roles (BLS, 2009f).

Speech-language pathology assistants are support personnel who perform tasks prescribed, directed, and supervised by American Speech-Language-Hearing Association (ASHA)–certified speech-language pathologists (SLPs). The SLPs are responsible for the services provided by the assistant. Different terminology is used in different states that refers to the support personnel in speech-language pathology (e.g., communication aides, paraprofessionals, and service extenders). These support personnel may have a different scope of responsibilities in the work settings based on their level of training (American Speech-Language-Hearing Association, 1997–2012).

The speech therapy process consists of the three main steps of identifying and assessing client's needs, planning, and intervening:

- *Assessment.* The assessment is individualized and is related to the client's communication skills. There are two steps in assessment:
  - Screen all areas of communicative function
  - A comprehensive assessment of the specific areas that may be challenging

  The assessment usually includes standardized and nonstandardized tests and clinical observations.
- *Planning.* The plan that includes short- and long-term goals of treatment is based on the results of the assessment. An individualized plan of care is developed on the basis of each client's needs.
- *Intervention.* The therapist will provide direct intervention for areas of weakness. The SLP will provide necessary instruction and strategies during therapy sessions to help achieve preset goals. The therapist will also use the session to go over the strategies and skills taught. Additional activities specific to a client's needs will also be provided by the therapist to increase the carry-over of skills learned within the therapy setting to the home environment.

The licensing requirements to be a speech-language pathologist are a master's degree from an accredited college or university; a passing score on the national examination on speech-language pathology; 300 to 375 hours of supervised clinical experience and 9 months of postgraduate professional clinical experience. Some states require continuing education for licensure renewal (BLS, 2009f). Speech-language pathologists may specialize in:

- Particular age groups
- Certain speech or language disorders
- Feeding and swallowing disorders (or dysphagia)
- There are no specific requirements similar to those for physical or occupational therapists to specialize in the field of gerontology yet.

To become a speech-language pathologist assistant, ASHA recommends completion of a 2-year associate's degree from a technical training program. The requirements to practice as an SLP assistant vary across the country, and the interested individuals should check with the state of intended employment for that state's specific requirements. State licensure boards currently regulating support personnel have training requirements that range from a high school diploma to a bachelors' degree plus graduate credit hours.

ASHA no longer has a recognition process for associate degree technical training programs nor a registration process for speech-language pathology assistants. However, ASHA's "Guidelines for Training, Use, and Supervision of Speech-Language Pathology Assistants" can provide the basis for the commonly used terms to identify SLP support personnel, training and educational requirements, and job responsibilities (American Speech-Language-Hearing Association, 2004).

AREAS OF WORK

Physical therapists rehabilitate people with physical disabilities and provide wellness and prevention programs. Occupational therapists use specialized knowledge to help individuals to perform daily living skills and achieve maximum independence. Speech-language pathologists specialize in the prevention, diagnosis, and treatment of speech and language problems as well as of swallowing (dysphagia) difficulties. The assistants and aides work under the supervision of the therapists and assist them to render cost-effective therapy services. They work with each other in a multidisciplinary approach as a team (BLS, 2009a).

These professionals treat older adults in multiple settings that may include, but are not confined to the following:

- Acute-care hospitals
- Home health/homes/home care programs
- Rehabilitation centers
- Adult daycare programs/day clinics
- Health/fitness centers
- Nursing homes
- Senior housing
- Skilled nursing facilities
- Private practices
- Outpatient clinics
- Hospices
- Community mental health centers
- Community-based rehabilitation programs
- Senior citizen centers
- Assisted-living facilities

ADMINISTRATION

Long-term care administration is gaining popularity as one of the most important healthcare fields. It is a business that needs a good administrator and management team to plan, direct, coordinate and supervise the delivery of care.

Health administrators have varying roles and functions depending on the size of the facility they oversee. They handle daily operations that include finances, facility operations, admissions, policy analysis, budgeting, and human resources. They may have some direct activities in the clinical areas, such as nursing, therapy, medical records, and health information. Their main goal in all settings is to improve quality and efficiency of health care, while controlling costs, as insurance companies and Medicare demand higher levels of accountability (BLS, 2009a).

Administrators and management have to work closely with each health professional providing care to patients, including nurses, physicians, surgeons, therapists, and technicians. Usually, an organization categorizes the expertises as specific departments. A director or department head who is very experienced in that specific clinical area handles each department. For example, a director of physical therapy is an experienced physical therapist who establishes and implements policies, objectives, and procedures for his or her department, evaluates the individuals and work quality, develops reports and budgets, and coordinates activities with other departments (BLS, 2009a).

A facility may have a rehabilitation department/unit in which the physical therapist, occupational therapist, and speech-language pathologist, along with their assistants and aides, provide services to the clients. Each patient has a written plan of care for services that include diagnosis and prognosis of condition and treatment regime intended to enhance and increase a patient's functional abilities. The physical therapist, occupational therapist, and speech-language pathologist are members of the multidisciplinary health team, and they may be employed (full-time/part-time) or be contracted with an organization, such as a hospital; skilled nursing, assisted living, or nursing home; or may have a private practice. Though the therapists mainly work in the clinical area, some of them do take up supervisory and administrative roles.

Physical, occupational, and speech therapist are important members of an organization, and they make their contribution in certain administrative areas that include, but are not limited to, the following:

1. Recruitment
   - Recruitment is one of the most important aspects of administration.
   - The administrator faces a few challenges while recruiting a therapist. The professional qualifications and credentials of the therapists have to be verified, and the administrator has to

determine whether the therapist's goals blend with the institution's mission and values.
- The therapist's licensures should also be verified before recruitment.
- The administrator may request permission of the therapist to contact previous employers in order to know more about the style of work of the therapist.
- In addition, the administrator should also be aware if the therapist's license has been revoked anytime and why.

2. Facilities and equipment
   - If a facility is to provide rehabilitation services to the patients, the administrative/management team has to provide adequate space, facilities, and equipment within the facility to fulfill the professional, educational, and administrative needs of the therapists.
   - The therapy director and the administrator need to work together to see that each service area is easily accessible to patients by means of transportation ordinarily available to the patients requiring the services.

3. Policies and procedures
   - These are usually developed by the director of rehabilitation services or by the designated medical staff committee in cooperation with representatives from the medical staff, the administration, the nursing service, and other services.
   - There are certain written personnel policies (that are to be kept current), including professional qualification and state licensure information.
   - There are written policies for patient-care practices and procedures established by a group of professional personnel, including physicians, physical or occupational therapists, or speech-language pathologists. These policies are evaluated at least annually and revised as necessary.

4. Treatment order
   - The therapy treatment can be initiated only upon written prescription of the responsible physician.
   - When the therapy is prescribed, the therapist determines the need of the service and then develops a plan of care.

5. Patient records
   · All kinds of therapy orders, procedures, and treatment need to be recorded in the patient's medical record.
   · The responsible therapist has to make notations in the patient's chart that reflect repeated evaluations of the patient's progress. Records are reviewed by the medical staff for evaluation of the service and to ascertain means of improving the quality of patient care.
   · Both the therapy department and management have to ensure that there is appropriate utilization of services (U.S. Government Printing Office, 2012).

ROLE OF PT, OT, AND SLP ASSISTANTS AND AIDES IN LONG-TERM CARE

As the population is aging, the function of their various organs and systems start to decline. The aging population has many coexisting conditions that require various types of services, including rehabilitative therapies. The day-by-day increasing work of therapists has led to the existence of the paraprofessionals—assistants and aides. They play a significant role in providing care to older adults, but their work usually goes unnoticed. Provided here are brief descriptions of the roles and tasks that assistants and aides can perform in the specific physical therapy, occupational therapy, and speech-language pathology fields under the direction and supervision of a PT, OT, or SLP.

Physical Therapy

According to the Bureau of Labor Statistics (2009e), the assistants and aides support physical therapists in rendering care to clients who need improvement in mobility and pain, and lessening of physical disabilities.

Assistants

Physical therapist assistants assist PTs in providing care to patients. They provide exercise instruction; therapeutic methods like electrical stimulation, mechanical traction, and ultrasound; massage; and gait and balance training. The assistants record the patient's responses to treatment and report the outcome of each treatment to the physical therapist.

Aides

Physical therapist aides are usually responsible for keeping the treatment area clean and organized, and for the preparation of each patient's therapy.

They help clients in their transportation, such as moving to or from a treatment area. The duties of an aide also include some office tasks, such as ordering needed supplies, answering the phone, and filling out paperwork (BLS, 2009e).

Occupational Therapy

According to the Bureau of Labor Statistics (2009c), the assistants and aides, under the direction of occupational therapists, provide rehabilitative care to patients with mental, physical, emotional, or developmental impairments.

Assistants

Occupational therapists develop a treatment plan, and the assistants follow the plan to provide rehabilitative activities and exercises to the clients. The tasks that an assistant can perform include, but are not limited to, teaching older adults the proper method of moving from a bed into a wheelchair and of stretching and limbering the hand muscles; monitoring the correctness of the activities performed by the client; encouraging independent activities; assisting professionals in administering diagnostic tests of clients' abilities; instructing clients and their families in home programs, basic living skills, and care and use of adaptive equipment; recording the client's progress for the OT and documenting the billing of the client's health insurance provider.

Aides

OT Aides usually prepare the work area and materials, and assemble equipment used during treatment. They are responsible for a range of clerical tasks, including scheduling appointments, answering the telephone, restocking or ordering depleted supplies, and filling out insurance forms or other paperwork. They help in the transportation of the clients to and from the therapy area. They report information and observations to their supervisors daily (BLS, 2009c).

Speech-Language Pathology

States use different terms to refer to the SLP support personnel, such as communication aides, service extenders, and paraprofessionals. Aides are not widely used in the field of speech-language pathology. However, the role of an SLP assistant is important. ASHA's (2004) "Guidelines for Training, Use, and Supervision of Speech-Language Pathology Assistants" must be followed. The tasks that an assistant may perform include assisting the therapist with speech-language and hearing screenings; informal documentation and, during assessment of patients/clients, following the written treatment plans formulated by the therapist; performing clerical duties (e.g., preparing work area, materials, and equipment used during the treatment; answering phone calls; scheduling activities; and filing paperwork); maintaining equipment; data collection for monitoring quality

State laws vary and may differ from ASHA guidelines. Specific state regulations should be checked for particular state's scope of responsibilities of an SLP assistant (American Speech-Language-Hearing Association, 2004).

BRIEF DESCRIPTION OF THE SURVEYS CONDUCTED

The main emphasis of the chapter is on the role of physical therapists, occupational therapists, and speech-language pathologists in the field of gerontological administration. The authors conducted a qualitative survey with questions related to their work in gerontology, and following are responses to the survey questions.

The physical therapists, occupational therapists, and speech-language pathologists that were interviewed all have long-term experience in the clinical and gerontology field.

Therapists were asked: what is the role of (or how would you define) a therapist (PT/OT/SLP) in long-term care? The therapists described their role as:

- The SLPs said their overall role is to assist clients to communicate in a functional manner to the best of their ability in which the norms for the population for speech and language are considered.
- PTs and OTs explained their role as assisting older adults with returning maximum function in regard to self-care activities, functional mobility, and finding a purpose in those activities. They also play a very important role in discharge recommendations.

When the researcher asked the therapists if they found any changes in their role in the present compared to the previous decade, the therapists mentioned that they believed there is more of a focus on evidence-based practice in the present. More therapy is based on efficacy studies so that techniques can be better defended. The insurance companies have become strict and are more closely scrutinizing the therapy methods and the evidence of functional gains. The therapists need to provide evidence as to why the therapy is needed for the patient in order for it to be paid for by Medicare/Medicaid.

The continuum of care plays a very important role in gerontology. The authors asked the therapists about their role in the continuum of care, and the therapists explained that their role is usually in the sub-acute setting, hospitals, home care, outpatient departments, rehab facilities, assisted living, skilled nursing facilities, and nursing homes. The PTs and/or OTs evaluate patients' functional status and make recommendations to modify the environment or provide adaptive equipment to improve their overall function. The SLP plays an important role in dysphagia, language/cognition/orientation for dementia (Alzheimer's) patients; speech or voicing for Parkinson's disease patients; and other voice disorder/aphasia cases.

On being asked about their opinions on impact of regulations/licensure on the delivery of therapy to the senior, the therapists commented that the regulations have changed from time to time and have become more direct and specific as to who is able to provide what kind of care to the aging population. The basic regulations needed by the therapists have been explained earlier in this chapter. The therapists believe that the regulations do have an impact on the delivery of the care to the seniors, as it helps them to stay up to date on new information, issues, and treatment related to older adults and the general population.

One of the questions the authors asked the therapists concerned the important issues regarding older adults that they faced on a regular basis and how they handle them. According to the therapists, the important issues regarding aging adults they faced on a regular basis are freedom and safety. Freedom and safety are very important and tend to be inversely proportionate. If one increases a patient's freedom, his/her safety may be jeopardized; and if one focuses on safety, a patient's freedom to do things may become limited. Thus, it is a challenging issue to balance the demands of independence and safety. For example, at home, orientation is maximized, the client is happier, but safety may be compromised. However, it is opposite in a facility where clients are safe, but their freedom is limited and they tend to become confused or disoriented.

The therapists were also asked about how they addressed the concerns of the senior residents and families. All the therapists' surveys emphasized that the Health Insurance Portability and Accountability Act (HIPAA) and clients' privacy rights should be kept in mind while addressing the issues and concerns of the client. However, they said that if the clients did not have an insight or were not aware of their deficits, they could involve the client's legal guardian in their plan of care.

On being questioned about the changes they found in the problems of the older adults over a period of time, the therapists said that the older adults are living longer and the number of facilities focusing on long-term care is gradually growing. The therapists are facing various ethical dilemmas while treating their clients. The general problem and difficult decision for the families and the therapists is to make recommendations and confirm to say when the elderly can no longer safely live at home under the conditions in which they have always lived.

The authors asked the therapists to describe ethical dilemmas that they faced while providing care to older adults. The SLP talked about a few ethical dilemmas with dysphagia clients' right of autonomy when their decision making may be compromised. For example, a client has dysphagia that could be very fatal. Medical advice says to stop eating (take only liquids) but the client tells the SLP that he is still going to eat. In this case, the SLP may teach some techniques to the client that would help reduce the chances of dysphagia (this is where the ethical dilemma arises). Another example was about a client suffering from an end-stage disease. The client is immobile, has great pain, and may not live long. Is it still acceptable to trouble the client by providing therapies that may not even treat the condition of the client? A client is over 100 years old and needs a speaking aid device that costs about $8,000. The cost of the device is to be paid by the patient, as insurance does not cover it. The client may not live long enough to utilize it. In this case, do you still recommend it or not?

The therapists were asked for their opinions on "Wii-hab" therapy and its usefulness for the aging population. The PT and OT emphasized that Wii-hab therapy is a new kind of therapy they adapted, in which they used gaming technology (the Nintendo Wii) for rehabilitation. Wii-hab therapy is helpful for the rehabilitation of patients with various diseases including, but not limited to, joint replacement, stroke, Parkinson's disease, and sports injuries. Some of the therapists interviewed by the author use Wii-hab as a method of therapy because the outcome results of the clients improved noticeably, especially in case of older adults.

The final question asked by the authors in order to know the impact was the role therapists have in gerontology administration. The responses received from the therapists were interesting. The therapists believe that their role does have a positive impact on administration related to gerontology. The OTs and PTs stated that they had a direct impact on the length of stay (LOS) of a client, because, before discharging a client, a PT/OT evaluation is necessary. This directly affects the finance or reimbursements for the health facility. They also have to ensure the safety of the client upon discharge by providing the necessary adaptive equipment. The speech-language pathologist who was interviewed mentioned that he made recommendations to the administration for monitoring client safety and enhancing the communication process with the older adult. He recommended rules in order to facilitate communication between the healthcare staff and the older residents so that the staff would be able to have easier interaction with the residents. For clients with dysphagia, a SLP recommendation may also have an impact on the rules for the kitchen.

SUMMARY

The aging population is increasing day by day, and so are their health problems. The most common health problems in the older adults are arthritis, poor nutrition, cardiac diseases, stroke, dysphagia, and neurological diseases that lead to a rise in the demand for healthcare professionals. This chapter provides a basic explanation about physical therapy, occupational therapy, and speech therapy and the steps of their processes. It includes details on the basic regulations and licensure for each healthcare specialty. Though they have different professional goals and responsibilities, they work with each other in a multidisciplinary approach as a team. They treat the elderly in multiple settings, such as acute-care hospitals, nursing homes, rehabilitation centers, home care, outpatient clinics, assisted-living centers, and community health centers. Long-term care administration is gaining popularity as one of the most important healthcare fields. Administrators have to work closely with each health professional providing care to patients, including nurses, physicians, surgeons, therapists (PT, OT, or SLP), and technicians. The ever-increasing work of the therapists has led to the existence of paraprofessionals—assistants and aides. Assistants and aides play a significant role in providing care to the older adults, but their work usually goes unnoticed. The role of the assistants and aides should be recognized in the field of gerontology as their demand is increasing with the rising Baby Boom generation. The physical, occupational, and speech therapists are important members of an organization, and they make their contribution in certain administrative areas that include, but are not limited to: recruitment, facilities and equipments, policy and procedures, treatment orders, and patient records. We can thus conclude by saying that the therapists play an important role in the care of the aging population and in gerontological administration.

Discussion Questions

1. How would you define the role of a therapist (PT/OT/SLP) in long-term care?
2. Describe the role of therapists in the continuum of care related to older adults.

3. What are the basic regulations needed for therapists to specialize in the field of gerontology? Do the regulations have an impact on the delivery of care to older adults?

4. Identify the different environments in which the therapists would treat the elderly.

5. Describe any ethical dilemmas that the therapists may face while providing care to the aging population.

6. What is the role of PT/OT/SLP assistants and aides in long-term care?

7. What is "Wii-hab" therapy? Is it feasible for an administrator to introduce it in his or her facility?

8. What impact does the role of therapists have on administration related to gerontology?

References

The AGS Foundation for Health in Aging. (2009). *What is geriatrics?* Retrieved March 13, 2012, from http://www.healthinaging.org/public_education/what_is_geriatrics.php.

American Board of Physical Therapy Specialists. (2011). Specialist certification: Geriatrics. Retrieved March 13, 2011, from http://www.abpts.org/Certification/Geriatrics/.

American Occupational Therapy Association. (2009a). AOTA Certification. Retrieved March 13, 2012, from http://www.aota.org/Practitioners/ProfDev/Certification.aspx.

American Occupational Therapy Association. (2009b). Program information. Retrieved March 13, 2012, from http://www.aota.org/Practitioners/ProfDev/Certification/Info.aspx.

American Physical Therapy Association. (2011). Role of a physical therapist assistant (PTA). Retrieved March 13, 2012, from http://www.apta.org/PTACareers/RoleofaPTA.

American Speech-Language-Hearing Association. (1997–2012). Speech-language pathology assistant (SLPA) FAQs. Retrieved March 13, 2012, from http://www.asha.org/certification/faq_slpasst.htm#b1.

American Speech-Language-Hearing Association. (2004). Guidelines for the training, use, and supervision of speech-language pathology assistants. Retrieved March 13, 2012, from http://www.asha.org/docs/html/GL2004-00054.html.

Bureau of Labor Statistics (BLS), U.S. Department of Labor. (2009a). Medical and health services managers. *Occupational Outlook Handbook, 2010–11 Edition.* Retrieved March 13, 2012, from http://www.bls.gov/oco/ocos014.htm.

Bureau of Labor Statistics, U.S. Department of Labor. (2009b). Occupational therapists. *Occupational Outlook Handbook, 2010–11 Edition.* Retrieved March 13, 2012, from http://www.bls.gov/oco/ocos078.htm.

Bureau of Labor Statistics, U.S. Department of Labor. (2009c). Occupational therapist assistants and aides. *Occupational Outlook Handbook, 2010–11 Edition.* Retrieved March 13, 2012, from http://www.bls.gov/oco/ocos166.htm.

Bureau of Labor Statistics, U.S. Department of Labor. (2009d). Physical therapists. *Occupational Outlook Handbook, 2010–11 Edition.* Retrieved March 13, 2012, from http://www.bls.gov/oco/ocos080.htm.

Bureau of Labor Statistics, U.S. Department of Labor. (2009e). Physical therapist assistants and aides. *Occupational Outlook Handbook, 2010–11 Edition.* Retrieved March 13, 2012, from http://www.bls.gov/oco/ocos167.htm.

Bureau of Labor Statistics, U.S. Department of Labor. (2009f). Speech-language pathologists. *Occupational Outlook Handbook, 2010–11 Edition.* Retrieved March 13, 2012, from http://www.bls.gov/oco/ocos099.htm.

Merck Manual for Health Care Professionals. (2009). Occupational Therapy (OT). Retrieved March 23, 2012, from http://www.merckmanuals.com/professional/sec22/ch336/ch336c.html.

U.S. Government Printing Office. (2012). *Title 42: Public health.* Retrieved March 24, 2012, from http://ecfr.gpoaccess.gov/cgi/t/text/text-idx?c=ecfr&sid=7db1f2e12d87847ec5d7a253a6fdb226&rgn=div6&view=text&node=42:5.0.1.1.1.4&idno=42.

WordIQ.com. (2010). Speech therapy—Definition. Retrieved March 13, 2012, from http://www.wordiq.com/definition/Speech_therapy.

World Confederation for Physical Therapy. (2011). Policy statement: Description of physical therapy. Retrieved March 23, 2012, from http://www.wcpt.org/policy/ps-descriptionPT.

World Federation of Occupational Therapists. (2011). *Occupational therapy.* Retrieved March 4, 2011, from http://www.wfot.org/AboutUs/AboutOccupationalTherapy/HowdoOTswork.aspx.

Chapter 4

Social Work in Geriatric Health Services

Doris Chechotka-McQuade, PhD, ASCW, LCSW

LEARNING OBJECTIVES

1. To develop understanding of the roles of social workers in varied multidisciplinary gerontological service settings
2. To increase understanding of the range of education, skills, competencies, and certifications required/requested of master's level professional social workers in the gerontological arena
3. To facilitate an examination of the interprofessional team mandate combined with professional experience required for successful gerontological service delivery across settings
4. To initiate an examination of how current and upcoming societal (and social work) trends and issues will affect administrative strategic planning in your organization

KEY TERMS

Social Work: The twofold task of helping individuals improve/maintain functioning and creating/supporting positive societal change for all (Barker, 2003)

Social Work Practice: The application of social work knowledge, skills, values, and techniques to provide social services to society (Barker, 2003)

Gerontological Social Work: A social work specialization with older persons

Gerontological Social Work Skills and Competencies: Defined as the development and use of multiple social work interventions with older persons

Interprofessional/Interdisciplinary: A team approach to service provision inclusive of multiple professions

INTRODUCTION

Think of this chapter as the resource for those frequently asked questions (FAQs) about the role(s) of social work in gerontological healthcare administration. Typically, in order, the four main questions are:

1. What do gerontological social workers do exactly?
2. What training/education/competencies and/certifications will a gerontological social worker possess?
3. How do these competencies fit/blend with the mission and work of my organization?
4. What's next?

WHAT DO GERONTOLOGICAL SOCIAL WORKERS DO EXACTLY?

Definition

"It depends" seems like a shadowy, even shallow response to that question, even though it's certainly true, and obvious that aspects of all four questions are interrelated. The best place to start, however, is with how the social work profession defines itself and its practice. Barker (2003), in the 5th edition of *The Social Work Dictionary*, utilizes the National Association of Social Workers (NASW) definition: "Social work is the professional activity of helping individuals, groups, or communities enhance or restore their capacity for social functioning and creating societal conditions favorable to this goal" (p. 408). Similarly, the International Federation of Social Workers includes in the definition promoting social change, social justice, problem solving, and empowering people as they interact with their environments.

Social Work Code of Ethics

The social work Code of Ethics (NASW, 1999) notes in the Preamble, the six core values of social work: service, social justice, dignity and worth of the person, importance of human relationships, integrity, and competence. These are essential for professional practice to implement social work techniques in a biopsychosocial and spiritually holistic manner. Gerontological social workers are social workers specializing in practice in the multidisciplinary field of gerontology.

Healthcare Settings and Interdisciplinary Methods

A well rounded explanation of varied healthcare settings and interdisciplinary methods is clearly explicated in the book *Days in the Lives of Gerontological Social Workers* (Grobman & Bourassa, 2007), which categorizes the professional practice stories of 44 contributors into 7 parts:

- Community
- Health care—hospitals, home health, and hospice
- Nursing homes
- Special populations—acute mental health inpatients, Parkinson's patients, persons with geriatric addictions, homeless older adults, and Alzheimer's patients and their families
- Nontraditional methods and settings—interprofessional teamwork with art therapy, intergenerational partnerships, law firms, private practice care management, and psychoeducational support groups in business and industry
- Policy and macro-practice—state government community organizing and gay, lesbian, bisexual, transgender (GLBT) aging
- Student, educator, and researcher perspectives—field/internship placements, qualitative research, racism, oral histories, and centenarians in India

This typology neatly describes varied settings, populations, and modalities, as well as other professional groups with which gerontological social workers practice. Through their practice stories, the contributors and editors also ensure that readers grasp the broader themes of interdisciplinary/interprofessional healthcare work, client-worker collaboration in creative problem solving, the global nature of gerontological work, and the essential issue of client self-determination within a cultural context.

The interrelatedness of the categories and the broader themes can be illustrated with an example from my practice as a hospice social worker. One patient was about to be admitted to the in-hospital hospice unit following a 1-day stay on a traditional patient floor. Neither the patient nor her husband spoke English; they were from India, visiting family in the United States when the patient became so ill she was rushed to the emergency room. While the hospital transport person handed me a chart for the patient, he did not know the patient or have any information about how the patient's medical history had been secured. What was clear was the hospital medical staff believed the patient was close to death from advanced cancer and had appropriately referred the patient to the hospice unit. The hospice nurses immediately attended to the patient's condition and comfort using smiles, reassuring gentle gestures, and show-and-tell style explanations of their work.

After this initial settling-in time and after I had checked with hospital admissions and nursing floor staff about how the medical and social information in the chart was gathered, I also met the patient with reassuring smiles and gestures. Shortly thereafter, the patient's husband arrived, very distraught because he had not been informed, or perhaps had not understood, the transfer to the hospice unit. He did understand some English and found his way to the hospice unit, but did not know what such a unit was, or what services could be provided. He was willing to share his son's New Jersey business card, indicating his permission to speak with his son, who had full command of the language and would involve as many family members in the United States as possible. He helped me understand that his son, and other adult children, did not know their mother had cancer, and he had not believed her illness to be so advanced or they would not have made the trip to the United States. Once his son was contacted, he visibly relaxed, speaking his primary language with his son translating, and they quickly were able to set up visiting arrangements.

A few hours later the husband's son, daughter-in-law, and older grandchildren arrived and everyone, including the nurse and aide, held a family meeting since the patient was by then determined to be actively dying/very close to death. It became clear that the patient's and family's Muslim faith tradition was extremely important, since performing customary rites was essential at that time. As they were not from the area, and this situation had not previously been encountered in the hospice unit, there were no existing policies or resources. So, I first found a local mosque and spoke to the imam (religious leader) who guided hospice staff by phone on proper procedures for the time of death and the period leading up to death (which were completely different than the standard Western hospice protocols). The imam came to the unit, prayed with and comforted the patient and family, educated the staff, and left appropriate materials for future reference.

The patient died while the family was having dinner that evening, and the staff made all appropriate arrangements, per the imam's instructions, for all time-of-death rites to be performed by the family on their return. Though grieving, the patient's husband and son sought me out along with the nurse and aide to express their gratitude for the physical, emotional, and spiritual care the patient had received from "strangers."

This practice example may read like a tailor-made story to illustrate the points about culturally competent, client-focused, interdisciplinary, solution-oriented, creative healthcare practice fitting the Grobman and Bourassa (2007) typology, but this is an actual patient/family example.

Gerontological social workers are not only hands-on practice professionals, usually part of an interdisciplinary team in health care, but also often hold specific supervisory and/or management and/or administrative roles. Their precise titles may vary by agency or field; however, there is no dearth of literature in the area of social service management and practice.

One example of a practice and thorough guide for social work managers/administrators is the 4th edition of *The Social Worker as Manager* (Weinbach, 2003), a text designed for a traditional single-semester social work course in management, which examines the context, definitions, and overlaps of management and administration, as well as the functions, varied tasks, and the strengths and stressors of a management position within an organization. Weinbach also provides a working definition of management: "certain functions performed by social workers at all administrative levels within human service organizations which are designed to facilitate the accomplishment of organizational goals" (p. 19). The book's chapters are designed to reflect the five traditional major management functions—planning, staffing, organizing, controlling, and leading—while also covering topics such as strategic planning, mission and vision, values, ethics, diversity, and volunteers. Weinbach's review of historical and current management and administrative theories concludes that our present management perspective is well rooted in the insights and context of the past while adapting more current psychosocial principles for practice.

One clear example of this is illustrated in the 2nd edition of *Issues in Aging* (Novak, 2009), which discusses the development of the United States healthcare system today. Changing contexts demographically, fiscally, and through medical advances have altered the initial planning of long-term care. We still retain the medical model, social model, and health-promotion model in our approaches to health care; however Medicare, Medicaid, and Medigap insurances have changed as the structural flaw of inadequate planning for large numbers of advanced old age and infirm citizens has become imminent. The five major management functions noted earlier are continually playing catch-up with the demographic and fiscal realities of not enough residential or community-based, long-term care services now, and in the near future, as evidenced by continually reported stories in local, national, and aging-specific newspapers and magazines. The March 2011 *AARP Bulletin,* a newspaper for persons 50 years and older, has no fewer than eight items and articles specifically related to long-term care services.

One article in particular, "Lowering Costs in the Doughnut Hole" (Barry, 2011) discusses the history of the "doughnut hole" (the coverage gap in Medicare's Part D drug benefit), how and why it will be reduced in 2011, who will qualify, what drugs will qualify, and how one goes about qualifying. This information is vital, good news for the hundreds of thousands of senior persons currently enrolled and enrolling in the program. By 2014, as President Obama's varied healthcare initiatives come into being, this "doughnut hole" issue should be completely eliminated. Managed care programs have attempted to bridge the gap by combining some community-based and residential program features. For example, in Pennsylvania, LIFE Geisinger, Living Independently for Elders, is one model of health care based on the national Programs for All-Inclusive Care of the Elderly (PACE) specifically designed to serve frail community elders who might otherwise be placed in a nursing home. Since the PACE program acronym is generally recognized as the national pharmacy program, in Pennsylvania it became the LIFE program (Hastie, 2011). The LIFE/PACE programs provide a full range of healthcare and recreational services on site, through an interprofessional team approach, enabling frail seniors to maximize their biopsychosocial functioning in their own homes and communities.

The most recent emphasis, fueled by current research, has been on primary and secondary prevention through the disease-prevention and health-promotion model. Health RAC, for example, is a program offering health risk assessments and education about healthy lifestyles (Novak, 2009). Social workers will also be found practicing at the national policy level to initiate new or remodeled policies through varied administrative levels in programs/services implementing those policies, including the 2010 healthcare reform applications.

Hasenfeld's (2010) 2nd edition of *Human Services as Complex Organizations* underscores the interrelatedness and complexities of sociodemographic changes (diversities of ethnic cultural structures, age groups, income, education, technologies, etc.) with the adaptive responses of the service organizations. While internal decentralization and external subcontracting have been past organizational adaptive efforts, current responses need to reframe the social problems, which will in turn alter service practices. "Ultimately, realizing that organizational effectiveness depends on the quality of relations between workers and clients, we need to understand the environmental and organizational factors that shape them" (Hasenfeld, p. 4). This worker–client emphasis has traditionally been the oversight responsibility of supervisors in the organization.

Social work supervision can be divided into clinical supervision and administrative supervision, though these distinct functions, roles, and tasks may be combined and performed by a single supervisory person (Dolgoff, 2005). Summarily stated, supervisors are mid-level managers who are part of a management team focused on the workflow of their units, but also responsible for the identification of environmental (client) needs and framing appropriate organizational responses. The profession acknowledged this fact by establishing an administration/supervision specialty practice section for those NASW members currently practicing at this level or intending to practice at this level. Furthermore, *Administration in Social Work* (a journal published by Routledge) has been reporting since 1977 on the varied connections between social policy planning, key issues in management and administration practice, and service delivery.

WHAT TRAINING/EDUCATION/COMPETENCIES WILL A GERONTOLOGICAL SOCIAL WORKER POSSESS?

While "it depends" may again be a perfectly legitimate response to this question, there are some required basics, or standards, and some extras depending on practice areas, per the Council on Social Work Education and the National Association of Social Workers. All bachelor-level (BSW) and master's trained social workers (MSW) are expected to demonstrate in their practice 10 core competencies explicitly named by the profession's academic accrediting body, the Council on Social Work Education (Council on Social Work Education [CSWE], 2008). These include:

- Identifying and conducting oneself as a professional social worker
- Applying social work ethical principles to guide practice
- Applying critical thinking to inform and communicate professional judgments
- Engaging diversity in practice
- Advancing human rights and social and economic justice
- Engaging in research to inform practice and vice versa
- Applying knowledge about human behavior and the social environment
- Engaging in policy practice to enhance service delivery and social and economic development
- Responding to varied contexts that shape practice
- Engaging, assessing, intervening, and evaluating individuals, families, groups, organizations, and communities (CSWE, 2008)

Social work education pays careful attention to ethical decision making and ethical practice behavior, through the professional Code of Ethics of the NASW (1999), the profession's legally recognized standard bearer. All

BSW and MSW students in CSWE–accredited schools of social work study social work ethics and follow the code of ethics in their field placements. The CSWE allows a wide range of options for ensuring ethical content; for example, some MSW programs have mandated specific ethics courses, and some programs have ethical material infused throughout their curriculum.

In addition to the 10 BSW and MSW core competencies, many schools of social work in the United States have a defined gerontological track or specialization, while other schools of social work offer one, or a variety of gerontological electives in their overall curricula. Additionally, many MSW programs offer one or more dual degree programs with a gerontological focus: for example, a dual MSW and master of science (MS) in gerontology, or an MSW and a master of public administration (MPA) degree. There are some universities and schools of social work housing gerontology institutes or geriatric education centers, which foster interprofessional research, study, and field experiences with gerontological continuum-of-care service providers. Some universities and schools of social work offer a post-master's certificate in gerontological practice, or a post-master's certificate in end-of-life care or other related area, with a variety of credits or hours of advanced study and practice with an experienced, credentialed mentor. There are also numerous schools of social work in the United States offering doctorate degrees with a gerontological focus from clinical through administrative, and social welfare policy (Geriatric Social Work Initiative, n.d.a).

Finally, there are 12 programs in the United States which have earned the distinction "Program of Merit" from the Association for Gerontology in Higher Education (AGHE), a unit of the Gerontology Society of America (see www.aghe.org). For example, the Certificate of Specialization in Gerontology offered through Marywood University's Gerontology Institute offers an interdisciplinary experience with nursing, counseling, public administration, social work, nutrition, and the physician assistant's program (Marywood University, 2009).

Those MSWs working in the gerontological arena should have additional knowledge and experience, as noted by the development of a clinical social worker in gerontology (CSW-G) certification by the NASW, which includes a master's degree from an accredited school of social work, no less than 2 years (3,000 hours) of work experience with older adults, completion of 20 hours of continuing education work relevant to older adults, a reference from a supervisor or social work colleague, advanced exam-based certification/licensure, and membership in good standing in the NASW professional organization (NASW–PA Chapter, 2008).

The NASW advanced social worker in gerontology (ASW-G) certification includes competencies in assessment, documentation/reporting, care and case management, service planning, and administration and clinical skills in micro and/or macro settings. Understanding the biopsychosocial changes and challenges of the population and their caregivers, the services and resources available, the specific legislative issues, and the ethical considerations are essential in securing this advanced certification. Additionally, the same NASW requirements noted earlier are applicable (NASW, 2011a).

While not specifically gerontology focused, though certainly relevant to gerontological healthcare practice, the NASW also offers the certified social worker in health care (C-SWHC) credential, which requires current NASW membership; an MSW degree from a CSWE–accredited institution; documented 2 years and 3,000 hours of paid, supervised, post-MSW healthcare social work experience; an evaluation by an approved supervisor and a reference from an MSW colleague; and either an ACSW, DCSW, and/or current state MSW-level license or an ASWB MSW-level exam passing score. The core functions cover psychosocial assessment and interventions, resource management, continuity of care planning, crisis intervention, health education, and interdisciplinary collaboration (NASW, 2011a).

Additionally, the NASW offers both the certified social work case manager (C-SWCM) and the certified advanced social work case manager (C-ASWCM) certifications. Core functions are engagement, assessment, planning, implementation/coordination, advocacy, reassessment/evaluation, and disengagement (NASW, 2011a). The certified hospice and palliative social worker (CHP-SW) credential and the advanced certified hospice and palliative social worker (ACHP-SW) credential are both joint credentials of the NASW and the National Hospice and Palliative Care Organization signifying national social work leadership and expertise by these healthcare professionals.

GERIATRIC SOCIAL WORK COMPETENCIES

The Social Work Leadership Institute, through the Geriatric Social Work Initiative (n.d.b), has developed a 5-section, 50-item list of competencies and skills that clarify how a social worker participates in the health services administrative team, from outreach and intake through supervisory, director, and policy-making roles.

Values, Ethics, and Theoretical Perspectives

1. Assess and address values and biases regarding aging.
2. Respect and promote older adult clients' right to dignity and self-determination.

3. Apply ethical principles to decisions on behalf of all older clients, with special attention to those with limited decision-making capacity.
4. Respect diversity among older adult clients, families, and professionals (e.g., class, gender, sexual orientation).
5. Address the cultural, spiritual, and ethnic values and beliefs of older adults and families.
6. Relate concepts and theories of aging to social work practice (e.g., cohorts, normal aging life-course perspective).
7. Relate social work perspectives and related theories to practice with older adults (e.g., person-in-environment, social justice).
8. Identify issues related to changes, transitions, and losses over the lifecycle in designing interventions.
9. Support persons and families dealing with end-of-life issues related to dying, death, and bereavement.
10. Understand the perspective and values of social work in geriatric interdisciplinary practice while respecting the roles of other disciplines.

Assessment

1. Use empathy and sensitive interviewing skills to engage older clients in identifying their strengths and problems.
2. Adapt interviewing methods to potential sensory, language, and cognitive limitations of the older adult.
3. Conduct a comprehensive geriatric assessment (biopsychosocial evaluation).
4. Ascertain health status and assess physical functioning (e.g., ADLs and IADLs) of older clients.
5. Assess cognitive functioning and mental health status of older clients (e.g., depression, dementia).
6. Assess social functioning (e.g., social skills, social activity level) and social support of older clients.
7. Assess caregivers' needs and level of stress.
8. Administer and interpret standardized assessment and diagnostic tools that are appropriate for use with older adults (e.g., depression scale, mini-mental status exam).
9. Develop clear, timely, and appropriate service plans with measurable objectives for older adults.
10. Reevaluate and adjust service plans for older adults on a continuing basis.

Intervention

1. Establish rapport and maintain an effective working relationship with older adults and family members.
2. Enhance the coping capacities and mental health of older persons through a variety of therapy modalities (e.g., supportive, psychodynamic).
3. Utilize group interventions with older adults and their families (e.g., bereavement groups, reminiscence groups).
4. Mediate situations with angry or hostile older adults and/or family members.
5. Assist caregivers to reduce their stress levels and maintain their own mental and physical health.
6. Provide social work case management linking elders and their families to resources and services.
7. Use educational strategies to provide older persons and their families with information related to wellness and disease management (e.g., Alzheimer's disease, end-of-life care).
8. Apply skills in termination in work with older clients and their families.
9. Advocate on behalf of clients with agencies and other professionals to help elderly clients obtain quality services.
10. Adhere to laws and public policies related to older adults (e.g., elder abuse reporting, legal guardianship, advance directives).

Aging Services, Programs, and Policies

1. Reach out to older adults and their families to ensure appropriate use of the service continuum (e.g., health promotion, long-term care, mental health).
2. Adapt organizational policy, procedures, and resources to facilitate the provision of services to diverse older adults and their family caregivers.
3. Identify and develop strategies to address service gaps, fragmentation, discrimination, and barriers that impact older persons.
4. Include older adults in planning and designing programs.
5. Develop program budgets that take into account diverse sources of financial support for the older population.
6. Evaluate the effectiveness of practice and programs in achieving intended outcomes for older adults.

7. Apply evaluation and research findings to improve practice and program outcomes.
8. Advocate and organize with the service providers, community organizations, policy makers, and the public to promote the needs and issues of a growing aging population.
9. Identify the availability of resources and resource systems for older adults and their families.
10. Assess and address any negative impacts of social and healthcare policies on practice with historically disadvantaged populations.

Leadership in the Practice Environment of Aging

1. Assess "self-in-relation" in order to motivate self and others, including trainees, students, and staff toward mutual, meaningful achievement.
2. Create a shared organizational mission, vision, values, and policies responding to ever-changing service systems to promote coordinated, optimal services for older persons.
3. Analyze historical and current local, state, and national policies from a global human rights perspective to inform action related to an identified older adult social problem to create change.
4. Plan strategically to reach measurable program, organizational, and community development objectives.
5. Administer programs and organizations from a strengths perspective to maximize and sustain human and fiscal resources.
6. Build collaborations across disciplines and the service spectrum to ensure access, continuity, and reduce service gaps.
7. Manage individual/personal and multistakeholder/interpersonal processes from community through intra-agency levels to inspire and leverage power and resources to optimize services for older adults.
8. Communicate to public audiences and policy makers through varied media, the mission, and outcomes of the organization's services for diverse client groups.
9. Advocate with and for older adults and their families for building age-friendly community capacity, including use of technology, and enhance the contribution of older persons.
10. Promote use of research, including evidence-based practice, to evaluate and enhance the effectiveness of social work practice and aging-related services.

In addition to joint certifications, in the interprofessional arena, The John A. Hartford Foundation's (2001) *Geriatric Interdisciplinary Team Training Manual* describes the social work role as "Assessment of individual and family psychological functioning and provision of care to help enhance or restore capacities; this can include locating services or providing counseling" (p. 4). It goes on to detail the care management, group work, liaison, advocacy, and community resource expertise roles, as well as the leadership/administrative roles that any member of the interdisciplinary healthcare team may facilitate, and which have been noted earlier in the various educational requirements, core skills, competencies, and post-MSW certifications of NASW and the Social Work Leadership Initiative.

The recent addition of elder mediation services provided by appropriately certified social work case managers to families in dispute is a good example of the integration of many skills applied to many issues across many generations that might previously have gone to a court of law, but are now settled by the parties themselves, communicating with the help of a trained third party. In fact, the nature of these interdisciplinary changes for gerontological social workers was highlighted again in the May 2010 issue of *NASW News*, noting the collaboration of NASW and the Case Management Society of America (CMSA) in revising the CMSA standards for case managers working in multiple healthcare settings, accommodating such trends as assessing client needs holistically and care planning accordingly. NASW has also developed Standards for Social Work Practice with Family Caregivers of Older Adults, Standards of Social Work Practice in Health Care Settings, Standards for Social Work Practice in Palliative and End-of-Life Care, Standards for Social Work Services in Long-Term Care Facilities, and Standards for Continuing Professional Education, all of which address the requirement for interdisciplinary competency.

Given the training, education, and certification available, social workers come to interprofessional teams with skill sets that foster team collaboration across the spectrum of healthcare service provision. Though there are many definitions of social work administration, all include a goal-oriented dynamic process that transforms social policy into service delivery. Planning, organizing, coordinating, staffing, supervising, and directing resources to achieve a goal are skills in every administrator's tool kit.

In summary, the essence of gerontological social work is maintaining and enhancing older persons' quality of life. Practice interventions are designed to intensify self-determination, dignity, and optimal functioning in every setting through biopsychosocial and spiritual assessments of strengths, as well as crisis situations. Health care's current emphasis on wellness and prevention are a great fit with social work's focus on strengthening existing support networks, ensuring responsive agency and program management and evaluation, resource/strategic planning, and socially just public policy initiatives.

How Do These Competencies Fit/Blend with the Mission and Work of My Organization?

This is certainly the perfect section for the "it depends" answer, since the vision, mission, goals, objectives, and staffing of your respective service organization are unique. There really is no "one-size-fits-all" answer as to how social workers can or will practice in your agency, since as you analyze the needs, trends, opportunities, and constraints of your organization's place in the healthcare continuum, you are in the best position to operationalize (or not) a social work role.

Social workers often come to gerontological practice by a somewhat convoluted route—2006–2007 figures indicate less than 50% of social work MSW students have any interest in working with older adults post-graduation (CSWE, 2010). The following edited interview with Dr. Janet Melnick, coordinator of the Human Development and Family Studies program at Penn State, Worthington Scranton illustrates both the serendipity and the recognition of the goodness of fit between the worker's skills and clients' and agencies' needs, as well as the rise and demise of a healthcare service organization.

An MSW's Journey into Aging Practice and Administration

My personal story into aging social work practice and administration has been an evolving, unplanned series of fortunate opportunities and near mishaps. I began my career as a van driver/recreation aid for the ARC of Lackawanna County, in Scranton, Pennsylvania. In the late 1970s, I worked with mentally disabled children while completing my undergraduate degree in human services. At this stage of my career, I did not have a specific career path nor client population planned or thought out. I merely wanted to gain experience and earn money to pay for college expenses.

After graduation, I was able to move to the Adult Day Services Client Care Manager position. It was during this time that I began working with adults. More importantly, one aspect of the program for "retired" clients was developed; a socially active, fun program without the necessity to work on specific goals or work-related tasks. This population was unique and challenging, but the work was a joy, and I confess spending more hours than necessary with my clients because here my love for working with the senior population was formed. Also, during this time, I started and completed my MSW degree at Marywood College (now Marywood University).

My next career step took me from private to public agency practice when a position as a client care manager became available at the Lackawanna County Area Agency on Aging. Although I enjoyed my work with the senior mental retardation population, it was a pure stroke of luck that this opening became available and I was able to secure it. My primary responsibility was assessing clients for services ranging from personal care to at-home attendant care. Since I was one of the few case managers who possessed a graduate degree, I was also assigned a large number of clients requiring "extra" management or clients that were in some type of imminent danger: from possible cognitive incompetency requiring assessment to determine appropriate level of independent or dependent living status, to cases of alleged physical, mental, or financial abuse or neglect. After working in the case management unit for about 3 years, the agency moved to establish a Protective Service Unit. Again, given my educational status and my familiarity with these situations, I secured the first protective service supervisor position. This was truly my first formal supervisory/administrative position, and I learned how to supervise and establish policies by trial and error. I did not study the administrative track in graduate school, as it never occurred to me that I would not only be promoted to such a position, but that I would also seek these positions out in future jobs.

I believe this is the case for most newly minted MSWs, and I speak with my current undergraduate students about acquiring information about many practice areas, since we really never know where our lives and careers will take us. This position was certainly an eye opener for me since now I not only was responsible for my own professional behavior and the welfare of my individual clients, but also for the case management staff in the unit as well. I excelled at my administrative duties, but was unprepared to handle the self-inflicted stress of taking the responsibility home and dwelling on case situations and court rulings. However, due to the outstanding work of my colleagues, the unit performed so well that we soon became a model for other Area Agencies on Aging. It was not until a few years after my departure from the unit that Pennsylvania adopted a protective service law that gave more authority to the workers in these units/agencies.

After 2 years I was recruited to work at a local nonprofit agency, Telespond Senior Services, as the Director of Rehabilitation Services. At this organization I honed my administrative style while again learning on the fly. I was responsible for two adult day care programs, which specialized in dementia care, in-home respite and personal care service, and a comprehensive outpatient rehabilitation facility (CORF). Administratively, this was my first interprofessional experience with staff management that included hiring, firing, budgets, and facilities' management. Trial by fire would be an understatement! I had no formal administrative training and it took a while to get my administrative feet under me. The easy part was the work with the geriatric clients and their families, since I was very secure in that aspect, understanding what needed to be done and how to do it. The interdisciplinary aspect of being responsible for the performance of the nursing staff when I had only a basic background in medical care of dementia patients, combined with managing the entire CORF and the responsibility of securing budgets was nearly overwhelming. Three days after I started my new position, I was on a plane to Pittsburgh, Pennsylvania to present and defend the CORF budget to our Medicare intermediary. This meeting would determine our per diem rate for all the therapies supplied by our CORF, as well as determine how much money we could recoup for administrative overhead; this could make or break an agency. Though successful, I knew I had a very limited knowledge of budgeting on this level and made sure I learned what I needed to know to ensure the mission and goals of the agency.

At the same time, the agency was opening a second adult day care facility in the northern end of the county, so I went from a supervisory role with some administrative experience to a completely administrative position in a matter of days. Also, the agency's executive director worked on a grant from the Robert Wood Johnson Foundation for adult day care funding, which began a 6-year relationship with the foundation. I was co-coordinator of this project, the Dementia Care and Respite Services Program. The intent of this $5.1 million, 4-year program was to demonstrate that nonprofit day centers could provide financially viable programs and services needed by persons with dementia and their caregivers. This grant not only provided funding, but also technical marketing and administrative information throughout the 4 years. The program was run like a business, not a social service, which was a radical concept back then, and though I learned a lot administratively, I struggled with balancing the social work aspects and the business aspects. Eventually, I became a grant reviewer and mentor to program sites in the second round of this Partners-in-Caregiving grant. I was now responsible for explaining, demonstrating, and encouraging other programs based on all that I had learned, especially in budget modifications, fundraising, and marketing.

Throughout this course in "business administration" and the various growth and changes through the 7 years of my tenure there, I tried to stay rooted in my social work code of ethics and beliefs, though it was never easy to do this. I would make ethically difficult business versus service decisions, with a focus on the greatest good for the clients.

After 7 years I moved to Marywood University as the assistant director of field for the School of Social Work, where I was responsible for the field/internship program. I also entered the interdisciplinary PhD program in human development started at Marywood during this time, though I had never even considered this degree or the possibility of teaching.

Once I earned my doctorate, I was hired in a contract teaching position in the Human Development and Family Studies (HDFS) program at Penn State University, Worthington campus. Initially, part of my job was field coordination, but my experience in gerontology allowed me to expand the curriculum and now I have two teaching specialty areas: field/internship and aging. After promotion to senior instructor, I also became the program coordinator for the HDFS program on campus. I have come full circle back to the administrative role! I have oversight responsibility for the unit, including budgeting and recruitment, and although not exactly stress-free, my previous administrative experiences have made this role easier to tackle.

My range of healthcare administration is quite broad, and over the years, has included positions on a number of community boards of directors. The one that had been the most enjoyable also became the most difficult 2 years ago. The local Family Service Association had been in existence for over 100 years, and it was where I had completed one of my MSW student internships. The agency had a good reputation in the community, but over time, it relied almost solely on United Way funding. I had the dubious honor of being board president during the final years as we lost funding and eventually had to close the agency.

Many anxious months of budget cutting, reorganizing, cutting staff, moving the offices to a less expensive space, and unsuccessfully seeking any possible funding source were the most difficult of my professional life, despite some board members' and a community agency's help. The community is a sadder place because of the loss of the counseling services, and there are probably clients falling between the gaps of remaining service providers. Though I know we did all we could to keep the agency vital, the gerontological social work administrator part of me still has a difficult time accepting the closure of an agency we once believed would always be there in the community.

In summary, general and gerontological social work competencies clearly fit with many healthcare organizations, as illustrated in Dr. Melnick's interview, though how they will be integrated with a particular interprofessional focus, in a particular organization, with unique social and economic contexts, will vary with client and agency needs.

WHAT'S NEXT?

Repetitive though it is, the response is still "it depends"... on the particular needs of the organization as a whole, the staff, changing environmental supports and environmental challenges, demographic trends, professional advances/retrenchment, and the interplay of the multiple areas discussed earlier. Still, there are certain trends that can be examined in a forward-into-the-future fashion.

Environmental Supports

Narrative gerontology is the term Greene, Cohen, Gonzalez, and Lee (2009) use to theoretically ground their book *Narratives of Social and Economic Justice*. While narrative gerontology encompasses our usual understanding of narratives as life stories/histories, reminiscences, or *life reviews*—a term credited to Dr. Robert Butler, the Pulitzer Prize winning, recently deceased (in July 2010) founding director of the National Institute on Aging—Greene et al. note it is "a scientific approach to [studying] human development, a field of research ... that offers a perspective or a way of gathering new insights on aging ... now used in theory building, research and practice" (p. 1).

StoryCorps is a national oral history project, which archives the recorded stories of Americans in the Library of Congress, portions of one interview air every Friday morning on National Public Radio (NPR) stations. Since this is a recent past and current event, how is it also an example of a "what's next" area? Greene et al. (2009) indicate the importance of individual cultural data aggregation by and on multiple social systems; person-in-environment crosses the micro, mezzo, and macro system levels and offers us tools in clinical practice: from mental and physical health care by its person-centered approach, to culturally based transformational social policy advocacy practice. There is no need to reinvent this wheel, just guide that wheel into some areas of practice that reflect the social work mandate, and society's need, to help improve the personal as well as social environment through a strengths- and evidence-based process. A simple example of this would be a review of all those StoryCorps recordings already stored in the Library of Congress, with the goal of researching/discovering the five most prominent themes for persons over the age of 65 (as an arbitrary cohort; any grouping serving your needs is possible) in the nation, then regionally where clear differences might be expected, then using that verifiable, evidence-based information to develop appropriate regional or national policies to address those themes. This type of research can be completed by healthcare service providers with their respective databases as an ongoing process to meet emergent needs before they become emergency needs—planning at its best.

This idea of theory informing public policy through the use of examining the life-course perspective is echoed by Marshall (2009) in the *Handbook of Theories of Aging*. While it has long been accepted that public policy and structures affect the life course, the Canadian Policy Research Initiative places aging persons in their broader life course, noting that developing policy to enhance their quality of life must begin earlier in the lifespan, not just after age 65. Aging is a lifelong process of transitions within a historical time and place, interdependent with the opportunities and constraints of the sociocultural environment. This is a person-centered approach, combing quantitative and qualitative cross-cultural databases to *develop*, not just analyze, public policy.

Retirement

The Oxford Institute of Ageing and Harris Interactive (2007) conducted research on 21,000 people aged 40–79, in 21 countries and reported globally on the good health and control they were experiencing. Three main topics/trends were the focus: the ways older persons contribute to society, the extent of family help, and the "health boost" of retirement. The realization that not all older persons are receivers of care, but active major contributors to society (billions of dollars in work, volunteer efforts, and taxes), caregivers *to* family members, and in better health for more years has significant implications for future planning.

This view of retirement was conditionally affirmed in *Aging: Concepts and Controversies* (Moody, 2010). In a chapter entitled "Is Retirement Obsolete?" the author stresses the dual nature of retirement for the person and the systemic policy impact on society, provides a history of retirement through time, and notes economic changes/swings that can drive the option of late-life leisure time. After a thorough investigation, which includes a Japanese cross-cultural perspective, Moody concludes that American society has not answered that question yet. Continued public debates over retirement timing, evident in 2011–2012 political party efforts to raise the age for claiming full Social Security benefits as one possible solution to ensuring Social Security's longevity, and limited program opportunities for voluntary or paid productive aging are indicative of the fact that "the experiment goes on, but . . . controversies about work and leisure demonstrate that we have not yet agreed on the key social values at stake."

The aspect of paid or voluntary productive aging may be well served with the expansion of existing programs, such as the Senior Community Service

Employment Program (SCSEP) established in 1965 under Title V of the Older Americans Act, a government-sponsored program for productive aging in the public service field. Government-sponsored volunteer programs encouraging productive aging, such as the Senior Companions Program, Foster Grandparents, or the Retired Senior Volunteer Program (RSVP) are run through the ACTION office of the Older American Volunteer Program. Many of these programs are in the community (e.g., libraries), as well as in healthcare sites such as nursing homes, and since they are successful existing programs with well prepared, educational materials available online (see www.aoa.gov or www.aarp.org), they can be integrated into your organization's services with relative ease; again, not reinventing the wheel.

Societal and Social Work Trends

These two areas are clearly intertwined. One summary of societal demographics. *An Aging World: 2008* (U.S. Department of Health and Human Services, 2009), identified nine trends that presented challenges for the future:

- The world population is aging: People over the age of 65 will soon outnumber children under the age of 5 for the first time in history.
- Life expectancy is increasing in most countries, raising questions about the potential lifespan.
- The number of the oldest old is rising: Persons 80 years and older will increase by 233% between 2008 and 2040.
- Some populations are aging while their total population size declines.
- Noncommunicable diseases are becoming a growing problem: Chronic noncommunicable diseases are the major cause of death among older people in both developed and developing countries.
- Family structures are changing, as will care options in older age.
- Patterns of work and retirement are shifting: The shrinking ratio of workers to pensioners with more years spent in retirement burden the health and pension systems.
- Social insurance systems are evolving: As costs increase, countries are examining the sustainability of these systems and reworking old-age security provisions.
- New economic challenges are emerging: The increased numbers greatly affect the social entitlement programs and labor supply globally.

As noted, given the ever-increasing numbers of aging persons, changing family structures, and varied economic challenges affecting both the social insurance and social entitlement programs, the importance of long-term continuum of care options becomes paramount. From community-based independent living, community-based assisted living, facility-based assisted living, and skilled nursing facilities; from naturally occurring retirement communities (NORCs) to continuing care retirement communities (CCRCs); gerontological social workers, along with other interdisciplinary team members, will be involved with service provision from the information and assessment roles through the supervisory, administrative, and policy advocacy roles (Hooyman & Kiyak, 2011).

McInnis-Dittrich (2009) notes society's increasing need for skilled end-of-life gerontological social work caregivers working multidisciplinarily to ensure the biopsychosocial, spiritual, and legal/policy supports for those persons at this life stage (pp. 284–311).

The Latino Age Wave: What Changing Ethnic Demographics Mean for the Future of Aging in the United States (Global Policy Solutions, 2011) reports an increase of 4 million Latino elders 65 years and older by 2015, the fastest growing ethnic population. As a group, they are generally concentrated in four highly populated states—California, Florida, New York, and Texas; are less educated; have lower incomes/higher poverty rates; receive a higher proportion of their income from Social Security; have lower rates of health insurance coverage; and lower rates of English speaking. "For Latino older adults, best and promising practices are often rooted in practical considerations of their unique culture, values, and familial relationships [and] can even vary among Latinos when there are significant differences among them" (Global Policy Solutions, 2011).

Three broad categories: health and wellness, communications, and one-stop-shopping services are considered best practices in serving older adults, regardless of ethnicity. It is clear that healthcare organizations, as well as governmental services, must build programs inclusive of these three areas in order to ensure appropriate quality provision for ethnically and/or racially diverse elders. In 2010, the U.S. Administration on Aging published online *A Toolkit for Serving Diverse Communities,* which provides an inclusive, respectful four-step process to proceed from program planning through implementation and assessment in a sensitive manner with all stakeholders.

Some of these trends/challenges can be directly seen in the social work profession itself, as many experienced gerontological social workers currently near or at retirement will create a service gap. NASW (2006b) published the *Licensed Social Workers Serving Older Adults, 2004* report, which indicated that "social workers in aging are more likely to plan to retire in the next two years than other social workers serving older adults," even though they believe opportunities in the field will increase. This finding held for nonprofit and for-profit aging service organizations. The *Licensed Social Workers in the United States, 2004 Supplement* (NASW, 2006a) noted certain negative changes in the practice of social work: increased caseloads, paperwork, assignment of non-social work tasks, and severity of client issues; and decreased levels of reimbursement, staffing, job security, and availability of supervision. Ensuring that your organization does not countenance any of these practices will facilitate maintaining an experienced workforce.

Whitaker, Weismiller, and Clark (2006) conclude that despite the aging out of current frontline social workers and the huge demand for health and social services for older persons, there are multiple initiatives underway in social work education to increase the numbers and competency of aging specialists in teaching, research, and practice, such as through the Gerontological Society of America, the Hartford Foundation, and the Robert Wood Johnson Foundation. In fact, using a positive strategy to mitigate the "looming shortage of licensed social workers" is addressed in the NASW 2009 *Professional Development Report* (Whitaker & Arrington, 2008), noting the membership's extensive continuing education interests, as well as requirements, for license maintenance. Employer/organizational support was noted as critical in the areas of providing time off, paying for and providing other incentives for continued training.

SUMMARY

The January 2011 issue of *NASW News* reviewed the many plans across the country to celebrate National Professional Social Worker Month in March. The theme was "Social Workers Change Futures," a fitting description of this chapter's material about the multiple roles, skills, and competencies of professional gerontological social workers in creatively tackling the challenges of gerontological healthcare provision from direct service through administration, now and in the future. The 2012 Social Work Month theme, "Social Work Matters," has developed the first Media Awards program to highlight social work–related stories of expertise across many fields of practice, as reported in the January 2012 issue of *NASW News* and echoing NASW's executive director Elizabeth Clark's 2009 directive to "...collectively craft a bolder and broader vision—a vision of social work that will carry us into the future" (p. 10). The March 2011 issue of *NASW News*—reporting on the development of the Healthy People 2020 initiative of the U.S. Department of Health and Human Services, which is designed to provide scientifically based data integrated with current trends and innovations with 10-year objectives to improve the health of all Americans throughout their lifespans—quotes Stacy Collins, the NASW senior practice associate who authored NASW's practice perspective on the topic: "It was important to have social work representation in the development of the objectives, because social workers are some of the strongest advocates for improving health status by addressing the underlying social and environmental determinants of health" (p. 6).

Discussion Questions

1. What are some roles that a gerontological social worker might fill in your organization, now and in the future?

2. Per your organization's mission and objectives, what specific social work skills and competencies would be considered essential in the varied roles noted in this chapter?

3. List and explain the opportunities and constraints of using interdisciplinary/ interprofessional teams in your organization.

4. Develop a "forward-into-the-future" presentation for the administration and board of directors of your organization that encompasses the retirement and workforce trends noted in this chapter as they relate to potential employees as well as potential service consumers.

5. Develop a "5-year plan" for marketing your organization that is culturally respectful of future service consumers as well as flexible in interpreting the organization's mission and goals.

REFERENCES

Barker, R. L. (2003). *The social work dictionary* (5th ed.). Washington, DC: NASW Press.

Barry, P. (2011). Lowering costs in the doughnut hole. *AARP bulletin, 52*(2), 18–19.

Clark, E. J. (2009). *A broader vision for the social work profession.* Washington, DC: NASW Press.

Council on Social Work Education (CSWE). (2008, revised). *Educational policy and accreditation standards.* Retrieved March 13, 2012, from http://www.cswe.org/ File.aspx?id=13780.

Council on Social Work Education. (2010). *Rationale for gero infusion.* Retrieved March 13, 2012, from http://www.cswe.org/CentersInitiatives/GeroEdCenter/ Students.aspx.

Dolgoff, R. (2005). *An introduction to supervisory practice in human services*. Boston, MA: Pearson Education.

Geriatric Social Work Initiative. (n.d.a). Experience exciting careers in social work and aging. Retrieved March 13, 2012, from http://www.gswi.org/CSW0908.pdf.

Geriatric Social Work Initiative. (n.d.b). *Geriatric social work competencies*. Retrieved March 13, 2012, from http://www.cswe.org/CentersInitiative/GeroEdCenter/TeachingTools/Competencies/History.aspx.

Global Policy Solutions. (2011). *The Latino age wave: What changing ethnic demographics mean for the future of aging in the United States*. San Francisco, CA: Hispanics in Philanthropy.

Greene, R. R., Cohen, H. L., Gonzalez, J., & Lee, Y. (2009). *Narratives of social and economic justice*. Washington, DC: NASW Press.

Grobman, L. M., & Bourassa, D. B. (Eds.). (2007). *Day in the lives of gerontological social workers: 44 professionals tell stories from "real-life" social work practice with older adults*. Harrisburg, PA: White Hat Communications.

Hasenfeld, Y. (2010). *Human services as complex organizations* (2nd ed.). Thousand Oaks, CA: Sage.

Hastie, M. (2011). *LIFE Geisinger*. Scranton, PA: LIFE Geisinger.

Hooyman, N., & Kiyak, H. A. (2011). *Social gerontology: A multidisciplinary perspective* (9th ed.). Boston, MA: Allyn & Bacon.

The John A. Hartford Foundation of NYC. (2001). *Geriatric interdisciplinary team training program*. New York: Hartford Institute, GITT Resource Center.

Marshall, V. W. (2009). Theory informing public policy: The life course perspective as policy tool. In V. L. Bengtson, D. Gans, N. M. Putney, & M. Silverstein (Eds.), *Handbook of theories of aging* (pp. 573–594, 2nd ed.). New York: Springer.

Marywood University. (2009). *Graduate catalog, 2010–2012*. Scranton, PA: Author.

McInnis-Dittrich, K. (2009). *Social work with older adults: a biopsychosocial approach to assessment and intervention.*(3rd ed.). Boston, MA: Pearson Education.

Moody, H. R. (2010). *Aging concepts and controversies* (6th ed.). Thousand Oaks, CA: Pine Forge Press.

NASW. (1999). *Code of ethics of the National Association of Social Workers*. Washington, DC: NASW Press.

NASW. (2006a). *Licensed social workers in the United States, 2004 supplement* (p. 23). Washington, DC: NASW Press.

NASW. (2006b). *Licensed social workers serving older adults, 2004*. Washington, DC: NASW Press.

NASW. (2010). Caseload guidance given to Veterans Health Administration. Paul R. Pace, News Staff. *NASW news, 55*(5), 1, 9.

NASW. (2011a). *NASW Credentials and specialty certifications*. Washington, DC: NASW Press.

NASW. (2011b). Social workers key to objectives development *NASW news, 56*(3), 6.

NASW. (2012). Media awards part of initiative. Paul R. Pace, News Staff. *NASW news, 57*(1), 1, 9.

NASW–PA Chapter. (2008). *The Pennsylvania social worker, May/June 2008*. Harrisburg, PA: Author.

Novak, M. (2009). *Issues in aging* (2nd ed.). Boston, MA: Pearson Education.

Oxford Institute of Ageing and Harris Interactive. (2007). *The future of retirement: The new old age*. Oxford, UK: Oxford University.

U.S. Administration on Aging. (2010). *A toolkit for serving diverse communities*. Retrieved March 13, 2012, from http://www.aoa.gov/AOARoot/AoA_Programs/Tools_Resources/DOCS/AoA_DiversityToolkit_Full.pdf.

U.S. Department of Health and Human Services. (2009). *An aging world: 2008*. Washington, DC: U.S. Government Printing Office.

Weinbach, R. W. (2003). *The social worker as manager: A practical guide to success* (4th ed.). Boston, MA: Pearson Education.

Whitaker, T., & Arrington, P. (2008). Professional development: NASW membership workforce study. Washington, DC: NASW Press.

Whitaker, T., Weismiller, T., & Clark, E. (2006). *Assuring the sufficiency of a frontline workforce: a national study of licensed social workers. Special Report: social work services for older adults* (pp. 1–7). Washington, DC: NASW Press.

Chapter 5

Nutritional Considerations for the Older Adult Population

Jessica Rae Bodzio, MS, RD, LDN, and Lee Harrison, PhD, RD

LEARNING OBJECTIVES

1. To recognize population trends associated with aging and how they interact with an older individual's nutritional status
2. To identify the expanded areas of healthcare services and the shift from a primary emphasis on medical issues and uniformity of care toward a holistic approach focusing on maintenance of health and quality of life through an individualized nutritional plan
3. To specify nutritional requirements of older adults
4. To acknowledge nutrition-related complications associated with the aging process
5. To understand the role of the health services administrator in the nutritional care of older adults

KEY TERMS

Quality of Life: Multidimensional concept that includes subjective evaluations of an individual's physical, mental, and social domains (Centers for Disease Control and Prevention [CDC], 2011)

Individualized, Liberal Diet: A menu plan that is customized to a persons' food and beverage preferences while considering their overall health and medical status

Disease-Specific, Therapeutic Diet: A menu plan that restricts an individual's choices in an effort to control for a specific disease without taking into account the individual's preferences or overall health and medical status

Undernutrition: Frailty, unintentional weight loss (10 pounds in past year), self-reported exhaustion, weakness (grip strength), slow walking speed, and low physical activity as a result of inadequate nutritional intakes, which may or may not be accompanied by cachexia (Fried et al., 2001)

Cachexia: A complex metabolic syndrome associated with underlying illness that may be a result of decreased energy intake or as a direct result of the metabolic ramifications of a disease process (Evans et al., 2008)

Sarcopenia: An age-related decrease in the synthesis of muscle protein mass and loss of muscle function that is a major component in the development of frailty in the elderly (Rolland et al., 2008)

Sarcopenic Obesity: A condition of low muscle mass in the obese person (Baumgartner, 2000)

Culture Change Movement: A concept based on the "core person-directed values of choice, dignity, respect, self-determination, and purposeful living" (Pioneer Network, n.d.)

Registered Dietitian (RD): A food and nutrition expert who has met academic and professional requirements as determined by the American Dietetic Association's (ADA's) Commission on Accreditation for Dietetics Education and is credentialed by the Commission on Dietetic Registration (CDR) (ADA, 2011a)

Dietetic Technician, Registered (DTR): A food and nutrition professional who has met academic and professional requirements and works in partnership with registered dietitians (ADA, 2011a)

Certified Dietary Manager (CDM): A dietary manager who has successfully met education, training, supervised experience, and professional requirements to competently perform the responsibilities of a dietary manager (Dietary Managers Association [DMA], 2011)

Nutrition Care Process (NCP): A systematic approach to providing exceptional, individualized nutrition care that formulates a nutritional plan through the following steps: nutrition assessment, diagnosis, intervention, and monitoring/evaluation (ADA, 2011b)

INTRODUCTION

This chapter is a brief overview of the nutritional considerations for the older adult population. It is intended to be a primer in geriatric nutrition for gerontology health services administrators and will enhance the reader's understanding of the importance of nutrition in successful aging and overall quality of life.

Successful management of health concerns in the older adult population cannot be accomplished without careful consideration given to the roles of nutrition and hydration. Dietary and liquid intake must meet the growth, sustained health, and recovery requirements of an individual at all ages of the lifespan. Appreciating the consequences of aging on organ systems, psychological status, and the combined effects of each, healthcare providers are offered unique challenges by the aging body. The status of an individual's nutrition and hydration, adequate or otherwise, has profound effects on multiple systems and subsystems of the body at any age.

Optimal nutritional and hydration status can be attained and maintained by following a balanced diet inclusive of nutrient-dense foods and beverages from the basic food groups and by consuming beverages at and between meals (Lichtenstein, Rasmussen, Yu, Epstein, & Russell, 2008; U.S. Department of Health and Human Services & U.S. Department of Agriculture, 2005). To achieve this goal, one must maintain a desire to eat and enjoy food and beverages. In older adults residing in healthcare communities, this is often achieved by offering an individualized, liberal diet, rather than a disease-specific, therapeutic diet, to promote optimal quality of life (ADA, 2000; ADA, 2010a; Scott-Smith & Greenhouse, 2007). This nutritional strategy is in accordance with the paramount goal outlined in *The State Operations Manual* of the Centers for Medicare & Medicaid Services (CMS), which states: "A facility must care for its residents in a manner and in an environment that promotes maintenance or enhancement of each residents' quality of life" (CMS, 2009). It is because of this collective goal that this portion of the text is dedicated to outlining nutritional considerations for the older adult population, specifically those individuals in healthcare communities.

Population Trends

The growth of the population age 65 years and older increased by 15% in 1 decade—from 35 million in 2000 to 40 million in 2010—with a projected growth over the following decade of 36%—to 55 million—in 2020. More specifically, the population age 85 and older increased by 36%, from 4.2 million in 2000 to 5.7 million in 2010, with an additional increase to 6.6 million projected for 2020 (Administration on Aging, 2009).

Nutrition plays a key role in the prevention and treatment of the most common chronic conditions plaguing Americans: heart disease and stroke, cancer, diabetes, arthritis, obesity, respiratory diseases, and oral conditions (CDC, 2009). Functional disabilities, such as the compromised ability to perform activities related to self-care and daily living, are associated with each of these chronic conditions (Hills, 2002). In 2008, 38% of older adults reported some type of disability, such as difficulty in hearing, vision, cognition, ambulation, and/or self-care to varying degrees. The number and degree of reported disabilities increase with age, with 56% of adults aged 80 or older reporting that they require assistance related to severe disabilities (Administration on Aging, 2009). Sensory impairment, especially dentition, is of particular importance when considering nutritional status, as it has the potential of significantly influencing food and beverage selection and preparation. In 2010, the prevalence of edentulism was reported at a rate of 20% for adults aged 65–74 and a rate of 34% for those aged 85 and older, with socioeconomic factors being the greatest influence on this rate (Federal Interagency Forum on Aging Related Statistics, 2010).

Appreciating that disease and disability are associated with the aging population, it can be surmised that the consumption of healthcare resources will have a growth rate that correlates to the projected population growth. As providers and managers of this care, we must approach health care with a flexible, adaptive perspective to maintain the quality of life of older adults in a variety of venues ranging from home care to long-term care settings with effective and efficient use of resources. One such strategy is to optimize older individuals' nutritional status through an individualized approach. This simplistic, yet effective approach in enhancing quality of life of older persons should be adopted by all health services administrators.

HEALTHCARE COMMUNITIES DEFINED

The need for healthcare services throughout the aging process is supported by the projected population growth, as well as a redistribution of government-funded financial support. In response to this need, community services and the range of housing accommodations for the elderly have expanded to include at-home care, continuing care retirement communities, board and care group homes, personal care homes, assisted living centers, short-term rehabilitation centers, skilled nursing or long-term care facilities, and hospice facilities (Federal Interagency Forum on Aging Related Statistics, 2010).

Moreover, the recent shift in the philosophy of health care from a primary emphasis on medical issues and uniformity of care toward a holistic emphasis on each person while providing individualized, client-directed care has aided in further defining the primary goals of these alternative care facilities to include maintenance of health and quality of life (ADA, 2010a; Federal Nursing Home Reform Act, 1987; White-Chu, Graves, Godfrye, Bonner, & Sloane, 2009). This culture change has allowed healthcare providers to encourage older adults to make informed choices regarding their medical, as well as their nutritional plan of care. It has placed a much-needed emphasis on respect for individuals' ethnic, cultural, religious, and other food and dining preferences, allowing them to be involved in such decisions as meal times, dining locations, and food selections (ADA, 2010b). Although the type of food and nutrition care offered at healthcare communities may differ, the emphasis on meeting the individual's specific nutritional needs remains constant.

NUTRITIONAL REQUIREMENTS OF THE OLDER ADULT

Nutritional requirements for a healthy older person are generally the same as those of the rest of the healthy adult population (de Groot & van Staveren, 2010). Consistent with the general adult population, older adults' dietary needs are relative to the person's individual physical activity level and health status, and should be accounted for by the nutrition professional when determining an individualized plan. Daily calorie requirements range from 1,600–2,000 kcal for women and 2,000–2,600 kcal for men aged 60 and older, with no more than 20–35% of these calories provided by fat (Lichtenstein et al., 2008). Carbohydrate intake should be greater than 130 grams per day to maintain an adequate supply of glucose for brain function and should supply 45–65% of total daily calories (Institute of Medicine [IOM], 2006). Tissue repair and regeneration require adequate protein intake. According to recent research, to prevent the loss of lean tissue, the older adult should consume 1 gram of protein per every kilogram of body weight daily or ensure that 10–25% of total calories are contributed by protein (Campbell, Carnell, & Thalacker, 2006; IOM, 2006).

With few exceptions, the elderly population has physical activity levels that are less than optimal (Singh, 2006). This contributes to, but is not the sole factor of, the progressive decline in lean body mass seen with the aging process (Thomas, 2007). Although calorie requirements decrease as energy expenditure declines, as with reduced physical activity and lean body mass, specific nutrient requirements remain constant, placing a greater emphasis on the necessity for nutrient-rich food and beverage choices of this population. Furthermore, the intake requirements of several nutrients, such as vitamins D and B_{12}, increase with the aging process; this warrants special attention to ensure adequacy of these nutrients (Lichtenstein et al., 2008).

Research regarding the many roles of vitamin D is still emerging. Nonetheless, there is substantial evidence to support adequate intakes of vitamin D for all adults (Holick, 2007). Additional supplementation of 800–2000 IU/day to achieve a recognized adequate serum 25-hydroxyvitamin D (25OHD) level of 75 nmol/L (30 mg/mL) is recommended for older adults (Dawson-Hughes et al., 2010). The prevalence of a vitamin B_{12} deficiency among community-dwelling older adults is not only dependent on intakes of the vitamin, but also on their ability to absorb the nutrient (Suter, 2006). Appreciating this, the recommended daily allowance (RDA) for vitamin B_{12} in the older population is set at 2.4 mcg/day and is to be obtained via fortified foods or supplementation (IOM, 2006).

NUTRITION-RELATED COMPLICATIONS IN THE OLDER ADULT

Aging is a dynamic process that is both ongoing and interrelated. Physiologic declines in the aging person, such as changes in body composition, activity level, sensory impairment, and hormone balance, can significantly impact a person's food and drink consumption (ADA, 2010a; Brownie, 2006). In turn, seniors with high nutritional risk have reported a decline in the assessment of their health-related as well as their overall quality of life (Keller, Østbye, & Goy, 2004).

A decline, gradual or sudden, in calorie intake can result in nutrient, vitamin, and mineral deficiencies and ultimately, unintended, precipitous loss in body mass (both fat and fat-free tissue); which, in turn, can place a person at increased risk for infection, illness, morbidity, and mortality. This weight loss due to undernutrition is known as nutritional frailty and may or may not be accompanied by cachexia, which is distinct from, and less common than sarcopenia (Bales & Ritchie, 2009). The clinical syndrome of frailty can be designated to an older person who has experienced "three or more of the following: unintentional weight loss (10 pound in past year), self-reported exhaustion, weakness (grip strength), slow walking speed, and low physical activity" (Fried et al., 2001).

Cachexia is a complex metabolic syndrome associated with underlying illness and may be a result of decreased energy intake or as a direct result of the metabolic ramifications of a disease process. It is characterized by a loss of approximately equal amounts of adipose and lean mass, maintenance of extracellular water and intracellular potassium, and is predictive of a decline in quality of life and an increase mortality rate (Evans et al., 2008; Rolland et al., 2008; Thomas, 2007). Cachexia is related to the following underlying diseases: cancer, acquired immunodeficiency syndrome, rheumatoid arthritis, chronic renal insufficiency, chronic obstructive pulmonary disease, ischemic cardiomyopathy, and infectious diseases (Thomas, 2007).

Sarcopenia is an age-related decrease in the synthesis of muscle protein mass and loss of muscle function, and is a major component in the development of frailty in the elderly (Rolland et al., 2008). Because of the correlation between lean body mass and intracellular water storage, the total water content of an individual declines as the proportion of lean tissue decreases, therefore placing the individual at greater risk for dehydration and its associated risks (Elmadfa & Meyer, 2008; Lindeman, 2009).

Sarcopenia can be present in underweight, normal weight, and obese older individuals. Appreciating that the prevalence of obesity (body mass index [BMI] ≥ 30 kg/m^2) is increasing in older adults aged 65 and older, it is important to consider this condition of low muscle mass in the obese person, a condition termed *sarcopenic obesity*, as well as the in under- and normal-weight individuals (Baumgartner, 2000; Rolland et al., 2008; Stenholm et al., 2008; Villareal, Apovian, Kushner, & Klein, 2005). Furthermore, loss of muscle mass in the elderly—at any weight—has been associated with a decline in functional capabilities, including the act of completing everyday tasks, and has been linked to the etiology and pathogenesis of frailty, which is predictive of disability and morbidity in the elderly (Cesari et al., 2006; Ferucci et al., 2004; Ranaten, 2003).

Older adults are not immune to the obesity epidemic of our time (Jensen & Hsiao, 2010). According to the National Health and Nutrition Examination Survey (NHANES), from 1999–2008, approximately 78% of all men and 68% of all women aged 60 or older are categorized as overweight, designated by a BMI of 25.0 kg/m^2 or higher, and 37% of men and 33% of women aged 60 or older are categorized as obese, with a BMI of 30.0 kg/m^2 or greater (Flegal, Carroll, Ogden, & Curtin, 2010). Age-related decreased muscle mass complicates the ability to carry the extra mass associated with obesity, thereby resulting in significant functional decline and subsequent loss of independence. Furthermore, the health implications of obesity are numerous and include cardiovascular disease, chronic obstructive sleep apnea, hypertension, osteoarthritis, diabetes, and some forms of cancer (Villareal & Shah, 2009).

One nutritional complication in the older adult not related to an individual's weight status is nutrient deficiency–related anemia. Nearly one-third of all anemia cases in older adults are related to a deficiency of iron (approximately half of all older adults) alone or accompanied by deficiencies in folate and/or vitamin B_{12}(Guralnik, Eisenstaedt, Ferrucci, Klein, & Woodman, 2004). Although the causes of nutrient-deficient anemia can be multifaceted, diet can be a contributing, controllable factor (Patel, 2008).

Another nutritional complication associated with nutrient deficiencies is the development and treatment of pressure-related wounds. Although undernutrition is not the sole contributing factor in the development of pressure ulcers in the older person, it is a significant, noteworthy influence (Shahin & Tannen, 2010; Thomas, 2009). Furthermore, nutritional deficiencies hinder the normal healing process and result in a decreased wound tensile strength, an increased incidence of infection and chronic wounds, and ultimately higher morbidity and mortality rates once a wound develops (Stechmiller, 2010).

Chewing and swallowing difficulties also present a unique challenge in meeting the nutritional requirements of the older population. Specifically, dysphagia is defined as a difficulty in the passage of a food or liquid bolus from the mouth to the esophagus, oropharyngeal dysphagia, or through the esophagus, esophageal dysphagia (Garcia & Chambers, 2010; Martin, Saunders, & Stattmiller, 2006; Robbins & Kays, 2006). Age-associated problems leave the older population at a greater risk for the development of dysphagia. Occasionally, compromised dental status or the absence of dentition can be the primary contributing factor to an older person's chewing problem. However, more often dysphagia is related to disordered neuromuscular status, such as musculoskeletal weakness, or neurological disorders, such as Parkinson's disease (Robbins & Kays, 2006). Nonetheless, adequate oral nutrition remains the primary goal to maintain health, even in the presence of dysphagia.

NUTRITIONAL STRATEGIES FOR OLDER ADULTS IN HEALTHCARE COMMUNITIES

The overriding objective of nutrition care in older adults is to maintain or enhance the health and quality of life of each individual by optimizing his or her nutritional status. Historically, attainment of this goal relied on disease-specific, nutrient-restricted, therapeutic diets. However, these modified diets can negatively impact the palatability and overall appeal to the older adult, thus resulting in decreased consumption and ultimately undernourishment. It is now recognized that the risk of undernourishment outweighs the benefits of therapeutic diets in the maintenance or enhancement of an older person's nutritional status, and that approaching nutritional interventions from a person-centered perspective provides overarching health benefits, even for those individuals coping with chronic diseases such as diabetes mellitus, cardiovascular disease, chronic kidney disease, and Alzheimer's disease (ADA, 2002; ADA, 2010a; ADA, 2010b). Because of this, an individualized approach to nutrition is recommended for older adults in all healthcare communities (ADA, 2010a). This individualized approach is consistent with the culture-change movement, which is based on the "core person-directed values of choice, dignity, respect, self-determination, and purposeful living" (Pioneer Network, n.d.). An individualized approach to diet allows the nutrition professional an opportunity to promote healthy meal choices that "include foods abundant in nutrients, flavor, color, and variety" (ADA, 2010b).

Successful attainment of optimal nutritional status through an individualized approach requires involvement from individuals or their caregivers and collaboration with one or more nutrition professionals who can assist individuals with food and beverage choices that will meet their personal preferences while also meeting their nutritional requirements. This person-centered collaborative approach should be reflected in the client's nutritional plan of care, developed by the registered dietitian (RD) through the utilization of the nutrition care process (NCP), and available for all providers of care to facilitate optimal health for that individual (ADA, 2010a; ADA, 2010b). In partnership with the RD, the dietetic technician, registered (DTR) can complete screening, evaluation, and education of older adults and can participate in overall health promotion (ADA, 2011b). Additional support can be provided by the certified dietary manager (CDM), who, in addition to expertly managing all operations of the dietary department, can work in concert with the RD to ensure optimal nutritional status of all older adults in healthcare settings (DMA, 2011). Although partnership between the health services administrator and each of these food and nutrition experts is optimal, collaboration with at least one of these professionals is necessary to achieve optimal nutritional status in older adults in all healthcare communities.

Creating menu options that offer variety and dining programs that meet social standards to better meet individual's expectations are two methods of optimizing the nutritional status of older adults in healthcare communities (ADA, 2010a; Bernstein et al., 2002). Three of the main menu styles that are consistent with the culture change movement are selective menus, nonselective menus with a variety of readily available substitutions, and restaurant-style menus (ADA, 2010b). Each menu style can be incorporated into a variety of dining programs that can meet the older client's expectations. Such dining programs include, but are not limited to the following: buffet-style dining, which appeals to the visual and olfactory senses of individuals and allows for individual choices; neighborhood dining, which allows for a small number of individuals to live and dine in a designated area within a larger facility; and family-style dining, in which food served on serving platters or bowls is passed around the table for residents to serve themselves their own desired food (ADA, 2010b). Offering five smaller meals throughout the day and/or incorporating food into social events are two other concepts that should be considered when attempting to enhance the nutritional status of older adults in healthcare communities (ADA, 2010b). Additionally, the menu can be adjusted to accommodate individuals with dysphagia while providing adequate nutrition. The National Dysphagia Diet (NDD) was created with the intention of standardizing mechanically altered diets and consistency-modified liquids (Garcia & Chambers, 2010; Robbins & Kays, 2006). This diet offers four standard levels of altered diets: Level 4 Regular—all foods allowed; Level 3 Advanced—allows most textures except for hard, sticky, and crunchy foods and requires that foods are presented in moist, bite-sized pieces; Level 2 Mechanically Altered—consists of all level 1 foods plus moist, soft-textured foods that can easily be formed into a bolus, meats are ground or minced to less than a quarter of an inch in size; Level 1 Pureed—allows foods pureed to a smooth, homogeneous, and cohesive consistency (similar to pudding) and excludes foods that require mastication, bolus formation, or manipulation (Garcia & Chambers, 2010; Robbins & Kays, 2006).

Nevertheless, registered dietitians should be intimately involved in each of these nontraditional approaches to dining to ensure nutritional adequacy while meeting the expanding expectations of the older adult population. Collaboration between the facility's/organization's administrator; food service/dining director; RD, DTR, and/or CDM; the clients of the facility/organization; and/or their caregivers is key to the success of an individualized approach to optimal nutrition for the older individual. The role of RDs is invaluable in that they utilize the Nutrition Care Process to create care plans that are consistent with needs based on nutritional and medical status and personal preferences. Additionally, the RD should be directly involved, and assisted by the DTR and/or CDM in the development of and education on facility/organization dietary policies (ADA, 2010a).

THE ROLE OF THE HEALTH SERVICES ADMINISTRATOR

The role of health services administrators is to ensure that nutrient-rich food and beverage choices are offered and readily available to the population they serve in order to maintain or attain optimal nutritional status. The first step in achieving this goal is to collaborate with one or more of the following food and nutrition professionals: RD, DTR, and/or CDM. After achieving this, the administrator should work to ensure that the main goal of nutritional services is to optimize the older person's quality of life through an individualized plan.

SUMMARY

Inadequate food and beverage intake can lead to compromised nutritional status that subsequently can lead to a variety of disease states and can even negatively affect perceived quality of life (Keller, Østbye, & Goy, 2004). Offering a varied, individualized diet can maximize nutrient consumption and prevent undernutrition and unintended weight loss in the older population (ADA, 2010a). This, in turn, can modulate the risk of additional health complications and enhance older individuals' quality of life. The health services administrator plays an integral role in attaining and maintaining optimal nutritional status of older adults in healthcare communities. The administrator should ensure collaboration with a qualified nutrition professional, who in turn, should be considered an essential component of a healthcare team.

Discussion Questions

1. What are the population trends associated with aging and how do they interact with an older individual's nutritional status?
2. How do nutritional requirements for older adults differ from those of younger adults?
3. Discuss the nutrition-related complications associated with the aging process. Are these modifiable? If yes, how?
4. Identify the food and nutrition professionals most often employed in healthcare communities and discuss each of their roles.
5. Discuss the overriding objective of nutrition care in older adults. How can the health services administrator achieve this goal?

ADDENDUM

Since the creation of the original version of this manuscript, several professional organizations related to the field of nutrition and dietetics and referenced throughout this chapter have officially revised their name. The following define these revisions:

- American Dietetic Association (ADA) is now the Academy of Nutrition and Dietetics.
- Commission on Accreditation for Dietetics Education (CADE) is now the Accreditation Council for Education in Nutrition and Dietetics (ACEND).
- Dietary Managers Association (DMA) is now the Association of Nutrition and Foodservice Professionals (ANFP).

REFERENCES

Administration on Aging. (2009). A profile of older Americans: 2009. Retrieved March 14, 2012, from http://www.aoa.gov/aoaroot/aging_statistics/Profile/2009/2.aspx.

American Dietetic Association (ADA). (2000). Position of the American Dietetic Association: Liberalized diets for older adults in long-term care. *Journal of the American Dietetic Association, 102*(9), 1316–1323.

American Dietetic Association. (2002). Position of the American Dietetic Association: Nutrition, aging, and the continuum of care. *Journal of the American Dietetic Association, 100*, 580–595.

American Dietetic Association. (2010a). Position of the American Dietetic Association: Individualized nutrition approaches for older adults in health care communities. *Journal of the American Dietetic Association, 110*, 1549–1553.

American Dietetic Association. (2010b). Practice paper of the American Dietetic Association: Individualized nutrition approaches for older adults in health care communities. *Journal of the American Dietetic Association, 110*, 1554–1563.

American Dietetic Association. (2011a). Nutrition care process. Retrieved March 14, 2012, from: http://www.eatright.org/HealthProfessionals/content.aspx?id=7077.

American Dietetic Association. (2011b). What are the qualifications of a registered dietitian? Retrieved March 14, 2012, from http://www.eatright.org/Public/content.aspx?id=6713.

Bales, C. W., & Ritchie, C. S. (2009). Redefining nutritional frailty: Interventions for weight loss due to undernutrition. In C. W. Bales & C. S. Ritchie (Eds.), *Nutrition and health: Handbook of clinical nutrition and aging* (pp. 157–182, 2nd ed.). New York: Humana Press.

Baumgartner, R. N. (2000). Body composition in healthy aging. *Annals of the New York Academy of Sciences, 904,* 437–448.

Bernstein, M. A., Tucker, K. L., Ryan, N. D., O'Neill, E. F., Clements, K. M., Nelson, M. E., & Singh, M. A. F. (2002). Higher dietary variety is associated with better nutritional status in frail elderly people. *Journal of the American Dietetic Association, 102*(8), 1096–1104.

Brownie, S. (2006). Why are elderly individuals at risk of nutritional deficiency? *International Journal of Nursing Practice, 12*(2), 110–118.

Campbell, W. W., Carnell N. S., & Thalacker, A. E. (2006). Protein metabolism and requirements. In R. Chernoff (Ed.), *Geriatric nutrition: The health professional's handbook* (pp. 15–22, 3rd ed.). Sudbury, MA: Jones & Bartlett.

Centers for Disease Control and Prevention (CDC). (2009). The power of prevention: Chronic disease—The public health challenge of the 21st Century. Retrieved March 14, 2012, from http://www.cdc.gov/chronicdisease/pdf/2009-Power-of-Prevention.pdf.

Centers for Disease Control and Prevention. (2011). Health-related quality of life. Retrieved March 14, 2012, from http://www.cdc.gov/hrqol/concept.htm.

Centers for Medicare & Medicaid Services (CMS). (2009). State operations manual: Appendix PP—Guidance to surveyors for long term care facilities. Retrieved March 14, 2012, from http://cms.gov/manuals/Downloads/som107ap_pp_guidelines_ltcf.pdf.

Cesari, M., Leeuwenburgh, C., Lauretani, F., Onder, G., Bandinelli, S., Maraldi, C., et al. (2006). Frailty syndrome and skeletal muscle: Results from the Invecchiare in Chianti study. *American Journal of Clinical Nutrition, 83*(5), 1142–1148.

Dietary Managers Association (DMA). (2011). CDM credential. Retrieved March 14, 2012, from http://www.dmaonline.org/About/CDM_CFPP_credential.shtml.

Dawson-Hughes, B., Mithal, A., Bonjour, J.-P., Boonen, Burckhardt, P., Fuleihan, G.E.-H., et al. (2010). IOF position statement: Vitamin D recommendations for older adults. *Osteoporosis International, 21,* 1151–1154.

de Groot, C. P. G. M., & van Staveren, W. A. (2010). Nutritional concerns, health and survival in old age. *Biogerontology, 11,* 597–602.

Elmadfa, I., & Meyer, A. L. (2008). Body composition, changing physiological functions and nutrient requirements of the elderly. *Annals of Nutrition and Metabolism, 52*(S1), 2–5.

Evans, W., Morley, J. E., Argiles, J., Bales, C., Baracos, V., Guttridge, D., et al. (2008). Cachexia: A new definition. *Clinical Nutrition, 27*(6), 793–799.

Federal Interagency Forum on Aging Related Statistics. (2010). Older Americans 2010 key indicators of well-being. Retrieved March 14, 2012, from http://www.agingstats.gov/agingstatsdotnet/Main_Site/Data/2010_Documents/Docs/OA_2010.pdf.

Federal Nursing Home Reform Act from the Omnibus Budget Reconciliation Act (OBRA) of 1987, 442 CFR 483.25 (vLex, 1987). Retrieved March 14, 2012, from http://cfr.vlex.com/vid/25-quality-care-19811696.

Ferucci, L., Guralnik, J. M., Studenski, S., Fried, L. P., Cutler, G. B., & Walston, J. D. (2004). Designing randomized, controlled trials aimed at preventing or delaying functional decline and disability in frail, older persons: A consensus report. *Journal of the American Geriatrics Society, 52*(4), 625–634.

Flegal, K. M., Carroll, M. D., Ogden, C. L., & Curtin, L. R. (2010). Prevalence and trends in obesity among U.S. adults, 1999–2008. *Journal of the American Medical Association, 303*(3), 235–241.

Fried, L. P., Tangen, C. M., Walston, J., Newman, A. B., Hirsch, C., Gottdiener, J., et al. (2001). Frailty in older adults evidence for a phenotype. *Journal of Gerontoly Series A: Biological Sciences and Medical Sciences, 56*(3), M146–M157.

Garcia, J. M., & Chambers, E. (2010). Managing dysphagia through diet modifications. *American Journal of Nursing, 110*(11), 26–33.

Guralnik, J. M., Eisenstaedt, R. S., Ferrucci, L., Klein, H. G., & Woodman, R. C. (2004). Prevalence of anemia in persons 65 years and older in the United States: Evidence for a high rate of unexplained anemia. *Blood, 104*, 2263–2268.

Hills, G. A. (2002). Activities of daily living. In C. B. Lewis (Ed.), *Aging: The health care challenge* (pp. 27–47, 4th ed.). Philadelphia, PA: F. A. Davis Company.

Holick, M. F. (2007). Vitamin D deficiency. *New England Journal of Medicine, 357*, 266–281.

Institute of Medicine (IOM). (2006). *Dietary reference intakes: The essential guide to nutrient requirements.* Washington, DC: The National Academies Press.

Jensen, G. L., & Hsiao, P. Y. (2010). Obesity in older adults: Relationship to functional limitation. *Current Opinion in Clinical Nutrition & Metabolic Care, 13*(1), 46–51.

Keller, H. H., Østbye, T., & Goy, R. (2004). Nutritional risk predicts quality of life in elderly community-living Canadians. *Journal of Gerontology: Medical Sciences, 59A*(1), 68–74.

Lichtenstein, A. H., Rasmussen, H., Yu, W. W., Epstein, S. R., & Russell, R. M. (2008). Modified MyPryamid for older adults. *American Society for Nutrition, 138*, 5–11.

Lindeman, R. D. (2009). Hydration, electrolyte and mineral needs. In C. W. Bales & C. S. Ritchie (Eds.), *Nutrition and health: Handbook of clinical nutrition and aging* (pp. 219–234, 2nd ed.). New York: Humana Press.

Martin, W. E., Saunders, M., & Stattmiller, S. P. (2006). Oral health in the elderly. In R. Chernoff (Ed.), *Geriatric nutrition: The health professional's handbook* (pp. 163–210, 3rd ed.). Sudbury, MA: Jones & Bartlett.

Patel, K. V. (2008). Epidemiology of anemia in older adults. *Seminars in Hematology, 45*(4), 210–217.

Pioneer Network. (n.d.) What is culture change? Retrieved March 14, 2012, from http://www.pioneernetwork.net/CultureChange.

Ranaten, T. (2003). Muscle strength, disability and mortality. *Scandinavian Journal of Medicine & Sciences in Sports, 13*(1), 3–8.

Robbins, J., & Kays, S. (2006). Swallowing problems in older adults. In R. Chernoff (Ed.), *Geriatric nutrition: The health professional's handbook* (pp. 163–210, 3rd ed.). Sudbury, MA: Jones & Bartlett.

Rolland, Y., Czerwinski, S., Abellan Van Kan, G., Morley, J. E., Cesari, M., Onder, G., et al. (2008). Sarcopenia: Its assessment, etiology, pathogenesis, consequences and future perspectives. *Journal of Nutrition, Health and Aging, 12*, 433–450.

Scott-Smith, J. L., & Greenhouse, P. K. (2007). Transforming care at the bedside: Patient- controlled liberalized diet. *Journal of Interprofessional Care, 21*(2), 179–188.

Shahin, E. S. M., & Tannen, A. (2010). The relationship between malnutrition parameters and pressure ulcers in hospitals and nursing homes. *Nutrition, 26*(9), 886–889.

Singh, M. A. F. (2006). The geriatric exercise prescription: Nutritional implications. In R. Chernoff (Ed.), *Geriatric nutrition: The health professional's handbook* (pp. 407–425, 3rd ed.). Sudbury, MA: Jones & Bartlett.

Stechmiller, J. K. (2010). Understanding the role of nutrition and wound healing. *Nutrition in Clinical Practice, 25*(1), 13–15.

Stenholm, S., Harris, T. B., Rantanen, T., Visser, M., Kritchevsky, S. B., & Ferrucci, L. (2008). Sarcopenic obesity—definition, etiology and consequences. *Current Opinion in Nutrition and Metabolic Care, 1*(6), 693–700.

Suter, P. M. (2006). Vitamin metabolism and requirements in the elderly: Selected aspects. In R. Chernoff (Ed.), *Geriatric nutrition: The health professional's handbook* (pp. 31–76, 3rd ed.). Sudbury, MA: Jones & Bartlett.

Thomas, D. R. (2007). Loss of skeletal muscle mass in aging: Examining the relationship of starvation, sarcopenia and cachexia. *Clinical Nutrition, 26*, 389–399.

Thomas, D. R. (2009). The relationship of nutrition and pressure ulcers. In C. W. Bales & C. S. Ritchie (Eds.), *Nutrition and health: Handbook of clinical nutrition and aging* (pp. 219–234, 2nd ed.). New York: Humana Press.

U.S. Department of Health and Human Services, & U.S. Department of Agriculture. (2005). Dietary guidelines for Americans. Retrieved March 14, 2012, from http://www.health.gov/dietaryguidelines/dga2005/document/pdf/DGA2005.pdf.

Villareal, D. T., Apovian, C. M., Kushner, R. F., & Klein, S. (2005). Obesity in older adults: Technical review and position statement of the American Society for Nutrition and NAASO, The Obesity Society. *American Journal of Clinical Nutrition, 82*, 923–934.

Villareal, D. T., & Shah K. (2009). Obesity in older adults—a growing problem. In C. W. Bales & C. S. Ritchie (Eds.), *Nutrition and health: Handbook of clinical nutrition and aging* (pp. 263–277, 2nd ed.). New York: Humana Press.

White-Chu, E. F., Graves, W. J., Godfrye, S. M., Bonner, A., & Sloane, P. (2009). Beyond the medical model: The culture change revolution in long-term care. *Journal of the American Medical Directors Association, 10*(6), 370–378.

Chapter 6

Enhancing Quality of Life for Older Adults Through the Creative Arts Therapies

Barbara Parker-Bell, PsyD, ATR-BC, LPC, and Sr. Mariam Pfeifer, IHM, MA, LCAT, MT-BC

LEARNING OBJECTIVES

1. To increase understanding of the roles of creative arts therapists in diverse older adult environments
2. To increase awareness of the professional qualifications required for the practice of both art therapy and music therapy
3. To increase understanding of the goals of art and music therapy interventions related to the older adult's diverse needs and levels of functioning
4. To increase awareness of diverse creative arts approaches related to the aging population
5. To heighten awareness of the effectiveness of creative arts treatment as evidenced by case reports and research
6. To address creative arts funding sources such as grants and other considerations that impact administrator incorporation of creative arts services

KEY TERMS

Art Therapy: A mental health profession that uses the creative process of art making to improve and enhance the physical, mental, and emotional well-being of individuals of all ages; a necessary health profession that demonstrates the power of art in healing (American Art Therapy Association [AATA], 2012)

Art Therapist: Healthcare professionals with a minimum of a master's degree in art therapy or a related field, who work in a variety of settings to help people address health and well-being

Music Therapy: The clinical and evidence-based use of music interventions to accomplish individualize goals within a therapeutic relationship by a credentialed professional who has completed an approved music therapy program (American Music Therapy Association [AMTA], 2006)

Music Therapist: A qualified person holding the credential music therapist–board certified (MT-BC) who uses music or music activities to facilitate the therapeutic process

Therapeutic Relationship: Considered one of the most significant curative factors in the psychotherapeutic process and is built on therapist and client agreement on therapeutic goals; therapist attunement to a client's needs, strengths, and limitations; and the interpersonal sensitivity and skills of the therapist to respond to these client characteristics and goals. A therapeutic relationship includes reflective and effective therapist responses to client materials that foster trust between therapist and client and assure emotional and physical safety

Therapeutic Environment: A physical and emotional space that is created to safely and effectively hold the emotional content and physical materials of verbal and creative processes. Characteristics of a therapeutic environment include: privacy; materials access and safety; therapist-facilitated safety in terms of acceptance of clients' verbal and musical expression and art production; and facilitation of appropriate boundaries and interaction between therapist and client, as well as among group members when group therapy structures are utilized

Creative Engagement: In the context of therapeutic treatment for the aging population, refers to the provision of opportunities for personal exploration and expression; response to visual, tactile, emotional, or physical stimuli in the environment; involvement in decision making; problem solving; and/or participation in the production of artistic or musical compositions on an individual or group basis

Life Review: A process where reminiscence and review of one's life experience is used in a therapeutic context to help an older adult resolve life conflicts and come to a greater sense of peace regarding one's spiritual life

Memory Retrieval: To recall to mind and the senses; for example, the ability to sing the words of a song learned earlier in life, even when unable to speak due to stroke or brain injury, or to move to music with familiar dance steps

Senescence: Describes the universal and inevitable decline in the efficiency of the body systems that are normal aspects of aging (Clair & Davis, 2008, p. 183)

Biological Age: Sometimes referred to as senescence, the duration or the measure of time of the process of aging beginning at conception and ultimately ending with death (Medical Dictionary, 2012a)

Psychological Age: How well a person responds to a changing environment and can adapt to new situations or experiences

Psychosocial Age: A type of aging that a person will experience that may or may not match his or her actual aging; similar to nonphysical maturity (Medical Dictionary, 2012b)

INTRODUCTION

> "Creativity allows us to alter our experience of problems, and sometimes to transcend them in later life. Part of the nature of creativity is its engaging and sustaining quality—no matter what our actual physical condition, we feel better when we are able to view our circumstances with fresh perspective and express ourselves with some creativity. Creativity strengthens our morale in later life. Creativity makes us more emotionally resilient and better able to cope with life's adversity and losses."
>
> —Cohen, 2000, p. 11

The creative arts therapies encompass a broad range of arts modalities, including art, dance, drama, movement, music, and poetry. Each of these modalities may be used to promote the achievement of diverse therapeutic goals specifically designed for older adults. For the purposes of this chapter, two of the creative arts therapies, art therapy and music therapy, are addressed. First, art therapy is described, followed by music therapy.

ART THERAPY

To begin to consider the incorporation of art therapy services into settings for older adults, an administrator needs to understand basic information about the art therapy profession. What are the professional standards for training, certification, and licensure? What scope of practice should be expected from art therapists? How do they work? And, of course, what sources of funding can support the presence of an art therapist?

The American Art Therapy Association (2012) is an organization of professionals dedicated to the field of art therapy. Its mission is to serve its members and the general public by providing standards of professional competence, and developing and promoting knowledge in, and of, the field of art therapy. The Associating defines art therapy as:

> a mental health profession that uses the creative process of art making to improve and enhance the physical, mental and emotional well-being of individuals of all ages. Research in the field confirms that the creative process involved in artistic self-expression helps people to resolve conflicts and problems, develop interpersonal skills, manage behavior, reduce stress, increase self-esteem and self-awareness, and achieve insight.

The AATA has defined the art therapy profession as follows.

ART THERAPIST: DEFINITION

Art therapists are master's level professionals who hold a degree in art therapy or a related field. Educational requirements include theories of art therapy, counseling, and psychotherapy; ethics and standards of practice; assessment and evaluation; individual, group, and family techniques; human and creative development; multicultural issues; research methods; and practicum experiences in clinical, community, and/or other settings. Art therapists are skilled in the application of a variety of art modalities (drawing, painting, sculpture, and other media) for assessment and treatment.

Art therapists are trained to work with people of all ages and impairments in a variety of settings, including hospitals, rehabilitation, psychiatric, medical, residential, educational, assisted-living facilities, and private practice (AATA, 2012).

Professional Qualifications

While the American Art Therapy Association sets the standards for education and practice, the Art Therapy Credentials Board (2010) serves "to protect the public by promoting the competent and ethical practice of art therapy." They offer credentialing programs that result in registration (ATR), board certification (ATR-BC), and credentialing as an art therapy certified supervisor (ATCS). The Art Therapy Credentials Board defines the benchmarks of professional achievement through the following registration and certification processes.

Registration and Board Certification

Becoming a registered art therapist (ATR) requires the completion of master's level education (including art therapy core curriculum, supervised practicum, and internship experiences) and post-education supervised clinical experience.

Upon receipt of the ATR, applicants are eligible to apply for the ATR-BC. Successful completion of the Art Therapy Credentials Board Examination (ATCBE) is required for the ATR-BC. The ATR-BC credential requires maintenance through proof of continuing education.

The art therapy certified supervisor (ATCS) is a newly available credential offered to board-certified art therapists (ATR-BCs) who are qualified and interested in demonstrating substantial supervision qualifications. This credential informs employers, prospective employers, supervisees, and prospective supervisees, that the individual providing art therapy supervision has met specific criteria for competency in the theories and practices of art therapy supervision (ATCB, 2010).

Other Credentials

In many areas of the United States, art therapists may hold additional credentials, such as, but not limited to, licensed professional counselor, marriage family therapist, or licensed creative art therapist. Most graduate art therapy programs provide coursework to help students meet eligibility requirements for state or regional mental health provider licenses. License qualification and requirements vary state by state, and most licensing processes include accumulation of supervised professional hours after the master's degree has been completed. Additionally, many licensing bodies also require that the art therapy board certification examination or other licensing examination be taken and passed. The opportunity for additional licensure has assisted art therapists and art therapy employers in finding additional means to provide and fund art therapy–based services.

What Do Art Therapists Do?

Art therapists' training meets certain educational standards. However, how therapists implement art therapy techniques depends on several factors, such as philosophical or theoretical orientation; developmental, cultural, family, personal, or cognitive needs of the client; the setting in which art therapy takes place; safety issues; and the timeframe available for art therapy services to be provided. The cases and experiences of art therapists described later in the chapter demonstrate how art therapy provision may shift in style and focus even within the narrower category of art therapy with older adults. Art therapists may work as independent practitioners, or may work as part of an interdisciplinary team. Art therapists work with clients individually, in groups, and with families. Some art therapists may look more like art teachers facilitating artistic mastery, while other art therapists may look more like psychotherapists who use art minimally as a tool for disclosure. Others appear somewhere in between. In each case, art therapists choose their approach carefully, through assessment, determination of treatment goals, and awareness of applicable treatment strategies. Art therapists acknowledge and honor the importance of their relationship with the client (the therapeutic relationship) and use the art as a mediator in the therapeutic process.

WHY ART THERAPY? ADVANTAGES OF ART AND IMAGERY

Wadeson (2010) describes several advantages of art therapy, including imagery, decreased defenses, objectification, permanence, spatial matrix, and creative and physical energy. While verbal skill has been highly valued in contemporary cultures, individual's conceptions of the world are often based on visual perception and imagery. Experienced imagery shapes our core experiences; therefore, using imagery can help access those experiences. Yet, when imagery is used in the context of therapy, defenses are often decreased. This reduction occurs because people are frequently less adept at controlling or disguising their visual expressions. Consequently, images may tell people's secrets without them being aware.

The advantages of objectification and permanence relate to the physical nature of the art product (Wadeson, 2010). Expression is externalized in the art form and allows the maker to achieve some separation from that expression. The emotional space created allows a person to distance, view, acknowledge, and integrate the symbolic communication. Fortunately, this symbolic communication does not evaporate into the air like conversation, but remains a visual testimony to the experience. Therefore, the artifact is witnessed and experienced by both patient and therapist. Like a cherished art work in a museum, it can be revisited time and again for appreciation or further exploration of meaning.

People are intrigued by artifacts and images in museums because they tell a story about a specific culture, person, place, or time in history that cannot be communicated in other ways. This advantage and appeal also applies to art therapy. Wadeson (2010) called the spatial matrix or visual/spatial nature of art an advantage because it can bring numerous fantasy- or reality-based elements into the same composition. In addition, relationships between the elements can be seen and experienced not just explained. Compare an artwork to a dream image. A dream image provides a snapshot of a story that has personal meaning. Yet, it is hard to verbally communicate all that it may represent. The linear nature of verbal communication demands a different type of expression, and it is at best a translation of what has been seen and experienced. Moon (1994) calls art therapy *metaverbal*, because the imagery created goes beyond words.

For some people, the most rewarding aspect of art therapy is the opportunity to work with creative materials. Visually and kinesthetically stimulating materials can enliven emotional and imaginative energy. Similarly, the action of art play can create physical energy (Wadeson, 2010). Ultimately, creative engagement generates energy that can be channeled into the constructive process of growth and healing.

WHY ART THERAPY WITH OLDER ADULTS?

> "Creativity is our greatest legacy. To be creative in later life provides an invaluable model of what is possible as we age, for our children, grandchildren, great grandchildren, and society."
>
> —Cohen, 2000, pp. 11–12

Addressing Developmental Issues of Later Life

In considering caring for older adults, one may initially be focused on deficits and losses of functioning that often accompany aging and the urgent medical needs that must be addressed. These associations appear limited and can be fixed on the destruction of what had been versus the strength of what remains, or the potential of what still can be. Gerontologist, Cohen (2000) challenged negative viewpoints about human potential during aging. Cohen asserted that creativity remains a positive component in the later stages of life:

> Aging and creativity intersect in distinctly different ways at different times to produce new opportunities for personal growth and discovery: Creativity that *commences* with aging, or first becomes apparent in later life . . . Creativity that *continues, sometimes changing* with aging, evident in those who continue to be creative in a particular field or focus . . . Creativity that *connects with loss,* which develops in response to loss and adversity (pp. 117–118).

Furthermore, Cohen (2000) saw opportunities for creativity that are well suited to needs evidenced in four later life stages. He named the four phases the "mid-life evaluation phase" (ages between 40 years and early 60s), a phase characterized by a quest to make life more gratifying; the "liberation phase" (ages between 60s and 70s), where a sense of freedom of creative expression is derived from the comfort and confidence built from past accomplishments; the "summing-up phase," when creative expression may spring from "the desire to find larger meaning in the story of our lives, and to give in larger way the wisdom we have accrued" (p. 79); and the "encore phase," which occurs during advanced age (80 years or older). Cohen described the creative purpose of the encore phase as an effort to "make long, lasting contributions . . . to affirm life, take care of unfinished business, and celebrate one's own contributions" (p. 79). Cohen saw his phases as reflective of the changing experiences of aging in our times and as an update to the age-based developmental stages defined by Erikson (1963).

Shore (1997) also referred to Erikson's stages in relationship to the creative process and the elderly. She asserted that "the struggle inherent in the creative art process" (p. 173) is an excellent means to examine the developmental struggle between integrity and despair. Erikson's (1963) description of the dynamic tensions of integrity and despair, where one may struggle to balance a sense of self-acceptance and -efficacy with feelings of hopelessness in the face of decline and end of life. Shore suggested that the use of art processes, in the context of a therapeutic relationship, may be used to address and resolve psychosocial developmental conflicts and promote attainment of wisdom. She states, "Evoking expression and evoking association are most helpful in stimulating active emotional struggle" (p. 173). However, art media and the level of structure provided must be thoughtfully selected to present the appropriate amount of challenge for the individual.

A creative example of how art therapy may be used to promote integrity is seen in Doric-Henry's (1997) quasi-experimental study, where she introduced elders at a residential nursing home to an 8-week pottery program. Participants of the program were selected based on their willingness to participate in activities that were active, creative, and expressive. Doric-Henry showed them how to prepare clay, work with clay on a potter's wheel, and to create clay pottery through this process. Doric-Henry measured success of the program via pre- and post-intervention measures related to self-esteem, depression, and anxiety. At the end of the study, Doric-Henry noted that many participants within her small sample size of 20 started with healthy levels of self-esteem, therefore significant change did not occur post-treatment. Yet, measured change was observed in behavior and attitude as many of the elders "were becoming more independent and showing a sense of accomplishment in their work," and it was "after making pottery that they felt good about themselves" (p. 171).

In an earlier study, Yaretsky and Levinson (1996) demonstrated that clay work can be used to address sensorimotor activation as well as psychosocial concerns. Yaretsky and Levinson facilitated a group art therapy process for eight geriatric patients residing in a rehabilitation setting. Each person had experienced physical limitations as a result of stroke or femur neck fractures. Some group members also experienced slight cognitive impairment. "The objective of the therapy was to combine bilateral sensorimotor activities of the upper limbs with social interaction directed towards future leisure-time activity" (p. 75). Participants were encouraged to use both hands (including the hand impaired by the stroke) in the clay processes, and spontaneous use of both hands increased through the weeks of clay therapy. Additionally, group facilitators selected the theme of "the home" for the clay works, as it is an especially important topic for elders who are struggling to stay independent or for those who are considering leaving home as care needs become greater.

After participants became familiar with clay, they learned step-by-step methods on how to build clay homes. The gradual process of building the home's external structure, moving to the indoor components and finally to the people that inhabited the home was designed not to overwhelm participants like a more comprehensive task introduction might have. While Yaretsky and Levinson (1996) did not discuss Erikson's developmental tasks, they appeared sensitive to seniors' vulnerability to despair and the importance of supporting an elder's sense of mastery or integrity.

Yaretsky and Levinson (1996) provided additional stimulation for the participants' creative process by bringing in images of work by a regional clay artist who explored home and neighborhood themes. The artist in question was also elderly. The strategy was to very purposefully expose participants to a successful role model. The intention of the leaders was to foster the perception that clay work and creativity was nonthreatening. In their own way, Yaretsky and Levinson were planting a seed of hope within them, the hope that they too could explore their own creativity, and that they too could express ideas about their intimate and familiar settings.

Hope and Community in the Face of Cognitive Decline

Riley (2001) also described the creative arts process and the home theme utilized by art therapists she observed working with elders experiencing significant cognitive loss. In preparation for such work Riley encouraged therapists to look at clients holistically through the lens of their entire lifespan.

She suggests that each person has a unique life story. If a therapist knows a person's past accomplishments of that life story, it may help the therapist connect to the client's inner world, even when the older adult appears disconnected or confused about the goings on in the outer world. Many older adults may experience more confusion when removed from the familiarity of home and their life-story setting. Therefore, utilizing a home-centered art theme may prompt associations with past memories and stories. To address the home theme, participants in the art therapy group observed by Riley were provided with small dimensional cardstock home structures. Subsequently, the group members enhanced the structures with markers, paint, and magazine cut outs. Although the therapists did not necessarily anticipate participants' abilities to engage and connect, they did find that when participants created their home and placed them in a table-top neighborhood drawing, their conversation and interaction increased. The stimulus of the home objects and the creation of a metaphoric community appeared to help participants create a moment of community connection.

Even if cognitive challenges exist as a result of dementia or other disorders, an older adult still deserves the opportunity to engage at their best capacity. Such an opportunity can be provided in a safe, creative arts space. Kasayaka (2002) states, "Being able to create a holding environment, a space that is safe and supportive, so that it can contain and catalyze whatever expression of experience or feeling that needs to happen is the first prerequisite of the healing arts therapist" (p. 15). Given a person-centered approach, where interventions are matched with a person's present capabilities, an art therapist can fulfill his or her core functions, "the reclamation, the regeneration and the celebration of the human spirit" (Kasayaka, p. 9). Kasayaka asserts that person-centered creative arts approaches "allow for and facilitate continued growth, expansion, and healing regardless of cognitive function" (p. 6).

The need for creative space and opportunity for creativity may be most felt in the long-term care setting (Sandel & Johnson, 1987). Sandel and Johnson state that the creative arts therapies enliven the long-term care environment and contribute to an elder's life by increasing orientation and activation, facilitating reminiscence, increasing self-understanding and acceptance, developing meaningful interpersonal relationships, and building communal spirit (pp. 8–9). Furthermore, Sandel and Johnson argue that "participation in creative arts therapies is an antidote to the dependency, passivity, and death that waiting expresses" (p. 9). Art therapy activities that invite elders to express, engage, and interact remind individuals of their own creative and productive natures.

Kates (2008) declares that in the long-term care setting, "the cognitively well" patients are "possibly overlooked in the institutional atmosphere," as staff efforts are often pulled to manage residents with immediate basic care needs (p. 11). In Kates's descriptive study with two physically frail but cognitively well long-term care residents, Kates provided art therapy services. Both residents were suffering from depression and withdrawal from activities not related to their physical challenges. Kates remarked that participants often complained about routines or meals, but that the deeper issues seemed to reflect fears of personal safety and loss of intimacy/relationship opportunities. Using a person-centered dynamic approach, Kates slowly introduced participants to visual engagement and art activities. The slow progression toward engagement was designed in direct response to the resident's confidence and ability to manage art making. In addition, Kates was sensitive to generational or culture attitudes or roles that may impact the residents' participation in an art-based activity. Art activities were then combined with use of family photographs, song, play, conversation, and life-review tasks to support the therapeutic process. After 12 weeks of sessions, the residents gained skills in using symbolic activity to support communication, expression, and connection to others.

Art-Based Life Review and Artistic Legacies

Perry Magniant (2004) confirms that the goals of art therapy with older adults can be varied. She describes that an art therapist may be charged with calming someone who is experiencing anxiety, helping someone to reduce depressive symptoms, supporting the use of undamaged parts of the brain in someone with dementia, helping someone through the grief process, supporting growth of self-esteem through emphasizing positive abilities, promoting creativity as a means to emphasizing those positive abilities, providing cognitive and physical stimulation to support maintenance of skills and energy, providing art and session structures that encourage relationships with the therapist or peers, and designing and engaging elders in tasks that help them maintain their sequencing and problem-solving skills. In addition, the art process or productions can be used to evaluate changes in behavior and thinking.

Yet, the focus of Perry Magniant's (2004) work has been the use of art therapy in the context of a life-review process that culminates in a product called the "lifebook." Perry Magniant asserts that the lifebook technique was developed to support the life-review process of the older adults she worked with in the long-term care setting, and to "capture the rich verbalizations that accompanied the pictures made by the older adults" (p. 54). Goals specific to the lifebook process are: to address grief and loss issues; to support life review using early memories; to support transitions and transfer trauma reconciliation; to promote self-expression, creativity, and self-esteem; and to leave a tangible memory.

Based on her experiences with older adults, Perry Magniant (2004) found that the defined structure and goal of completing a book supported the elder's "sense of importance and pride" (p. 55). The lifebook process also gave them a way to honor the events of their lives in a formal, creative package to be shared with others. In a spiralbound sketchbook, residents would illustrate their life stories from earliest and most vital memories to the present. Perry Magniant provided more than art supplies when she met with the elders; she supplied the long-term care residents with a trusting environment, verbal and artistic stimulus, and support to recall, select, depict, and write stories about their lives. During each session, Perry Magniant would review all previously created artworks and stories to help some regain memories and reorient the participant to the task and stimulate the telling and depiction of the next important story. It is important to note that artistic talent was not a requirement of participation. Because the art therapist is knowledgeable about art techniques that support expression, the art therapist can provide structure and techniques suited to diverse skill levels that enable communication and mastery. The safety built by the development of a positive therapeutic relationship also reduces anxiety for those who may initially feel less comfortable with artistic tasks. When the lifebook content is completed, the older adult designs and creates a formal finished design for the cover. In the end, the lifebook holds a lifetime of memories that can be easily transported and shared.

When the end of life is near and the elder is placed in hospice care, there is often more urgency to share memories and make final connections with family members. According to Wadeson (2000), art therapy can facilitate these important processes. Specifically, "art therapy can contribute to the hospice objective of elevating the quality of life for the dying patient and for family members" (p. 388). In addition, increased activity levels, autonomy, communication, and reduced isolation may be outcomes of art therapy provided in the hospice setting. Artwork made independently or in collaboration with the art therapist can be presented to family to assist with sharing final thoughts. Like a lifebook, the concrete art product created during the hospice experience provides a tangible keepsake for family members to cherish.

Community and Home-Based Art Therapy

As types of care environments for elderly have expanded, so have environments for the provision of art therapy. Today, art therapy services may be found in day hospital settings, continuing care settings, and home settings (Brett-MacLean & Magid, 2004; Canuto et al., 2008; McElroy, Warren, & Jones, 2006). Studies have been conducted to explore differences in art therapy intervention and the outcomes of those interventions. For example, Canuto et al. (2008) conducted a longitudinal assessment of psychotherapeutic day hospital treatment for elders experiencing depression. Using the geriatric depression scale (GDS), short-form survey (Sheikh & Yesavage, 1986), depression was assessed at 3-, 6-, 9-, and 12-month intervals. The multidimensional treatment approach evaluated during the research process included art therapy groups, as well as a psychomotricity group focusing on movement and music, psychodynamic psychotherapy groups, and sociotherapy groups that encouraged social relationships and interactions. While 85% of participants were treated with psychotropic medications such as antidepressant and anxiolytic drugs, comparisons were made between admission and discharge dosages and no significant differences were observed. GDS scores at admission confirmed depression at the beginning of the study and demonstrated remission of depression symptoms at discharge. Importantly, the remission of symptoms occurred at a statistically significant level.

Brett-MacLean and Magid (2004) provide more anecdotal evidence of positive client outcomes based on their experiences with the Artworks Studio. The Artworks Studio is an expansive studio that sits at the heart of a continuous care center for elderly veterans. Residents can come to the studio and be instructed or engage in fine art and craft processes on a daily basis. Drawing and painting, sculpting, textile arts, woodworking, ceramics, and computer-based arts are some of the offerings available to residents. Theme-based workshops are also offered to residents on occasion and may include short-term holiday crafts. Adaptive tools and gripping aids, and cutting and visual aids are used to help keep older adults involved in projects as long as possible. When older adults become infirm and unable to leave the hospital-like units that are a part of the center, trained staff members facilitate art-based activities to sustain life-enhancing activity at those locations. The authors assert that the art-making components of the center contribute to "a sense of well-being, connection, and community, within an institutional care setting and beyond, as veteran residents experience and share their art making with others" (Brett-MacLean & Magid, p. 70).

When an older adult's treatment occurs in the home setting, art therapy can still be a part of a treatment plan. McElroy, Warren, and Jones (2006) and Sezaki and Bloomgarden (2004) have shown successful adaptations of art therapy in the home setting. Given the home environment and the likely presence of a caregiver, the dynamics of art therapy may be significantly different than institutionally based art therapy. To address this hypothesis, McElroy, Warren, and Jones conducted a qualitative study (with five participants) to explore and describe home-based art therapy goals and effectiveness. Participants in the study were selected based on convenience, participant age (over 65), diagnosis of a functional mental health disorder, participant and caregiver consent, and general willingness to have an art therapist come to the home 1 hour per week for a maximum span of 8 weeks. Participants in the study also met criteria for being homebound either by virtue of physical infirmity or mental health issues such as agoraphobia.

Unlike an art class or activity therapy that follows a particular curriculum, the art therapy interventions administered in the research process involved a person-centered approach to art therapy treatment. Participants were interviewed and engaged in goal setting to determine therapeutic goals that were personally relevant to each participant. Goals identified by participants included: to make sense of how I am feeling, to work on anger, to become more motivated. When the interventions were implemented, art therapists used simple art materials that could be transported to the home, such as markers, clay, paint, color pencils, pens, oil pastels, charcoal, and paper. For participants who had difficulty expressing themselves in words, the art therapist modeled and encouraged expression in colors, symbols, and assorted imagery.

At the end of the research, participants cited that they preferred the homey environment to institutional or day care environment, and that the support and guidance of the art therapist helped them feel more confident about their art and their ability to express themselves nonverbally. Frequently, participants noted that they enjoyed individual treatment as opposed to the group treatment that was experienced or anticipated to be provided in other community or institutional settings. This feedback may indicate that the therapeutic relationship between client and art therapist is an extremely important part of therapy satisfaction and engagement. Therefore, not surprisingly, participants also felt that the art therapy process made them feel "friendlier" or more connected to others. Caregivers observed that in some instances their loved one appeared more motivated to engage after treatment was provided and that the positive art exposure became a catalyst for a new hobby (McElroy, Warren, & Jones, 2006). More research is needed to confirm the efficacy of home-based art therapy care.

Gibson (as cited in Sezaki & Bloomgarden, 2004) was one of the first art therapists to identify specific goals for home-based art therapy care. These goals were designed to address depressive symptoms, monitor for suicide ideation, identify specific anxiety and fears not otherwise expressed, and provide opportunities for creative problem solving that could be applied to other life challenges, including: goals related to mood enhancement; reconciliation related to physical illness, chronic pain, or body-related losses; providing a safe place to address issues related to sexuality; identification of family conflicts that impact the person's well-being; and guidance in developing coping mechanisms to address these later life issues.

With these goals in mind, as well as sensitivity toward family, family culture, and home dynamics, Sezaki (Sezaki & Bloomgarden, 2004) provided art therapy care to identified individuals in the home setting. Similar to the approach of McElroy, Warren, and Jones (2006), Sezaki conducted assessments and created individualized care plans in accordance with client goals. Goals identified by clients related to expression of feelings, exploration of interaction methods, improvement or maintenance of quality life, relationship improvement, increasing life enjoyment through the creative process, implementation of coping skills, improved communication, and family engagement.

In the two cases described by Sezaki and Bloomgarden (2004), the approach to art therapy treatment was very different. Given the needs of one client experiencing early signs of dementia and his wife/caregiver's distress, Sezaki provided structured art conversation tasks that prompted the client to provide artistic and verbal responses to simply drawn scribbles or symbols. At times, the caregiver was also involved in these activities as the caregiver had expressed distress regarding their reduced ability to communicate. The structure of the activity and the support of the therapist helped the caregiver see that making pleasant, personal connections with her husband was still possible.

In the second case, more attention was focused on the client's adjustment to debilitating medical issues and reduced independence and resources for expression and social engagement. Through the initial interview with the client, Sezaki (Sezaki & Bloomgarden, 2004) discovered that the client had studied fine art at one time, and built on that experience to reacquaint her with the creative process. Although the client remained restricted to the home environment, she found a fulfilling way to be creative through exploration of the previously familiar watercolor media. The client used postcards made from watercolor paper and adorned them with messages and images of the plants and flowers that were in her home. She then renewed her communication with others outside of her home by sending them the outcomes of her creative experiences. During the long-term therapeutic process, artistic tasks changed along with the therapeutic relationship. It is important to note that although art therapy interventions may appear to have an art activity/art education focus, the goals are resolutely focused on the social emotional sustenance that the artistic and therapeutic process can support. Art therapists who have ventured into the home setting have realized that art therapy can be beneficial in the home setting. In that context, art therapy can be personalized in a very meaningful way.

Art Therapy Stories: Two Graduate Art Therapy Students Discuss Their Experiences with Older Adults

Story 1: Mandy Gwiazdowski, Graduate Art Therapy Student, Marywood University

As an art therapy student, I have experienced a few different populations during practicum study (on-site, graduate-level clinical art therapy training conducted under on-site and school-based group supervision). My latest experience was with older adults at the Wilkes-Barre Pennsylvania Veterans Association (VA). I worked with many groups of people that came in for the adult day care program. Most of these veterans were high functioning and made crafts and talked about their families. They also reminisced about their "younger years." It was interesting to hear their life reviews. It was also disheartening to see the decline in their present thought process in which they knew where they had been stationed during World War II or the Korean War, for instance, but they couldn't recall what they had for breakfast that morning.

The most enjoyable experience at the VA was the dementia unit, also known as "memory lane," which is a locked ward where the veterans lived. It was locked because the veterans needed constant supervision. I worked each week with many of these veterans, creating artwork, painting, coloring with crayons and markers, and using Model Magic, a nontoxic clay that is soft and pliable. One experience that was very fascinating involved a man who painted a wooden box with acrylic paint. He chose his colors independently and while painting this box over several sessions he talked about his life. As he painted the outside of the box green he discussed his fear while working in the coal mines, the fear of being lowered into the mine. While painting the inside of the box he talked about his money, coins specifically, and where he thought they might be in his room. He was unsure where he put them at the time. Another wonderful experience was with a man in his mid-80s with fairly moderate-stage dementia; he liked to draw with markers and pencils. His drawings were interesting in that he would draw an image with elements that typically didn't fit together. Some of his drawings were representative of his confusion and thought distortions that particular day. We had a one-on-one session where he worked on a drawing for approximately 30 minutes. When he was finished, he talked about it. He spoke of each element in the drawing separately. When asked how it all fit together, he just replied that he "wasn't sure," but those were the things that were on his mind at the moment.

The older adults are a wonderful group with whom to work. They have a wisdom that is genuine and they've had experiences that can teach future generations to embrace life. They are grateful for each day and each encounter. I was very grateful for the opportunity to relate to them through art experiences.

Story 2: Teresa Toth, Graduate Art Therapy Student, Marywood University

When working with an older adult population, I think a key consideration is to always help each individual keep his or her independence in some way. Oftentimes the hardest adjustment for older adults is the loss of their independence. Some ways that I thought helped my participants maintain their independence was to offer tasks or group projects that allowed each individual to improvise or create his or her own idea. This strategy was something that I found to be successful, because each individual had different levels of physical dexterity and cognitive capability. If a given task was presented with a narrow, "this is the way to do the activity" approach, it often left people more frustrated and more aware of their limitations. Accordingly, I provided a variety of artistic options so that each individual could find a comfortable way to explore his or her experiences and memories.

I found that opportunities to share memories and experiences were important to the people with whom I worked. One way I facilitated this need was to focus on memories using a memory book. Individuals could search through magazines that evoked memories, or they could use their own family photos. The book was designed to be fairly small so they were able to have a book of memories to carry with them. In my opinion, it created beautiful interactive opportunities. First, participants expressed themselves in a book, with page after page filled with thoughts and memories that only they knew. But by creating the book, they were literally able to show their memories and explain to others what each page represented. The images prompted memories that they may not have retrieved otherwise. When thinking of adults at the end stage of their lives, I felt that helping them express what they felt to be important helped them pass on their legacy not only to their family, but also to the people who surround them, such as friends and caregivers. Legacy is an important concept when working with this population, because it is important for people to leave behind their thoughts, their history, and their traditions.

A general thing that I learned when working with this population was that it is important to always be aware of your nonverbal cues. For example, it was important to be aware of the differences in movement and processing speed between myself and the older adult. I noticed that participants would get frustrated if I moved too fast and did not give them enough time to figure out the directions given. I also became more sensitive to how they handled stimuli and found that it was important to not be overwhelming in one's approach or enthusiasm. I found that individuals were often comforted by a set plan for their day. Finally, I learned to honor their routines. In that regard, I facilitated group rituals or routines to increase comfort during sessions.

In terms of art, I found that introducing art in a nonformal way worked better because I discovered that art can be intimidating to the elderly, especially when a blank piece of paper and markers were presented with instructions to draw freehand. I also found that when cutting rectangular pieces of paper around the edges so that the paper was rounded off or circular, participants were more receptive to the art process. It appeared that the participants found the rounded paper somehow more inviting, or less intimidating.

I have several ideas I will try with the older adults in the future. For example, I would like to create comfort blankets with them. To make blankets, participants would select or create personally important images to be transferred onto fabric with fabric paints or other techniques. The decorated fabric could then be sewn into a quilt or blanket that can be used on their bed or lap, or be hung in their room for display. I would also like to combine art making and gardening. In collaboration with an older client, I would grow a flower or plant from seed, nurture it, and watch it grow week after week. We would map the plant's progress through drawing or painting, using the plant as a subject for a still life. The intention would be to help them be mindful of the growth and beauty that still occurs around them. Finally, when I think about older adults, I feel the greatest gift I can give to them is lend an ear and to use my skills to help them leave their legacy in an artistic way.

Student Story Reflection

During the 10 years Parker-Bell has worked with graduate art therapy students, there has been a growth of interest and willingness of students to work with the aging population. Initially, many students were hesitant or afraid to go into elder-care environments for practicum training, as they had visions of infirmity and the end-of-life somberness associated with those places. In most cases, once students began using art to reach the older adults with whom they worked, they found ways to connect with them that provided rich and valuable experiences for all involved. Well trained art therapy students and art therapy professionals use proven art therapy strategies as well as their own creativity to respond to the needs and capabilities of the older adult, no matter where the person may reside. In the context of a safe therapeutic relationship, meaningful dialogues arise and older adults are supported to assert their creative abilities. Creative engagement provides people of all ages an opportunity to enhance their sense of joy and to tell their stories.

SUMMARY

Art therapists are master's level professionals who have been trained and have met specific educational standards and experiences to deliver art therapy services. Art therapy methods of treatment can be of particular help to adults who must face developmental issues that include loss and grief over loved ones, physical and cognitive challenges, and diminishing skills and independence. As services to older adults span different treatment environments—from the home setting, to the community setting, to long-term care settings—so too does the use of art therapy. The creative process of art, within the hands of a well trained art therapy professional, can activate and enliven the spirit, increase activity and engagement, foster memory retrieval and communication, and help the older person experience the last phase of his or her life with creativity and integrity.

In this next section of the chapter, the focus turns to the creative art of music, beginning with words of the musician, Yehude Menuhin. He creatively describes the therapeutic possibilities that lie within the elements of rhythm, melody, and harmony that are comprised in the medium of music. Music therapists transform and utilize the qualities of music to enhance quality of life for the aging population.

MUSIC THERAPY

"Music creates order out of chaos; for
rhythm imposes unanimity upon the divergent,
melody imposes continuity upon the disjointed, and
harmony imposes compatibility upon the incongruous."

—Yehudi Menuhin

Introduction to Music Therapy

One of the most intriguing uses of music today is its application to all aspects of the health care and maintenance of the individual. From this connection grew the discipline of music therapy (Scartelli, 1987, p. 20). Music has power that resonates through generations, traverses the boundaries of linguistic differences, and permeates the spirit. A song can instantly propel you back to a certain time, place, and emotional state (Sochoka, 2004, p. 12). Dr. E. Thayer Gaston (1968, p. 7), who is often referred to as the "father of music therapy," writes, "Music, a form of human behavior, is unique and powerful in its influence." As an art, music is enjoyed for its aesthetic and entertaining value. It is obvious that humankind uses music and even exploits the effect of music to nonaesthetic or nonentertainment ends. Music is integral to social, business, educational, and religious functioning. Music pervades all aspects of our daily lives.

In attempting to define music therapy, Michel (1981) delineates the meaning of therapy and related words, such as "therapeutic means to attend" (p. 5). He goes on to say in his introduction that "Masserman finds in the Greek root of the word, therapy to mean 'service,' and that…'serving the best interests of a fellow human being, whether stranger, friend, client, or patient, is the purpose of all treatment as well as the hallmark of civilization'" (Masserman as cited in Michel, 1981, p. 5).

To provide a deeper understanding of music therapy, responses to the following list of questions will be answered: What is music therapy? With whom does a music therapist work? What are the professional standards of education and clinical training? What is the entry-level credential and the scope of practice required? What qualities can be expected of a board-certified music therapist? How does music therapy enhance the quality of life of the older adult? What are some approaches used in the practice of music therapy? What funding sources are available that support music therapy services for aging adults? Following a brief review of basic terms, a description of the biological age, psychological age, and psychosocial age, and possible music therapy goals for each, this section addresses each of these questions and provides a few personal case examples. These examples relate specifically to the potential of meeting goals that can improve the quality of life of the older adult population.

Gerontological Concepts and Music Therapy Treatment Goals

Music therapists who work with an aging population must be aware of basic theoretical and practical concepts related to the process of aging. As life-spans continue to increase, some people ask, "When is a person considered old?" There is no designated time indicating when an individual becomes old, as aging is a gradual process involving physical, psychological, psycho-social, and cognitive changes beginning at birth. Gerontology is among the fastest growing scientific disciplines of the past 5 decades and is defined as the systematic study of the phenomena of aging, involving the normal biological, psychological, and psychosocial aspects in the processes of growing old (Ferraro as cited in Clair & Davis, 2008; Harris as cited in Clair & Davis, 2008). A gerontologist is a person who specializes in one or more aspects of aging. This study is multidisciplinary and draws upon research findings and experiences of various disciplines, including music therapy. Senescence describes the inevitable decline in the efficiency of the body systems that is a normal aspect of aging. Senescence is slow and progresses at various rates in different people. It leads to a decrease in energy, eventual organ-system failure, and ultimately, death. Music therapy can compensate for senescence by helping to provide the elderly person with a more satisfying and useful life (Clair & Davis, 2008).

Biological age refers to the time period when a person starts to show physical signs of aging, usually beginning around the age of 40 years. Characteristics such as a slight decrease in stamina and strength, the appearance of wrinkles, gray hair, and changes in weight and body composition begin to occur. Concomitant there are changes in bones, muscle strength, and endurance. Bones become brittle; joints become less flexible and lose density; stooped posture, loss of height, and body fat increase with aging. Cellular, molecular, and organ functions become less efficient with age (Markson as cited in Clair & Davis, 2008; Waters as cited in Clair & Davis, 2008). The music therapist's goals addressing biological aging would most likely focus on:

- Increasing upper and lower extremity strength
- Increasing mobility and range of motion
- Strengthening sensory training

Psychological age can be defined as the impact that growing old has on memory, learning, personality, and emotions. This relates to how well a person responds to a changing environment and is able to adapt to new situations or experiences. A person who does little to vary his or her routine may be considered psychologically old (Erber as cited in Clair & Davis, 2008; Harris as cited in Clair & Davis, 2008). Music therapy, in an attempt to remedy some effects of psychological aging, might set the following goals to:

- Stimulate long-term memory
- Improve short-term memory
- Increase reality orientation
- Increase self-esteem
- Promote relaxation and stress reduction
- Enhance life experiences with reminiscence

Psychosocial age is usually determined by society's criteria as to how a person should act or what one should be doing at certain stages of life. American society idealizes youth and discounts much of the experience, wisdom, and knowledge that the elderly population has to offer. Ageism is discrimination against elderly people. Older adults are often portrayed as insignificant or ugly in some children's literature. Clair & Davis (2008) observe that they may be described as "over the hill," "old fool," or "old maid." Often they are portrayed negatively in movies, television, or in music. The Beatle's song, "When I'm Sixty-four," is an example of this—even though musically upbeat, the lyrics describe aging as an unpleasant process. Many other cultures hold their elderly members in esteem and an older person is looked to for wisdom and guidance. In the United States, emphasis is on maintaining youthful beauty (p. 185).

Music therapy psychosocial goals are aimed to:

- Improve and increase social interaction
- Diminish feelings of isolation
- Increase verbal interaction
- Maintain levels of participation/adherence to creative treatment program
- Improve communication skills
- Reduce agitation
- Decrease wandering
- Improve personal hygiene (Clair & Davis, 2008)

WHAT IS MUSIC THERAPY?

Regarding music therapy, Hanser (as cited in Pfeifer, 1982) states:

> Music is a complex form of expression which defines us as human. It opens us to vivid images, moves us to tears, speeds up our heartbeat, and transports us to other places and times. The most incapacitated people respond to music, and sometimes only to music; those most capable express a world that is not definable and often with indescribable feelings and thoughts through music.

The power of music provides an extremely effective medium in therapy with the elderly. A music therapist–board certified (MT-BC) is well prepared to bring a quality of joy to the life of the elderly through the basic music foundation gained through studies. Not that an administrator needs to pursue this program of study, but to become an advocate one needs to appreciate the vast training required to become board certified. Functional skills in voice, piano, guitar, percussion; improvisation techniques; knowledge of composition, music theory, and music history; conducting and arranging skills; and an understanding of the many musical styles are other competencies music therapists must possess. Flexibility in choosing appropriate music and instruments "in the moment," is a must during the delivery of effective music therapy sessions. The therapist is able to select or create music that may alleviate pain, make communication easier, and help the client express his or her feelings when words fail. The trained therapist is able to engage in healthy interactions with clients, which lead to the unfolding of a therapeutic relationship. Developing a therapeutic relationship is essential for therapy to be effective. In order for people to thrive as social human beings, meaningful relationships are necessary. Professional members of the American Music Therapy Association (AMTA, 2012) embrace and strive to live the spirit of the mission: to advance public awareness of the benefits of music therapy and to increase access to quality music therapy services in a rapidly changing world.

The AMTA mission was exemplified when Sr. Mariam was invited by Vestal Nursing Home's administrator, Denise Johnson, to become a consultant. This nursing home is located in Vestal, New York, on the Southern Tier of the state. Johnson had been listening to her staff as they commented about the positive effect that music seemed to have on participants. The residents appeared more attentive, wandered less, smiled more, were more vocal, and in general seemed happier when the programs involved music.

From this input and her own observations, Johnson understood and valued the benefits of music and was anxious to find a way to employ a music therapist. She was convinced that this would be a way to enhance the quality of life for her residents. What would she need to do to make this a reality? Noticing once again that dementia research grants were available from the New York State Office of Health, she considered whether it would be worth trying for one. Writing grants is always a risk-taking job. She had applied unsuccessfully before. Would she attempt this again? She was not one to give up and decided to try again. The dementia grant program called for the completion of a research study that would measure the effects of music therapy. As a true advocate for music therapy, Johnson called the author for an appointment and drove an hour and a half to meet. Upon returning to her facility, she engaged a grant writer, who also made the trip to meet and asked more questions that gave him additional insights about the music therapy profession. The proposal was written and submitted. This time, Vestal Nursing Home was awarded a sizeable grant that provided funds to hire a director for the research project, two music therapists, the purchase of necessary equipment needed to implement the music therapy program, and other necessary consultants.

The author helped design a scholarly study that would reliably measure the effects of music therapy versus activities only on the residents. The program director was responsible for the major part of coordinating the research project. The study investigated the effects of music on agitation and wandering of those in early stages of Alzheimer's dementia as compared to those who engaged in only daily living activities. Music therapy was shown to be more successful than other provided activities at decreasing agitated behaviors. The results showed that a 15-minute individual session could significantly decrease agitated behaviors for up to 7 hours. There was also a significant difference in favor of music therapy when measuring attention and participation. Johnson stated that, aside from the statistics, she had observed that music therapy had a positive impact on the lives of the residents at the Vestal Nursing Center. The residents receiving music therapy were more attentive and participated during their individual sessions. They were less agitated than those residents who received other activities. It was reported that residents often made the statement, "I love it!" when referring to the music therapy.

This new program contributed greatly, not only to residents' quality of care and quality of life, but also in alleviating levels of stress for the caretakers and for families, as well. The program served to increase the body of research showing the effects of music therapy for the elderly. As mentioned earlier, the administrator understood the value of music therapy and was truly an advocate for incorporating it into programs for her residents. This experience culminated with Denise Johnson receiving the Advocacy Award from the Mid-Atlantic Region of the National Association for Music Therapy.

MUSIC THERAPISTS

As a profession, music therapy in the United States can be traced back to 1950 with the founding of the National Association for Music Therapy, now known as the American Music Therapy Association (AMTA). Bruscia (1998) reminds us that the identity of music therapy as a profession has not yet fully emerged within the education and health communities, but is "still developing; it is still in the process of becoming" (p. 15). Bruscia provides an overview of the evolution of music therapy in his book, *Defining Music Therapy,* which includes many additional definitions.

The AMTA (2006) fact sheet, *Music Therapy and Alzheimer's Disease,* offers the following definition: "Music Therapy is the clinical and evidence-based use of music interventions to accomplish individualized goals within a therapeutic relationship by a credentialed professional who has completed an approved music therapy program" (p. 1). Research in music therapy supports the effectiveness of intervention in many areas, such as facilitating movement and overall physical rehabilitation, increasing motivation for one to engage in treatment, providing emotional support for clients and their families, and creating an outlet for expression of feelings. Because music therapy is a powerful and nonthreatening medium, unique outcomes are possible. Music therapy is used with all ages and disabilities. Music therapy interventions can be designed to: promote wellness, manage stress, alleviate pain, express feelings, enhance memory, improve communications, and promote physical rehabilitation. Research in music therapy supports its effectiveness in a wide variety of healthcare and educational settings.

Music therapists complete a bachelor's degree in music therapy or the equivalent at an AMTA–approved college or university program. Currently, the AMTA is highly considering creating a master's level in order to gain more advanced, in-depth knowledge or additional training in an area of specialization. Often, pursuing a master's degree is driven by fulfilling the requirement to apply for licensure, which frequently increases the possibility for receiving third-party reimbursement for services. The bachelor's degree (or the equivalent) includes successful completion of 1,200 hours in a supervised internship following the completion of the academic studies.

The curriculum is competency based in three main foundational areas: musical foundations, clinical foundations, and music therapy foundations and principles, as specified in the AMTA professional competencies. Completion of the academic studies and the culminating internship training provides eligibility to take the national board certification examination for music therapists administered by the Certification Board for Music Therapists (CBMT).

What Are the Credentials and Educational and Clinical Requirements?

Graduates of college or university programs approved by the AMTA who have completed the undergraduate academic and clinical component of a minimum of 1,200 hours of internship training or the equivalent are eligible to take the national board certification examination for music therapists. Those who pass the national board certification exam for music therapists merit the credential, music therapist–board certified (MT-BC), qualifying one for entry into practice. As in other related healthcare professions, one must become recertified every 5 years through ongoing continuing music therapy education (CMTE) or the retaking of the exam in the 4th year of the 5-year cycle. Content of continuing education courses must relate to a scope of practice that is revised every 5 years. As of 2011, one continuing education music therapy course must be in ethics.

The CBMT administers the national board examination, awards the credential (MT-BC), and coordinates the ongoing recertification program. The CBMT is an autonomous organization with the primary role of providing the MT-BC credential through administering a national certification examination for music therapists and the recertification program. This credential is primarily an effort to protect the consumer.

With Whom Does a Music Therapist Work?

In the past, music therapists worked primarily with persons with behavioral and emotional disorders and those with intellectual disabilities. With increased emphasis on preventative health care, the integration of children with disabilities into public schools, and increasing services to the aging population, music therapists are expanding services into several new clinical areas. Music therapy is now used in pain control, stress management, infant stimulation, adult day care, nursing homes, wellness programs, childbirth, prisons, medical care, private practice, and more.

How Does Music Therapy Make a Difference for Older Persons?

Research results and clinical experiences attest to the viability of music therapy even in those who are resistive to other treatment approaches. Music is a form of sensory stimulation that provokes responses due to the familiarity, predictability, and feeling of security associated with it. For example, stroke patients unable to speak are often able to sing the words of songs learned earlier in life. In practice, the author experienced this a few years ago when a relative of a sister spent time at the author's residence following a stroke that left her speechless. Her lifestyle prior to the stroke involved a deep love for hymn singing. During her stay, this therapist brought her to the chapel and facilitated music therapy sessions in that setting. With organ accompaniment provided by the author, she became engaged in singing every word of many of her favorite hymns, although she could not speak a sentence. This type of memory retrieval also takes place readily with persons in various stages of dementia when they are unable to speak with meaning any longer. The rhythm and melody of familiar songs are processed and sung with expression and comments. Music organizes the disorganized.

What Does a Music Therapist Do?

The music therapist takes referrals and during the first few sessions assesses the strengths and needs of each client. This provides information about what should be entered on a treatment plan that is designed with goals and objectives aimed to meet the needs of an individual. With this information, the therapist is ready to implement the plan which involves the client in music and musical activities. Music therapists may choose to structure the use of both instrumental and vocal music strategies to improve functioning areas of need that facilitate changes that will transfer into daily life. The therapist may improvise or compose music with clients, accompany and conduct group music experiences, provide instrument instruction, direct music and movement activities, or provide music listening opportunities. Music therapists are members of the team of therapists who implement programs with groups or individuals that display a continuum of needs ranging from leisure-time activities to community involvement to bedside care. Following each session, the therapist documents the outcomes and periodically writes a progress or termination report.

Following a referral, the music therapist completes an assessment of the strengths and needs of the client. From this information, a treatment plan is designed with long- and short-term goals, objectives, and strategies to address them. Implementing the program is the next step, by utilizing and contributing to evidence-based music therapy practice. A competent therapist has a good musical, music therapy, and clinical foundation and is well prepared to select or create music and when necessary to adapt the elements of music that will best treat the patient's/client's needs. Documentation of the responses is compiled and data are collected. From this information, periodic progress reports are written and presented on the outcomes and benefits that music therapy has provided. Evaluations of these findings are ongoing, from which decisions about continuing or terminating music therapy services are made.

The music therapist profession was incorporated over 60 years ago. Much progress has taken place over this timespan, as more research increases "best practice" as in other allied health professions. While not yet mandated, the trend is moving toward requiring a master's degree or advanced level of competence for entry-level practice. Many therapists currently pursue advanced degrees that may lead to state licensure or simply the desire to embrace and use various special techniques or approaches in their practice: for example, the Nordoff-Robbins creative music therapy approach using improvisation, the Bonny Method of Guided Imagery and Music (BGIM), psychoanalysis, Orff-Schulwerk method, and many more. It is a very exciting and rewarding time to be a professional music therapist reaching out to the many needs of the day. As of this writing, there are 5,072 active MT-BCs and there is a greater demand for music therapists than those who are prepared to practice in the profession.

It is important to distinguish between music therapy and recreation therapy. While both are beneficial for providing a quality of life for the elderly, the goals are different. Music in recreation therapy serves as a diversion and entertainment primarily, whereas in music therapy, the use of music is intended to bring about specific changes identified in an assessment of the individual. From this information gathered, a specific program plan is designed with goals and objectives to be met and documented. Implementation of the music therapy program may be done with groups or individuals who displayed a vast continuum of needs from bedside care to leisure-time activities in the community.

MUSIC THERAPY OUTCOMES

Participants do not need to have a music background to benefit from the life-giving benefits achieved through music therapy, although, with the elderly, a musical background is often present. Some outcomes of a music therapy program with the elderly are:

- Memory recall which contributes to reminiscence and satisfaction with life
- Positive changes in mood and emotional states
- Sense of control over life through successful experiences and opportunities to choose
- Awareness of self and environment which accompanies increased attention to music
- Anxiety and stress reduction for older adult and caregivers
- Nonpharmacological management of pain and discomfort
- Stimulation, which provokes interest even when no other approach is effective
- Structure, which promotes rhythmic and continuous movement or vocal fluency as an adjunct to physical rehabilitation
- Opportunities to interact socially with others (AMTA, 2006)

Clinical practice involves the deliberate and purposeful use of music by a credentialed music therapist to meet these areas of needs. Again, interventions are supported by evidence-based research, and outcomes are associated with what is needed to increase an individual's quality of life in a community. Therapeutic outcomes from music therapy interventions are gathered through ongoing assessments of cognitive, physical, and psychosocial skills that transfer to life functions. These skills contribute to a quality of life primarily through successful experiences in domestic life, self-care, personal satisfaction, spiritual life, and community involvement (Clair & Davis, 2008, pp. 194–195). Music therapy interventions require the development, strengthening, and maintenance of skills that transfer readily in "real-world" experiences. Music activities serve as a strong motivator that facilitates skill strengthening and new skill development that transfers readily to family and community life.

The development of a therapeutic relationship with professionally trained music therapists helps individuals learn, adapt, and develop in ways that contribute to their well-being. The ultimate goals of music therapy are the achievement of the best possible functioning, and a good understanding of "normal" according to Clair and Menmot (2008), who are specialists with the older adult population. The clear understanding of strengths and limitations provides the basis of a new self-concept, where individuals are empowered to be all that they can be as they participate in the activities of life.

In her video documentation of music therapy as a treatment modality for those with dementia, Clair (1991) demonstrated the effectiveness of music therapy with one client. This excerpt from a music therapy session was played at the U.S. Senate Hearing in 1991. In the scene shown, a gentleman sat awaiting Clair's arrival for therapy. He was not just seated, but was engaged in making loud, desperate garbled noises while waving his arms in large movements in an effort to convey his message. This interesting gentleman demonstrated several characteristics found in patients with Alzheimer's-type dementia. His frustration with his inability to verbalize his needs was obvious. As he continued, one could witness an increase in agitation—his muscle tone was filled with tension that was observed in his gross arm movements. He continued attempting to communicate verbally until his therapist entered and greeted him respectfully by name. She sat directly facing him, and proceeded to tune her guitar. One could see him beginning to relax, even during the short tuning process. The therapist moved into a gentle song that seemed to elicit his undivided attention and to change his agitated state into one of total relaxation. Although he appeared to be passively participating, suddenly, in that very short time, the music therapy provided prompted him to conclude the song by pointing to the fingerboard of the guitar, and in a clear voice, articulate the words, "I like that, don't you?" Once again, the therapist experienced firsthand, *music organizing the disorganized.*

THE OLDER AMERICANS ACT

As stated previously, Clair's video was shown at the Committee on Aging U.S. Senate Hearing held in Washington, DC in 1991 as an example of the effects music can play in providing a quality of life for the elderly. Like administrators, the senators were seeking answers to the question: How can we provide a greater quality of life for older adults? Since that time, there has been a considerable increase in research on the topic, and modern technology has taken away much of the mystery of what happens in the nervous system, the brain, the memory, and our entire being. The body, mind, and spirit are surely one, integrated in a very complex system that once seemed a bit mysterious. Music therapy, art therapy, and other creative arts therapies are among those disciplines recognized and utilized to meet the various needs of the aging population. As of 1992, creative art therapies have been added to the list of viable treatments in the Older Americans Act (PL 102-375). This came about through the cooperation, commitment, and collaborative efforts of the National Association for Music Therapy (now known as the American Music Therapy Association) by organizing this hearing. As a result, funding was provided to increase research on the subject. This funding stimulated a proliferation of older adult-focused research studies. Results of these studies continue to be disseminated and utilized by music therapy professionals to this date.

The proceedings of the hearing before the Special Committee on Aging of the U.S. Senate (1991), were published as *Forever Young: Music and Aging*, and still impact us today. The many messages of witnesses and those giving testimony heightened the awareness of the role and benefits of the creative arts in the lives of older adults. The committee's findings emphasized music therapy's benefits for older adults and that music should no longer be looked on as something "trivial or only used for performance." Dr. Oliver Sacks, the famous neurologist, and the late Dr. Mathew Lee from the Rusk Institute (of New York University) stressed this point in their testimonies. Senator and coordinator, Harry Reid, from Arizona opened the session by reminding everyone that, "Music therapy is an innovative approach that will not widen the deficit but can help millions of older Americans live happier and more fulfilling lives—and we can get this impression as the saying goes, for a song" (Special Committee on Aging, 1991).

Dr. Oliver Sacks, the popular and well known neurologist portrayed in the film *Awakenings*, spoke to the Special Committee on Aging (1991) from a practical and intuitive sense. He ended his testimony with these inspiring words:

> Music and music therapists are crucial and indispensable in institutions for elderly people and among neurological disabled patients. I think what is pragmatic and intuitive is that one needs to know what goes on and the need for research and funding for this purpose. I think there needs to be proper awareness and respect for Music Therapists, so that it is not looked on as just something trivial and entertaining.

In closing his testimony, Dr. Mathew Lee, professor of medicine at the Rusk Institute in New York City, entered into an interesting dialog with Senator Reid that is worthy of reflection for future administrators. Dr. Lee told Senator Reid, "My experience in the medical world has brought me to realize the importance of the creative arts and specifically music therapy." Senator Reid interjected the following question, "Dr. Lee, do you think music therapy can save on federal expenditures, and, if so why, do you say that?

Dr. Lee responded by saying,

> The answer is yes. I will give you an example. If one looks at the amount of medication that is given in nursing homes, primarily they would fall into two categories—one, to help a patient sleep; the other, to reduce pain.. It is my contention and my clinical observation up to this point in time that if we play music or introduce any form of creative art, we'll reduce the amount of medication that is given. What I would like to do, then, is to translate this money that is saved in the pharmacy

department and use it to hire a music therapist (Special Committee on Aging, 1991).

This hearing (Special Committee on Aging, 1991) resulted in an allocation of $385,000 to the National Association for Music Therapy to further research in music therapy for the elderly. This allocation of funds became six grants to be used in research by music therapists. An explosion of research has occurred over the decades that followed that continues to show the effects of music therapy on the elderly.

WHO PAYS FOR MUSIC THERAPY SERVICES?

The Administration on Aging (AoA) was reauthorizing the Older Americans Act in 2011. Music therapy and the creative arts are a part of the act, and Judy Simpson, the government relations specialist in the AMTA Office, has provided testimony to the AoA as part of the reauthorization process and is networking with the National Center for Creative Aging. The following information was provided by Judy Simpson (AMTA, 2011b).

Skilled Nursing Facilities

Since Medicare payments for skilled nursing facilities (SNFs) are preset year to year based upon factors identified within the related prospective payment system (PPS), it is not possible to bill Medicare for music therapy as a separate service. That does not mean, however, that music therapy cannot contribute to the treatment offered and be included within the PPS reimbursement. In fact, music therapists can frequently provide successful interventions that enhance the existing program and ultimately assist the facility to implement cost-effective services.

Music therapists can contribute to the restorative care program documented on the Minimum Data Set (MDS), positively impacting the daily PPS reimbursement rate from Medicare. Several interventions and techniques that music therapists offer in skilled nursing facilities can be considered restorative care, including strategies that address range of motion or communication. Documentation of music therapy interventions within resident records can then be counted toward the restorative care total for those individuals identified as restorative care candidates on the MDS assessment.

Music Therapy and the Minimum Data Set (MDS)

The MDS 3.0 assessment tool utilized in SNF PPS and in residential placement programs lists music therapy under "Section O. Special Treatments, Procedures, and Programs O0400. Therapies, F. Recreational Therapy (includes recreational and music therapy)." This listing provides a more accurate vehicle for documenting physician-ordered music therapy services in settings utilizing the MDS and helps to validate the inclusion of music therapy as a part of the PPS daily rate.

Music therapy has been identified since 1994 under Medicare as a reimbursable service under the benefits for Partial Hospitalization Programs (PHP). According to the AMTA, under the heading of activity therapy, using the Healthcare Common Procedure Coding System (HCPCS) code G0176, music therapy must be considered an active treatment by meeting the following criteria: (1) a physician's prescription, (2) reasonable and necessary for the treatment of the individual's illness or injury, and (3) goal directed and based on a documented treatment plan (Simpson, J., personal communication, February 16, 2011).

As mentioned earlier, under Medicare's PPS, music therapy is not billed as a separate service. Music therapists contribute to a facility's treatment program and are included within the PPS reimbursement, assisting the facility to implement cost-effective services. Within some SNFs, utilizing the MDS assessment, music therapists provide and document restorative care programming, which can positively affect Medicare reimbursement. Private insurance is another means for private payment for the provisions of music therapy services. The number of success stories involving private insurance reimbursement for music therapy services continues to grow. Companies like Blue Cross Blue Shield, Aetna, Cigna, Greatwest Healthcare, and others have reimbursed for music therapy services case by case, based on medical necessity.

Music therapists provide required documentation for insurance industry representatives to make informed decisions about music therapy coverage. Board-certified music therapists record assessment results, propose treatment plans, outline functional outcomes of interventions, provide diagnostic and procedure codes, and present research evidence to support the reimbursement process. Music therapy typically requires preapproval and is reimbursable when deemed medically or behaviorally necessary to attain the treatment goals of the individual client.

Other Sources

Additional sources regarding reimbursement and financing of music therapy include state and county department of developmental disabilities, workers' compensation, TRICARE, private auto insurance, Individuals with Disabilities Education Act Part B–related services funding, foundations, grants, and private pay (AMTA, 2011a).

SUMMARY

It is important to acknowledge that the creative art therapies have a significant role in the care of older adults. Music therapy was specifically included in the 1992 amendment of the Older Americans Act because of its demonstrated effectiveness. Music therapists, as well other creative art therapists' early experiences with older adults show that the creative arts therapies are viable treatment approaches that enhance the quality of life for the aged. In his testimony at the Senate hearing discussed earlier, Dr. Mathew Lee (Special Committee on Aging, 1991) stated that the medical ". . . world is truly beginning to realize the importance of the creative arts and specifically music therapy" in health care.

As a review, music therapy may address issues specific to later life that relate to biological, psychological, and psychosocial ages. Music therapists meet specific educational and clinical requirements established by the AMTA. In addition, the music therapist must also pass the CBMT national board certification examination to practice as a music therapy professional. After establishing themselves as professionals, music therapists may also pursue advanced competencies in an area of specialty or may pursue state licensure when applicable. These trained and credentialed music therapists use evidence-based practices to determine appropriate assessments, treatment plans, and implementation of music interventions for the older population. Music therapy services are always offered within the context of a therapeutic relationship.

Music therapy and art therapy represent two professions in a broader group called creative arts therapies. Formally trained music therapists and art therapists, in accordance with the regulations of their professional associations and credentialing bodies, use their creative and therapeutic training to help older adults more fully engage in expressive tasks that allow their lives to be more fulfilling. When one is in the last stages of life, when losses are great, one can potentially lose hope. Engagement in the creative arts therapies can instill hope and activate positive processes of change even in later life. As Aldridge and Aldridge (1992) state, "Creative art therapies can be powerful tools in such a process of change" (p. 91).

Discussion Questions

1. How do professional creative arts therapy services delivered by credentialed music therapists and art therapists differ in focus, approach, quality, and content from services delivered by recreational therapists, activity aides, or activity therapists?

2. Describe the aging process from a biological, psychological, and psychosocial perspective.

3. What later life developmental issues are the creative arts therapies well suited to address?

4. When older adults experience symptoms related to dementia or stroke, why would the creative arts therapies be a preferred treatment option in comparison to verbal therapy?

5. Based on the information in the chapter, where might older adults obtain creative art therapy services, and in which care settings are creative arts therapy treatment strategies effective?

6. How was the amendment of the Older Americans Act of 1992 influential in establishing creative arts therapy as a viable service for older adults?

7. What are ways that administrators may obtain payment for creative arts therapy services?

ADDITIONAL RESOURCES

The American Art Therapy Association: www.americanarttherapyassociation.org

Art Therapy Credentials Board: www.atcb.org

American Music Therapy Association: www.musictherapy.org

Certification Board for Music Therapists: www.cbmt.org

Beyond Words: Art Therapy with Older Adults (film). Expressive Media: www.expressivemedia.org

Older Americans Act, Administration on Aging: www.aoa.gov/AoA_programs/OAA/index.aspx

FURTHER READING

Bright, R. (1993). *Music therapy and the dementias: Improving the quality of life.* St. Louis, MO: MMB Horizon Series, MMB Music.

Cevasco, A. (2010). Effects of the therapists non-verbal behavior on participation and affect of individuals of Alzheimer's Disease during group music therapy sessions. *Journal of Music Therapy, 47*(3), 282–299.

Clair, A., Bernstein, B., & Johnson G. (1995). Rhythm playing characteristics in persons with severe dementia, including those with probable Alzheimer's type. *Journal of Music Therapy, 32*(2), 113–131.

Lipe, A. (1995). The use of music performance tasks in the assessment of cognitive functioning among older adults. *Journal of Music Therapy, 32*(3), 137–151.

O'Konski, M. B. (2010). Comparative effectiveness of exercise with patterned sensory enhanced music and background music for long-term care residents. *Journal of Music Therapy, 47*(2), 120–136.

Ravid-Horesh, R. H. (2004). 'A temporary guest': The use of art therapy in life review with an elderly woman. *Arts in Psychotherapy, 31*(5), 303–319.

Smith. D., & Lipe, A. (1991). Music therapy practices in gerontology. *Journal of Music Therapy, 28*(4), 193–210.

Sole, C., Mercadal-Brotons, M., Gallego, S., & Riera, M., (2010). Contributions of music to aging adult's quality of life. *Journal of Music Therapy, 47*(3), 264–281.

REFERENCES

Aldridge, D., & Aldridge, G. (1992). Two epistemologies: Music therapy and medicine in the treatment of dementia. *The Arts in Psychotherapy, 19*, 243–255.

American Art Therapy Association (AATA). (2012). *About us.* Retrieved March 14, 2012, from http://www.americanarttherapyassociation.org/aata-aboutus.html.

American Music Therapy Association (AMTA). (2006). *Music therapy and Alzheimer's disease.* Retrieved March 14, 2012, from http://www.musictherapy.org/assets/1/7/MT_Alzheimers_2006.pdf.

American Music Therapy Association. (2010). *Professional competence.* Retrieved March 14, 2012, from http://www.musictherapy.org/about/competencies/. AMTA Standards of Education and Clinical Practice.

American Music Therapy Association. (2011a). *Music therapy makes a difference: Resources & trends in music therapy reimbursement* (Brochure). Available from American Music Therapy Association, Silver Springs, MD: Author.

American Music Therapy Association. (2011b). *Resources on reimbursement: Personal interview with Judy Simpson, AMTA office.* Silver Spring, MD: Author.

American Music Therapy Association. (2012). *Music Therapy Mission Statement.* Retrieved March 24, 2012, from http://www.musictherapy.org.

Art Therapy Credentials Board. (2010). Welcome to the Art Therapy Credentials Board, Inc.! Retrieved March 14, 2012, from www.atcb.org.

Brett-MacLean, P. J., & Magid, M. M. (2004). Fostering well-being and community in a continuing care setting: The George Derby Centre artworks program. In

R. C. Perry Magniant (Ed.), *Art therapy with older adults: A sourcebook* (pp. 69–98). Springfield, IL: Charles C. Thomas.

Bruscia, K. (1998). *Defining music therapy* (2nd ed.). Gilsum, NH: Barcelona Publishers.

Canuto, A., Meiler-Mititelu, C., Herrmann, F., Delaloye, C., Giannakopooulos, P., & Weber, K. (2008). Longitudinal assessment of psychotherapeutic day hospital treatment for elderly patients with depression. *International Journal of Geriatric Psychiatry, 23*(9), 949–956.

Clair, A. (Producer). (1991). *Case study presented at the Older American Act hearing* [Videotape]. (Available from the American Music Therapy Association, 8455 Colesville Road, Suite 1000, Silver Spring, MD 20910.)

Clair, A., & Memmot, J. (2008). *Therapeutic uses of music with older adults.* Silver Spring, MD: American Music Therapy Association.

Clair, A., & Davis, W. (2008). Music therapy and elderly populations. In W. Davis, K. Gfeller, & M. Thaut, *An introduction to music therapy: Theory and practice* (pp. 181–207). Silver Spring, MD: American Music Therapy Association.

Cohen, G. (2000). *The creative age: Awakening human potential in the second half of life.* New York: HarperCollins.

Doric-Henry, L. (1997). Pottery as art therapy with elderly nursing home residents. *Art Therapy: Journal of the American Art Therapy Association, 14*(3), 163–171.

Erikson, E. (1963). *Childhood and society.* New York: W. W. Norton.

Gaston, E. T. (1968). *Music in therapy.* New York: Macmillan Publishing.

Kasayaka, A. (2002). Introduction. In A. Innes & K. Hatfield (Eds.), *Healing arts therapies and person-centered care* (pp. 9–17). London, UK: Jessica Kingsley.

Kates, N. (2008). Individual art therapy for elderly clients. *The Canadian Art Therapy Association Journal, 21*(1), 11–17.

McElroy, S., Warren, A., & Jones, F. (2006). Home-based art therapy for older adults with mental health needs: Views of clients and caregivers. *Art Therapy: Journal of the American Art Therapy Association, 23*(2), 52–58.

Medical Dictionary, The Free Dictionary. (2012a). Biological age. Retrieved March 14, 2012, from http://medical-dictionary.thefreedictionary.com/biological+age.

Medical Dictionary, The Free Dictionary. (2012b). Psychological age. Retrieved March 14, 2012, from http://medical-dictionary.thefreedictionary.com/psychological+age.

Michel, D. E. (1981). *Music therapy* (p. 5). Tokyo, Japan: Ongaku-No-Tomo-Sha.

Moon, B. (1994). *Introduction to art therapy: Faith in the product.* (1st ed.). Springfield, IL: Charles C. Thomas.

Perry Magniant, R. C. (2004). Lifebooks with older adults: Making memories last. In R.C. Perry Magniant, *Art therapy with older adults* (pp. 53–68). Springfield, IL: Charles C. Thomas.

Pfeifer, M. (1982). *Music Therapy Brochure*, Marywood University, Scranton, PA.

Riley, S. (2001). *Group process made visible: Group art therapy.* Philadelphia, PA: Brunner Routledge.

Sandel, S., & Johnson, D. R. (1987). *Waiting at the gate: Creativity and hope in the nursing home.* New York, NY: Haworth Press.

Scartelli, J. (1987). *Music and self-management methods: A physiological model.* St. Louis: MMB Horizon Series, MMB Music.

Sezaki, S., & Bloomgarden, J. (2004). Home-based art therapy for older adults. In R. C. Perry Magniant, *Art therapy with older adults* (pp. 123–142). Springfield, IL: Charles C. Thomas.

Shore, A. (1997). Promoting wisdom: The role of art therapy in geriatric settings. *Art Therapy: Journal of the American Art Therapy Association, 14*(3), 172–177.

Sheikh, J. & Yesavage, J. A. (1986). Geriatric Depression Scale (GDS): Recent evidence and development of a shorter version. *Clinical Gerontology, 37,* 2.

Sochoka, S. L. (2004) Music's healing power. In *Marywood Impressions*, Fall/Winter, Vol. II p. 12.

Special Committee on Aging, U.S. Senate. (1991). *Forever young: Music and aging* (One Hundred Second Congress, First Session). Washington, DC: U.S. Government Printing Office.

Wadeson, H. (2000). *Art therapy practice: Innovative approaches with diverse populations.* New York: John Wiley & Sons.

Wadeson, H. (2010). *Art psychotherapy.* (2nd ed.). New Jersey: John Wiley & Sons, Inc.

Yaretsky, A., & Levinson, M. (1996). Clay as a therapeutic tool in group processing with the elderly. *American Journal of Art Therapy, 34*(3), 75–82.

Part

II

SPECIAL TOPICS

Chapter 7

Financing Long-Term Care

James Pettinato, MHSA, RN

LEARNING OBJECTIVES

1. To list reasons long-term care needs continue to increase in today's healthcare market
2. To develop an understanding of the costs, expenses, and revenues related to providing long-term care services
3. To be able to identify long-term care services available through various payer sources
4. To identify individual responsibilities and the government's role in planning for long-term care services and reimbursement
5. Develop an understanding of how long-term care providers need to balance revenues, expenses, and productivity
6. List potential solutions to future long-term care needs

KEY TERMS

Per Diem Rate: Global reimbursement payment covering multiple services

Indemnity Insurance: Comprehensive insurance plan for sick care, also known as traditional health insurance

Out-of-Pocket Cost: Expense paid by the insured in addition to insurance plan payment; usually has a limit that is paid based on insurance plan details

Skilled Nursing Facility (SNF): Care facility that provides short-term rehabilitation services including nursing, therapies, and custodial care

Case Mix Index: Measure of patient illness severity used by third-party payers

Deductibles: Expense paid by the insured before insurance plan payment

Alternative Care: Nontraditional care that supports physical needs of a patient

Premium: Money paid to an insurance company for coverage

Costs/Expenses: Deductions from revenue for operations and provision of service

Centenarians: Individuals 100 years old, or older

Accountable Care Organization: Healthcare provider(s) entering into a capitation arrangement to take care of a given population of patients

INTRODUCTION

As with any aspect of healthcare administration, managing finance issues is an integral part of providing services. With the ever-changing healthcare environment, it is expected that long-term care (LTC) needs in the United States will continue to rise, and the ability to obtain funding for these services will become more complex.

Mosby's 2008 Medical Dictionary defines long-term care as:

> The provision of medical, social, and personal care services on a recurring and/or continuing basis to persons with chronic physical or mental disorders. The care may be provided in environments ranging from institutions to private homes. Long-term care services usually include symptomatic treatment, maintenance, and rehabilitation for patients of all age groups.

This type of care is paid for through a diverse payer system with multiple providers. This design challenges LTC administrators in coordinating care, maintaining regulatory compliance, and securing reimbursement for the services provided, as different rules and regulations for reimbursement can be applied to similar patients and settings where care is rendered. For example, two patients in the same long-term care institution who require care may be reimbursed differently and through use of different resources based on the payer source.

It is important to remember reimbursement for LTC comes from a variety of payers and is not restricted to nursing homes. Other settings where LTC is provided include, but are not limited to, in-home care services, assisted-living facilities, and in other community-based settings such as adult day care and outpatient centers. Other community organizations sponsor programs such as Meals on Wheels and Serving Seniors that augment services in these various settings. It is also important to remember that long-term care involves skilled care, such as nursing, physical therapy, or other professional healthcare services, and also includes custodial care.

Custodial care encompasses cooking, cleaning, and the performance of activities of daily living, including eating, bathing, dressing, transferring, and toileting. Assistance with activities of daily living (ADLs) makes up the greatest percentage of need for those living outside a healthcare institution (Olshansky et al., 2005).

While custodial care makes up the greatest need, there has been a steady growth in many other LTC settings over the last several years. Reasons for this increase include the ever-changing healthcare environment, political polarization regarding healthcare reform, and the lack of public funding for needed services. Other contributing factors are related to advances in technology, medicine, and pharmaceuticals. Collectively, these advancements will increase lifespans and thereby increase LTC needs even more. Regardless of lifespan changes and these advancements, conditions such as Alzheimer's, dementia and other degenerative diseases including diabetes, stroke, heart problems, cancer, and Parkinson's disease will likely result in an expansion of LTC service needs in all settings (Olshansky et al., 2005).

Despite this growth, payers and policy makers remain cautious about addressing funding for these needs. Most ordinary health insurance policies, including Medicare, do not generally reimburse long-term care expenses for extended timeframes. Without long-term care insurance, or substantial financial planning early in life, savings of individual patients could be eroded quickly. Affording LTC insurance or accumulating a savings can also be impacted by the fact that many of the degenerative diseases themselves could inhibit individuals from remaining in the workforce until their full retirement age. If this were to occur, their ability to maintain health insurance could also be impacted, thereby increasing their financial burden for illness care, as well as LTC, because of a poor health status early in life. In essence, a perfect storm is created between the inability to maintain health, pay for insurance, and save enough to afford care that might have otherwise been cheaper if the person could have avoided a debilitating illness to begin with.

As a LTC administrator, the goal of balancing access with quality service to the available reimbursements across the healthcare continuum will be a primary focus. There may be little you can do to impact the perfect storm discussed earlier, but understanding how to utilize diversified resources to meet patient needs, maximizing patient benefits without duplicating services, and controlling expenditures will allow you to operate a successful LTC service. Proper utilization of diversified resources involves coordination of these resources to achieve the desired outcomes. Duplication of resources causes waste in the delivery system, and on a larger scale, reduces the available resources across the continuum as a whole.

Administrators need to focus on eliminating waste, improving access to care, providing quality services, and reducing expenditures to maximize profits and be successful in all LTC settings.

LIFESPAN AND GROWING NEED FOR LONG-TERM CARE

There has been a consistent increase in life expectancy over the last 1,000 years. The only variance in this pattern was related to epidemics, pandemics, famines, and wars. By the beginning of the 19th century, control of infectious diseases, improved living conditions, and advances in public health and medicine reduced these variances.

Since 1980, life expectancy in United States did decrease slightly relative to this historical pattern, but some believe life-extending technology may still result in a longer life expectancy in years to come (Olshansky et al., 2005). LTC Tree (2011) and the National Advisory Center for Long Term Care Insurance (2008) note an increase in the number of centenarians living today and the harsh realities facing an aging population. These include:

· 50% of people over the age of 65 will eventually need long-term care
· Men live an average of 80.9 years
· Women live an average of 84.5 years
· 50% of seniors 85 years and older have Alzheimer's or some other debilitating disease as the number one reason for needing long-term care

In addition, America's Health Insurance Plans (AHIP) published a *Guide to Long-Term Care Insurance* in 2004, citing that by the year 2020, 12 million older Americans will need long-term care. AHIP also predicted 40% of people over 65 years of age will be cared for at home by family members and friends. Many of these individuals will risk entering a nursing home, and about 10% will stay there for 5 years or longer.

AHIP also points out that while the focus is on individuals over 65 years of age, the need for long-term care can happen at any point in life. The U.S. Government Accountability Office (as cited in AHIP, 2004) estimates that 40% of the 13 million people receiving long-term care services are between the age of 18 and 64 years. To compound this issue, individuals 85 and older are now the fastest growing segment of our population today. This combination will result in an increase in the number of people entering nursing homes, resulting in longer lengths of stay and further burdening an already taxed delivery system.

This increase is related to advances in medicine and pharmaceuticals. These have led to better management of disease processes and extended lifespan for some medical conditions. To demonstrate how aggressively these advancements have been funded, one could look at the total budget for the National Institutes of Health (NIH) in 2000 in comparison to pharmaceutical companies' budgets. The NIH spent $15 billion compared to the $20 billion per pharmaceutical company for research and development that was focused on the big killers—including heart disease, cancer, and diabetes. As more attention is focused on an aging population, it is expected even more of these funds will be funneled into research specific to anti-aging (Klein, 2003).

These anti-aging cures may involve genetic manipulation (since the human genetic code has now been mapped), stem cell regeneration, and use of small biomechanical devices for invasive monitoring and the repair of aging cells and organs (Klein, 2003).

While there is still a lot of work to be done to achieve some of these milestones, life extension and the potential for "immortality" could soon be at hand. Centenarians are the best example of how prolific these estimations may be. Klein (2003), in an article on human lifespan, discussed the U.S. Census Bureau's projection of the population of centenarians—people over the age of 100—through 2050 (see **Table 7.1**). The data demonstrate an increase in the number of centenarians since 2000 with some future projections (Kinsella & Wan, 2009).

This aging population faces significant challenges in how care will be accessed due to the lack of funding related to the nation's healthcare programs limiting reimbursement for LTC. Adminstrators will be faced with the challenge of providing access with limited reimbursement. Knickman

Table 7.1 Projected Number of U.S. Centenarians

Number of Centenarians	Years
72,000	2000
131,000	2010
214,000	2020
324,000	2030
447,000	2040
834,000	2050

Source: Data from Krach, C. A., & Velkoff, V. A. (1999). U.S. Census Bureau, U.S. Department of Commerce, *Centenarians in the United States* (P25-199RV). Retrieved March 7, 2012, from http://www.census.gov/prod/99pubs/p23-199.pdf.

and Snell (2002) echoed this position and further predicted that by 2030, other challenges in caring for the elderly will include:

- Making sure society develops payment and insurance systems for long-term care that work better than existing ones
- Taking advantage of advances in medicine and behavioral health to keep the elderly as healthy and active as possible
- Changing the way society organizes community services so that care is more accessible
- Altering the cultural view of aging to make sure all ages are integrated into the fabric of community life

There are different opinions on whether lifespan is changing or not, but the numbers of centenarians are clearly on the rise. Advancements in medicine and technology are changing the face of healthcare delivery today, and the need for long-term care continues to grow beyond the available resources.

Complications for those living past age 65 will burden both private and public funding for health programs and impact public policy. Furthermore, it may not be expanding life expectancy that causes the bankruptcy of Social Security, but rather the increase in health costs related to obesity, cardiovascular disease, diabetes, renal failure, hypertension, asthma, cancer, gastrointestinal problems, and other illnesses. Unless more focus is placed on these issues, the increasing lifespan seen for the last 1,000 years could be reversed. Public policy makers are challenged to take action to prevent this from occurring (Olshansky et al., 2005).

Despite different beliefs about lifespan extension, one cannot ignore the fact people are living longer than they did 40 or 50 years ago when Social Security and Medicaid programs were formed. Advances in healthcare technologies and pharmaceuticals are extending lifespans to some degree, which is also increasing the need for long-term care. If one considers the Baby Boomer impact in addition to increased life expectancy, it is obvious the demand for long-term care will only increase in years to come.

Additionally, current public policy has not addressed issues of prevention and financing or focused on disease management programs to any level that might offer a solution to decreasing LTC needs in the future. As healthcare administrators and policy makers, we need to recognize the major threats to health and the longevity of our younger generations today. Doing so will reduce future demands on LTC and allow for a continued expansion of life expectancy (Olshansky et al., 2005).

PERSONAL ACCOUNTABILITY IN LONG-TERM CARE

Many people believe it is the government's responsibility to make public policy to address LTC needs and services. This author believes individuals also have a responsibility to make provisions for LTC early in life through proper planning, and most importantly, by maintaining a good health status.

Clark (2008), from Laborers' Health and Safety Fund of North America (LHSFNA), stated, "it is generally perceived that personal habits are one's own business, but personal habits have social and financial impacts especially in matters of health care." LHSFNA is a group that enhances jobsite safety and health and improves the competitiveness and strength of Laborers' International Union of North America (LIUNA). This group discusses personal accountability in the healthcare cost equation. They believe that individuals should take more responsibility for their own health behaviors.

Unfortunately, Clark's (2008) position on this matter is generally not well received in a climate where many Americans see healthcare benefits as an entitlement. Given the fact that many Americans generally do not take good care of themselves, and sole reliance on public programs to provide for long-term care needs is not in the foreseeable future, other alternatives need to be sought.

One method for taking personal accountability in meeting long-term care needs is to utilize one's own financial nest eggs to fund LTC. One way to do this is to use life insurance policies. Tenenbaum and Batis (2005) discussed using life insurance benefits to pay for long-term care. This is done by using the front-end spending clause of a permanent policy called the accelerated death benefit (ADB). If the policy has this provision, it will pay part of the face value prior to death to be used for LTC expenses. In some cases, it may even pay out completely prior to death, thereby completely eliminating the death benefit entirely. Other more reasonably affordable insurances could then be used for death benefits such as term life insurance plans.

Another method of maintaining personal accountability is to purchase long-term care insurance, and/or develop a savings program to set money aside for LTC expenses. Skowronski (2010) indicated that a nursing home bed costs $229/day and a personal care facility bed costs $110/day on average. The article also indicated home care aide services ranged from $20 to $22/hour and made up one of the largest components of LTC services provided outside facilities. Over the last few years, costs have increased in these service areas and even outpaced medical care inflation. The only exception to this trend is seen in the home care aide arena, where costs have remained below medical care inflation. Families continue to provide the lion's share of this care, but paid care at these rates can devastate even the best futuristic fiscal plan. Given this rate of inflation and rising costs for paid care, long-term care insurance is gradually climbing in popularity.

Unlike other health insurance policies, long-term care policies generally cover skilled care and ADLs, which include bathing, dressing, transferring from bed to chair, toileting, eating, and continence care. Accessing these services can usually be done through coordination with a family physician and a social service agency, or by directly contacting the insurance carrier for assistance in enacting the benefits.

In addition to the traditional services covered in long-term care plans, some policies will also cover "alternative care." This is nonconventional care and services where a licensed healthcare practitioner looks for alternatives to traditional care needs that are more cost effective for both the patient and insurer. For example, a healthcare provider may make a recommendation for medically necessary modifications to bathrooms or kitchens that allow wheelchair accessibility, or address individual handicap patient's needs to keep them as independent as possible and out of a facility. These modifications are paid by the insurer to avoid higher healthcare costs related to being placed in a facility (AHIP, 2004).

Another option is to use self-funded programs where money can be set aside early in life for use later when healthcare needs increase. This can be done through use of a health savings account (HSA), individual retirement account (IRA), and other saving methods including, but not limited to, investing in a specialized bank account, employer retirement program, or stock and bond investments.

The Laborers' Health and Safety Fund of North America places an emphasis on personal accountability, starting with wellness programs and changing behaviors that intensify healthcare needs later in life. These include smoking-reduction programs, healthy diet habits, weight control, and enrollment in disease management programs. Early enrollment in these programs, or engaging in behaviors that reduce complications later in life, directly impact the need for long-term care in later years.

In summary, personal habits and accountability have both social and financial impacts, especially in matters of health care. Since 2008, employers have been pressing Americans to take more responsibility for their own personal health behaviors both on and off the job. As healthcare administrators, we should reinforce this focus in programs that promote health and reduce expenses related to long-term care needs in the future. As the healthcare dollar continues to shrink and the population needing LTC grows, resources will continue to become scarce and can only be extended by improving quality, both in the direct provision of care and prevention of medical complications in those needing care (Clark, 2008).

EXPENDITURES AND PRODUCTIVITY

The increased demand for LTC services and escalating healthcare costs are forcing providers to closely monitor productivity. Larkins's (1997) article on measuring productivity defined productivity as the ratio of output to input. It measures the resources used to achieve results. She further indicated the benefits of measuring productivity, which include:

- Facilitating efficiency between a financial plan and the projection of resources needed to provide services
- Providing additional information about direct and indirect expenses
- Predicting revenues based on projected total expenses
- Assessing how much time staff is spending in direct service (activities that directly benefit the client or caregiver) and indirect service (activities that result in no direct benefit to the client or caregiver)

Productivity measurements also provide useful information to administrators regarding length of stay, staffing needs, reimbursement patterns, and can be compared to patient outcomes. Analyzing these data allows administrators to project personnel needs in the future, improve staff effectiveness, and control expenses (Larkins, 1997).

LTC staff members are being asked to demonstrate their productivity to meet both established fiscal targets and the demand for their services. Evaluation of staff productivity is a useful tool used by administrators to determine how well the organization is operating overall. Patient outcomes have to be examined very closely when looking at productivity as well, since financial targets are only part of the equation. For example, patient falls or medication errors that lead to poor outcomes may impact a facility's bottom line through reduced referrals, fines, or failure to collect payment on services provided. Maintaining productivity standards may provide cost savings on the front end, but unless patient outcomes are maintained also, long-term expenses could cut into those savings. Balancing productivity with good outcomes is a dynamic process that constantly needs reevaluation in any healthcare setting.

While productivity is a key component in measuring an organization's fiscal performance, there are other measurements, or "management tools" that contribute to this evaluation as well. These include monitoring the percentage of occupancy, case mix index, and overall patient census. LTC providers must have these types of monitoring systems in place to evaluate fiscal performance and make adjustments when results fall below established guidelines.

Costs and Expenses

Costs and expenses are two terms used interchangeably by many people in healthcare administration. *Cost* is defined as resources used to produce a good or service, and *expense* is defined as a measure of the resources used to generate revenue and/or provide a service (Cleverley & Cameron, 2002). Since the term *expense* measures the resources used, it is more commonly seen in the healthcare accounting for determining unit of service, or units of measure (Larkins, 1997).

In long-term care, *costs* may be seen in the purchase and/or renovation of facilities, purchase of computers and other healthcare equipment, hiring fees associated with employing staff, the development of support systems for information technologies, establishing and maintaining billing functions, and administration to manage the operation. These types of expenditures are usually referred to as *indirect costs* and do not necessarily produce revenue, but rather support the production of revenue (Cleverley & Cameron, 2002).

Capital expenses fall into this category and refer to items needed to deliver care that could be reused on multiple patients, such as beds, lifts, and specialty chairs. The items themselves do not produce revenues directly, but they support operations to produce revenues.

Other expenses involve paying staff salaries, purchasing disposable supplies, providing medications, paying for linen services, and purchasing food and other items needed to render care. These expenditures, when allocated, should result in the production of revenue. Controlling these expenses is a key function of any LTC administrator. If these expenses exceed revenues collected, the facility, or provider, is in danger of bankruptcy if the pattern continues for any extended period of time.

Inflation

Both "for-profit" and most "not-for-profit" organizations strive to assure revenues exceed expenses to cover the expenditures related to providing service. Both costs and expenses are rising in the healthcare arena at a rate surpassing inflation. Control of these expenditures is a challenge to any healthcare executive while also trying to maintain an organization's market share in a highly competitive environment.

Philosophies do differ somewhat between for-profit and nonprofit entities in health care. The main difference is that nonprofit entities tend to be more "mission based" and typically provide services at much lower margins, or at "break even" levels compared to for-profit organizations that usually seek to gain a certain revenue margin on the services provided. Also different is that some nonprofits may operate at a loss and accept donations to offset those losses to carry out their missions.

According to Skowronski (2010), private-room nursing home rates rose 4.6% in 2010 at an average of $83,585 per year, per patient. Cost in this case refers to the amount billed to either the patient, and/or third-party payer (if qualified). This is typically referred to by a provider as *charges*, since the cost is transferred to the payer. Charges reflect the amount billed, but not always the amount collected. Sometimes there are *contractual allowances* that are deducted from the amount collected as a condition of accepting a particular payer's business. This is a common practice in Medicare, Medicaid, and many managed care programs. **Table 7.2** provides some information on charges (cost to patients) and the rate of increase between 2009 and 2010.

When looking at the table, note there was no increase in some settings over the year, and that it only reflects averages. The actual amount charged may vary based on geography and individual market settings; therefore, rates will differ significantly in different areas of the country.

Case Mix Index

Case mix index is an indicator of the level of severity of patients' conditions treated by a provider. In any case, administrators and admission staff in these facilities need to carefully evaluate the services they will be providing prior to accepting an admission. Careful calculation of patient needs must be compared to the potential reimbursement for those needs before

Table 7.2 Average Increase in Charges in Select Long-Term Care Settings (2009–2010)

Setting	% Increase from previous year	Charges (Costs to patients)
Nursing Home	4.60%	$83,585/year
Assisted Living	5.20%	$39,516/year
Home Care Aides	0.00%	$21/hour
Adult Day Care	0.00%	$67/day

Source: Data from Skowronski, J. (2010, 29 October). Cost of long-term care rises. *Newsweek*. Retrieved March 14, 2012, from http://www.thedailybeast.com/newsweek/2010/10/29/cost-of -long-term-care-rises.html.

accepting the patient. In some situations, providers may accept a high-needs patient when a higher acuity may increase expenses, but maximize reimbursement from a payer. This scenario is seen in skilled and acute rehabilitation facilities that must carefully maintain a balance of patient types. Their goal may involve having a balance of different payers at different levels of acuity to maximize the reimbursement opportunities, while simultaneously controlling expenses.

At times, providers may refuse a patient admission based on the mix of patient types, and overall acuity it may currently have in its program or facility. Subsequently, patients requiring IV therapy, wound care, or renal dialysis are often difficult to place in any long-term care setting as they consume a lot of resources and have high expenses related to their daily care. These types of patients pose compliance, legal, and ethical dilemmas to LTC administrators. Knowing LTC regulations, plan benefits, and facility policy and practices could help avoid the occurrence of compliance and ethical issues.

Occupancy/Census

In addition to evaluating patient types and needs, a facility or provider must also look at its organization's percentage of occupancy. This is the ratio of the actual number of patient days compared to capacity. In *The Introduction to Health Care Administration*, Davis (2000) gives the following example for calculating percentage of occupancy. It is calculated by taking the total number of facility beds and multiplying by the total number of days those beds are available to calculate resident days. For example:

$$175 \text{ beds} \times 30 \text{ days} = 5{,}250 \text{ possible resident days}$$

Then, multiply the actual number of those beds filled with patients to calculate the actual resident days. For example:

$$150 \text{ beds} \times 30 \text{ days} = 4{,}500 \text{ actual resident days}$$

Then, divide the actual resident days by the possible resident days to get the percentage of occupancy:

$$4{,}500 \div 5{,}250 = 85.7\% \text{ occupancy}$$

While this is a common measurement used in facilities, a similar one exists in other settings and with different providers. For example, in home care, there is a certain amount of staff and resources dedicated to seeing a minimum number of patients. If the number of visits, or patients, declines below the minimum expected census (or visits), the organization will lose money and jeopardize its ability to provide care. See **Figure 7.1**.

In any LTC setting, occupancy may be measured in units of service, volume of patients, daily census, or some other measureable variable that allows administrators to determine the activity level of the organization. This activity level is usually tracked, trended, and used to budget resources on an ongoing basis.

Measuring Performance

Methods of measurement may differ in each LTC setting, but the overall goal is to be sure expenditures do not exceed revenues for extended periods of time. It is not uncommon, however, that not-for-profit groups may have a higher tolerance for marginal revenues, or even work at a deficit if they can cover its losses through some other philanthropic source, investment, or business line.

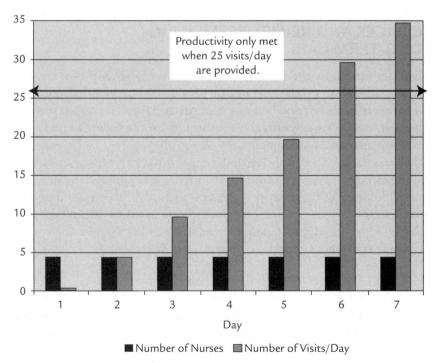

Figure 7.1 Home Care Productivity Example

Analysis: Days with less than 25 visits are considered non-productive since the number of nurses/day did not change. Over a 7-day period, the average number of visits/day is 16.43. This is well below the required 25 needed to maintain expenses.

Putting It All Together

While case mix index, average daily census, productivity standards, and control of expenditures are critical to maintaining a sound financial operation, there are other factors that may influence the overall performance of an organization. These include, but are not limited to, the level of services being provided, the size of the provider's organization and overhead costs, geographic location, and ability to maintain quality care and services. The ultimate goal in almost all healthcare settings is to maintain a balance of costs and expenses with revenues that results in some profits and while fulfilling the mission of the organization. Even not-for-profit LTC providers generally cannot suffer sustained losses for long intervals. LTC administrators must use several different tools to monitor financial performance and make adjustments when any one of the indicators changes to maintain a balance. The ability to drill down and determine the true cause for the change will allow the administrator to make focused adjustments to correct a problem, or capitalize on a gain.

SERVICES AND REIMBURSEMENT IN LONG-TERM CARE

There are various methods of reimbursement for long-term care services, and it is dependent on the level of care provided. In many situations, only skilled services are covered by most third-party payers. Custodial care, on the other hand, is usually only covered through private payments and some government-sponsored programs.

Unfortunately, there are also many gaps in the payment systems that require facility and service administrators to be watchful of their accounts receivable. Some of these payment systems include, but are not limited to, private long-term care insurance, managed care (fixed payments), medical assistance, private payments, and combinations of both public and private funds either in addition to these sources, or as solo payers.

Settings and Payers

In most settings, you will also find combinations of reimbursement from a variety of these sources for each patient. LTC administrators have a responsibility to maximize the available dollars in a cost-effective manner that meets the patient's needs and results in a surplus (or profit) for the organization providing the services. These long-term care settings include, but are not limited to:

- Adult day care (sponsored by various agencies both public and private, as well as religious)
- Specialty facility/elder care service (psychiatric, Alzheimer's, dementia, etc.)
- Home care/hospice
- Respite care programs
- Retirement communities
- Nursing home/swing bed program
- Rehabilitation units
- Veterans centers/government retirement programs

Table 7.3 identifies the major payers, covered services, benefits, limitations, and facts related to reimbursement in long-term care.

Table 7.3 Long-Term Care Payers, Services, and Benefits

Payer Source	Type of Service(s) Commonly Covered	Benefits/Limitations/Facts/Profit Margins
Medicare Part A	· Skilled care including nursing, therapy, and social services · Some custodial care coverage is provided while skilled need is present	· Usually applies to most patients over 65 years of age or those with end-stage renal disease (ESRD) · Typically short-term coverage and has copayments and deductibles · Pays providers 80% of allowable charges based on federal rates, case mix adjustment, and geographic region · Does not provide for long-term care after 100 skilled days/year (first 20 skilled days paid at 100% less deductible, the next 80 days have a 20% copay) · Profit margin for providers is limited as reimbursement is only calculated at 80% of an allowable charge, and not based on expenses actually incurred
Medicare Part B	· Outpatient services	· Covers physician office visits, outpatient therapies, ambulance service, durable medical equipment, prosthetics, orthotics, and some medical supplies
Medicaid	· Skilled care including nursing, therapy, and social services	· Major payer in long-term care for patients requiring institutional services and assistance with ADLs

(Continued)

Table 7.3 Long-Term Care Payers, Services, and Benefits *(Continued)*

Payer Source	Type of Service(s) Commonly Covered	Benefits/Limitations/Facts/Profit Margins
	· Will also provide for long-term custodial care once personal finances are "spent down"	· Limited by the fact patients must spend down life savings before qualifying for coverage · Limits for coverage vary from state to state both from financial qualification to degree of functional limitations for eligibility requirements · Payments to facilities also vary state to state and in some cases require a percentage of charity care (to the state) contribution before reimbursement is made · Profit margin for providers is limited and usually is offset by other payers and cost shifting
Commercial Insurance/ Managed Care	· Mostly only covers skilled care, limited custodial coverage, unless provision for LTC is included in plan/policy	· Premiums are generally costly to enrollees · Provides coverage for long-term care needs unlike other government programs if LTC policy purchased · Usually have deductibles and out-of-pocket expenses · Despite recent focus on purchasing plans, cost has been prohibitive by most that will need it · Diverse plans, confusing to consumer · Profit margins usually better than Medicare and Medicaid; opportunity to participate in risk sharing and negotiate rates with payer and used to offset losses from other payers
Private Pay	· Any service can be requested	· Patients do not need financial approval, or meet functional requirements · Limited by financial resources available · Usually results in consumer paying usual and customary charges, unless negotiated for lower rate by patient/legal guardian · Most states still require physician orders for care being requested · Allows for larger profit margins and individual negotiating of rates for services rendered; usually used to offset losses from other payers
Federal Long-Term Care Insurance Program	· Similar to Medicare and Medicaid service coverage	· Limited to federal employees and other qualified members; covers Federal and U.S. Postal employees with certain medical conditions · Certain medical conditions could lead to being disqualified from the plan · Limited profit margins as rates are similar to Medicare and Medicaid

Compliance and Reimbursement

In addition to having multiple payers contributing to the care being provided, there is also the possibility of multiple services providing care simultaneously. This combination of multiple providers and payers places a significant challenge on healthcare administrators not only to assure billing and receivables are done correctly, but also to avoid fraudulent billing practices through incorrect charging of services to a payer source. An example may be someone being cared for in long-term care facility under Medicaid who requires a skilled service covered by Medicare for an acute problem while enrolled in a hospice program. Clearly, this combination of services increases the level of complexity in coordinating care and billing appropriate charges for the services rendered to the proper payer.

Organizations that participate in government-funded programs such as Medicare and Medicaid are required to have a Corporate Compliance Plan to help assure services are rendered and charged in the proper manner. Such a plan outlines methods for monitoring for fraud and abuse through confidential reporting, compliance audits, and education of the organization's staff about proper billing practices. The board of directors, owners, and management team have an obligation to be sure compliance programs are followed and updated as laws change.

An organization's overall financial success is dependent on following insurance guidelines and laws governing reimbursement as fines and penalties can be levied when either care or billing is performed incorrectly. In many cases, even errors made without malicious intent can be interpreted as fraudulent and punishable under law. Corporate Compliance Programs need to be followed carefully and provided in an environment that promotes nonpunitive reporting internally. This type of reporting requirement is essential to identifying problems and facilitates correction without fear of reprisal against anyone making the report.

To summarize, services in long-term care need to be provided within the established guidelines of the patient's benefits and charges need to be accurately submitted to avoid what may be considered to be fraudulent activity. Many times benefits and program allowances are left to interpretation by the provider. When the provider fails to clarify benefits, or chooses to make loose interpretations of those benefits, the risk of rendering free care and loss of profit increases. According to the Coalition Against Fraud (n.d.), Medicare and Medicaid made an estimated $23.7 billion in improper payments in 2007. These included $10.8 billion for Medicare and $12.9 billion for Medicaid. Money paid out by third-party payers, governmental agencies, and private individuals for billing errors continues to plague the healthcare industry, and long-term care is not immune.

METHODS OF PAYMENTS AND REIMBURSEMENT

A variety of payment methods are used in long-term care. The most common method is what is referred to as per diem payment. According to Centers for Medicare & Medicaid Services (CMS) (2012), with the implementation of the Balanced Budget Act of 1997, services furnished to eligible beneficiaries in a skilled nursing facility (SNF) will be reimbursed using the prospective pay system (PPS). This is very much different from the previous payment methods where reasonable costs, or low volumes, were examined to determine payment to the provider.

These PPS payments are adjusted for case mix, geographic variations in wages, and cover all costs and expenses of furnishing SNF services. This concept of per diem payments has now extended beyond skilled care. Many third-party payers will reimburse based on a fee schedule according to the level of care being provided. Even personal care facilities now charge a per diem rate that includes all costs and expenses related to caring for the patient.

In most settings, providers are reimbursed based on the evaluation of patient acuity, need, and ability to be rehabilitated or treated. Acuity in this sense usually refers to the amount of services, or care, a patient will require. Patients with significant medical needs may have higher acuity and require more resources. Occasionally, despite high acuity and need, there are restrictions on services, as not all services are covered in every setting. Methods of assessment and determination of payments also differ, but medical need and appropriateness of the care being provided are common. The following are some examples of how medical necessity, acuity, and reimbursement are calculated in various settings.

Skilled Nursing Facilities/Short-Term Care

In long-term care facilities, a resident classification system called Resource Utilization Groups (RUG) is used to determine acuity of each resident, which then helps determine per diem payments per patient. RUG was developed in the United States in the 1980s, specifically for measuring day-to-day resource use in the long-term care of elderly people. Patients are placed into a RUG category determined by the completion of a resident assessment instrument (RAI) and relative weights are developed from staff time data. This assessment data is used to complete the Minimum Data Set (MDS), which is a powerful tool for implementing standardized assessments and for facilitating care management in nursing homes and noncritical access hospital swing beds (Carpenter, Main, & Turner, 1995).

Swing beds are used to provide skilled services while the patient is still in a hospital, and before transfer to a skilled facility, or discharged to home. This program allows noncritical access hospitals to "swing" an acute care bed to a "skilled bed" status and change the level of services being provided from acute to skilled. There are restrictions on the percentage of patients that may be in this category, which are monitored by the facility staff on a regular basis. This type of program works very well for patients who need short-term rehabilitation prior to discharge since the patient remains in the same care continuum. This avoids transfer and admission to another facility and also reduces overall costs to providing care.

An RAI is still required to be completed, and a RUG category must be assigned. Days of service used in a swing bed do count against the beneficiary's allowable skilled nursing benefit and are not considered additional services. Copays and deductibles for skilled services also apply to swing bed programs as they do in skilled nursing facilities.

In either setting, RAIs are important in determining the RUG category the patient may fall into. The CMS (2008) published a Resident Assessment Instrument manual, which helps staff gather information to be used to assess and plan the care for residents, as well as providing information used for payment to the provider. Upon collection of this data, the patient is placed in a case mix group (CMG), which then results in a per diem fee/day of service to the facility. The average range of reimbursement is usually between $200 and $400 per day and is applied to mostly all care needs of the patient. Some services a patient receives in these settings can be billed separately in certain circumstances, especially if they are not part of the original plan of care.

Registered nurse assessment coordinators (RNACs) are nurses who have been specially trained to complete RAIs in SNFs. They utilize a variety of screening tools to determine where a patient may score on a RUG prior to admission. Information collected by the RNAC typically begins at least 7 days prior to the intended admit date to a skilled nursing service; therefore, patients with significant medical problems and high-cost treatment needs could be difficult to place. This is done through medical record review and face-to-face visits to the patient while the patient is still in the acute-care setting. Specific time intervals are outlined where information about the patient's condition is "locked" and submitted to the payer source, usually Medicare, and that determines the rate of reimbursement. Patients must have a qualifying acute care admission within 30 days of being admitted to an SNF to avoid expensive out-of-pocket costs.

In-Patient Rehabilitation Facilities/FIM Scores

Per the Centers for Medicare & Medicaid Services (2004), a different system is used to determine acuity in in-patient rehabilitation facilities. It is called functional independent measurement (FIM) scoring. These acuity levels are correlated to one of three tiers for reimbursement to a provider for each patient. To determine the tier level, facility staff completes five types of FIM assessments, which include admission, goals, interim, discharge, and follow up. The FIM assessments are further used clinically to monitor the outcomes of rehabilitative care. Improvement in FIM scores through the course of care impact reimbursement opportunities. Providers may be reimbursed from a payer several thousand dollars per day for a patient's care if the scores improve from date of admission to discharge.

Again, all services the patients require need to be provided under this single payment system. Reimbursement is calculated based on timed reassessments of each patient after an initial evaluation. Subsequent reassessment data are submitted during the patient's course of care, and, similar to those processes used in skilled nursing and swing bed systems, these timed intervals are "locked" and submitted to the payer source, usually Medicare. This information determines the rate of reimbursement.

FIM is based on a 7-point rating scale, measuring 18 separate activities. The activities include self-care, bowel and bladder management, ability to transfer, locomotion/ambulation, communication, and social cognition. Each area is evaluated as independent (no help needed), modified dependence (help needed), or complete dependence. The FIM information comes from a combination of the patient, family, medical records, medical staff, and direct observation. Improvements in FIM scores from admission to discharge help determine the amount of money reimbursed for those services. The more improvement noted in the scores as the patient progresses through the rehabilitation process, the better the reimbursement to the provider. Failure to progress, or failing to achieve established outcomes, will result in lower payments.

As explained in this section, case mix index (or acuity), improvement in functional status, and average daily census are some of the driving factors behind the reimbursement a facility receives. As mentioned in previous sections, controlling costs and expenses is critical to the financial survival of the provider organization.

Home Care/Hospice

Home care programs are primarily designed to keep patients out of facilities, and allow them to achieve a maximum functional level of independence in the home. The goal in home care programs is to allow the patient to achieve the best possible health status and be the least reliant on others as possible.

Hospice carries this one step further by providing support for families and significant others caring for a terminally ill patient. Comfort care in this setting is critical to a successful program and allowing the patient to achieve end-of-life care in a dignified and comfortable manner. The hospice benefit is different from all other Medicare benefits, as it does not reimburse for curative measures. It is focused on reimbursing for palliative care resulting from a terminal illness or injury. The main focus is on providing care and support to the patient and family to optimize the quality of life and reduce suffering.

Both services have specific admission requirements and are subject to copays and deductibles depending on the payer source. Physician orders are required in most all cases, with few exceptions noted only in personal care services cases.

For the most part, both of these services are provided based on medical need that is gathered in an initial assessment done by a registered nurse. Initial assessments could be ordered by the physician, along with continuing care orders, or requested by the patient. The requested needs are validated by the registered nurse and approved by physician caring for the patient.

There were significant regulation changes in 2010. These changes require a patient being serviced to be examined by the physician authorizing the service within 90 days prior to, or 30 days after the first home care visit. Not only does the regulation require the exam occur in that time period, but the reason the services are being ordered needs to be related to that exam. In other words, a physician could not order services based on a "well visit" or "checkup" and then order home care services for a new problem without reexamining the patient again. These exams are usually referred to as "face-to-face" encounters and need to be arranged and coordinated with the home health or hospice agency to insure they occur in the required time periods (CMS, 2011).

Once the physician requirement is met regarding the exam, reimbursement in home care is based either on a per diem fee received for each visit done or on a lump sum payment for a given diagnosis, depending on the payer. Much like in skilled facilities and rehabilitation centers, these payments will cover all services ordered except for some services like medications and durable medical equipment (DME). In some managed care and hospice programs, however, rates could be negotiated to include some of these other services.

Personal Care Services

As mentioned earlier, personal care services do make up a large portion of long-term care programs. For the most part, third-party payers usually cover skilled care and rehabilitation services, both in facilities as well as at home. However, private pay reimbursement to providers is usually the main source of revenue for personal care services. Provisions for homemaking and ADL services allow many individuals to remain independent in their home setting and avoid entering an institution.

Personal care facilities are typically funded through private payments. There are instances where government-sponsored programs do contribute to care of patients in these settings, but are very limited. The terms *home* and *personal care facilities* are used synonymously, despite the big difference between being home versus a facility. Being in a personal care home is considered the person's home even if the stay is temporary. No skilled or rehabilitative services are usually provided in relationship to payments received in these settings. If skilled services are required, then patients may be transported to a facility, or have home healthcare services provided. Some facilities do specialize in specific patient populations, such as dementia, psychiatric, and other disease processes, and have engineering controls designed and staff specially trained to address those needs.

Reimbursement for these services vary significantly. A survey by this author of rates for 2010 in northeast Pennsylvania ranged on from $1,200 to over $5,000 per month. Excluded in many of these rates are medications and DME.

Home care agencies also provide a great deal of personal care services. These services may be provided in the patient's home or in a facility. While this may be considered a duplication of services, private funds can be spent to the patient's ability and liking. In many states, even personal care services still need to be ordered by the physician, or provided under physician direction. As mentioned earlier, rates hover around $21 per hour and have had the least increase over the last few years. Certification of care providers is not always required, but in many settings is preferred.

Another source providing these services includes nursing registries and private caregivers. Typically these caregivers are not certified or trained through formal classes, but rather have on-the-job training. Caution needs to be advised to patients seeking these services from anyone not affiliated with a reputable organization, as it is an area of concern for theft, poor care, elder abuse, and fraudulent activities.

Some facilities or organizations do not permit private caregivers to render care to patients in their facility or program for liability reasons, but this is a common request when the patient or family wants to provide additional services beyond those being rendered. An example of this may include a family wanting to hire a private-duty caregiver to help care for a patient in a hospital or skilled facility.

Usually the rendering of personal care services through private payments does not disqualify the patient from receiving services from third-party payers. Unless there are restrictions by an individual facility or program, personal care services may be provided in conjunction with other skilled care on a private-pay basis. Alternately, personal care services may be part of the skilled plan of care being prescribed for the patient, and covered by a third-party payer. An example of this can be seen in home care and hospice settings when skilled services are being given to the patient, and home health aide care can be rendered as an included service. When the skilled care is completed, aide services are then discontinued.

Personal care services do make up the largest portion of long-term care, but are not always covered by third-party payers. Private pay for personal care at home or in a facility is costly and can drain life savings quickly. Augmenting community programs for elderly, such as adult day care, Area Agency on Aging programs, Meals on Wheels, community centers, and other public programs can help defer direct costs and increase care to the patient. As discussed previously in this chapter, coordination of services and avoiding duplication are key actions to balancing access, quality, and cost.

SUMMARY

In summary, given the rising need for long-term care services and limited coverage and reimbursement under federal and state programs, administrators in LTC are going to need to look for ways to provide access to quality care in a cost-effective manner. One approach in controlling future expenses is to look at personal accountability of individuals by reducing health complications through preventative care. Controlling disease processes will help reduce future expenses, and help reduce the need for extensive care needs in the future. Also important is managing expenditures, maximizing reimbursement within the established guidelines, avoiding duplication of services, avoiding fraudulent billing practices, and focusing on providing quality care.

Additionally, coordinating services between different providers and payers, while controlling expenses, will increase the overall availability of services to the community at large. Preserving services across the continuum of providers and payers will help control rising costs and stop the accelerated rate of LTC expenses beyond the inflationary rates. Careful placement of patients in the setting that meets individual needs and not providing more services than necessary will not only preserve services, but also promote independence of the patient when and where possible.

In an article titled "Long Term Care: Coming of Age in the 21st Century," Stone (1999) stated that an estimated 15% to 20% of nursing home patients could live in a residential care setting. Stone went on to say that integrating acute and long-term care services through insurances and delivery systems with the guidance of case managers, protocols, interdisciplinary teams, and centralized medical records could help reduce the expense of LTC. A quality oversight system combined with integrated financing and flexible funding tied to incentives for good performers could align payers and providers in the elimination of cost shifting. This concept can be seen today in the healthcare reform act regarding the development of accountable care organizations where the government is encouraging organizations to be all-encompassing providers.

This author believes maintaining patients at the best possible level of health and functional independence throughout life also ties directly back to personal accountability in reducing LTC needs and expenses. Preparing for LTC through these actions may be the only real solution to the disparity we are experiencing between need for quality services and the access to those services in a cost-effective manner. Profit margins will continue to be reduced if the health status of the population needing LTC continues to deteriorate and providers are unable to meet those needs.

Discussion Questions

1. Who are the major payers in long-term care? Where is the largest portion of services being provided?
2. How will the changes in lifespan impact LTC needs? Is lifespan the only element affecting LTC needs?
3. What are some of the benefits, advantages, and disadvantages among the primary payers in long-term care? What services are covered and how does an LTC administrator maximize reimbursement?
4. What are some ethical dilemmas that LTC administrators may be confronted with regarding coverage, benefits, and patient needs?
5. What can be done to control the rising LTC needs in the future?

REFERENCES

America's Health Insurance Plans. (2004). *Guide to long-term care (LTC) insurance.* Retrieved March 14, 2012, from http://www.pueblo.gsa.gov/cic_text/health/ltc/guide.htm.

Carpenter, G. I., Main, A., & Turner, G. F. (1995). Casemix for the elderly inpatient: Resource Utilization Groups validation project—RUGs. *Age and Ageing, 24*(1), 5–13.

Centers for Medicare & Medicaid Services (CMS), UB Foundation Activities, Inc. (2004). *The inpatient rehabilitation facility—patient assessment instrument (IRF-PAI) training manual.* Retrieved April 26, 2012, from http://www.cms.gov/Medicare/Medicare-Fee-for-Service-Payment/InpatientRehabFacPPS/downloads//irfpaimanual040104.pdf.

Centers for Medicare & Medicaid Services. (2008). *Long-term care facility resident assessment instrument user's manual.* Retrieved April 11, 2010, from http://www.hpm.umn.edu/nhregsplus/Resources%20and%20Publications/Federal_Resources/RAI/Complete%20RAI.pdf.

Centers for Medicare & Medicaid Services. (2011). *Medicare benefit policy manual Chapter 7—home health services.* Retrieved March 23, 2012, from https://www.cms.gov/manuals/downloads/bp102c07.pdf.

Centers for Medicare & Medicaid Services. (2012). *Case mix prospective payment for SNFs Balanced Budget Act of 1997.* Retrieved March 23, 2012, from https://www.cms.gov/SNFPPS/.

Clark, S. (2008). Personal accountability part of health care cost equation. *Laborers' Health and Safety Fund of North America.* Retrieved March 14, 2012, from http://www.lhsfna.org/index.cfm?objectID=E9E41541-D56F-E6FA-9BD7527C8BDF4A5A.

Cleverley, W. O., & Cameron, A. E. (2002). *Essentials of health care finance* (5th ed.). Gaithersburg, MD: Aspen Publishers.

Coalition Against Insurance Fraud. (n.d.). Fraud statistics. Retrieved March 14, 2012, from http://www.insurancefraud.org/stats.htm.

Davis, W. (2000). Financial Management. In *The Introduction to Health Care Administration* (pp. 131–161). Bossier City, LA: Professional Printing & Publishing.

Klein, B. (2003). Human lifespan—Is there a limit? Retrieved March 14, 2012, from http://www.longecity.org/forum/topic/680-human-lifespan-is-there-a-limit-bruce-klein/.

Knickman, J. R., & Snell, E. K. (2002). The 2030 problem: Caring for aging Baby Boomers. *Health Services Research, 37*(4), 849–884.

Larkins, P. G. (1997). Measuring productivity: Finding the right quality quotient. American Speech-Language-Hearing Association. Retrieved March 14, 2012, from http://www.asha.org/slp/healthcare/productivity.htm.

LTC Tree. (2011). *Long term care insurance.* Retrieved March 23, 2012, from http://www.longtermcareinsurancetree.com/.

National Advisory Center for Long Term Care Insurance. (2008). *Long term care insurance*. Retrieved April 11, 2010, from http://www.longtermcareinsurance.org/.

No author. (2008). *Mosby medical dictionary* (9th ed.). St. Louis, MO: Mosby.

Olshansky, S. J., Passaro, D. J., Hershow, R. C., Layden, J., Carnes, B. A., Brody, J., et al. (2005). A potential decline in life expectancy in the United States in the 21st century. *The New England Journal of Medicine, 352,* 1138–1145.

Skowronski, J. (2010). Cost of long-term care rises. *Newsweek.* Retrieved March 14, 2012, from http://www.thedailybeast.com/newsweek/2010/10/29/cost-of-long-term-care-rises.html.

Stone, R. (1999). Long term care: Coming of age in the 21st century. Retrieved March 14, 2012, from http://www.familyimpactseminars.org/s_wifis12c01.pdf.

Tenenbaum, M., & Batis, E. (2005). Financing long-term care: The life insurance solution. Retrieved March 14, 2012, from http://www.ltlmagazine.com/article/financing-long-term-care-life-insurance-solution.

Kinsella, K., & Wan, H. (2009). U.S. Census Bureau, International Population Reports (P95/09-1), An aging world: 2008. Washington, DC: U.S. Government Printing Office. Retrieved March 14, 2012, from http://www.census.gov/prod/2009pubs/p95-09-1.pdf.

Chapter 8

Meeting Spiritual and Religious Needs in Long-Term Care

Gail Cabral, IHM, PhD

LEARNING OBJECTIVES

1. To provide evidence for the ubiquity of the spiritual in human life
2. To describe the evidence for a positive effect of religion on health, and for some of the reasons suggested for this relationship
3. To distinguish between religion and spirituality
4. To elaborate on three ways in which caregivers can assist the elderly in meeting spiritual and religious needs: provision of religious counseling, provision of services in facilities, and understanding the effectiveness of religious coping
5. To summarize the role of the administrator in teaching staff the importance of religious coping, and the possibilities of change in religion and spirituality among the elderly

KEY TERMS

Religion: Beliefs and actions related to supernatural beings and forces (Miller, 2007)

Spirituality: (1) The part of one's identity concerned with purpose and meaning in life, interdependence with others, inner peace, and transcendence (Muse-Burke, 2004); (2) experiences or practices that pertain to the transcendent and existential aspects of life

Faith: That which gives meaning and purpose to our lives

Gerotranscendence: Theoretical concept that in old-age individuals may develop a new and deeper perspective, which includes wisdom, greater concern for that which is spiritual and cosmic, and redefinition of perceptions of life and death (Tornstam, 2005)

INTRODUCTION

The residents of gerontological facilities have a right to have their needs met, and some (or perhaps many) of them have religious or spiritual needs. The nursing home administrator is expected to be a professional. Nursing home personnel are expected to be and act professionally. In addition, personnel do not necessarily share in the religious affiliations of their residents. These two facts may cause uneasiness for the healthcare administrator in a nursing home when religion or spirituality is discussed. The following section seeks to ask why we are sometimes reticent about the place of religion in our facilities. What is the relationship between religion and health? What may (and should) administrators do to help residents with their spiritual needs? This chapter discusses the answers to these questions.

RELIGION IN THE MODERN AGE

Human beings are complex, integrated beings with physiological, cognitive, social, and spiritual dimensions. The importance of physiological functions, with their great impact on health and well-being, is seldom debated, and is certainly assumed in healthcare settings and in dealing with the elderly. Indeed, all of us can understand the impact of pain or disability on the experience of life. A toothache or the experience of sore feet diminish the quality of life for any of us and color the hours in which we attempt to do our work or participate in social activities. There are other reasons for a focus on the physical, and a relative neglect of the spiritual. To understand that focus, let us look briefly at the history of the "modern world" over the last 400 years.

The focus on only the materialistic aspects of life probably began around the time known as the age of the Enlightenment several centuries ago. This was a time of emphasis on reason rather than the established authority of church or king, and a beginning of reliance on objectivity and science as means to truth. Associated with this emphasis on scientific knowledge was an increased emphasis on the freedom and independence of the individual thinker. As a result, the contemporary Western world increasingly came to value and respect the accomplishments of science. Science is both an enterprise of discovery in practical and theoretical realms, and a methodological approach, a "way," that relies on empirical data and logical analysis. The assumptions of the scientific method—objectivity, reliance on facts, and disavowal of anything but the most parsimonious interpretation of those facts—have strongly affected the mindset of most of us. The result is a very strong perception that only that which is material can be real. This strong materialistic emphasis in Western cultures convinces us, perhaps unconsciously, that the material realm is the "real world," and any other dimension to human life is "less real," perhaps even fanciful.

This belief is actually a type of philosophical conclusion. There are other understandings of what is real, both in philosophy and science. For example, there are philosophies that believe that ideas are more real than that which is physical or material. There are also descriptions in contemporary science, for example, quantum physics, in which physical surfaces, like the pages of the text before you (or screen of your e-reader), are made up of spaces between electrons and neutrons, and are not hard, continuous surfaces at all. In addition, the late 20th and early 21st centuries have seen an intentional rejection, or at least a questioning, of the assumptions of a material and scientific worldview under the term *postmodernism*. In our everyday lives, however, that which is material is usually seen as real. We pound the table or the book in front of us when we want to specify reality. This brief explanation of the materialistic bent of our time and place is meant to introduce you to the context in which religion and spirituality will be discussed, namely a text in a discipline (elder care) that is highly influenced by scientific fields.

On the other hand, research since 1990 has indicated that religion is strongly correlated with health (Benjamin, 2004; Krause, 2008; Lee & Newberg, 2010; Levin & Chatters, 2008; Levin, Chatters, & Taylor, 2011; McFarland, 2010), and the role of religion has come to be studied scientifically in medicine, psychology, sociology, and other fields. Before we summarize some of that research, we will make some observations about the words "spirituality" and "faith," in particular, their meaning apart from "religion" per se.

RELIGION AND SPIRITUALITY: DEFINITIONS AND DISTINCTIONS

This section differentiates between the two terms, *religion* and *spirituality*, so that one can identify them and provide examples. Religion may be defined as "the service and worship of God or the supernatural" or "a personal set or institutionalized system of religious attitudes, beliefs, and practices" (Merriam-Webster, 2012a). These definitions include a belief or commitment to gods, God, or supernatural forces. Belief, practice, and commitment on the part of the individual may be included, as well as the presumption of something outside the person. Religion often implies acceptance of an external system of beliefs.

The term *spiritual* was originally used to mean "sensitivity or attachment to religious values" (Merriam-Webster, 2012b). Since the late 20th century in Western nations, attachment to organized religions has weakened. Many people hold some, but not all of the beliefs of the organized religion in which they were raised. Nevertheless, they are loath to describe themselves as wholly separate from transcendental beliefs or experiences. In this context, people began talking about "spirituality" as an important dimension of life, but one not directly tied to the tenets of institutional religion. This broader view of spirituality implies an openness to that which is "beyond the material" or that which is beyond the mundane, everyday world. Spirituality also is a very inclusive term; people without a specific belief system may both declare themselves spiritual and be viewed that way by others because of their openness to experience, a positive view of the world, and an appreciation of nature, art, and other people.

The Relationship of Religion and Spirituality

Richards and Bergen (2000) describe "spiritual" as:

> Those experiences, beliefs, and phenomena that pertain to the transcendent and existential aspects of life (i.e., God or a Higher Power, the purpose and meaning of life, suffering, good and evil, death, etc.) . . . We view religious as a subset of the spiritual. Religious has to do with theistic beliefs, practices, and feelings that are often, but not always, expressed institutionally and denominationally as well as personally (p. 13).

The organization of the terms in this way explains "religion" as a subset of the "spiritual." Spirituality is a broad term that has to do with closeness or connection to the transcendent; religion is a particular way of being spiritual. The transcendent may of course mean God or a Higher Power, but it may also mean awareness of beauty, nature, or art—anything that is more than the superficial or temporal. This accounts for people who say, "I'm not religious, but I'm spiritual." Researchers in psychology and other social sciences have begun to analyze dimensions of spirituality. Muse-Burke (2004), for example, suggests that spirituality includes purpose and meaning in life, interdependence with others, inner peace, and transcendence.

Richards and Bergin's (2000) schema not only provides for the phenomenon of people who are spiritual but not religious, but also allows people who are religious to be spiritual. It also implies that people whose motives for religious practice or association are completely due to extrinsic, nonspiritual ends may be considered religious but not spiritual. An example would be someone who belongs to or attends a church in order to make profitable connections, but who has no interest in the actual beliefs or experiences associated with religion.

Other Dimensions of Religion

Religion has been described as both personal and social (Paloutzian, 1996). The personal dimension is concerned with how religion operates in a person's life. William James, an early American psychologist who wrote a seminal work on religious experience, said that personal religion is concerned with "the inner disposition of man himself [sic] his conscience, his deserts, his helplessness, his incompleteness" (James, 1902 as cited in Paloutzian, 1996). Religion can also be viewed as a social reality. Used in this way, it refers to a person's relationship to a religious organization, which itself has at least some of the following elements: a cognitive or belief structure, a moral code, and a set of practices for worship or prayer. In addition, people who "follow" a religion usually also have an experiential dimension to their religious lives—that is, there are feelings or inner experiences associated with rituals and religious behaviors.

In addition to personal and social dimensions, Paloutzian (1996) divides definitions of religion into functional and substantive dimensions. As a result, he uses four categories: personal functional, social functional, personal substantive, and social substantive. This author would like to show some inferences from Paloutzian's classification system. When religion is viewed according to the functions it performs, the content of religious belief can be ignored. Religion can be investigated according to its effects on individuals or its societal effects. Much of recent research in psychology on the effects of religion would fit into the personal functional category.

Paloutzian's (1996) substantive dimensions include the beliefs or practices unique to particular individuals (personal substantive), and the general beliefs and practices of a group—that is, the dogma and practice of an organized religion (the social substantive). As noted earlier, it has become common in 21st-century discourse for people to say that they are "spiritual but not religious." Thus, it would seem that when people disavow a religious dimension to their lives while emphasizing a spiritual one, they are explicitly separating themselves from social substantive aspects of religion—from the expectations of a formal creed or common practice. It seems that they are eager (perhaps even anxious) to support an attitude of independence and freedom (see earlier discussion of Enlightenment) and a separateness, which emphasizes the value of the individual. Nevertheless, they want to verify the importance and reality of "something beyond" the mundane, the everyday, and the material. They are, according to Paloutzian's scheme, focused on the personal, and not the social. They may stress the functions spirituality plays in their lives (e.g., how a practice makes them feel), or their individual beliefs (the substance or content of their personal faith).

Occasionally contemporary research suggests that there are important social effects of religion. Sometimes people suggest that society needs religion for its ability to assist in the development and encouragement of moral behavior. Others feel religion assists in promoting the common good. Before we discuss the influence of religion and spirituality on physiological and psychological health, let us discuss *faith* as a term related to religion and to human well-being and development.

Faith as a Developmental Phenomenon

Piaget (1969) described children's thinking as characterized by a fixed sequence of cognitive stages in a long series of research studies whose conclusions became highly influential in the middle of the 20th century. Following Piaget's success at delineating developmental changes, other developmental theorists sought to describe universal, progressive structures in other dimensions, including personality (Erikson, 1982; Loevinger & Blasi, 1976), moral development (Kohlberg, 1976), and even faith (Fowler, 1981). These approaches included some of the assumptions which came from the Enlightenment: the importance of the individual and freedom, the possibility of change and progress, and a reliance on skepticism and reason in order to produce more logical and just solutions to problems. The ability of the developing person to critique the moral judgments of the surrounding community and the beliefs of his or her religious faith show a direct trajectory from the stance of the enlightenment.

In this developmental psychology context, psychological theorists have struggled to define faith apart from the doctrines of particular religions. They have tried to describe stages of faith in which the individual personally appropriates to him- or herself a deep belief that transcends the particular tenets of the religion he or she was raised in. As a result, the theorists have needed an understanding of faith broader than a person's acceptance of particular dogmas. James Fowler, a developmental psychologist who has described six stages of faith, defines faith as the makeup of an individual's main motivation for life (Green & Hoffman, 1989 as cited in Hart, Limke, & Budd, 2010). Faith is that by which a person gives meaning to his or her life.

This view that faith is whatever is used to give meaning to life underscores the humanness of faith and spirituality, and the universal character of the spiritual dimension in human beings. It removes the association of spirituality with specific religions or particular doctrines or practices. It seems natural for human beings to "make meaning"—to attempt to give meaning to their lives. Indeed, the existential psychoanalyst, Viktor Frankl (2006), discovered in his observations in a Nazi concentration camp, that those who perceived meaning in their lives were much more likely to survive the horrors of their circumstances. Those who seemed not to have meaning soon succumbed to illness and death (Frankl, 2006).

This introduction to a broad view of faith and spirituality is meant to bolster your understanding that attention to a resident's spirituality is not predicated on an acceptance of any particular religion or its tenets. Like all of us, the elderly have spiritual needs—needs that go beyond those of food, warmth, medicine, and health care. Also, like the rest of us, the elderly will use their spiritual beliefs in every aspect of their lives.

THE UBIQUITOUS NATURE OF SPIRITUALITY

This discussion of religion and spirituality helps us to understand why professionals are somewhat loath to engage in conversation about religion, especially in a highly pluralistic society such as the United States. It also explains why a broader term like *spirituality* is more comfortable and has become more widely used. The broader term certainly allows us to assume that all human beings are spiritual, and that this dimension of human existence should be recognized and cultivated.

The reason this is important for long-term care (LTC) staff and administrators is twofold. First, the view of human beings as spiritual should bolster humane, dignified, and respectful treatment of residents in our facilities. Human beings are deserving of such respect because they are, in the terms used in human service professions, bio-psycho-social-spiritual beings. This is true despite limitations of age or cognition.

Secondly, this broad view of religion and spirituality needs to be understood by staff who themselves may have more limited understanding of this dimension of life. There is a spiritual dimension to the life of each person, whether or not the person is a practicing member of a religion, and whether or not he or she verbalizes beliefs or spirituality. Staff will need sensitivity and an understanding of diversity within the population of residents. As the United States becomes more diverse, there will be greater incidence of residents from non-Western traditions and cultures.

A concept related to spirituality but not coterminous with it is that of *gerotranscendence*. This is an idea that in late life individuals are able to transcend or go beyond the worldview that dominated their middle age. The concept of gerotranscendence bears some similarity to ideas of wisdom and ego integrity, often suggested as characteristics that are more likely to be found among the elderly. Included in gerotranscendence is a decrease in interest in material things and superficial social interactions. There is less self-centeredness, and a greater need to spend time in reflection and meditation.

The Relationship of Religion and Spirituality to Health

The last couple of decades have provided a great deal of evidence that religion is often positively correlated with health and longevity (McCullough, Friedman, Enders, & Martin, 2009; McCullough, Hoyt, Larson, Koenig, & Thoresen, 2000). The reasons proposed for this relationship are summarized in this section. Thoughtful authors have also noted that religion may not always lead to contentment and positive ways of coping. Religion may provide a negative way of coping, leading to bitterness, disappointment, or fear; a thorough discussion of these dual effects of religion is beyond the scope of this chapter.

The scientific study of religion has its roots in the seminal writings of William James in the late 19th century, with many empirical studies completed over the last 40 years (Schaie, Krause, & Booth, 2004). Since 1996, there have been efforts to conceptualize the dimensions of religion and to devise measures of those dimensions (Fetzer Institute & National Institute on Aging Working Group, 1999; Krause, 2002b). In addition, there has been considerable research investigating relationships between religion and health following early studies conducted at Duke University (e.g., Gillum, King, Obisesan, & Koenig, 2008; Lucchetti et al., 2011; Rippentrop, Altmaier, Chen, Found, & Keffala, 2005; Schnall et al., 2010). Such research has investigated mortality rates, quality of life, and physiological and psychological health.

Having established that there is a connection between religion and health, research is now seeking to understand *how* religion affects health and well-being. Two ideas suggested to explain the relationship of religion and health have been social support (Krause, 2002a) and avoidance of unhealthy behaviors. There is a large body of literature that demonstrates that people who have social support (family, friends, acquaintances, people to help in time of need) enjoy greater psychological well-being. Perhaps religion, especially attendance at religious events, provides a kind of "social capital," a network of connections that increases psychological health, and provides support for physical needs. Moreover, clergy are often the preferred counselors in situations requiring emotional support; therefore, having a religious leader often provides access to counseling even if that term is not used. In addition, many religions advocate avoidance of, or at least moderation in, alcohol and drug use, smoking, overeating, and other unhealthy behaviors. As a result, religion may encourage people to have healthy lifestyles. There is support for the idea that religious participation has part of its influence on health in these ways.

In many of the studies of the association of religion with health, church attendance has used as the measure of religion. McCullough has suggested that the role of private religious behavior needs to be a focus of future research (McCullough, 2001). *How* does religion affect health and longevity? In addition to the idea that social support and healthy life styles promote health, Idler (2004) argues that being religious also provides "frameworks of meaning." These frameworks provide comfort, security, and understanding when people are faced with the difficulties of life. The specific needs and difficulties faced by LTC residents are discussed later in this chapter. Other recent research has looked at other dimensions of religiosity, including prayer, religious coping, and forgiveness.

Does prayer correlate with better health? Several studies have found that religious devotion appears to provide a degree of protection from depression (Musik, Koenig, Hayes, & Cohen, 1998; Nooney & Woodrum, 2002); other studies found conflicting results (Ellison, 1994). Prayer has been associated with higher subjective health and life satisfaction (Musick, 1996, and Ellison, Gay, & Glass, 1989, both cited in Levin, 2004). Levin provides an epidemiology framework for the study of the relationship between prayer and health. He then attempts to suggest answers to the question: why does prayer affect health? He suggests that regular prayer helps us to maintain a sense of our relationship to God. In turn, this sense of relationship engenders motivation, connection, meaning, hope, love, and transcendence. Levin encourages the study of these effects as variables that may explain the relationship between prayer and health.

In addition to discussions of prayer, religious coping has been explored in several studies. Results indicate that religious coping is correlated not only with psychological well-being, but also with physiological functioning and spiritual health (Pargament, Koenig, Tarakeshwar, & Hahn, 2004). An analysis of several studies suggests that the relationship may not always be positive. Certain types of religious coping may decrease measures of health; negative religious coping that centers on "a dissatisfying relationship with God" was correlated with higher mortality rates (Pargament & Ano, 2004, p. 126).

To summarize, the relationship of religion to both physical and psychological health has been the subject of many studies. In general, religion has been positively correlated with good health, but some studies have failed to find such a relationship. The early literature investigated religious attendance, but more recent research has been interested in the effects of prayer, the meaning of religion for the participant, and, in particular, the uses of religion when people face transitions or losses in life.

NEEDS OF THE ELDERLY IN LONG-TERM CARE

Transitioning into long-term care entails several kinds of loss: the loss of home, the loss of independence (at least in some ways), and the loss of routines and familiar surroundings. In addition, elderly people who are moving into long-term care have often recently suffered the loss of loved ones, and are faced with less frequent contact with family and friends. Diminishing independence and these other losses may cause depression; depression itself may lessen physical and social activities, leading to a cycle of decreasing engagement and decreasing strength, which then increase depression. In addition, perceptions of staff may be affected in that judgments of disability may be exaggerated because of the effects of depression and decreased activity level. As a result, staff expectations may decrease inappropriately, leading to continued decreased engagement by the elderly person.

Dealing with Religious/Spiritual Needs in Various Settings

Residential care, personal care, or assisted living (RC/AL) may provide spiritual care in various ways: spiritual counselors or pastoral workers, religious services at the facilities, or even transportation to the resident's house of worship for services. These options are similar to those found in nursing homes. One interesting phenomena more feasible in the RC/AL setting is the leadership or initiative of residents themselves. In both religiously based and nonreligious institutions, residents may organize regular prayer groups. The recitation of the rosary, a popular Catholic devotional practice, or scripture study groups organized by residents themselves, are common in assisted-living facilities whether the institutions are faith based or not.

Activity directors quickly (and appropriately) add these resident-initiated activities to their published schedule of what is available to clients.

In comparison to assisted-living facilities, nursing homes (NHs) have been more likely to be religiously affiliated, to provide hospice services, and to have a hospice unit (Hamilton, Daaleman, Williams, & Zimmerman, 2009). Nursing homes and new-model, assisted-living facilities were more likely to provide counseling by clergy and religious services. (New model AL facilities in the cited study were larger facilities that catered to residents with different degrees of needs, had either a licensed practical nurse or registered nurse on duty at all times, and included residents who required assistance in transfer, or were incontinent. See Hamilton et al. for detailed criteria of this schema based on a stratified sample of facilities in Florida, Maryland, New Jersey, and North Carolina.)

Role of the Administrator in Providing Spiritual Care

Spirituality in the nursing home involves a general atmosphere of respect for persons; this will include respect for residents and respect for staff, and thus leadership has an extremely important role to play in the culture and climate of the facility. In addition, administrators need to organize the use of pastoral caregivers, both professional and volunteer, to help meet the needs of residents.

Religious and Spiritual Activities

In general, there are two realms of spiritual care provided in long-term care facilities: one-on-one counseling and public services. These may be offered by an in-house chaplain, or by religious professionals from the community.

The In-House Professional Chaplain

In an article providing a rationale for chaplains employed by long-term care facilities, Vance (1997) provides persuasive arguments and reacts to perceived barriers for in-house chaplains. After noting that two White House Conferences on Aging recommended that LTC facilities should have a chaplain and that Congress, hospitals, and military and police organizations typically have chaplains, he summarizes the reasons why LTC units frequently do not. Vance's position is that most people think that cost is the prohibitive factor. He argues first that chaplaincy is not generally understood, and secondly that having a well trained chaplain as part of the care team will decrease costs.

By a chaplain, Vance (1997) means a person who is a highly trained specialist; he does not think a "minister is a minister" or that any volunteer or clergyperson will necessarily be adequately prepared. He assumes the professional chaplain will have a master's degree and at least 400 supervised hours of clinical training. Secondly, as he details the work of the chaplain, he suggests that attention will be paid to residents, to family members, and to staff. Vance assumes the chaplain will probably work out of the social services department and will often be the initial counselor, or the preferred counselor.

In regard to working with residents, the chaplain's attention to residents' fears, losses, and grief may prevent the build-up of rage, depression, and complaints that often cost the facility a great deal of tension and money. Families are often ambivalent about the loved one's transition to long-term care, and their emotions lead to difficulties and accusations with the staff and with the administration or corporate office. Vance believes that the chaplain, though she or he works for the organization, provides confidentiality and a sense of fairness to residents, their families, and staff. The ability to meet the needs of overworked and emotionally exhausted staff also contributes greatly to reducing staff turnover and the costs associated with it (Vance, 1997).

The Use of Religious Professionals and Volunteers

For both one-on-one counseling and public worship services, administrators should develop and maintain contact with religious professionals in the broader community, such as ministers, priests, rabbis, and imams. This will be necessary even if there is a chaplain on staff, as residents will want to maintain contact and closeness with their previous religious leaders. The degree of religious pluralism in a community will affect the degree to which a variety of professionals should be involved. Even in the case of less diversity, for example, a mainly Protestant community, residents will come to the NH with attachment to particular religions, and within a particular religion, to particular churches and parishes.

Volunteers from local parishes or community groups can play a huge part in dealing with one of the greatest needs of in-care elderly: isolation and loneliness. The type of activities they do may range from church-related rituals (e.g., communion) to study of scriptures, or to general visiting. If the volunteers are members of the resident's former religious parish or church group, there is the additional benefit of maintaining connection to one's former life. Perhaps the most important point to make, and to reinforce among staff at all levels, is that religious ministry volunteers should be welcome to visit, and to offer individual counseling, prayer and comfort to residents who desire these meetings.

END-OF-LIFE ISSUES

People are now more likely to die in long-term care facilities than they are in hospitals or at home (Shield, 2004). A recent study by Hamilton et al. (2009) compared the extent of religious and spiritual care at end of life in nursing homes and in three types of assisted-living facilities. Information was received from family members of deceased residents as well as from facility administrators. The degree to which religion and spirituality were important for the decedent was correlated with the degree of attention given to religious and spiritual care. The other demographic characteristic that played a significant role was race. African Americans were more likely to receive spiritual help; they were also more likely to indicate that spirituality was important to them.

End-of-life issues are also related to loss and grief in general. Elderly residents are likely to have lost a spouse and sometimes a child or grandchildren, as well as friends to death. In addition, the residents are in an environment in which decline and death are frequently evident. In a study that investigated depression in nursing home residents and their coping mechanisms, participants indicated that "It is most depressing to make friends and then they die. . . . Having to see them going down, down, down—that is depressing" (Choi, Ransom, & Wyllie, 2008, p. 542). The authors also indicated that the most common way of coping was "stoicism" and religious coping. Almost all of the interviewees considered themselves religious. Acceptance of their lives was rooted in "trust in and gratitude toward God" (Choi et al., 2008, p. 543).

End-of-life issues also affect staff. The acceptance of a spirituality mindset in an institution provides a way for staff to make meaning of mortality, of their own questions about faith and doubt, and of their own difficult, yet essential role in meeting the needs of highly dependent and fragile residents.

SUMMARY

Although the scientific worldview has often contributed to materialism in the Western world, issues of aging and death demonstrate the role of religion and/or spirituality in LTC facilities. Religious and spiritual coping increase life satisfaction among residents, and help to prevent burnout among staff. Administrators need to understand their obligation to provide religious services and pastoral counseling to residents, and the varying ways that can be done. Administrators need to see their encouragement and support of staff as contributing both directly and indirectly to a climate that fosters spiritual well-being. In addition, careful analysis suggests that the relief provided to both staff and residents outweighs the costs related to providing such opportunities.

Discussion Questions

1. How can you differentiate between religion and spirituality? Reflect on spiritual experiences in your own life. Can you provide examples of spiritual experiences that include organized religion, and examples that do not?

2. Reflecting on religion and spirituality in your own life, what are examples of a personal function or experience? What are examples of a social facet or function?

3. What are some of the ways in which you think an administrator can support the religious/spiritual needs of nursing home residents? Can you think of ways that were not suggested in this chapter?

4. How can an administrator encourage employees to respect diverse religions in the nursing home?

5. In what ways can religion provide a positive coping mechanism when people are faced with loss? Can you think of times when religion might make coping more difficult?

Worksheet Questions

1. Review Paloutzian's (1996) delineation of religion into personal and social, and functional and substantive aspects. The result is a two-by-two table with the following categories.

   Personal-functional   Social-functional

   Personal-substantive   Social-substantive

   In which category would each of the following comments fit?

   a. I always feel better when I pray.
   b. I believe I need to be with others in a religious community to meet the needs of poor people in the world.
   c. I go to church (synagogue, mosque) because this is how I connect with my *Jou* traditions.
   d. I believe in the rituals and dogma of my religious group.

e. I like to discuss religion, especially the scriptures of my religion.

f. I find that the contact with nature brings me feelings of oneness with all reality.

2. If an older person moves to an LTC facility, which of these categories of religion/spirituality are most likely to be affected?

REFERENCES

Benjamin, M. R. (2004). Religion and functional health among the elderly: Is there a relationship and is it constant? *Journal of Aging and Health, 16*(3), 355–374.

Choi, N. G., Ransom, S., & Wyllie, R. J. (2008). Depression in older nursing home residents: The influence of nursing home environmental stressors, coping, and acceptance of group and individual therapy. *Aging and Mental Health, 12*(5), 536–547.

Ellison, C. G. (1994). Religion, the life stress paradigm, and the study of depression. In J. S. Levin (Ed.), *Religion in aging and health: Theoretical foundations and methodological frontiers.* Thousand Oaks, CA: Sage.

Ellison, C. G., Gay, D. A., & Glass, T. A. (1989). Does religious commitment contribute to individual life satisfaction? *Social Forces, 68,* 100–123. Cited by J. Levin, in K. W. Schaie, N. Krause, & A. Booth (Eds.). *Religious influences on health and well-being in the elderly.* New York: Springer.

Erikson, E. (1982). *The life cycle completed.* New York: Norton.

Fetzer Institute & National Institute on Aging Working Group. (1999). *Multidimensional measurement of religiousness/spirituality for use in health research.* Kalamazoo, MI: Fetzer Institute.

Fowler, J. W. (1981). *Stages of faith: The psychology of human development and the quest for meaning.* New York: HarperCollins.

Frankl, V. (2006). *Man's search for meaning.* Boston, MA: Beacon.

Gillum, R. F., King, D. E., Obisesan, T. O., & Koenig, H. G. (2008). Frequency of attendance at religious services and mortality in a U.S. national cohort. *Annals of Epidemiology, 18*(2), 124–129.

Hart, J. T., Limke, A., & Budd, P. R. (2010). Attachment and faith development. *Journal of Psychology and Theology, 38*(2), 122–128.

Hamilton, V. L., Daaleman, T. P., Williams, C. S., & Zimmerman, S. (2009). The context of religious and spiritual care at the end of life in long-term care facilities. *Sociology of Religion, 70*(2), 79–95.

Idler, E. (2004). Religious observance and health. In K. W. Schaie, N. Krause, & A. Booth (Eds.), *Religious influences on health and well-being in the elderly.* New York: Springer.

Kohlberg, L. (1976). Moral stages and moralization: The cognitive developmental approach. In T. Lickona (Ed.), *Moral development and behavior: Theory, research, and social issues* (pp. 31–53). New York: Holt.

Krause, N. (2002a). Church-based social support and health in old age: Exploring variations by race. *Journal of Gerontology: Social Sciences, 57B,* S332–S347.

Krause, N. (2002b). A comprehensive strategy for developing closed-ended survey items for use in studies of older adults. *Journal of Gerontology: Social Sciences, 57B,* S263–S274.

Krause, N. (2008). Religion, health, and health behavior. In K. W. Schaie & R. P. Abeles (Eds.), *Social structures and aging individuals: Continuing challenges* (pp. 73–95). New York: Springer.

Lee, B. Y., & Newberg, A. B. (2010). The interaction of religion and health. In D. A. Monti & B. D. Beitman (Eds.), *Integrative psychiatry.* New York: Oxford University Press.

Levin, J. (2004). Prayer, love, and transcendence. In K. W. Schaie, N. Krause, & A. Booth (Eds.), *Religious influences on health and well-being in the elderly.* New York: Springer.

Levin, J., & Chatters, L. M. (2008). Religion, aging, and health: Historical perspectives, current trends, and future directions. *Journal of Religion, Spirituality and Aging, 20*(1–2), 153–172.

Levin, J., Chatters, L. M., & Taylor, R. J. (2011). Theory in religion, aging, and health: An overview. *Journal of Religion and Health, 50*(2), 389–406.

Loevinger, J., & Blasi, A. (1976). *Ego development: Conceptions and theories.* San Francisco, CA: Jossey-Bass.

Lucchetti, G., Lucchetti, A. G., Badan-Neto, A. M., Peres, P. T., Peres, M. F., Moreira-Almeida, et al. (2011). Religiousness affects mental health, pain and quality of life in older people in an outpatient rehabilitation setting. *Journal of Rehabilitation Medicine, 43*(4), 316–322.

McCullough, M. E. (2001). Religious involvement and mortality: Answers and more questions. In T. G. Plante & A. C. Sherman (Eds.), *Faith and health* (pp. 53–74). New York: Guilford Press.

McCullough, M. E., Friedman, H. S., Enders, C. K., & Martin, L. R. (2009). Does devoutness delay death? Psychological investment in religion and its association with longevity in the Terman sample. *Journal of Social and Personality Psychology, 97,* 866–882.

McCullough, M. E., Hoyt, W. T., Larson, D. B., Koenig, H. G., & Thoresen, C. E. (2000). Religious involvement and mortality: A meta-analytic review. *Health Psychology, 19,* 211–222.

McFarland, M. J. (2010). Religion and mental health among older adults: Do the effects of religious involvement vary by gender? *The Journals of Gerontology: Series B: Psychological Sciences and Social Sciences, 65B*(5), 621–630.

Merriam-Webster. (2012a). Religion. Retrieved March 13, 2012, from http://www.merriam-webster.com/dictionary/religion.

Merriam-Webster. (2012b). Spirituality. Retrieved March 13, 2012, from http://www.merriam-webster.com/dictionary/spirituality.

Miller, B. (2007). *Cultural Anthropology*. Boston, MA: Pearson Education.

Muse-Burke, J. L. (2004). *Development and validation of the inclusive spirituality index*. (Doctoral dissertation). Retrieved from UMI Dissertation Services.

Musik, M. A., Koenig, H. G., Hayes J. C., & Cohen, H. J. (1998). Religious activity and depression among community-dwelling elderly persons with cancer: The moderating effect of race. *Journal of Gerontology: Social Sciences, 53B*, S218–S237.

Nooney, J., & Woodrum, E. (2002). Religious coping and church-based support as predictors of mental health outcomes: Testing a conceptual model. *Journal for the Scientific Study of Religion, 41*, 359–368.

Paloutzian, R. F. (1996). *Invitation to the psychology of religion* (2nd ed.). Boston, MA: Allyn & Bacon.

Pargament, K. I., Koenig, H. G., Tarakeshwar, N., & Hahn, J. (2004). Religious coping methods as predictors of psychological, physical and spiritual outcomes among medically ill elderly patients: A two-year longitudinal study. *Journal of Health Psychology, 9*(6), 713–730.

Pargament, K. I., & Ano, G. G. (2004). Empirical advances in the psychology of religion and coping. In K. W. Schaie, N. Krause, & A. Booth (Eds.), *Religious influences on health and well-being in the elderly* (pp. 114–136). New York: Springer.

Piaget, J., & Inhelder, B. (1969). *The psychology of the child*. New York: Basic Books.

Richards, P. S., & Bergin, A. E. (Eds.). (2000). *Handbook of psychotherapy and religious diversity*. Washington, DC: American Psychological Association.

Rippentrop, E. A., Altmaier, E. M., Chen, J. J., Found, E. M., & Keffala, V. J. (2005). The relationship between religion/spirituality and physical health, mental health, and pain in a chronic pain population. *Pain, 116*(3), 311–321.

Schaie, K. W., Krause, N., & Booth, A. (Eds.) (2004). *Religious influences on health and well-being in the elderly*. New York: Springer.

Schnall, E., Wassertheil-Smoller, S., Swencionis, C., Zemon, V., Tinker, L., O'Sullivan, M. J., et al. (2010). The relationship between religion and cardiovascular outcomes and all-cause mortality in the women's health initiative observational study. *Psychological Health, 25*(2), 249–263.

Shield, R. (2004, Nov.). End of life in nursing homes: Experiences and policy recommendations. Retrieved March 13, 2012, from http://www.aarp.org/home-garden/livable-communities/info-2004/end_of_life_in_nursing_homes_experiences_and_polic.html.

Tornstam, L. (2005). *Gerotranscendence: A developmental theory of positive aging*. New York: Springer.

Vance, R. E. (1997). The role of the chaplain. *Nursing Homes: Long Term Care Management, 46*(8), 59.

Chapter 9

Meeting Psychological Needs in Long-Term Care

Gail Cabral, IHM, PhD

LEARNING OBJECTIVES

1. To provide basic understanding of relevant terms: life satisfaction, gerotranscendence, activity theory, disengagement theory
2. To identify basic theories of successful aging and the implications of those theories on healthcare providers
3. To identify and reflect on stereotypes about the aged
4. To provide suggestions for ongoing development of the older individuals, as well as their family members and the staff who care for them
5. To identify the functions that can be performed by psychological professionals in the long-term care setting

KEY TERMS

Activity Theory: The belief that older persons will enjoy life satisfaction and psychological well-being to the extent that they remain as active as possible

Ageism: The stereotypic generalization of characteristics to people of a certain age, usually used to denote negative attitudes toward those who are elderly of advanced age; rigidly held and oversimplified beliefs that people, by virtue of their age alone, possess distinct psychological traits and characteristics

Benevolent Ageism: The stereotypic generalization of positive traits and behaviors in the elderly; rigidly held and oversimplified positive beliefs about the aged

Disengagement Theory: The belief that it is natural and helpful for the aged to withdraw from activities and responsibilities in a timely way, that is, at the time when other people are ready to take on their responsibilities

Gerotranscendence: The theoretical concept that in old age individuals may develop a new and deeper perspective on life, death, time, and space; developments may include changes in concepts of the self, and in social and personal relationships (Tornstam, 2005)

Protectionism: The tendency to overgeneralize from the older person's actual needs for assistance to needs inferred without justifiable evidence

Life Satisfaction: Life satisfaction is an overall assessment of feelings and attitudes about one's life at a particular point in time ranging from negative to positive. It is one of three major indicators of well-being: life satisfaction, positive affect, and negative affect (Diener, 1984 as cited in Buetell, 2006)

Stress Appraisal: The process by which human beings judge the potential harm or challenge in a situation, and simultaneously decide whether their resources are sufficient to deal with the situation (Lazarus, 1999)

Dementia Care Mapping: The system devised by researchers at Bradford University in England to evaluate which activities and which staff behaviors are able to engage residents and meet their unique (and changing) needs

Horizontal Stressors: The stress which occurs because of lifespan transitions (Carter & McGoldrick, 1999)

Vertical Stressors: The factors which influence stress that come from the genetics, family, culture, and history of a person; vertical and horizontal stressors interact in a person's experience of change and stress (Carter & McGoldrick, 1999)

INTRODUCTION

This chapter addresses the psychological needs of the aged population. The emphasis is on those in nursing homes and other residential care facilities, but other life transitions are addressed. In addition, the needs of staff are also addressed. The chapter begins with an overview of assumptions of the author, a description of the older population from a developmental and lifecycle perspective, and a delineation of basic and sometimes paradoxical human needs. Following a description of some of the stereotypes about the elderly, the next section discusses some of the theories about aging, and how those stereotypes and theories may manifest themselves in long-term care (LTC) facilities. The chapter concludes with the role psychologists can play in assessing and intervening in various behavioral and health problems of older residents in the community and LTC facilities.

Assumptions of This Chapter

This section discusses the assumptions of this chapter, and the complexity of human beings, before a detailed description of human needs and how they manifest in older adults is presented.

1. Every human person is a biopsychosocialspiritual being.
2. Every human person has complementary (and sometimes conflicting) needs for autonomy and connectedness.
3. In addition, each human person, no matter his or her age or physical or mental condition, desires and deserves to be treated with dignity and respect.
4. Human persons, of any age or condition, desire identity confirmation, recognition, and meaning.
5. Life transitions present stressful adjustments at any age. The social-cultural context at the moment of change, and the genetics, history, family dynamics, and generational pressures found in the person's family interact with his or her adjustment during life transitions.
6. One of the most important duties of administrators is to help staff develop an understanding of the geriatric resident. Psychologists and other mental health workers are in a very good position to help them do this.
7. There is great variety among human beings on any characteristic that can be measured. In old age, the amount of diversity is greater than at earlier ages.
8. The question of whether people change or stay the same throughout their lifespan is not empirically settled. Our belief about this theoretical question influences our expectations.

Consider the case of Mrs. Mary Jane Swartz. She is 85 years old, and has been noticing changes in herself, and so have her family members and her doctor. They all agree she should move to an assisted-living situation. List some challenges present in this brief and simple scenario: challenges for Mrs. Swartz, for her family members, and for staff at her new living facility.

Human persons are always multifaceted, complex beings, constantly developing and adapting. All of this development and adaptation takes place in a series of social interactions within varying social relationships and complex social systems. As human beings develop, they face biopsychosocial tasks—that is, they must adapt to physiological changes and changes in social expectations and roles. Personality develops, in part, from how we adapt to changes in our lives; how we adapt is influenced by our personality, our temperament, and our history. The context of our lives, our families, our relationships, our historical time, and our culture also play a part in how we adapt. How do these general facts about complex, developing, and integrated human beings fit the scenario involving Mrs. Swartz?

Mrs. Swartz and her family may be aware of some physical deterioration, and some memory loss. Since noticing changes, her family has begun to take a more active part in the decisions that affect Mrs. Swartz. Although Mrs. Swartz agrees she needs more help, and is open to moving to assisted living, she is aware not only of the changes within her, but also of other people's changed perceptions of her. She is also aware that the move to assisted living will require many kinds of adjustments and definite losses. This simple example includes physiological changes interacting with social role changes, environment changes, and psychological perceptions of people who interact with each other (Mrs. Swartz, her family, and the staff of the assisted-living facility). In addition to Mrs. Swartz's need to adjust to these changes and their implications, Mrs. Swartz will need to "make sense" of these transitions. Making sense of our lives is an ongoing human need. It is discussed in light of other needs Mrs. Swartz shares with all of us.

THE HUMAN BEING IS COMPLEX, AND ALWAYS DEVELOPING AND COPING WITH STRESS

Human beings are complex, integrated beings with physiological, cognitive, social, and spiritual dimensions. The importance of physiological functions, with their great impact on health and well-being, is certainly assumed in healthcare settings and in dealing with the geriatric residents. Indeed, the placement of a person in a long-term care setting is usually the result of an evaluation which has determined that the person is not able to meet all of his or her needs while living alone. A related factor may be that these needs cannot be met by family members or friends either. These needs are frequently related to illness and disability, or to a decline in cognitive functioning.

Human beings are always changing and developing both within themselves and in response to changing circumstances around them. Carter and McGoldrick (1999) suggest that all life transitions produce stress. Those life transitions are situated in a family lifecycle, and often revolve around changes in the family structure; for example, the inclusion of a new daughter- or son-in-law, the addition to the family of new children and grandchildren, the moving out of the home of young adults, or the relocation of one's adult children. In any case, many of the life transitions related to aging produce stress and/or reduce one's resources to deal with stress.

One of the most frequently cited explanations of stress is the perception of needs that one does not think one has the resources to meet (Lazarus, 1999). In this view of stress, psychological stress refers neither to a specific list of stimuli or events in the environment, nor to specific emotional reactions in themselves, though both environmental stressors, and the experience of feeling stress are part of the reality. In Lazarus's relational view of stress, stress is concerned with the relative balance or imbalance "between the power of the environmental demands to harm, challenge or threaten, and the psychological resources of the person to manage these demands" (p. 58). In other words, what is stressful will vary from person to person. A reasonable amount of demand, like the deadline for writing this chapter, produces a certain livable amount of stress if I feel I have the resources to complete my assignment. I feel challenged, excited, and engaged. A course that primarily repeats material you learned in another course offers too little challenge. Here, the outcome may be boredom or indifference. A course (or reading) that requires previous knowledge of many concepts you have not been exposed to, and which you do not think you have the ability or time to learn, causes negative stress. You think, "I do not have the resources to deal with what I must face."

Note that a central part of evaluating stress is done by the person's perception, or better yet, by his or her "appraisal" of both the situation and his or her ability to handle that situation. Individual differences will make what is seen as stressful for one person an interesting or pleasantly challenging opportunity for someone else.

Part of Lazarus's (1999) theory assumes that human beings make appraisals of their ability to deal with the stressful situations in their lives. How does this general theory of stress and its appraisal fit with the topic of life change in the elderly? First, once again, what are the environmental stressors typical in the lives of the aged?

Many authors assume that all changes, even highly positive changes, produce stress. Some of the changes experienced by the elderly may be viewed as positive (more time during retirement, more freedom from social restrictions, less interest in keeping up with the Joneses). Some are less positive, and some require major shifts in daily life. The life transitions related to gerontology include the following: changes in workplace responsibilities, retirement, "downsizing," relocation, using home health care, moving to assisted living, moving to an LTC facility, entering hospice, and facing death. Not every older adult goes through all of these, but many older adults face several of these transitions.

There are also changes related to physiological and mental functioning. Some elderly appear impervious to these declines associated with aging. However, many people do find themselves facing decreasing physical skills, and those who come to assisted living or nursing home facilities are probably seeing some declines in some of their functions. In relation to Lazarus's (1999) theory, therefore, there are new demands (dealing with a new residence) at the very time of, and because of, changes in one's resources (increasing frailty, for example). So the very move from one's own house has some essential loss ("I lost my home"), and some accompanying losses ("I have less control over my surroundings at a time I am less able to deal with relocation than I would have been earlier").

Carter and McGoldrick (1999) discuss a developmental (or horizontal) axis of change: The individual meets the need for change and adapts to these changes as he or she goes through the lifespan. Carter and McGoldrick include an additional vertical axis of potential stressors, including genetics, cultural and societal history, stereotypes, social hierarchies, and beliefs which come from one's family of origin. Each of these vertical stressors weighs down on the person undergoing a life transition; each influences how much stress a person is experiencing in the life transition of the moment. Let us look again at Mrs. Swartz.

What did Mrs. Swartz learn from her family of origin that affects her during this process of transition to assisted living? Was there an unspoken expectation that elderly parents would age and die in the home of one of their children? Does she come from a family whose ethnic background assumes that daughters will remain local in order to be available to meet the needs of aging parents? Does she remember parents or grandparents who suffered from dementia and were placed in a nursing home in which they seldom received visits from family members? Does she remember formal, superficial, and tense visits with relatives in long-term care (LTC)?

Mrs. Swartz is not facing this process of transition as a blank slate. She comes with memories, expectations, beliefs, and stereotypes of her own. Whether these background (vertical) realities will make her adjustment easier or more difficult depends on what they are, and her reactions and resources. Nevertheless, Carter and McGoldrick's (1999) description of horizontal (developmental) changes, and vertical stressors that impinge on us from cultural, social, and familial backgrounds is important. It allows us to see the complexity of humans in their life transitions, and the various factors which influence the residents we see in assisted or LTC facilities.

UNIVERSAL HUMAN NEEDS

This section discusses universal human needs and their presence in the elderly, along with transitions and losses of many kinds. The most important point is that the elderly are more like the rest of us than different. Needs for dignity and respect, and dangers to such needs in LTC are discussed first.

Psychosocial needs described by the psychologists Erik Erikson and Robert F. Peck are then summarized. Needs which seem antagonistic to each other, individuation and belonging, are used to explain some of the difficulties elders find in life transitions.

The assumption of this chapter is that human beings are more alike than they are different. All human beings are born, experience babyhood and childhood, experience joys and disappointments, and will die. Human beings have the same types of reactions, for example, pleasure when faced with that which is attractive or interesting, and fear or anger when faced with whatever threatens. However, throughout our lives, different objects arouse these common reactions. Also, although human beings experience the same feelings, we may not express them the same way. And human beings, no matter their age or condition, have basic human needs. One of the truisms related to this point says, "That which is most personal is most universal."

The next section discusses the need for dignity and respect, and how each person needs to feel his or her identity is recognized and confirmed. We then discuss paradoxes in human needs and how those competing needs affect life transitions, and paradoxical stereotypes of the elderly.

Human Dignity and Respect in Long-Term Care

The mission statements of care facilities speak to the need to treat all clients with dignity and respect. They sometimes indicate that the facility focuses on the residents' unique needs and goals; they say they will use a holistic approach in their care of the elderly. Such statements indicate the highest desires of care workers at all levels of the institution, and the expectations of accrediting and governing agencies. Nevertheless, the pressure of work at all levels may militate against these generally agreed upon ideals. Some examples follow.

There have been egregious examples of mistreatment of nursing home patients, including neglect, disparagement, and physical, psychological, and sexual abuse. State organizations attempt to control and eliminate such abuses. However, in the context of this text, which is focused on administration, the attitudes of workers and the stresses of the job may be seen as contributors to an atmosphere in which a very small minority of care workers manifest tremendous disrespect for the clients they serve.

The cost of staffing is the largest part of a facility's expenses. In direct care, and in the decisions which affect direct care, there is a tendency to manage a facility with as few staff as possible. The net impact of staffing decisions of this type is to lower the morale of the "first responders"—those interacting most directly with residents. In addition, the direct-care staff are pushed to the limit to get the necessary work done as quickly as possible.

Extreme pressure on workers leads to several adverse effects: less personal interest in the residents while attending to their physical needs, less attention to signs of physical change until they become serious, and greater turnover of staff. The latter phenomenon brings with it a set of cascading effects. The time lag while the administration attempts to hire increases the stress and pressure on continuing workers. The necessity of training and orienting new staff delays optimal service. In addition, the residents are required to learn and adjust to new workers. This will be particularly difficult for those who are cognitively or psychologically deteriorating, or who are just beginning to feel they are comfortable in their new home.

Administrators at any level must convey their commitment to the ideals of the mission, even as they make practical decisions every day. Staff who participate in direct care are quick to judge administrators who "talk the talk" but do not "walk the walk" when the ultimate care of the patients is not reflected in decisions. In this regard, administrators should take considerable care in the communication of decisions which affect care in any way.

A climate of respect and dignity for all employees results when administrators listen to staff from all levels of the organization. This willingness to listen goes a long way toward creating an atmosphere in which dependent elderly are treated with respect. Since human beings have psychosocial, or biopsychosocial needs, it is helpful to delineate some of them; the next section provides such a description.

Psychosocial Needs: Identity, Intimacy, Generativity, and Integrity

Erik Erikson (1968) describes eight psychosocial stages, overviewing life issues from infancy to death. Each requires the solution to a crisis or paradox, a choice between two natural but seemingly opposing poles. Each person composes her or his unique solution that indicates a movement toward one of these two poles. Erikson's first stage, associated with infancy, poses this dilemma: "Acquiring a Sense of Trust versus Acquiring a Sense of Mistrust." For Erikson, the real solution is not to trust blindly. Such a person would not be able to live well in a real world. Rather, the infant and the person the infant becomes will formulate an individualized solution that includes a measure of trust in a good world, *and* a measure of mistrust that will allow prudence and discernment. Each stage follows this dialectical and dynamic process and each produces an ego strength that affects individuals throughout the rest of their lives.

The central stage of Erikson's (1968) theory is the active choice of a personal identity; this is formed in the context of the person's social world. Erikson calls this the crisis of "identity versus identity diffusion." Although usually associated with adolescence, identity remains an essential component of personality in each age of a person's life in Erikson's theory. Actually, Erikson sees each "stage" as holding elements of each other stage. In particular, the last four of his stages, identity versus identity diffusion, intimacy and solidarity versus isolation, generativity versus self-absorption and stagnation, and integrity versus despair—though most often associated with adolescence, young adulthood, middle adulthood, and old age, respectively—overlap many phases of the life of adults.

In the last stage of life, the individual is faced with a choice between *integrity and despair*. Integrity in this context means that one's sense of oneself and one's historical time, one's life choices, and one's experiences are perceived to have a unity and wholeness. While each of Erikson's stages has an unavoidable negative pole, it is hoped that the individual's response to each stage will include more of the positive pole. Thus, some regret will be present in old age, along with the knowledge that there is neither time nor opportunity for redress or doing things over. Thus, there may be some "despair." However, the psychologically healthy elder will also have an ability to remember the good with gratitude, to enjoy the present with aplomb, and to cope well with the difficulties life may inflict.

Applying the need for respect and dignity with the lifelong issue of identity helps us to understand that older people, like all human persons, need to have their identity confirmed. Each person needs to be treated as an individual. Each person needs a sense of him- or herself as unique, and related to others. We are all affirmed when a new leader in our workplace quickly learns and uses our name. Our self-worth is supported when our efforts are noticed or praised, when our contributions are named. Here, the treatment of employees again colors the atmosphere of the whole facility, providing an indirect and implicit safety net for residents. Employees who are well treated, who feel respected in the workplace, are much less likely to provide shoddy care, be dismissive toward residents' complaints, or neglect or abuse those under their care. When staff are respected as individuals, they are much more likely to stay in the facility, to be open to ongoing learning and development, and to treat residents with respect.

In the direct care of residents, whatever confirms them as individuals—the use of their name, the recognition of their past accomplishments, the banter that remembers what they said yesterday, their favorite sports team, or the names of their beloved grandchildren—each and every instance of such personal contact confirms the person in his or her uniqueness, and demonstrates respect.

The last two stages of Erikson's (1968) theory were more elaborately described by the developmental psychologist Robert Peck (1968). Peck extended Erikson's concept of integrity versus wisdom as the central issue in old age. He suggested three more specific developmental tasks related to Erikson's concept. The first is the crisis, or the pattern, of redefinition of self versus work-role preoccupation. This challenge relates to either changes in work responsibilities or retirement itself. It is also related to the loss of roles. Someone who defined herself primarily as mother and wife may be at a loss to understand what she should be doing now, or how her life has meaning. **Table 9.1** summarizes Erikson's psychosocial stages for adolescence and adulthood and Robert Peck's extension of the latter two by more specific crises or life tasks.

The Paradox of Needs: Independence and Inclusion

Criticism of psychological theories has often revolved around the idea that they have a subtle sex bias, very common in the Europe and the United States. This is an overvaluing of qualities usually associated with masculinity—in particular, an emphasis on individuality and independence. Carter and McGoldrick (1999) make such a criticism of developmental theories. Here,

Table 9.1 A Comparison of Erikson's and Peck's Descriptions of Psychosocial Tasks of Adolescence and Adulthood

Age	Erikson's Psychosocial Stages	Peck's Developmental Tasks
Adolescence	Identity vs. identity diffusion	
Young Adulthood	Intimacy vs. isolation	
Middle Adulthood	Generativity vs. stagnation, self-absorption	1. Socializing vs. sexualizing 2. Valuing wisdom vs. physical strength 3. Emotional flexibility vs. rigidity 4. Cognitive flexibility vs. rigidity
Later Adulthood	Integrity vs. despair	1. Role differentiation vs. work-role preoccupation 2. Body transcendence vs. body preoccupation 3. Ego transcendence vs. ego preoccupation

Source: Adapted from Erikson, E. (1968). *Identity: Youth and Crisis*. New York: Norton; and Peck, R. C. (1968). Psychological developments in the second half of life. In B. L. Neugarten (Ed.), *Middle age and aging*. Chicago: University of Chicago Press.

we apply their critique to Erikson's (1968) theory and review a developmental theory that attempts to describe complementary needs.

Central to Erikson's (1968) stages are characteristics related to autonomy and independence. Carter and McGoldrick (1999) criticize developmental theorists as likely to focus on the development of the individual, using a male model of increasing independence as a standard of maturity. They suggest that "healthy development requires finding an optimal balance between connectedness and separateness, belonging and individuation, accommodation and autonomy" (2005, p. 9). This description is very similar to main ideas in the theory of a thoughtful developmental psychologist, Robert Kegan (1982).

Kegan (1982) presents the idea that there are some paradoxical aspects of universal human needs, which he calls "the deep yearnings of the human heart." These two deep and always present human desires are the need to be connected to others—that is, to belong and be included—and the complementary need to be independent, unique, and autonomous. Both kinds of needs are hypothesized to be present in each person, though they are probably not present in equal measure at every moment. In his book on adult development, *The Evolving Self*, Kegan suggests that human development occurs through a process of constructing meaning over a series of stages. In each stage, we are called to "know" and to "experience," to understand and to reflect with the heart.

Kegan's (1982) dynamic concept suggests the alternation of these two pulls or needs. The adolescent wants to be autonomous and seems to move away from parents. At the same time, she or he will move closer to friends or romantic partners. The college student who chafes to live away from home may find herself calling home repeatedly, eager for an inclusion in family almost contradictory to her independent stance. Kegan's dialectical approach is relevant to the difficulties in all relationships when two people are "out of sync" or asynchronous with each other—that is, when one wants togetherness at the same time the other seeks distance. And yet, each will, at some point, experience the other deep human need. The following sections discuss these human needs for inclusion (belonging) and independence and provide examples of how these ideas apply to senior citizens in life transitions.

Need for Inclusion and Belonging

The need for belonging is the first need. The infant who barely knows his or her separateness is naturally comforted by being held or touched by someone; for the very young infant, being held by anyone brings pleasure and comfort. Small children like to be covered, to hide in small spaces, to be enclosed. Our need for belonging is so strong that we will occasionally do things that bring us pain or danger in order to be part of a group; so great is our need to be included. A recent ad for a smoking cessation product shows a young man and a young woman relegated to the outside of a party because they are smoking. The man says, "To think I started to smoke because I wanted to belong."

One of the most poignant vignettes about the elderly shows an elderly woman in a rocking chair, saying, "Nobody touches me." She reminisces about her mother touching her when she was a child, her husband touching her, and hugging and kissing her children. She ends by saying, "Now nobody touches me."

As adults age, life transitions occur which may strain our sense of belonging. These include work changes and separation from family members through relocation or death. Retirement separates us from coworkers. When the largest portion of a person's identity has been tied to his or her role in the workplace, identity itself is threatened when employment outside the home ceases. Retirement may loosen bonds with acquaintances in the workplace. The elderly may find themselves losing connections in other ways. One may find oneself too frail for certain activities which one used to enjoy, and friendships which were tied specifically to those activities may disappear. Moving to new housing, a new apartment, or a house in a new town, will disrupt contact with friends and neighbors. Having to give up driving is a major loss of independence in itself, but it also lessens one's ability to connect with others. Moving to an assisted-living facility or a nursing home will surely modify one's pattern of social interaction.

The death of friends and relatives may decimate one's social circle. Decreasing verbal or cognitive skills in the elderly or their friends may cause visits with loved ones to feel "different," less close, and less enjoyable. Carstensen (1992) has proposed a socioemotional selectivity theory of shrinking social circles. Her hypothesis is that as physical energy declines, elderly people will deliberately narrow the number of social contacts or social activities they want to participate in. They will drop social activities and relationships that are peripheral or superficial, and concentrate on their ties with family members or close friends.

There is some evidence to support Carstensen's (1992) hypothesis. However, the general principle of individual variation must be remembered; there are some elderly who continue to make new friends and to widen their social circles until the end of their lives. To the extent, however, that older people have become content in later life with a small social circle, they are in greater danger of loneliness, when losses occur among those close family members and friends.

Inclusion Needs in Long-Term Care (LTC)

A few suggestions follow regarding dealing with the need for belonging in long-term facilities, in particular, the provision of individual attention and the confirmation of residents' social identities.

We all know what it feels like to have someone inattentive when we are speaking, or to have someone texting or listening to another conversation in the background. We feel disrespected, dismissed, disregarded. We also know how empowering it is when someone seems to be willing to engage us, is interested in listening to what we say—in short, is eager to *pay attention* to us. Whatever connects or includes should be stressed in our dealings with elderly residents: names on bedrooms and at dining room tables, the use of "we" and "our" when referring to residents, the use of residents' names in conversations, and more than anything else, nonverbal and verbal personal attention.

Another aspect of belonging is the recognition of those groups to which we *have* belonged. I remember an elderly resident who was very surprised I knew the family she belonged to and the locally well known family business her father and brother had run. At the other extreme is the resident who repeatedly and proudly tells you of family members, old social connections, and the successes of children and grandchildren. The repetition may be partly due to memory loss and cognitive decline. It is also, however, a sign of the identification with others by which we each define ourselves. It is a statement that "I am a person," and "I am connected." Thus, older adults seek affiliation or cohesion with others, even as circumstances may take them from their homes and families to new settings in nursing homes or other facilities.

The aged may retire, change their residences (perhaps several times in middle adulthood and early old age), move to an independent living arrangement in a continuum of care facility, require additional care from family members or in-home care, move to an assisted-living situation, and then finally move to a long-term care institution. Each of these life transitions will demand physical, psychological, and social adjustment. It is not unusual for a person to experience several of these changes. Each transition changes relationships or creates possibilities for new relationships. Each requires letting go and relearning: learning a new locale and/or a new place in one's old social group, or a place in a new group.

Need for Autonomy and Independence in the Elderly

Elder people are not different from us, and will seek competence and independence. The retiree will need to find roles that fit and provide a sense of accomplishment. As you read this text, your perspective is that of the future administrator/caregiver. Thus, those of us in gerontological studies are poignantly aware of the lack of independence that usually has propelled the elderly to need assistance at home, or through assisted-living arrangements and nursing home placement. While considerable attention is often given to activities of daily living, in this context of the need for autonomy and independence, we find a broader concept, one that can include much more limited activity. Very simple choices can be offered which will allow a resident to feel some autonomy. Expressions of gratitude to an elder who participates in simple actions like getting dressed, will convey the sense that the other person is a contributor, and has a dignity in his or her own right.

The great human "yearning" for autonomy and independence cries out, "I am somebody," "I can do things;" in brief, "I have value." None of us likes to feel inept. We are embarrassed or shamed when we cannot do what we attempt. For older adults, the problem is heightened by the memory of former skills. An elderly woman was actually quite flexible doing physical therapy exercises at 92. She could bend and touch her shins quite well. But she said, "I used to be able to touch my toes."

Each of us, at any age, needs to be cognizant of what we can do; each of us needs to rejoice in the simple skills of self-care and mobility. When we care for those with diminished skills, we need to comment and extend gratitude for the partial activities which help us: helping us put arms in sweater sleeves, extending limbs, holding objects—all of these are small, not entirely independent actions. Nevertheless, they are actions related to dressing or other care. They are little partnering acts that should be recognized. Even if they interfere, we need to recognize the attempt. "Thanks for helping. Let me . . . [do it this way]" at least conveys attention, gratitude, and recognition of effort.

This confirmation of identity and autonomy fits both Erikson's view of the centrality of identity and Kegan's (1982) description of the need for independence and agency. Kegan's description of a paradoxical relationship between the desire for independence and the desire for inclusion, however, remind us of a basic ambivalence in all of us. We sometimes want contradictory things. We seem to be seeking always, and our goals are ambiguous. Human beings are not perfect, and we do not perfectly know even what it is we seek. The next section specifies some of the needs that our residents may present at times of transition, and at the end of life.

Needs at the Time of Transition to the Facility

Persons who move to assisted-living facilities or nursing homes have, by definition, suffered a loss of what is familiar. The staff, supervisors, and administrators are new to them. New residents are uncertain that they will be taken care of. They may have had little choice in the decision to relocate. Staying at home, staying with what is familiar, is usually a person's first choice. This tendency is heightened when one feels some diminishment in energy, health, or skill, the very situations that cause a change in one's living situation to be beneficial.

The decision to transition is never without some loss. In these circumstances, one of the early goals must be to provide enough attention so that the new residents have a sense that they will find here in this new place "care that can be trusted." Secondly, that care should, to the extent possible, reflect the fact that the person maintains some control and autonomy. Attention to personal likes and dislikes, for example, in regard to food, clothing, choice of TV programs, and the like, will help the resident to feel this is a place where they can still be themselves (the identity idea again).

Another area where personality differences demonstrate the paradoxical needs of autonomy and belonging is the area of nonintrusion. Here we have the delicate balance of making sure residents' needs are met, and respecting privacy. Supervisors will need to provide oversight to staff regarding these individual differences. Extraverted residents will thrive when staff engage them often, even with little warning. Introverted residents will easily feel somewhat infringed upon, especially by extraverted staff, and especially when they are new to the facility. A related issue is that of roommates. A recent study found that the lack of privacy involved in having a roommate was one of the most pervasive difficulties mentioned by residents (Choi, Ransom, & Wyllie, 2008). These issues of individual preferences preview the next major section of this chapter, the ubiquity and importance of human differences.

Needs Related to Death and Dying

One of the issues for everyone involved in LTC—administration, family, staff and residents—is the ubiquitousness of death. We live in a culture that tends to hide or deny death. The reality that death is coming to everyone, that death is one of the very few certainties of life, cannot be easily disguised in a nursing home. Certainly, the fact that one comes to know and to have feelings for elderly clients leads to the loss that comes both with seeing their diminishment, and then with their loss through death. This can be an issue for both staff and residents. Dealing with the frequent presence of death could certainly be a topic for staff workshops given by psychologists. In addition, the role of the chaplain, or visiting clergy, becomes especially important when people are faced with the death of friends, spouses, or themselves. Opportunities for spiritual counseling should come early in the resident's stay at a nursing home. This will assist the elderly in having a natural and familiar relationship with someone with whom to discuss, wonder, and pray.

The other main suggestion for LTC facilities is the use of hospice programs. The need for hospice programs is crucial if nursing homes are to meet their missions and goals. In a very positive review of *The Handbook of Religion and Spirituality* (Paloutzian & Park, 2005), David Balk (2007) notes the relative lack of attention to death and dying. He explains that this may be due to the influence of positive psychology, an emphasis on "living well" rather than on "dying well." Balk also notes that religion sometimes plays a part in alleviating death anxiety. In any case, death is a central reality in all life, including life in nursing homes, and needs to be explicitly recognized by staff and administration. Only in that way will residents receive the help they need to cope with their last great task.

In the next section, we examine some of the stereotypes about the elderly, theories of aging, and how both of these may impact staff behavior. This section of the chapter revisits Erikson's (1968) task of old age and analyzes its relationship to a newer concept called *gerotranscendence*.

STEREOTYPES, DIVERSITY, AND EXPECTATIONS

The problem with discussing the elderly in general terms consists in the wide diversity among older adults. It is commonplace in psychology textbooks to summarize general findings about human behaviors and tendencies. It is also usual to accompany such generalizations with reminders that human beings vary on almost anything that can be measured. Although this principle of human variability is verbally accepted, it conflicts with the human tendency to stereotype people. Age stereotypes appear in descriptions of other ages; we talk about "the terrible 2s" and the moodiness and critical nature of teenagers. Stereotypes of the elderly, however, may be the most harmful of the age stereotypes for two reasons. One, if by old age we mean everyone from the 60s to death, we have the largest range of possible ages. Stereotypes, therefore, are bound to be drastically inaccurate in many cases. Though one cannot predict exactly how someone will be just by knowing that person is 15 or 20 years of age, we are even more likely to be in error when we try to predict what someone will be like just because the person is 70 or 80 years of age. Secondly, the stereotypes of the old (and the theories that describe them) are likely to be formulated by those in midlife, who have not yet been old. The following sections show that developmental theorists may bring the values of their part of the lifespan and impose them on the elderly.

Stereotypes of the Elderly

Stereotypes of the elderly fall into several categories. They are all examples of ageism, a tendency to make judgments about people or to restrict opportunities for people, based on age alone. The first type of stereotype about the elderly might be called benevolent ageism; it views the elderly as benign, wise, calm, and pious. The aged population is seen as good and kind. What, you may ask, is bad about this? Well, despite the positive nature of this bias, it brings with it unrealistic expectations. Senior citizens are not saints (at least not in the sense of perfect thought and action). The elderly may have admirable traits; they may have wisdom and understanding which come from their long experience, and the rest of us may benefit from such wisdom and reflection. Nevertheless, when expectations are unrealistically high, humanity will indirectly be denied and eventually people will react negatively when seniors turn out to be less than exemplars of wisdom and patience.

Two other stereotypes of the elderly need to be discussed. The first focuses on dependence and lack of ability. The decline in certain skills in the elderly evokes in us a feeling of pity, perhaps accompanied by a feeling of superiority. This emphasis on diminished skills and dependence exacerbates the idea that senior citizens are less than adult, and are in a state of misery. This stereotype does, however, motivate family and staff with a sense of the importance of their caregiving. Another stereotype, the idea that the elderly are cranky, mean, and stubborn, allows staff to personalize the frustrations and difficulties of giving care by providing a target on which such frustrations can be vented. All three of these stereotypes of the elderly (saintly and cute, dependent and helpless, mean and stubborn) are present in our society simultaneously. This means that we hold them covertly and use them at different times and in different circumstances.

Our stereotypes affect both our theories about old age and our behaviors. Our stereotypes and our behaviors and expectations are also influenced by theories about what *should* constitute "healthy coping in old age." In the general literature on ways of coping with old age, two conflicting theories were originally described as hypotheses about how a person could successfully adjust to old age: the disengagement theory and the activity theory. The disengagement theory suggested that every aging person should "cut back" and leave the fields of work, responsibility, and power to others who are ready to take control. In this theoretical approach, effectiveness and productivity are viewed as highly important values. This fits with the importance of work and productivity in the lives of middle-aged theorists, and the emphasis on these qualities in U.S. culture. It also exacerbates the tendency to lower expectations of the aging population, and perhaps even to infantilize them. The second theory, the activity theory, suggested that the healthy elder should stay as active as possible, and that healthy aging will thereby be enhanced. This approach implies that continuation of midlife activity is valued, and should be maintained as long as possible. What is the evidence for these conflicting theories, and what are the practical implications of these theories in LTC?

There is evidence that staying active assists healthy elderly living in the community to maintain physical and psychological health. For those whose health requires living in LTC, participating in activities, either those planned by the facility or those which the elder chooses and can carry out alone, are highly beneficial. Nevertheless, there are differences among human beings in their desire for interaction and types of interaction.

A relatively recent concept, *gerotranscendence*, has attempted to provide an alternative perspective to the activity theory. Tornstam (2005) suggests that the experience of those in middle age in Western culture causes them to value very highly productivity, independence, and effectiveness. As a result, those who do not work are thought to be weak, dependent, and lacking in value. We may feel disdain for those who do not work. However, we also have, in Western tradition, a belief that elders should be treated with respect and honor. The result is a view of the aging population as weak, but needing to be comforted and protected. We transform our condescension into "kind pity" or sometimes fond warmth for those who do not compare to us in strength and productivity. There may also be connotations of lesser intelligence and value, though these judgments would seldom be expressed or consciously entertained.

Tornstam's (2005) concept of gerotranscendence is based on the fact that certain cognitively healthy elderly are able to transcend the reality of their diminishment with peace, calm, acceptance, and wisdom. Assumed to occur among the very old, gerotranscendence suggests that some elderly become "less self-occupied and more altruistic . . .[and] more selective in their choices of social and other activities . . . They express a greater need for 'alone time' for thought and meditation" (McCloy, 2009, p. 1).

Given the variability that we know exists among the elderly, it is probably unwise to expect any one of these theories (activity, disengagement, or gerotranscendence) to be applicable in every case. Nevertheless, such theories, combined with the stereotypes discussed in this section, lead to certain behavioral tendencies. These tendencies may serve to diminish or to distort views of the aged population. When caregivers (administrators, staff, or family) come face to face with the diminishment of the elderly, they (and we who are writing and reading this text) are likely to react with a kind of *protectionism* and/or *denial*. Both of these reactions may be found in the elderly person as well.

By "protectionism," I mean an exaggerated reaction to truly diminished powers in one area with an assumption of disability in other skills or powers. An example from a family situation follows. A daughter realizes her mother's poor eyesight is keeping her from being able to maintain her checkbook. The elderly mother shows no signs of dementia. The daughter takes care of the mother's finances, but neglects to keep the mother informed of her banking situation. The daughter might say, "She doesn't need to worry about that," or "It's probably too much for her." However, this behavior on the daughter's part takes from the mother information and a sense of control. The other part of this reaction of minimizing the responsibilities of the elderly is related to their slower reaction time. Because in our culture we associate quickness with intelligence, we may be prone to dismiss the efforts of elders out of fear that they cannot do the task, or because of impatience. This kind of reaction removes opportunities from the elderly that are still appropriate, and may begin an unnecessary downward cycle; fewer activities may lead to decreased confidence, which leads to fewer activities, and so on.

The other reaction, a type of denial, is an exaggerated interest in keeping the elderly person doing everything he or she used to do. People in the United States are much more likely to embrace the activity theory than the disengagement theory. As young or middle-aged people, we value our own productiveness and energy, and assume that the elderly need to be as busy as they used to be (or as busy as we are). Indeed, residents who are active socially are less likely to feel isolated, and the activity directors in our facilities are charged with providing many opportunities for activities and socializing. There are several caveats that need to be made, however: (1) Every activity is not for every person, and (2) the need for social interaction will differ among residents.

These concerns relate to the basic psychological principle of human individuality or individual differences. People who never liked Bingo will not suddenly become enthusiasts. In addition, there are two other considerations. One is Tornstam's (2005) idea of gerotranscendence, which suggests that the old-old may be less willing to engage in superficial social interaction. A second theory, socioemotional selectivity, indicates that the old-old will narrow their social circles. They will be just as eager to interact with close friends and family, but will be uninterested in interacting with acquaintances or strangers (Carstensen, 1992).

These theories and the research which supports them suggest that administrators should help staff to understand the diversity of human preferences that are normal and healthy. Of course, encourage new residents to meet new people and try new activities. Of course, activity directors should seek to offer a diversity of activities that meet the social and physical needs of residents. But expect diversity among the elderly, and respect it.

Another Difference: How Do the Elderly Cope So Well?

Satisfaction with life is not completely correlated with material wealth (Diener & Seligman, 2004). Peak physiological functioning is not a guarantee of happiness either. Thus, it seems that we must hold a multifaceted view of humans, one which is sometimes evoked by the term *biopsychosocialspiritual*. This idea implies that each person has many facets and that a person should not be defined purely by his or her medical condition or disability. It also implies that happiness may not be directly related to physical functioning.

One of the conundrums of aging is the fact that the elderly are often happy and content despite experiencing many losses. This is particularly noticeable in the comparison of life satisfaction in the elderly with those in adolescence and young adulthood. In general, young adulthood is a time of peak physical health and functioning. Old age is often a time of declining physical powers and increases in illness and disease. Studies of life satisfaction have noted many life events that entail loss in the lives of the elderly: death of a spouse, serious illness and hospitalizations, and loss of close relationships through relocation or through the death of friends (Rapkin & Fischer, 1992). Despite these losses, there is some evidence that life satisfaction is higher in older adults than in younger adults. In the United States in particular, old age is associated with less satisfaction and happiness. Both the elderly and the young think youth is a happier time of life (Nagourney, 2006). However, when asked to describe *their own experience*, the ratings of the elderly were higher than those of younger people.

Other research reveals that emotional responses may differ when older and younger adults are compared (Charles & Carstensen, 2008; Fung & Carstensen, 2004; Nielsen, Knutson, & Carstensen, 2008). Elderly persons differ in their goals; their degree of life satisfaction may reflect the specific goals they choose, and their judgments of their ability to reach those goals (Fung & Carstensen, 2004). Some may want stability, safety, and a relative disengagement from activity. Others may desire maintaining their social network interactions at previous levels. Once again, the general principle of diversity is clear.

Overall, life satisfaction has been shown in several studies to be higher in the elderly than in younger people (Isaacowitz & Blanchard-Fields, 2012). In one study, participants were faced with negative appraisals of themselves by others; older and younger adults responded equally with sadness, but younger adults were more likely to respond with anger, and with negative attributions about the source of the comments (Charles & Carstensen, 2008). The fact that the older adults show greater life satisfaction in the face of difficulties may be related to greater capacity for coping in the elderly. It also may be related to different levels of acceptance—acceptance of self, acceptance of other people, and acceptance of the vicissitudes of life. This ability to accept reality, including its occasional negative conditions, may be part of the wisdom associated with the old. In addition, the higher ratings of satisfaction among the elderly may be related to different *levels of expectation*. Healthy elderly may be comparing themselves to what they would have expected in old age, and also may be comparing themselves to friends or relatives. They are liable to know aged peers who are more disabled or ill than they are. The paradox of satisfied elderly may be a function of realistic and downward comparison. That is, the young person may be looking upward at those who have more, while the satisfied elder is looking downward at those who have less, and experiencing gratitude. In these comparisons, the lives of the aged seem positive to them, and they are grateful for the abilities and circumstances they enjoy. Older adults may be more likely to focus on positive aspects of situations, avoiding a negativity bias found in younger adults (Nielsen et al., 2008).

Summary of Psychological Needs, Theories, and Stereotypes

This section has summarized the similarity of the elderly to all human beings in their need for respect, dignity, affirmation, affiliation, and control. It has also suggested that the biases that overvalue productive work and physical perfection may lead to negative stereotypes about the elderly. Even psychological theories may slant our expectations of the elderly, and cause us to narrow our expectations unfairly or to impose impossible standards on those in our care. Those with leadership in LTC facilities need to be aware of these possible pitfalls, first in themselves, and secondly (and perhaps more importantly) in their staff. Continued attention to the differences among residents, both through in-service training, and flexible policies will support a level of quality of life in our nursing homes. The next section of this chapter discusses the roles professional psychologists and other mental health workers can play in working with the aging population.

THE USE OF PSYCHOLOGISTS IN LONG-TERM CARE

Zarit and Knight (1996) report that psychotherapy can be very effective in treating the aged population, despite popular misconceptions that the elderly find it difficult to change. There is evidence that a great number of LTC residents present mental health problems of varying kinds; the greatest proportion, however, have a diagnosis of dementia. Dementia may be accompanied by other difficulties, including depression, anxiety, lack of impulse control, and inability to adapt to new surroundings.

One of the ways a psychologist's role differs in the nursing home setting from that of a private practice has to do with the need to provide consultation with staff. Spayd and Smyer (1996) delineate effective interventions with nursing staff, attending physicians, social workers, families, administrators, and recreational therapists.

Training of Psychologists

For the purposes of this chapter, a psychologist is a person educated in the understanding of human behavior and experience who has completed training and is licensed in the state in which he or she is working. *Psychologist* is a protected term in Pennsylvania and in many other states. This means that no one may use the term in offering his or her services who is not licensed as a psychologist by the state. The national organization of psychologists, the American Psychological Association (APA), has recommended for a long time that a doctoral degree be a prerequisite for licensure as a psychologist. This recommendation has gradually been broadly accepted. At the time of this writing, a bill mandating doctoral training for psychologists is being debated in West Virginia, the lone exception to the doctoral requirement for psychologists.

Those who have master's degrees and the requisite background may work as psychologists under the supervision of a licensed doctoral-level psychologist. Ordinarily a licensed psychologist has completed a 4-year doctoral degree in clinical or counseling psychology, has participated in numerous practica, has completed a year-long internship, and has amassed hundreds of hours of clinical experience before taking and passing a state licensing exam. Administrators need to know these general standards and to be sure those they hire meet these criteria.

When can a psychologist assist in LTC? The answer is both at the time of admission and later. How can psychologists assist? By assessment, by behavioral management consultation, and by providing training.

Assessment and Diagnosis

Psychologists can assess cognitive and behavioral functioning to ascertain the care needs of potential residents. Whether someone is suitable for assisted living, for regular placement in a nursing home, or for a specialized dementia unit is important for the organization as well as for residents and their families. Because of the large number of LTC residents with dementia, and the stereotypes related to dementia in the elderly, it is possible that mental illness that is not dementia may be overlooked by family and by admission personnel. The services of a psychologist will be especially useful in these cases which require differential diagnosis.

A recent article discussing guidelines for the evaluation of dementia and age-related cognitive decline (APA, 2011) quotes from an earlier set of guidelines. The article notes that although some healthy aging persons maintain the cognitive level of their earlier years, many of the aged experience a decline in memory and other cognitive processes that mirror physiological decline in other areas, for example, reaction time. This kind of decrease is called "age-related cognitive decline" and is not considered pathological. Psychologists, using neuropsychological tests and cognitive testing, are able to provide "the most effective differential diagnostic methods in discriminating pathophysiological dementia from age-related cognitive decline, cognitive difficulties that are depression related, and other related disorders" (as cited in APA, 2011, p. 2).

Overview of Dementias

Dementia refers to a chronic or persistent disorder of the mental processes caused by brain disease or injury and marked by memory disorders, personality changes, and impaired reasoning. The root of the word means "out of one's mind" and thus was synonymous with madness. It was at one time used to refer to any severe mental illness. Today, dementia refers to a loss of brain function that accompanies certain diseases. It is a set of symptoms that are severe enough to interfere with ordinary functioning. The functions that are affected may include memory, thinking, language, perception, and behavior (PubMed Health, 2011).

When cognitive or personality changes seem severe and irreversible, it is assumed that there is an underlying disease, such as Alzheimer's disease (AD) or Lewy body disease. In fact, there are changes in the brain that accompany aging itself. Some of those changes may affect brain functions, but some may not. Whether those changes are severe enough to allow the person to be classified as having a "disease" is a matter of some discernment. Today, dementia is used as a generic term for neurological changes that have functional consequences. Changes in memory in particular are noted as characteristic of dementia in the elderly.

The other term that has come to be used in common parlance as a synonym for dementia is *Alzheimer's disease*. This is a misuse of the term. Alzheimer's disease is one of several dementias. Severe memory loss and other cognitive changes in the elderly can be due to other diseases. These include vascular disease or strokes and Lewy body disease, the presence of abnormal protein structures in the brain. In addition, there are several other diseases that may be accompanied by memory loss and dementia; examples are Parkinson's disease, multiple sclerosis, Huntington's disease, Pick's disease, and progressive supranuclear palsy. Infections such as HIV/AIDS and Lyme disease may also cause changes in brain functioning.

Although the connotation of the term *dementia* suggests an irreversible pattern of cognitive deterioration, there may be brain dysfunctions that can be reversed if the underlying condition is treated. This is a particularly important point. Given the stereotypic assumption of cognitive decline with aging, changes in memory are often assumed to be due to Alzheimer's disease (AD) by medical personnel, family members, and nursing home staff. Examples of other sources of cognitive changes are brain tumors, metabolic changes (e.g., changes in levels of sodium, blood sugar, or calcium), low levels of Vitamin B_1 or B_{12}, and certain medicines. (For more information about metabolic changes, see PubMed Health, 2010.)

Accurate diagnosis is particularly important given the prognosis of Alzheimer's disease. The implication of AD or other dementias is that the condition will not be able to be reversed and often is progressive. However, depression may cause changes that appear to be signs of dementia. Other acute illnesses may mimic dementia. Deterioration due to fever, infection, or other treatable conditions is probably reversible. When cognitive changes occur rapidly (over a few days) the diagnosis often is that of delirium. The importance of this difference is related to the chance of recovery.

There may be changes in the behavior or personality of residents over time; residents may display psychotic symptoms and sudden onset of memory problems. A psychological assessment will help to distinguish dementia from delirium or from depression. Psychotic symptoms may also occur as a result of illnesses, such as urinary tract infections or pneumonia. In brief, the diagnostic role of the psychologist in dealing with the onset of memory, personality, and other cognitive changes is crucial in avoiding misdiagnosis, and in providing early and appropriate treatment and care.

Behavior Management

Psychologists may assist staff in dealing with depressed residents, acting out residents, and conflict in relationships. Staff may find it helpful to consult with a psychologist either when they find a particular resident difficult to work with, or when there is a general problem that could use some continuing education for all the staff. Psychologists may evaluate the environment to help the staff differentiate what particular actions or stimuli "set off" a resident, and what characteristics of rooms or hallways confuse residents and lead to outbursts or negativity. They may make suggestions about how to post things, and how to introduce new activities or medical procedures. An example of a simple suggestion: the posting of large "STOP" signs at the end of hallways is liable to trigger a conditioned response in some residents with dementia and decrease wandering off of a unit.

Psychologists may help to mediate conflicts between roommates, between staff and residents, between administration and family members, or among staff. In addition, psychologists may provide training for staff on various issues, including stress management workshops to help staff deal with burnout. Training may be offered for staff related to dealing with stroke patients, aphasic residents, clients with dementia, and the impact of the transition from living at home in the community to a facility.

The general concept of human variability, and different expectations of aging related to gender, ethnicity, culture, personality, and background, certainly could be a suitable topic for staff. The concept of gerotranscendence, discussed earlier in this chapter, might well be an important topic for staff-development sessions. Encouraging residents to socialize and take part in facility activities needs to be balanced with an understanding of an increased need for solitude in some, and an increasing self-transcendence and decreased interest in material things (Tornstam, 2005).

A Special Case of Behavior Management: Dealing with Residents with Dementias

The early part of this chapter deals with universal human needs such as identity, control, belonging, dignity, and respect. Other writers have agreed with those descriptions and added others, such as trust, bonding, occupation, and comfort (University of Bradford, 2011). It may appear that the quality of life these needs would provide are out of the realm of possibility for someone who suffers from advanced dementia. In addition, direct-care staff members have to deal with the deterioration of residents. They see firsthand the loss of abilities to communicate, remember, and understand. Though they may intend to provide the best care possible, they may be disheartened by the changes they see and the diminishment of pleasure in the lives of their charges.

One of the responsibilities of administrators is the training and orientation of new staff; even as this is being done, novice staff may be learning to give impersonal care as they emulate those already working in the facility. Burnout is a common phenomenon among direct-care workers in dementia units.

In an attempt to form practical strategies to provide high quality of care based on a person-valuing perspective, researchers at the University of Bradford in Great Britain have devised an approach called "dementia care mapping" (see www.brad.ac.uk/health/dementia/). This approach attempts to see the environment and interactions occurring in the facility from the point of view of residents, even if they have considerable deterioration from dementia.

In brief, dementia care mapping (DCM) provides a detailed method of observing the resident with dementia for engagement and affect. The process involves coding every 5 minutes for the activity the person is doing (e.g., eating), for the affect the person portrays (positive or negative mood), and for the degree to which the person seems engaged in the activity. Each interaction with a staff person is also coded. Interactions may be seen as personally enabling the resident, or in the contrary situation, undermining one of the person's needs, such as comfort, attachment, or inclusion. These interactions are called personal enhancers, or personal detractors, respectively. In the record of these observations, the names of staff are never noted. The emphasis is on the experience of the resident. Individual differences discussed earlier in this chapter are addressed by the review of the resident's behavior when the coding is complete. The person with dementia may be unable to say, "I don't want to be ignored while you're feeding me and talking to another person." Nevertheless, the data of mood changes and activities will signal staff about which types of interactions are most beneficial to this particular person at this stage of his or her dementia.

An advantage of this process of DCM is its promise of providing staff with the information they need to deliver quality care to clients with dementia. Listening to a resident talk about her family in an early stage of dementia may engage the client, and increase her quality of life. This behavior on the part of staff (listening) may be less useful as the disease progresses and speech skills decline. This routine decrement in skills may be discouraging to the direct-care provider: "The way I used to get her to smile no longer works." DCM will assist staff to change their own level of interaction with the client gradually as clients' abilities change. This method affords great opportunity to match clients' needs for identity, comfort, and attachment with clear, appropriate individualized planning that meets their needs.

SUMMARY

Human beings have a diversity of needs, including the need for respect and dignity, for confirmation of identity, and for both inclusion and independence. Despite their many losses, the elderly are often satisfied with life, especially if they are able to engage in downward comparison. Indeed, they may be more satisfied with their lives than young adults. However, it is essential that staff members at all levels of long-term care facilities are able to understand the psychological as well as physical needs of the elderly. It is the responsibility of administrators to provide both the atmosphere and the direction that will encourage staff to meet the needs of the elderly in their care. Ongoing training and consciousness raising about subtle and implicit stereotypes would be helpful for most people who work with the elderly. Administrators also should understand the role psychologists can play in meeting the needs of LTC residents, including the diagnosis of problems, the provision of behavior management strategies, and the training of staff to continue such strategies. An awareness of the individuality of each person we interact with, and an empirical and reflective approach on the part of caregivers, will help us to recognize needs in others, and to meet those needs in appropriate ways.

Discussion Questions

1. On a scale of "1" to "10," where would you rate your own thinking about the following theories? ("1" means you think this theory is false most of the time, and "10" means you think this theory is true most of the time.)

    _____ The disengagement theory

    _____ The activity theory

    _____ The gerotranscendence theory

    _____ Socioemotional selectivity theory

2. Can you think of an example in which your own needs for independence and your needs for inclusion were at odds with each other? Can you think of an example in which the needs of two people for inclusion and independence were at odds, and led to difficulties in a relationship? (The relationship can be of any kind—work, friendship, romantic relationship, marriage, etc.)

3. What life transitions have you experienced in the last 20 years? Which were the most challenging? Why? Which were fulfilling and/or exciting? Why?

4. What situations would make you, as an administrator, react according to a protectionism mindset? A denial mindset?

5. Can you think of examples in which someone reacted with age-related stereotypes? It may be a personal example, or you may use your creativity to imagine a hypothetical scenario.

6. The LTC facility is a multidimensional institution, with care being offered directly and indirectly by people of varying backgrounds and educations. In what ways might psychologists act as mediators when difficulties arise between and among the many actors in the nursing home situation?

7. What is an example of a recent stressful situation in your life? Analyze it in terms of the environmental demand (or challenge or threat), and in terms of your appraisal of the resources you have to deal with the demand. How does this experience change if you change your perception of the threat? How does it change if you vary your belief in your ability to handle it? What does this example teach regarding your work with staff, with elderly residents, or with families of residents?

8. The dementia care mapping system provides a clear way of matching the needs of patients with dementia with well planned interactions with staff. As an administrator, how can you analyze the needs of staff and residents in order to do your job better?

REFERENCES

American Psychological Association. (2011). Guidelines for the evaluation of dementia and age-related cognitive change. *American Psychologist, 67*(1), 1–9.

Balk, D. E. (2007). Life over death in the psychology of religion and spirituality. *Death Studies, 31,* 383–387.

Buetell, N. (2006). *Life satisfaction, a Sloan work and family encyclopedia entry.* Retrieved March 13, 2012, from http://workfamily.sas.upenn.edu/glossary/l/life-satisfaction-definitions.

Carter, B., & McGoldrick, M. (1999). *The expanded family life cycle: Individual, family, and social perspectives* (3rd ed.). Boston, MA: Allyn & Bacon.

Carstensen, L. L. (1992). Social and emotional patterns in adulthood: Support for socioemotional selectivity theory. *Psychology & Aging, 7,* 331–338.

Charles, S. T., & Carstensen, L. L. (2008). Unpleasant situations elicit different emotional responses in younger and older adults. *Psychology & Aging, 23,* 495–504.

Choi, N. G., Ransom, S., & Wyllie, R. J. (2008). Depression in older nursing home residents: The influence of nursing home environmental stressors, coping, and acceptance of group and individual therapy. *Aging and Mental Health, 12*(5), 536–547.

Diener, E., & Seligman, M. (2004). Toward an economy of well being. *Psychological Science in the Public Interest, 5*(1), 1–31.

Erikson, E. (1968). *Identity: Youth and Crisis.* New York: Norton.

Fung, H. H., & Carstensen, L. L. (2004). Motivational changes in response to blocked goals and foreshortened time: Testing alternatives to socioemotional selectivity theory. *Psychology & Aging, 19*, 68–78.

Isaacowitz, D. M., & Blanchard-Fields, F. (2012). Linking process and outcome in the study of emotion and aging. *Perspectives on Psychological Science, 7*(1), 3–17.

Kegan, R. (1982). *The evolving self: Problem and process in human development.* Cambridge, MA: Harvard University Press.

Lazarus, R. S. (1999). *Stress and emotion: A new synthesis.* New York: Springer.

McCloy, C. (2009). Gerotranscendence offers reflection, acceptance for elders. Retrieved March 15, 2012, from http://www.all-things-aging.com/2009/06/gerotranscendence-offers-reflection.html.

Nagourney, E. (2006, June 20). Aging: Getting older along with the bluebird of happiness. *New York Times*, p. 6.

Nielsen, L., Knutson, B., & Carstensen, L. L. (2008). Affect dynamics, affective forecasting, and aging. *Emotion, 8*(3), 318–330.

Paloutzian, R. F., & Park, C. L. (2005). *Handbook of the psychology of religion and spirituality.* New York: Guilford Press.

Peck, R. C. (1968). Psychological developments in the second half of life. In B. L. Neugarten, (Ed.), *Middle age and aging.* Chicago: University of Chicago Press.

PubMed Health. (2010). Dementia due to metabolic causes. Retrieved March 13, 2012, from http://www.ncbi.nlm.nih.gov/pubmedhealth/PMH0001703.

PubMed Health. (2011). Dementia. Retrieved March 13, 2012, from http://www.ncbi.nlm.nih.gov/pubmedhealth/PMH0001748.

Rapkin, B. D., & Fischer, K. (1992). Framing the construct of life satisfaction in terms of older adults' personal goals. *Psychology & Aging, 7*(1),138–149.

Spayd, C. S., & Smyer, M. A. (1996). Psychological interventions in nursing homes. In S. H. Zarit & B. G. Knight (Eds.), *A guide to psychotherapy and aging.* Washington, DC: American Psychological Association.

Tornstam, L. (2005). *Gerotranscendence.* New York: Springer.

University of Bradford. (2011). Cornerstones of person-centered dementia care. Retrieved March 13, 2012, from http://www.brad.ac.uk/health/dementia/dcm/CornerstonesofPerson-CentredDementiaCare.

Zarit, S. H., & Knight, B. G. (1996). Psychotherapy and aging: Multiple strategies, positive outcomes. In S. H. Zarit & B. G. Knight (Eds.), *A guide to psychotherapy and aging.* Washington, DC: American Psychological Association.

Chapter 10

Nurse Satisfaction in the Long-Term Dementia Care Environment: Fostering Relationships Between Administration, Nurses, Staff, and Residents

Barbara Parker-Bell, PsyD, ATR-BC, LPC

LEARNING OBJECTIVES

1. To identify sources of motivation and support that influence nurse engagement and satisfaction in the long-term dementia care environment

2. To identify sources of stress that may contribute to burnout symptoms and turnover of staff

3. To identify coping practices and systems of support that may help nurses manage stressors or reduce experiences of stress

4. To identify practices that support the value of relationships and quality of care

5. To identify interview and hiring strategies that support acquisition and maintenance of quality nurses for the long-term care geriatric environment

Key Terms

Burnout: A response to prolonged chronic, emotional, and interpersonal stressors on the job; in reaction, people with burnout experience exhaustion, cynicism, and detachment from the job, as well as a sense of ineffectiveness and lack of accomplishment (Maslach, Schaufeli, & Leiter, 2001)

Conservation of Resources: An alternative stress and coping model that examines the fit between personal resources and environmental resources and demands

Eden Alternative: A model for transforming nursing care centers from dehumanizing to humanizing environments through the integration of plants, pets, and children into the care environment (developed by Thomas, 1994)

Green House Concept: A model developed by Thomas (1994) to transform the long-term care environment through radical changes to facility design and organizational structures to create more homelike environments that blend into neighborhoods

Person-Environment Fit: Another coping theory that addresses demands and resources and includes concepts of supplies-values (SV) and demands-abilities (DA); SV fit refers to the match between personal values and supplies available in the environment to fulfill those values, and DA refers to the match between a person's abilities and the environmental demands; a mismatch between these factors may cause employee stress

Value of Relationship: A model developed by Parker-Bell (2008) that emphasizes the impact of nurses' strong motivation for relationship on nurse perceptions of job stress and satisfaction

Turnover: The rate at which an employer gains and loses employees. This rate may impact the quality of resident care and financial health of the long-term care setting

INTRODUCTION

Alzheimer's disease and related disorders (ADRD) affect more than 1.9 million Americans age 65 and older (Wisniewski et al., 2003). More often than not, family members in the home provide for their care (Goode, Haley, Roth, & Ford, 1998; Wisniewski et al., 2003; Wright, Litaker, Laraia, & DeAndrade, 2001). Yet, family members may also be compelled to seek professional care for their loved ones in a long-term care setting. In either setting, providing health care for a person with dementia may lead to caregiver distress or strain. This distress often results in reduced physical and emotional health of the home caregiver (Alspaugh, Stephens, Townsend, Zarit, & Greene 1999; Goode et al., 1998; Patterson & Grant, 2003; Pinquart & Sorenson,

2003). Consequently, numerous psychologists have designed and investigated interventions for caregivers that may help them learn how to use systematic problem-solving strategies and maintain personal wellness while in the caregiver role (Eisdorfer et al., 2003; Elliot, Shewchuk, & Richards, 2001; Houts, Nezu, Nezu, & Bucher, 1996).

Similarly, professional nurse caregivers may experience job stress or burnout when providing care in the long-term care setting (Debring, McCarty, & Lombardo, 2002; Goergen, 2001; Robison Porter, Wong, & Wild-Wesley, 2004) leading to turnover of nursing staff (Castle & Engberg, 2005). Significantly less attention has been paid to assess and remediate this issue (Rodney, 2000; Streim, 2005; Zimmerman, et al., 2005).

This chapter includes literature that describes and supports the need to examine professional caregiver challenges and successes. Topics examined include descriptions of Alzheimer's disease, disease progression and transitions in care, family and professional caregiver challenges, occupational stress and job satisfaction factors and theories, special considerations related to the occupation of nursing, and specific concerns related to professional dementia caregivers.

In addition, this chapter outlines results from a qualitative study that was conducted to gather direct information from professional caregivers. Nurses were interviewed regarding work-related stressors, aspects of their work that they find rewarding, and methods they utilize to cope or remain engaged in their work. Direct information from professional nurse caregivers is used to build theory regarding job satisfaction, stress, and coping processes. Supplementary literature and outcomes from an interview with a successful long-term care director of nursing support are also included to provide examples of strategies and methods that enhance physical and organizational environments.

CHALLENGES OF DEMENTIA

Alzheimer's Disease Challenges

To understand the dynamics of caring for a person with Alzheimer's disease, it is important to understand the nature of the care recipient's disease. According to the *Diagnostic and Statistical Manual of Mental Disorders* (*DSM-IV-TR*; American Psychiatric Association [APA], 2000), dementia of the Alzheimer's type is a gradual decline of cognitive functioning that is characterized by the development of memory impairment and at least two of the following disturbances: aphasia, apraxia, agnosia, or disturbances in executive functioning that significantly differ from the individual's previous higher level of functioning. In addition, individuals with Alzheimer's-related dementia may or may not present behavioral disturbances such as wandering or agitation.

Alzheimer's disease is a progressive illness. Feldman and Woodward (2005) identify the stages of Alzheimer's disease as mild cognitive impairment (a prodromal stage of the disease), mild Alzheimer's disease, moderate Alzheimer's disease, and severe Alzheimer's disease. In the early stage of mild Alzheimer's disease, affected individuals demonstrate forgetfulness, short-term memory loss, repetitive question asking, loss of hobbies and interests, difficulty completing tasks that require planning, and difficulty naming objects or recognize words. In the moderate stage of Alzheimer's disease, cognitive deficits increase (Feldman & Woodward, 2005); at this stage, the person with Alzheimer's may exhibit loss of remote memories, some incoherence in speech, poor comprehension of others' speech, incidences of getting lost, difficulty copying figures, delusions, depression, agitation, and insomnia (Corey-Bloom, 2004). In addition, those with moderate stage Alzheimer's disease may need assistance to complete their basic activities of daily living, such as bathing and toileting. At this stage, transitions in care often occur. Families may refer the family member to adult day care or nursing home services (Feldman & Woodward, 2005).

In the final, severe stage of Alzheimer's disease, complete institutional care is often needed. Individuals may become mute, often become extremely agitated, have severe difficulty with sleep patterns, lose basic motor skills, experience incontinence, and rely completely on others to complete their basic activities of daily living (Feldman & Woodward, 2005). Feldman and Woodward state that individuals live an average of 4–9 years after the initial diagnosis of Alzheimer's disease. Additionally, lifespan post-diagnosis appears related to age of onset. Those who are diagnosed at 65 or younger live an average of 8.3 years post-diagnosis. In contrast, a person who is diagnosed with Alzheimer's disease at 90 years old may expect to live approximately 3.4 years.

More recently, efforts have been made to reconsider and reclassify disorders such as Alzheimer's disease. Jeste et al. (2010) have proposed a new category, Neurocognitive Disorders, to replace the category that currently exists in the *DSM-IV-TR* (APA, 2000), Delirium, Dementia, Amnestic, and Other Geriatric Disorders. Three new syndromes are defined—delirium, major neurocognitive disorder, and minor neurocognitive disorder. It is important to note that a neurocognitive disorder as defined by Jeste et al. only applies to individuals who experience a decline from a level of functioning that they had been able to sustain previously. Depending on the severity of the symptoms, a person with Alzheimer's disease could be diagnosed with either major neurocognitive disorder or minor neurocognitive disorder. Areas of cognitive functioning that would be evaluated for severity and diagnostic purposes include complex attention, executive ability, learning and memory, language, visuoconstructional-perceptual ability, and social cognition. The construct of neurocognitive disorder is intended to be a broader category than the current dementia diagnostic category, which was modeled on the symptoms of Alzheimer's disease. The proposed category of neurocognitive disorder does not require that memory impairment symptoms associated with Alzheimer's disease be present for diagnosis. Final configurations of the new diagnostic categories will be included in the *DSM-V*. It will be important for administrators, professional caregivers, and family caregivers to be aware of the upcoming changes, as they will support accuracy of diagnosis, increased understanding of symptoms, and better formulation of care plans related to an individual's level of functioning.

Family Caregivers

Given the certain progression of debilitating cognitive and functional decline, it is easy to understand how family members may experience distress or strain during the years of caregiving. Numerous studies have been conducted to assess strain and ways to remediate the strain experienced (Alspaugh et al., 1999; Patterson & Grant, 2003; Pinquart & Sorenson, 2003; Schulz & Beach, 1999). Pinquart and Sorenson (2003) assert that there are five main areas of family caregiver challenges related to the care of someone with ADRD:

1. Dementia-related behavioral problems, disorientation, and shifts in personality
2. The increased need for supervision and lack of spare time
3. The isolation of the caregiver due to the care receiver's behavior problems
4. The limited ability of care receivers to express gratitude and the associated reduction in uplifts of caregiving
5. The progressive deterioration of the care receiver, which reduces or eliminates visible positive long-term effects of caregivers' engagement (p. 4)

While family caregivers are not the focus of this chapter, understanding the strain of family members may contribute to a broader understanding of concerns facing professional caregivers. It is important to note that family members or other informal caregivers care for approximately 75–80% of the individuals who experience ADRD (Boise, Heagerty, & Eskenazi,

1996). Therefore, over a million people living with dementia rely on family caregivers to provide adequate supervision and administration of most of healthcare interventions in a home setting.

How does caregiving for a person with dementia differ from caring for an elder without dementia? Pinquart and Sorenson (2003) conducted a meta-analysis of dementia caregiver literature. The authors considered measures of life satisfaction, positive affect scales, and single-item indicators related to happiness as indicators of subjective well-being. Among their findings, Pinquart and Sorenson discovered that dementia caregivers report significantly more stress and less self-efficacy when compared to caregivers who care for elderly family members without dementia. Unfortunately, between 46% and 83% of dementia caregivers are estimated to experience significant symptoms of depression (Alspaugh et al., 1999).

In addition to emotional distress, caregivers may also experience physical distress. Researchers Patterson and Grant (2003) found that spousal caregivers who experience strain relating to their dementia caregiver role show a higher rate of physical ailments, mild hypertension, and vulnerability to chronic illnesses than control groups. Both caregiver and noncaregiver control groups were selected from random samples stratified by age groups 65–74, 75–84, and over 85. Individuals were excluded from the study if they did not meet the requisite physical health conditions established by the researchers. After following participants for a period of 4 years, Schulz and Beach (1999) found that spousal caregivers were 63% more likely to succumb to life-threatening circumstances than the noncaregiver control group.

Transitions in Care Provision

Given the demands of caregiving and the impact it can have on caregiver health, many family caregivers will not be able to provide home-based care through the final stages of their loved ones' diseases. Fortunately, families have several care options, such as adult day care, assisted living, and nursing homes. Cohen-Mansfield and Wirtz (2007) found that families often seek community resources, such as an adult day care center, prior to admitting a loved one to a nursing home. Day care centers provide services for care recipients, such as cognitive stimulation, physical exercise, reminiscence, and opportunities for social interaction. Care recipients who attend adult day care participate in programming an average of two to three times per week.

Although adult day care usage relieves some of family members' burden, adult day care involvement does not delay or prevent care recipients' admission to nursing homes. In fact, care recipients who attend adult day care centers may be at a greater risk of nursing home admission (Zarit, Gaugler,

& Jarrot, 1999). Zarit et al. suggest that use of adult day care may help family members gradually relinquish control of care of their loved ones. Once some control of care is released to others, family members appear to feel more comfortable with accepting comprehensive levels of care provided by nursing homes.

In a related study, Cohen-Mansfield and Wirtz (2007) studied 201 adult day care clients with dementia to determine which characteristics of day care clients or their family members would predict nursing home admission. The authors found that increased caregiver perception of burden predicted nursing home admission. In addition, care recipient characteristics such as care recipients' race (Caucasian), age, additional psychiatric diagnoses, level of depressed affect, and agitation (wandering, nonaggressive verbal outbursts) predicted nursing home placement. Additionally, a care recipient that experienced diminished socialization with relatives or friends was more likely to be admitted to a nursing home.

Yaffe et al. (2002) also explored factors that may influence nursing home admission. Based on their study of more than 5,000 dementia patients living in the community, Yaffe et al. concluded that the decision to institutionalize a loved one with dementia is complex and based on both patient and caregiver characteristics. Specifically, Yaffe et al. identified patient characteristics that predicted nursing home admission included ethnicity. Hispanic and African American dementia patients were less likely to be admitted to nursing homes. In addition, patients with one or more dependencies in activities of daily living, high cognitive impairment, and one or more difficult behaviors were more likely to be admitted to nursing homes. Caregivers who were between the ages of 64 and 74, age 75 or older, and those who rated their burden highly were prone to relinquishing care responsibilities to a nursing facility. Over a period of 3 years, 52% of dementia patients in the study were admitted to nursing homes. Indeed, 91% of the dementia patients who were identified as having characteristics that put them at risk for admission experienced admission to a nursing home by the end of the 3-year study.

Similarly, Wilson et al. (2007) stated that most persons with dementia are eventually placed in a nursing home. To learn more about dementia and the use of adult day care and nursing home services, Wilson et al. studied more than 400 people with dementia living in the community. Some participants in the study were already enrolled in adult day care at the onset of the research. During the 4 years of the study, participants were assessed for cognitive function, physical disability, day care use, and nursing home placement. The mean age of research participants at the beginning of the study was 80.3 years.

Wilson et al. (2007) used several measures to assess participants' cognition. These measures included a mini-mental status examination, logical memory tests, verbal fluency tests, body part identification, digit span backward, and figural recognition tests. Overall, Wilson et al. discovered that most participants experienced a gradually accelerating rate of global cognitive decline. Those who used day care at the baseline of the study demonstrated a lower level of cognitive function at baseline. However, day care use did not appear to interact with participants' rates of cognitive decline.

During the study, 35.9% (n = 155) of the participants were placed in a nursing home. Nursing home placement was associated with a lower level of cognitive function on admission and an accelerated rate of cognitive decline once residence was established. Participants who were younger at the time of nursing home admission showed a slightly slower rate of accelerated decline than older participants. Additionally, those who had a greater use of adult day care prior to nursing home admission had less dramatic acceleration of decline after establishing nursing home residence. Wilson et al. conjectured that individuals who used day care prior to admission to the nursing home had an easier time adjusting to nursing home care. A better level of adjustment seemed to provide some protection from swifter functional decline.

These findings demonstrate that the challenges of caring for residents might accelerate after nursing home admission. Not only do people arrive at the nursing home with lower functioning and cognitive levels than they had in the community, but also their decline levels often increase rapidly when residence is established. Nurses may be distressed when they witness residents' rapid loss of function and increased dependence; nurses may also be distressed because of the rapidly accelerating care needs and demands they must satisfy.

Complexity of Nursing Home Residents

To better understand the professional caregivers who work in long-term care, it is important to understand some of the challenges they might encounter. For example, nursing home administrators have reported a high prevalence of both dementia and mental illness among residents since the 1980s (Streim, 2005). In fact, more people with mental illness currently live in nursing homes than in psychiatric facilities. The American Psychiatric Association Task Force on Nursing Homes and the Mentally Ill Elderly (1989) noted that movements to deinstitutionalize state mental hospitals caused an influx of the mentally ill elderly into nursing home settings during the 1970s and 1980s. Approximately half of the hospitalized chronically mentally ill elderly became nursing home residents. This shifted the cost of mental health care from the state hospital system to the Medicaid program. Administrators are motivated to send elderly mentally ill patients to nursing homes because nursing home care costs less than state hospital treatment. Others consider nursing homes to be "community-based" care and perceive them as preferable to hospitalization. Therefore, it is likely that elderly people with mental illness and cognitive/functional declines will continue to account for a substantial number of nursing home residents.

Regrettably, nursing facilities are often unprepared or ill equipped to provide psychosocial rehabilitation services for the elderly mentally ill. Nursing staff members have found themselves faced with "belligerent, explosive patients, wanderers, or patients whose problems are too many and too complex to be managed in a low intensity system" (American Psychiatric Association, p. 4). Admission of the elderly with mental illness or mental retardation to nursing homes has taxed the resources of facilities with limited psychiatric resources.

In the nursing home setting, the house physician will often prescribe any needed psychiatric medications. Consultation with a psychiatrist may be limited to times when funds are available and/or in cases where gross behavioral disturbances have been noted by staff. The American Psychiatric Association (1989) suggests consultation with a psychiatrist even when residents' symptoms are subtle and less problematic. Unfortunately, professional caregivers might not be informed about the subtle symptoms that precede more serious emotional or behavioral problems. When a psychiatrist is not used as a resource to assist residents or train staff, professional caregivers are often faced with serving complex residents without adequate preparation or support.

Increasing Age: Decreasing Function

As a whole, long-term care professionals currently serve an older, less functional population. Decker (2005) asserts that nursing home residents are significantly older at the time of admission than they have been in the past. According to the National Survey of Nursing Homes (NCHS: National Center for Health Statistics) in 1977, 35% of residents were older than 85 years, while in 1999, 47% of nursing home residents were older than 85 years. Decker also notes that residents arrive at nursing homes with greater limitations of self-care skills than in the past. For example, in 1977, 30% of nursing home residents could dress without assistance. In contrast, only 13% of residents could dress themselves in 1999, according to NCHS study statistics (Decker, 2005).

Decker attributes these phenomena to the availability of alternative community resources, such as assisted living centers. Individuals may transition from home care to assisted living prior to nursing home admission. Since other resources are available, long-term nursing care residence is increasingly reserved for those with greater medical needs and more severe functional impairment.

Zimmerman et al.'s (2005) findings confirm Decker's (2005) descriptions. Zimmerman et al. reported that 15–37% of individuals currently living in assisted living facilities present impairments in three or more core dependencies, such as dressing, eating, and transferring. In addition, 37–49% exhibit the behavioral symptoms of moderate to severe dementia. These percentages are even more significant when one considers that more than 1 million elders live in assisted living settings (Golant, 2004). Therefore, approximately 370,000 to 490,000 assisted living center residents with cognitive and functional declines will likely become residents in a nursing home in the very near future. Nursing home staff must be prepared for coping with and serving this impaired population.

NURSING CONCERNS

In long-term care settings, nurses express great concern about the complexity of the residents they serve. Most frequently, nurses complain about the aggressive behaviors they have to manage (Rodney, 2000). However, comparatively little research has been done to determine how professional caregivers are coping with the stress of their care recipients' decreasing cognitive functioning and behavioral disturbances (Streim, 2005; Zimmerman, et al., 2005).

Streim (2005) asserts that more research needs to be conducted regarding professional dementia caregivers' occupational stress and coping strategies. He emphasizes that research regarding professional dementia caregiving needs to address factors that are unique to paid professionals. Factors that differ between family caregivers and professional caregivers include the level of emotional attachment to the patient, incentives for caregiving, and the extent of direct contact time (due to shift work, availability of multiple caregivers).

The differences between these groups may influence the level and type of stress experienced. For example, a professional caregiver may not experience the same degree of grief a relative may experience when witnessing the person's functional decline. It is possible that less emotional attachment may buffer the professional from more intense grief processes. Even if the professional caregiver experiences stress regarding care situations, he or she may have more time than the family caregiver to attend to self-care activities. A family caregiver may often give up a vocation and/or recreation time to care for a family member. Unlike a family caregiver, a professional caregiver has a work-life and a home-life that are separate. He or she does not provide around-the-clock care to residents with dementia. The professional caregiver shares the responsibility of care with several other shifts of professionals who all experience time away from the caregiving relationship and setting.

Zimmerman et al. (2005) assert that professional caregivers may be faced with stressors that family members do not experience. These stressors may include workplace problems, such as low pay, coworker problems and conflicts, and lack of resources to complete their jobs in a satisfactory manner. Additionally, nurses may experience poor interaction with residents due to lack of knowledge of resident personality and characteristics prior to the onset of dementia. Compared to family members, nurses may have less investment in engaging and retaining a positive relationship with a difficult resident. Furthermore, some professionals may lack specific interest in dementia care, but do the work for monetary gain. Additionally, a professional caregiver may lack personal qualities or professional skills necessary to respond productively to resident demands. A professional may retain his or her job even after demonstrating a lackluster performance due to the administration's concern over staff shortages and hiring challenges. Consequently, Streim (2005) recommends that researchers examine work-related distress and job satisfaction instead of the constructs of depression and physical health frequently examined in the family caregiver population.

Stressors, Job Satisfaction, and Job Performance

Robison et al. (2004) examined the high levels of pressure experienced by dementia caregivers. They noted that frontline care staff in dementia units experienced difficulty in the several areas. For example, professional caregivers may have difficulty establishing appropriate relationships with care recipients due to their cognitive impairment. Caregivers may also have to endure being the target of care recipients' acting-out behaviors, including physical violence and verbal abuse. Unfortunately, verbal abuse and negative behaviors may include racially motivated biases against the care provider and verbal abuse such as racial slurs. Since many care recipients and direct care staff members have diverse racial and cultural backgrounds, this occurrence is sadly common. In addition, professionals may witness family neglect and be disheartened by lack of family involvement in care and support of the nursing home resident.

Goergen (2001) found that work-related stress in the nursing home has a significant negative impact on worker behaviors toward patients. In response to his questionnaire, 79% of the 79 professional caregivers participating in the study reported that they had abused or neglected a resident at least once during the previous 2 months. Sixty-six percent of the participants stated they had also witnessed at least one other worker abusing or neglecting a patient in that time period. Abuse consisted of yelling at the nursing home residents, calling them names, or intentional ignoring of needs that would result in resident discomfort, and inappropriate or nonprescribed use of physical restraints.

On the whole, the professional caregivers who responded to Goergen's (2001) survey attributed the abuse or neglect to staff shortages and time pressures. They stated that they experienced conflicts with residents because they expressed wishes for care and attention that they could not fulfill. They also reported that they felt they (professional caregivers) were victims of abuse from difficult residents and wanted to vent and/or take it out their frustrations on the residents.

It is important to note that Goergen's (2001) sample of nurses was a small sample of convenience. Therefore, research results cannot be assuredly generalized to a broader caregiver population. In this vein, Goergen addressed the challenge of finding research participants. Goergen stated that nursing homes with alleged abuse reports might refuse to participate in neglect/abuse studies, while quality care facilities might readily participate, impacting the research sample. Once questionnaires are distributed at a nursing home, a researcher cannot control who responds or refuses to complete the questionnaire. Professionals who provide quality care may respond more readily than nursing staff that have neglected or abused clients. Many professional caregivers are hesitant to consider and report their own neglectful abusive behavior, even if requested to do so in a confidential format, due to the discomfort of such disclosure.

Professional Caregiver Characteristics and Perceptions

In a different study, Zimmerman, et al. (2005) examined relationships between staff characteristics and attitudes, stress, and satisfaction. Measures utilized included approaches to dementia (Lintern, Woods, & Phair, 2000), work stress inventory (Schaefer & Moos, 1993), and staff experience with demented residents (Astrom, Norberg, Sandman, & Winblad, 1991). Zimmerman et al. reported that professional caregivers were more likely to report stress and job dissatisfaction if they had been working as a dementia caregiver for only 1–2 years. Zimmerman et al. suggest that limited quantity of experience and training may be increasing nurses' perceptions of stress. Consequently, the authors recommended that increased training and reassurance regarding skill competency be provided to new employees in the nursing home setting. In contrast, Hall (2004) found that nurses with less than 2 years' experience attributed their stress to low levels of pay. Nurses interviewed by Hall stated that salaries for nursing home care did not seem to match the intensity and importance of their responsibilities.

Zimmerman et al. (2005) noted that nurses' perceived adequacy in training and their age also impacted stress and satisfaction. Older workers reported less stress and more satisfaction than younger workers. In addition, the authors found that caregivers with higher educational levels and 1–2 years of experience were more likely to hold person-centered attitudes. This attitude focus reflects the professional caregiver's desire to treat the person with dementia as a person deserving respect and choices. Zimmerman et al. suggested that nurses who worked more than 2 years were vulnerable to losing a person-centered focus due to burnout. Yet, those who felt better about the quality of their training continued to express a more person-centered focus.

Similarly, Brodaty, Draper, and Low (2003) examined nursing home staff perceptions of residents with dementia, as well as job strain and job satisfaction. The authors surveyed 12 nursing homes and found that the most prevalent perceptions of residents with dementia were negative. Specifically, more than 88% of the staff agreed completely or partly with the following description of residents with dementia: Residents with dementia are anxious, unpredictable, lonely, frightened and vulnerable, and lacking control of their difficult behavior. Nursing home staff reported that they had the most difficulty coping with behavior that was unpredictable, aggressive, or hostile; behavior that showed evidence of poor control; or behavior that appeared stubborn, resistive, and deliberately difficult. Sixty-four percent of the nurses surveyed (n = 253) found these resident attributes to be difficult or quite difficult to cope with. Thirty percent of the nurses surveyed stated that they were not provided with enough opportunities at work to discuss the psychological stress of the job.

Consequently, Brodaty, Draper, and Low (2003) examined the possibility that negative perceptions about patients, strain, and job satisfaction were correlated. The authors found that nursing staff members who reported a more negative evaluation of patients' functioning levels reported less strain, but also reported less job satisfaction. No definitive explanation was provided as to why nursing staff experienced less strain when they perceived patients as being more impaired. However, Brodaty et al. suggested that nursing staff who perceived the clients' impairment as more difficult were also less involved in their work. The authors further hypothesized that a lower involvement in work resulted in lower job satisfaction. However, they did not address the impact of organizational characteristics or dynamics on strain and job satisfaction. Utilization of survey questions regarding organizational stressors might have helped Brodaty et al. understand and describe job satisfaction levels more clearly.

Job Rewards, Satisfaction, and Commitment

It is important to note that professional caregivers can identify positive aspects of providing care for residents with dementia. Brodaty et al. (2003) also found that the majority of staff members were able to describe positive aspects and outcomes of their work experience. To gather the caregivers' opinions, Brodaty et al. utilized the English version of the Swedish satisfaction with nursing care and work assessment scale (SNCW; Hallberg, Welander Hansson, & Axelsson, 1994). The SNCW presents statements about quality of care that can be endorsed partially and completely on a Likert scale. Ninety percent of staff agreed, at least in part, with statements relating to confidence that quality of care was being provided, the importance of empathy with the patient's experience, beliefs that adequate delivery of information to relatives was occurring, experience of enjoyment during work, and the quality of their workplace as a whole.

Debring, McCarty, and Lombardo (2002) acknowledged that nurses perceive the demands and rewards of dementia care in varied ways. They reviewed studies that sought to explain the links between demands and rewards in the field to job satisfaction, but found few studies that addressed worker motivation. Debring et al. determined that it would be important to know what factors motivated nursing staff to work as dementia caregivers and if the type of motivation, extrinsic or intrinsic, influenced job satisfaction and career commitment. In this situation, extrinsic motivation refers to rewards that come from agents outside the person, including pay, benefits, and status. Intrinsic rewards refer to gains experienced internally by the work, such as growth and a sense of identity.

In their study, Debring et al. (2002) hypothesized that extrinsic factors such as hours of work, hours of direct patient care, pay, and job role would relate to level of career commitment. They predicted that high levels of patient contact, low pay, and low job status, would relate to lower job commitment. In addition, they hypothesized that those who found intrinsic rewards from their work, including personal growth, desired contact with patients and their families, and a greater sense of professional identity would have greater job and career commitment. Furthermore, the authors proposed that those who reported higher levels of burden related to their work would have lower job and career commitment.

Debring et al. (2002) surveyed 77 professional caregivers working in residential special dementia care programs. The professional caregiver group included nursing assistants (n = 52), licensed practical nurses (LPNs; n = 37), registered nurses (RNs; n = 13) nurse administrators (n = 3), social workers (n = 4), and recreation therapists (n = 7). Sixty-five percent of the professionals worked in the dementia care residence 40 hours or more per week. Thirty-one percent (n = 24) reported 21–36 hours of patient contact per week; 35% (n = 27) reported 37 or more hours of patient contact per week. On average, research participants had been at their current jobs for 8 years and had been professional caregivers for 13 years. Debring et al. asked this group several questions about job commitment. Results showed that 50% of the professionals surveyed were thinking of looking for another job and 25% of the sample was actually looking for new work. Of those thinking or looking at other jobs, 56 professionals (75%) were planning to stay in dementia care. Most professional caregivers who were not committed to the dementia caregiver career reported low commitment to their jobs.

In regard to the research hypotheses outlined earlier, Debring et al. (2002) found that some caregivers did keep their jobs because of extrinsic factors, but this was not the case for the majority of workers. Only 18% (n = 14) stated they stayed in their jobs because of the pay. Another 30% of the professionals stated they stayed in their jobs because of provided benefits.

Concerning intrinsic factors, 22 nurses, 29% of the research participants, stated that they stayed in dementia care because of contact with the care recipients' families. Perhaps when caregivers had contact with family members, they felt supported in their work. Or perhaps when caregivers had opportunities to meet with a family, they began to regard the care recipient as a valued person and part of a caring family. In this scenario, the caregiver may apply a more person-centered approach and find greater satisfaction in the caregiver–care recipient relationship.

Additionally, 59 professionals, 77% of the dementia caregivers, stated that they stayed in the profession because of opportunities for learning and professional identity as a dementia specialist. According to the study (Debring et al., 2002) this type of intrinsic motivation was highly correlated with career commitment, but not with job commitment. Career committed caregivers may still seek other work sites with better work environments or demands. More information about what motivates professional caregivers to stay in dementia care may also be elicited in the interviews proposed by the study.

Patient Contact, Perception of Burden, and Job Satisfaction

The final conclusions of Debring et al.'s (2002) study relate to the caregivers' perception of their work being burdensome. A high score on the professional caregiver burden index (PCBI), a measure created to assess perception of burden in dementia caregivers, was positively correlated with caregivers' thoughts about quitting their jobs and careers in dementia care. Additionally, the authors found that caregivers who reported the greatest amount of direct contact time with residents identified the least amount of commitment to their jobs. The group with the most contact with residents also was the most likely group of caregivers to be actively looking for new jobs.

Professional caregivers in the nursing home range from nurse administrators, to RNs, to LPNs, to certified nurse assistants (CNAs). CNAs have both the greatest contact with nursing home residents with dementia and the greatest turnover rate among nursing home staff (American Health Care Association [AHCA], 2010). In the state of Pennsylvania, the 2008 turnover rate of CNAs was 53.8% annually. In other states, the CNA annual turnover rate has reached up to a rate of 93.25%, as demonstrated in Indiana. Sixteen states have significant CNA turnover rates that exceed 60%. Therefore, it is important to ask: Do other factors contribute to the certified nurse assistant turnover rate? Do some of the factors impacting CNAs also impact other ranks of professional caregivers in nursing homes?

Certified Nurse Assistants and Empowerment

Gruss, McCann, Edelman, and Farran (2004) wanted to understand the type of stressors the CNAs experienced when caring for residents, as well as variations in the nursing home setting that may contribute to stress and turnover. First, they identified two categories of nursing homes: empowered environments and nonempowered environments. Gruss et al. defined an empowered environment as a place of employment that cultivates employee perceptions of having control and having access to power within the organization. Empowering environments also provide access to resources, education, and information.

In their study, Gruss et al. compared CNAs' perceptions of job-related stress in empowered and nonempowered nursing home units. In the empowered environment, identified stressors pertained to resident issues, such as behavioral or mood challenges, or terminal illness of a resident. In the nonempowered unit, which mirrors more traditional nursing home units, the top stressors were job related. Job-related concerns included wages,

workload, and lack of staff. Gruss et al. found that turnover on the empowered unit was 0%, compared to the 13% turnover on the traditional unit.
More information is needed regarding the nursing staff's perception of the
nursing home work climate. Professional caregiver interviews may provide
additional descriptions of work climate factors that are impacting worker
commitment to nursing home work.

Turnover of Caregiver Staff

Debring et al.'s (2002) study demonstrated that the nursing home setting
is particularly vulnerable to the low commitment of its workers to stay on
the job for longer than 1 year. According to Castle and Engberg (2005), the
average 1-year turnover rate for nursing aides and LPNs in nursing facilities
is 85.8%. Registered nurses (nurses who completed a more extensive 4-year
degree) showed greater longevity on the job, as evidenced by a lower, but still
significant turnover rate of 54.4% in a 1-year period. Additionally, nurses
in long-term care administrative roles have been shown to demonstrate a
turnover rate of 40% or higher (Angelelli, Gifford, Shah, & Mor, 2001). The
AHCA's (2010) most recent survey suggests slightly more modest rates of
turnover. Nationally, nurses with administrative responsibilities turnover
at a rate of 34.2%, staff RNs at a rate of 42.8%, and LPNs at a rate of 43.0%.

In a study of New York State nursing homes, Angelelli et al. (2001) found
that a small percentage of nursing homes (3.6%) may experience a turnover
of three administrators in a calendar year. But more often, administrators
represent the most stable nursing force in the nursing home. After examining data spanning from 1991 to 1997, the authors found that the average
job tenure for the nursing home administrator was 4–5 years. However, in
Debring et al.'s (2002) study, 100% of the small number of administrators
($n = 3$) surveyed stated they were thinking about quitting their current jobs,
and a third of that group were actively looking for new positions.

Turnover Impact on Care Recipients

Because nursing home residents are highly dependent on professional caregivers for physical, mental, and social needs, high staff turnover may be
detrimental to care recipients' health. Knapp and Missiakoulis (1983) and
Staw (1980) proposed that turnover interferes with continuity of care in a
number of ways. They suggested that turnover increases the number of inex-
perienced workers, weakens standards of care, causes psychological distress
for some residents, provides additional expense to the facility that may lead
to diversion of funds from care, and increases workload on remaining staff.

Castle and Engberg (2005) studied data from 354 nursing homes in four states related to nursing home staffing. They randomly selected two states that had reported high turnover rates and two states that reported low turnover rates in the AHCA data from 2002. Subsequently, 526 nursing facilities in those states were randomly selected to receive questionnaires. After collecting and analyzing data, Castle and Engberg found that turnover and quality of care had little relationship at lower levels of turnover. However, as turnover increased, significant reduction in the quality of care was noted. For example, when turnover reached 50%, nursing homes reported increases in the following quality factors: adverse events requiring restraints, catheter use, contractures, and pressure ulcers. When occurrence of these factors is high, the quality of care is considered poor. To avert poor care of nursing home residents with dementia, further examination of professional caregivers' stressors, coping practices, job-coping options, job rewards, and satisfaction must occur.

NURSE STRESS AND DEMENTIA CARE

How do stress and coping processes unfold in the dementia care environment? Rodney (2000) looked at several factors in the stress appraisal and coping processes of nurses who work with people with dementia. Specifically, Rodney explored how patients' aggressive behavior impacted nurses' perception and experience of stress. Measures were utilized to assess care recipient aggression, hardiness of the nurses, nurse appraisal of threat and challenge, experience of stress, and the type of coping strategies utilized. Overall, the nurse participants appraised patient aggression as moderately threatening and challenging. However, Rodney found that a higher evaluation of patient aggression was associated with greater nurse distress. To alleviate distress or change the stressful situation, the nurses tended to use active coping responses. Rodney did not find correlations between hardiness, active coping, and reduced distress.

Berg and Welander Hansson (2000) examined the role of clinical supervision in nursing dementia care. Optimally, clinical supervision provides opportunity for support and distribution of information that will bolster active coping responses to stressful patient situations. To evaluate the effectiveness of supervision, Berg and Welander Hansson designed a qualitative study to gather narrative responses from nurses. Additionally, participants were asked to complete a survey about their perception of supervision's value. Each nurse interviewed was part of a systematic clinical supervision intervention. The supervision process was provided in two ways:

clinical group supervision and supervised individual nursing care–planning sessions.

In their findings, Berg and Welander Hansson (2000) discovered that nurses found value in both aspects of the supervision. The nurses identified helpful results of supervision to be: experience of respect from other nurses, increased knowledge of nursing care, improvement of skills and the ability to enact them in clinical situations, and a deeper understanding of their patients and their nursing needs. Additionally, the nurses found that the supervision helped them see their patients as unique human beings. As a result of recognizing their humanity, they felt better able to offer individualized and affectionate care. When they provided this new level of care, the nurses found that conflicts with care recipients were reduced. Finally, nurses valued a greater level of communication and support among peers as a result of the clinical group supervision. Unfortunately, some nurses noted an increase in stress due to their perceptions that they were being asked to be more responsible, or were faced with more demands after completing the supervision interventions.

When Work-Related Stress Leads to Burnout

What is burnout? Maslach, Schaufeli, and Leiter (2001) define burnout as a response to prolonged chronic emotional and interpersonal stressors on the job. In reaction, people with burnout experience exhaustion, cynicism, and detachment from the job, as well as a sense of ineffectiveness and lack of accomplishment. Maslach et al. clarify that burnout and its symptoms are only related to the work context, and therefore burnout is different from depression. Comparatively, depressive symptoms impact a person's life more globally. The authors also clarify that burnout is seen to manifest itself in people who have not previously evidenced psychopathology.

Furthermore, Maslach et al. (2001) state that burnout theories were developed to address the impact of interpersonal stressors that arose from care provider and care recipient relationships, but have expanded to include industrial and organizational psychology constructs and applications. In this regard, burnout research often looks at situational factors related to the work context. These factors pertain to quantitative job demands, such as too much work for available time, and qualitative job demands, such as role conflict and role ambiguity. Other studies have focused on demographic characteristics, such as age and marital status, as predictors of burnout. Lastly, relationships between burnout and personal characteristics of employees, for example, hardiness, have also been examined.

Maslach and Leiter (1997) developed a burnout model that focuses on the degree of match or mismatch between employees and the characteristics of their work environment. The work characteristics identified include workload, control, reward, community, fairness, and values. Maslach et al. (2001) suggest that values play a central mediating role in the employee and workplace match. In the work setting context, value mismatches often refer to ethical concerns or discrepancies in purported missions and organizational actions. Other mismatches, according to the authors, may be tolerated if other work rewards are present.

The authors (Maslach et al., 2001) also note that the study of burnout has been influenced by the study of human strengths and optimal functioning addressed in positive psychology literature. This influence can be seen in the augmentation of the burnout models with factors of engagement, involvement, and efficacy. Maslach et al. describe engagement as a "positive affective-motivational state of fulfillment in employees that is characterized by vigor, dedication, and absorption" (p. 19). Maslach et al. believe that a system that reflects a spectrum between burnout and engagement will have value for future research efforts. Maslach et al. (2001) suggest that values play a central mediating role in the employee and workplace match. In the work setting context, value mismatches often refer to ethical concerns or discrepancies in purported missions and organizational actions. Other mismatches, according to the author, may be tolerated if other work rewards are present.

Stress and Coping: The Conservation of Resources Theory

Zellars, Perrewe, Hochwarter, and Anderson's (2006) focus on positive affect as a resource is tied to conservation of resources (COR) theory (Hobfoll, 2001; Hobfoll & Lilly, 1993), an alternative model used in the study of stress and coping. COR theorists explain that resource loss is the most significant component in the stress process. Compared to appraisal theories of stress and coping, COR theorists put more emphasis on objective and cultural factors in the environment. Due to this emphasis, COR has been applied to organizational settings, health settings, and trauma situations. Yet, Hobfoll (2001) considers COR theory an integrative theory that takes into consideration both the environment and the individual within the environment. He emphasizes that the experience of stress is predominantly situated in social contexts, or alternatively, influenced by social consequences. Therefore, when examining stress from a resource-based theory, the researcher examines the fit between personal resources and environmental resources and demands.

When considering COR, it is important to understand the concept of *resources*. Hobfoll (2001) describes resources as "objects, personal characteristics, conditions, or energies" (p. 339). These factors may be valued independently, or valued because they assist the person in developing or maintaining important resources. Hobfoll asserts, "The basic tenet of COR theory is that individuals strive to obtain, retain, protect, and foster those things that they value" (p. 341). He states that stress occurs when individuals' resources are threatened with loss, are actually lost, or when individuals fail to gain resources after a significant investment of resources. Although he admits that appraisal can be used to assess loss, he argues that most resources can be objectively determined or are observable.

Hobfoll (2001) describes several principles that characterize COR theory. First, he asserts that resource loss has significantly more weight than resource gain. Accordingly, given equal amounts or resource loss and gain, loss would have more impact on the individual. Hobfoll and Lilly (1993) originally researched the loss-gain principle in a study of university students. Students completed the conservation of resources evaluation (COR-Evaluation; Hobfoll & Lilly, 1993) that includes a list of losses and gains related to personal, social, economic, and other areas. Subsequently, participants rated their identified losses and gains that occurred in the past year. Next, losses were rated on a Likert scale of 1 to 7, representing little loss to great loss, and little gain to great gain. Loss/gain factors were compared with anxiety and depression measures. Hobfoll and Lilly's results showed a correlation between losses and distress.

Gains appeared to reduce distress, but were secondary in impact when compared to loss.

Person-Environment Fit Theory

The person-environment fit (PE-Fit) theory is another coping theory that addresses demands and resources (Chemers, Hays, Rhodewalt, & Wysocki, 1985; Edwards, 1996; Takase, Maude, & Manias, 2005). Edwards (1996) explains that the PE-Fit theory is conceptually well suited to organizational settings because it represents cognitive appraisal as the subjective comparison of person to environment. In theory, subjective appraisals can be compared and distinguished from actual outcomes. Specifically, Edwards examines the supplies-values (SV) and demands-abilities (DA) versions of the PE-Fit theory.

The SV-Fit refers to the match between personal values and supplies available in the environment to fulfill those values (Edwards, 1996). According to Edwards, supplies can be objective or subjective. The area of interest to the researcher is to test the difference between perceived and desired amount of supplies or conditions. In general, strain occurs as supplies fall short of values. In contrast, excess supplies may reduce strain immediately, or may be conserved or carried over to fulfill other values. However, Edwards notes that excess supplies may, on occasion, hinder fulfillment of values. For example, too much attention and direction from a manager may inhibit the employee from acting as autonomously as he desires.

Demands-abilities (DA) fit refers to the match between a person's abilities and the environmental demands (Edwards, 1996). In this equation, abilities include skills, knowledge, time, and energy that can be utilized to meet the demands of the environment. On the other side of the equation, demands refer to the amount and type of requirements asked of a person. These demands may be objective and include things such as a specific work-day length, or may be something related to social concerns, such as expectations and norms. Edwards states that only when a person perceives demands is he or she vulnerable to the impact of those demands. Generally, DA-Fit theory suggests that when demands exceed abilities, strain may occur. Similar to supplies, abilities may be conserved and carried over to meet other demands. However, a great excess of abilities may reduce engagement in work, or allow skills to atrophy. Edwards suggests that a balance between demands and abilities is optimal.

Studies Related to Work-Related Person-Environment Fit

To test PE-Fit theory, Edwards (1996) conducted an empirical study of SV-Fit and DA-Fit with a master's level student population. The students were presented with specific tasks, asked to report on the evaluation of the tasks, and to complete measures of job dissatisfaction and tension. Based on the data gathered, the author found correlations between challenges in SV-Fit and job dissatisfaction. Additionally, Edwards found that challenges in the DA-Fit were correlated with tension.

Chemers et al. (1985) also examined the environment-fit theory as it pertained to work-related stress. Specifically, the authors aimed to determine if the administrators who were "in match" with their work environment experienced less stress than those who were "not in match." Chemers et al. assessed the match by looking at leadership (personality factors) and levels of situational control (environmental factors). Participants also completed questionnaires related to job stress, health, and days missed from work. Chemers et al. found that the interaction between leadership style and situational control predicted job stress. Particularly, when those "not in match" with the environment experienced low to moderate situational control, greater levels of distress were indicated.

Nurse Stress and Stress Outcomes

Edwards and Burnard (2003) systematically reviewed research regarding occupational stress and mental health nurses in order to identify overarching themes in the research. Particularly, the authors aimed to identify stressors, moderators, and outcomes related to stress, burnout, and job satisfaction. Based on a review of 70 relevant articles, the authors found three main sources of external stress for nurses. These sources of stress include: specific occupational stressors, major life events, and "hassles"—an accumulation of small daily stressors. For mental health nurses, the ability to work together with other nurses or supervisors appeared to be the most important determinant of work stress. Additionally, moderators in work stress were identified in the research as high levels of self-esteem, positive social support networks, hardiness, positive coping skills, mastery and personal control, emotional stability, and effective physiological release.

Edwards and Burnard (2003) also reviewed both positive and negative stress outcomes. Positive outcomes were related to psychological health and job satisfaction, and negative stress outcomes were related to psychological illness, burnout, and low job satisfaction. Work elements associated with positive stress outcomes included interesting work to do, responsibility at work, and good interpersonal relationships. In the studies reviewed, burnout was defined as a syndrome consisting of three dimensions: emotional exhaustion, depersonalization, and personal accomplishment measured by the Maslach Burnout Inventory (MBI; Maslach & Jackson, 1986). Predictors of burnout included intensity of occupational stress, changes in life stress, social support, and work setting characteristics.

Many effective stress management interventions were identified in the studies examined. Effective strategies to reduce stress or burnout included training in behavioral techniques, stress management and relaxation techniques, stress management workshops, training in psychosocial interventions, and clinical supervision. Unfortunately, Edwards and Burnard (2003) noted that broad implementation of these interventions has not occurred, or has not been documented in available literature.

Nurses, Occupational Stress, and Job Satisfaction

Fortunately, researchers have already begun examining elements that contribute to occupational stress and job satisfaction in the nursing profession (Fillion, Tremblay, Truchon, & Cote, 2007; Hayhurst, Saylor, & Stuenkel, 2005; Lu, Hong, While, & Barriball, 2006; Shader, Broome, Broome, West, & Nash, 2001; Takase, Maude, & Manias, 2005). Administrators have learned from experience and research, and have also offered recommendations to increase satisfaction and reduce turnover in the long-term care setting. Accorinti, Gilster, and Dalessandro (2000) suggested three underlying themes for care programs to be built upon in order to support quality care as well as support nurse and direct-care worker retention. The three guiding themes include "respect and recognition of the individual; staff inclusion in decision making and planning of resident care and for the organization; and maintaining a work environment dedication to education and support of staff" (Accorinti et al., p. 12). In addition to these themes, the authors advocate for six administrative practices. These six practices include, hiring right, providing appropriate orientation, holding routine staff meetings, using rewards frequently, creating a fun environment to work in, and conducting staff surveys.

The authors (Accorinti et al., 2000) explain that "hiring right" entails taking time with a prospective employee to explain the center's philosophy, as well as the job responsibilities involved in caring for people with dementia. In addition, a tour of the facility where the person can witness residents at various stages of dementia is important. A "good hire" buys into the philosophy of the center and clearly understands care needs and job expectations. When employees are hired, it is important to further orient them to the care center. For example, the authors recommend assigning new employees to a more experienced mentor to help the new hire succeed. Additionally, provision of frequent, ongoing education programs enhances new and more seasoned workers' skills and demonstrates that the staff is valued. Another way to show that staff members are valued is to conduct routine staff meetings where active discussions and problem solving related to concerns and issues occur. Freedom of expression and administrator consideration of staff ideas and recommendations are key factors for promoting a positive meeting and an overall positive working climate.

Administrators can also promote a positive work environment by noticing and rewarding staff performance and achievement (Accorinti et al., 2000). Monetary awards, recognition awards such as employee of the month, and simple thank-you notes from the administrative team for good work or helpful suggestions can be very motivating for employees. In addition, when administrators offer fun events such as celebrations and gatherings, these too can help lift spirits, ease tension, and build camaraderie. Finally, Accorinti et al. recommend asking staff directly about their work satisfaction using formal, anonymous surveys. The authors suggest that turnover may be reduced when survey responses are collected and well considered. Ultimately, employees who feel their ideas are heard and considered in the development of the work environment will feel more satisfied with their work

To explore these ideas more formally, this chapter author conducted research related to professional dementia caregiver work engagement and satisfaction specific to the long-term care environment. Consequently, the following research was designed and implemented.

EXPLORING PROFESSIONAL DEMENTIA CAREGIVERS' EXPERIENCES: A QUALITATIVE STUDY

Study Design

To explore and achieve an increased understanding of nurses' experiences in the context of long-term dementia care, this contributor (Parker-Bell, 2008) designed and conducted a qualitative study based on grounded theory processes. Nurses were interviewed and information was gathered to assist in identifying, developing, and relating concepts that help formulate theory about the coping process of dementia care nurses.

Participants

Professional dementia caregivers currently employed in a long-term care facility were the subjects for this study. Specifically, LPNs and RNs who have worked at least 6 consecutive months in a unit serving dementia patients were considered for participation. To be eligible for the study, nurses had to work full time on the first or second shift. Nurses of both genders between the ages of 32 and 61 were included. Participating nurses had sufficient time available to contribute 1 hour to the interview sessions.

Nurses working the overnight shift were excluded to assure that participants had maximum opportunities for interaction with residents. In addition, nurse administrators who did not have work duties on the unit were also excluded from the study. Finally, due to the investigator's language limitations, the participating nurses were required to be fluent in the English language.

Nurses were recruited from long-term care facilities in the Northeast Pennsylvania region. Letters describing the study were sent to long-term care settings, and a phone call to the chief administrator followed. Permission for recruitment of nursing staff was obtained from the long-term care facility administrators prior to the distribution of research announcements. Announcements were then provided to employees of facilities via mail or hand delivery to the participating facilities. Next, the researcher arranged visits to the facilities to schedule appointments with nurses. Names were taken and appointments were scheduled. Consent forms were provided for review as appointments were made, and the forms were signed prior to the interview/recording sessions.

Method

The qualitative research design was based on the grounded theory methods of Strauss and Corbin (1998). Participants were asked to complete a form regarding demographic information, and a short information form regarding the facility in which they work. After these tasks were completed, the interview was conducted with the participating nurse. After the interview, participants were asked to complete the positive affect and negative affect scale (PANAS; Watson, Clark, & Tellegen, 1988). This measure was included in the study process so that additional information about the study participants could be gathered. Interview questions focused on career satisfaction, stressors, and coping techniques utilized to sustain interest and engagement in work. Questions are listed and explained as follows.

1. *What are the best and worst aspects of a career in dementia care?*
   This question provided an avenue to open dialogue about nurses' appraisals of their career in dementia care. Asking about best and worst career characteristics simultaneously opened the interview without a particular bias toward positive or negative responses. The question focused on career as opposed to job in order to solicit descriptions about challenges in dementia care overall, versus specific job-/worksite-related concerns. Additionally, best and worst questions were designed to invite automatic responses that divulge previous assessments of situations or settings.

2. *Describe the most satisfying aspects of your work in dementia care.*
   Folkman and Moskowitz (2000) stated that positive and negative responses co-occur in stressful caregiving situations. In addition, Folkman and Moskowitz identified the need to gather more information on positive responses. This question provided the opportunity to explore the rewards of professional caregiver work and potential "uplifts," attributions of meaning, or experiences that buffer work-related stressors. In addition, responses to the question illuminated how individuals perceived their fit or match with dementia care work in the long-term care setting. Finally, the focus on positive aspects of dementia care prior to the focus on stressful

aspects of dementia care allowed for an easier beginning dialogue with research participants.

3. *What kind of stressors do you encounter as a professional dementia caregiver?*

   Responses to this question provided information about the scope of stressors that are experienced by professional nurse caregivers. Researchers have explored several categories of stressors, including organizational concerns, limited physical and human resources, role ambiguity, and care recipient challenges such as potential for violence. This question helped the researcher identify what types of stressors were most salient to the research participants.

4. *How do you cope with these stressors?*

   This question provided an opportunity for participants to identify specific coping strategies they used related to their specific experiences and work context. Having an open-ended question allowed nurses to identify how they coped with work-related stressors at work, home, or other settings. Gottlieb and Gignac (1996) explored family dementia caregiver coping strategies in different contexts and found that caregivers used different coping strategies related to different stressors and contexts.

   This question also illuminated nurses' appraisals of situations and coping responses to situations perceived as stressful. For example, nurses' description of experiences may have related to Billings and Moos's (1981) categories of coping that include: active cognitive, active behavioral, and avoidance strategies. In addition, responses to the question were explored to determine use of problem-focused coping, emotional-focused coping, and meaning-focused coping styles.

5. *Have you been, or are you burned out? If so, what have you thought, felt, or done to reduce or eliminate your experience of burnout?*

   This question allowed nurses to describe the impact that work-related stressors have had on their personal level of energy, attitude, engagement, and sense of accomplishment. Maslach, Schaufeli, and Leiter (2001) described burnout as a group of symptoms that impact energy, attitude, engagement, and the sense of accomplishment that occur as a result of work-related stressors. It was important to explore how nurses perceived their burnout status. If a nurse felt he or she has experienced burnout, it was also important to explore the means they utilized to reduce this feeling or experience.

6. *Tell me about the things that you do, and how you think and feel, in order to maintain your interest and engagement in dementia care.*

Maslach et al. (2001) identified a new emphasis in burnout research described as job engagement. According to Maslach et al., engagement is evidenced by energy, involvement, and self-efficacy, the opposites of the three main burnout dimensions—emotional exhaustion, cynicism, and reduced self-efficacy. This question provided an avenue for the researcher to determine if the nurses remain engaged in their work, and what aspects of the work helped them maintain that engagement.

7. *Of all your personal qualities and abilities, which do you find most important and/or helpful in your work as a professional dementia caregiver? Please describe.*

This question allowed the researcher to explore the concepts of person-environment fit. Specifically, nurses identified personal and professional qualities that they deemed necessary for successful work in dementia care. Takase, Maude, and Manias (2005) stated that nurses bring their particular attributes to the work situation, and they may or may not match the work environment. The authors asserted that it is important to explore the complex relationship between nurse attributes and the environment in order to answer questions about what leads to dissatisfaction and turnover.

Research Results: Interviews

For the purposes of this chapter, the qualitative results of the study are emphasized. Not surprisingly, it is the richness of the interviews, individually and collectively, that provides a window into the world of professional dementia care nurses. It is important for the organization that administrators have a greater understanding of nurse viewpoints and the processes that contribute to those viewpoints.

Descriptive Findings

Best and Worst of Dementia Care

According to many of the nurses interviewed, the best aspects of dementia care related to making meaningful contact with residents and seeing residents' moments of lucidity, calm, pleasure, or engagement. Some nurses described these moments as evidence of a quality of life. Others explained the occurrences as evidence of connection. Nadine described her version of the best, and identified the factors that may contribute to quality of life for residents. She stated,

> I think the best aspects are truly helping somebody with a better quality of life, to be able to understand, or help them understand, and come to establish a daily routine for them, and to make it is as close to home as possible.

According to several nurses, finding a way to understand or connect with residents was important to them. For example, Tammy described,

> The best is when you can get into their world, and you can sit there and you could be that sister that they're, you know, trying to get on the bus and go meet, or the daughter they haven't seen in a while and you look just like them, and you know, and they give you the kisses, and the hugs, and you know, you just get into their little world.

Several themes arose when nurses identified the worst aspects of dementia care.

Themes included watching residents decline, frustration with communication problems when the resident is confused, frustration with unreasonable expectations of family members, and the hectic pace and multiple demands of caring for the needs of many.

The most frequent response related to the decline of residents. Laura stated,

> It's hard to watch the progression. Some of them have been here a number of years when I came to work here, and some of them I admitted. And to watch the decline, the progression of the diseases from the time they [came] here to now, it hurts.

Communication problems also ranked as one of the worst aspects of dementia care. Tammy stated,

> I guess the worst is when you just can't get into that resident's head to help them, no matter how hard you try. You know, to try to be a family member, try to—you always have a little bit of their background and try to get back into their world and you just can't get into that world, and you get frustrated that you just can't help them when they are yelling out or crying, or [with] their actions, actions that you know they would normally you know, be horrified by.

Most Satisfying Aspects of Dementia Care

When nurses were asked to elaborate on the most satisfying aspects of dementia care, many continued to discuss the rewards of relationships with their residents. Nurses expressed satisfaction in taking care of and protecting people in need, enjoying interaction with residents, seeing positive results of interventions, and receiving comments of appreciation from residents or their families. For example, Tina explained that the most satisfying aspect of dementia care was being a part of the resident's life. She then talked about love,

> You love them just as much as you would if somebody remembered you. You still love them just as much, and you do get to be a part of their life and knowing that you're taking care of them the best way you can because they can't. So making sure that they're taken care of properly, because they don't know what is right or wrong . . . Just making sure they're safe in their environment.

It appears that work on a dementia care unit transcends literal job descriptions: "It's not just a med pass." Leslie explained,

> You bond with the patients, so it's kind of like your family. They look to you for answers, the guidance, love, because some of them don't have people that come in here, so you're their only family. It's just like a friendship kind of thing. It's not work.

Stressors Encountered in Dementia Care

More often, caregiver stressors and stressful experiences have been examined in research forums. Data from interviews with this study's participants confirmed that several types of work-related stressors exist. These types of stressors included staffing concerns, families who impose unrealistic expectations or demands, difficulties satisfying multiple demands due to limited resources, failure of or restrictions on interventions that are intended to reduce suffering, and the impact of communication problems on medical assessment and treatment.

Leslie asserted that the biggest stressor was "not enough staffing." Leslie stated this was a particular problem for the Alzheimer's unit, because, "First of all, other people don't like to come to our floor because they can't deal with dementia. Secondly, . . . our residents don't know them and may be unwilling to accept care from the less familiar staff." Leslie continued,

> A lot of people do not know how to care [for] Alzheimer's patients. They [staff] get frustrated and aggravated. And then it only makes

things worse, because the patients get frustrated and aggravated, and then you know, it's just a big mess.

The presence of regular staff was highly valued, particularly by nurses designated as team leaders or charge nurses. When there were only new staff members or staff members less trained in dementia care available, work was deemed more stressful because of the impact on residents. Fran, one of the team leaders, stated,

> Sometimes we get a lot of people who are not used to working over there
> . . . and they don't know the resident and they don't know the little tricks
> that you [use to] get them to accomplish things. You don't want to lose
> ground that you've made because you have new people taking over.

Nurses often described experiences that reflected an imbalance of demands and resources. Molly illustrated one example of a stressful situation where too many demands were involved:

> A patient [is] physically going downhill, and you have to put a lot of
> time and attention there and you are needed somewhere else. You're
> kind of splitting yourself up, and you know, dealing with a lot of things
> at one time.

She described herself in other situations as, "trying to be all over the place, listening for bells."

On a continual basis, nurses are exposed to sounds and behavioral symptoms of dementia that may be stressful. Nurses seemed to find the symptoms most stressful when they were unable to reduce the symptoms through intervention. Tammy describes this stressor clearly:

> The stressful times are when you try everything, anything, magazines,
> movies, newspapers, bringing them around, taking them for a walk,
> showing them different things, trying to do an activity with them, and
> just cannot get into their world. You get frustrated that there's some-
> thing that you should be [doing] and you just can't, you just can't pick
> that one piece out of the puzzle that could turn them, and it's just very
> frustrating.

Coping with Stressors

According to nurses' interviews, a variety of methods are utilized to cope with stressors associated with dementia care. However, the most frequently reported work-time response to stressors involved some version of giving oneself a time-out. Time-outs came in several forms, including taking a deep breath, removing oneself from the situation, walking down the hall, taking a break off the unit, and planning a day off.

Additionally, time-outs included stepping away from a challenging resident to spend a little time with a resident who was having a good day. Tammy provided this example,

> If I see another resident is having a really good day, I'll go over there and just start talking to them, just [do] activities with them, having ice cream with them if that's what they like, you know, just to get the stress level down. But, you will still concentrate on that person sitting across the room that you couldn't get through to, "Well, I couldn't get through to Mr. John, but Miss Gloria over here is just giving me a wonderful morning and you know, I'm not a miracle worker, but we try."

Many addressed attempting to soothe themselves by changing their thoughts about their work. Elaine said she started with a deep breath, and then she would tell herself a few things such as, "This is what I need to do, and . . . these people are relying on me . . . to overcome these hurdles and get done what I need to do." Or, "I don't have to live with these people, I am here 8 hours, and I am able to go home."

Instead of self-talk, some nurses talked to others to release emotions, to seek support, or to make requests for help or ideas. Sources of support included coworkers, supervisors, family members, or an employee assistance program representative. Pat stated,

> I vent to the managers, supervisor, or whoever's there, and then it's over because there is nothing they can do about it either . . . You explain to them that now you have four aides to take care of 60 people, and they'll tell you that they can't take care of it, and you say, "well okay, that's fine, then we're not doing this today, we're not doing that today" . . . let them know what's going on and then miraculously, usually somebody appears . . . It's just letting them know the situation whether they choose to do anything about it or not.

Laura sought support related to the death of a cherished resident. She remarked,

> You know that the nursing supervisor is with you, and maybe the unit secretary, and aids. They feel the same way and you're not embarrassed. You're one big family who is patting each other on the back, saying we'll get through it. It's okay. We did the best we could . . . They were comfortable and they weren't gasping. They were okay and we made them able to take that next journey.

Types of support received in response to emotional expression varied in different settings and circumstances.

Maintaining Engagement and Interest

As stated earlier, this group of nurses has been very successful in achieving longevity in long-term care dementia work. Therefore, they may be considered experts on maintaining interest and engagement. In contrast to burnout themes, participants seemed very willing to share this area of expertise. Themes that arose during interviews included a family-like love for the residents, joy in caring for others who may not have anyone else to care for them, working collaboratively with a team of coworkers, having a sense of pride in their identity as a nurturing person able to accomplish a difficult job, feeling comfortable with the job because it was a good fit, daily variety and learning opportunities, and setting very small goals each day that can be accomplished.

The most prominent theme was family-like love and commitment to residents. Tina stated,

> Well, like I said, I don't have grandparents, so I just think of them all as my grandparents, and that's [what] makes me want to come here and take care of them . . . I just feel that if I'm not here who's going to take care of them?

Jane spoke similarly, "I just want to make things better for them, just like you would for your own children, you want to make things better for them, you want to make them feel good." Gina confirmed,

> I love the residents. You form relationships with them, or with the family members, and I mean after 9 years, this is just like a second home. But I think what keeps people coming back is the relationships, the bonds they form.

Personal Qualities and Abilities Important for Dementia Care

When participants were asked about the important qualities and abilities they brought to dementia care, they emphasized several different themes. These themes included a commitment to residents, commitment to compassion and caring, knowledge of dementia and dementia interventions, and creativity in implementing interventions and assessments. Additionally, nurses spoke of needing a positive outlook, patience, flexibility, adaptability, assertiveness, organization skills, and an ability to maintain relationships with residents, coworkers, and families.

The most prevalent themes related to commitment to and compassion for the residents as people, not patients. Accordingly, responses to this question often reflected earlier responses that focused on loving residents in a family-like manner. Betty asserted,

> You have to love them. You can't work here and not love them. You know what I mean. It's like, all right, you're nice and I'm sure you're a wonderful person, however, you're *not one of us*. You gotta go. That's why I'm not in human resources.

Betty seems to suggest that if you can't love the residents, you will not last in dementia care. A nurse who cannot "love" may not choose to stay, or may be asked to leave.

Loving seemed to be an umbrella term for attitudes that nurses felt and projected while working with residents. Loving attitudes may encompass patience, understanding, and a positive outlook or approach. Betty's scenario demonstrates how a nurse may have to work to maintain a loving attitude in a care situation:

> You can't be like, "Oh, come on, I just took you to the toilet 10 minutes ago." It's like, "Oh, you have to get to the bathroom again? Oh, can you wait just a minute?" A lot of them go, "I want to go to the toilet, I want to go to the toilet, I want to go to the toilet." It's like that all up here. They don't have to go to the bathroom: They want to do something. And it's like, "Why don't you wait a minute, we're gonna go watch a movie." And it's like, "Oh, a movie?" and all of a sudden they don't have to go anymore. And it's like, "let's just go for a walk. We can do that." They didn't have to go to the bathroom at all, they just remembered . . . "Wait a second I have got to go to the bathroom."

Many nurses seemed very proud of the knowledge and creativity they utilize to assess and treat their residents. Elaine described her own strengths as follows: "my knowledge, my clinical skills, and my ability to adapt my clinical skills to this population, and to be creative with my assessments and things."

As a final note, it is important to mention that even when participants' responses to this question began with a list of their specific abilities, the topic of love would resurface. Laura provided an example of this process:

> I am over-organized . . . other than being ultra-organized like that, I can't say that it's a great understanding of these residents it's just—I truly love what I do . . . I think you really have to see it as something more than giving out medicines and assessments. You have to really

believe that you're making a difference in these people's lives. Or, if [it's] end of life and they're dying, you made them comfortable and you made them okay with going. You made it okay for them to let go. And you just have to really, really love what you do.

Themes and Processes

Two models were constructed to depict the themes, processes, and the core phenomenon of research findings. The first model, **Figure 10.1**, depicts the themes from each category: best of dementia care, worst of dementia care, most satisfying aspects of dementia care, stressors, coping strategies, and caregiver abilities and strengths. Included in each category are the themes that were most frequently endorsed by the participants.

In addition, a process is suggested and outlined. The process is explained as follows. Nurses who select a dementia care career in long-term care facilities appear to seek work that will provide opportunity for relationships because they value relationships. Nadine shared her experience of her brief departure from long-term care nursing and her subsequent return:

> I was in long-term care when I first came out of nursing, and then I thought this wasn't my calling, this was not what I wanted to do. And so I went into the operating room, and that experience led me right back here . . . [In the operating room] your patients don't talk to you, except for "Hi, I'm here for surgery," and I say, "Okay you'll be going to sleep now," and that's pretty much it. And it taught me a lot as far as biology goes and anatomy, and what to expect after surgery . . . So it gave me that, but not being able to please a person and see their reaction, and see their emotion—nope, not for me.

Given the valuing of relationship, nurses perceive the best and worst aspects of dementia care as relationship related. The best of dementia care becomes about seeing evidence of relationship; the worst is when resident decline interferes with that relationship, and the nurse must acknowledge the eventual death of the resident and therefore the end of the relationship. Similarly, nurses perceive the most satisfying aspects of dementia care as relating to bonding with residents, residents' families, and coworkers in a family-like manner. Bonding is experienced as satisfying because it fulfills their desire for relationship. In contrast, nurses appraise situations as stressful when demands challenge nurses' resources and interfere with their valued commitment to providing quality care to residents with dementia. When events are appraised as stressful, nurses may experience distress. However, nurses use their personal resources (abilities and traits) and coping strategies in order to maintain engagement and achieve caregiving/

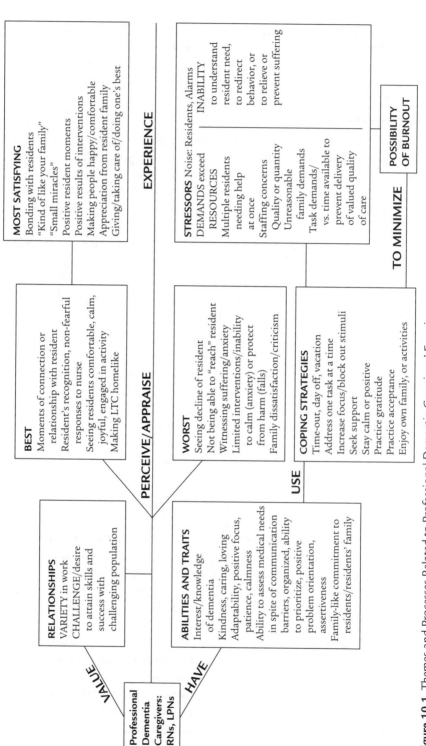

Figure 10.1 Themes and Processes Related to Professional Dementia Caregivers' Experiences

relationship goals. Burnout was seen as something to be avoided, as it also interfered with nurses' ability to maintain positive relationships with residents. Therefore, coping strategies were also utilized to minimize burnout.

Based on the interview data, this author developed the value of relationship model (**Figure 10.2**) to distill these factors even further. The value of relationship is depicted as the central theme to which all categories are connected. Professional dementia caregivers seek and value relationships with others. Therefore, the rewards of dementia care relate to the relationships that have been achieved, and perceived stressors relate to obstacles that interfere with honoring those relationships. Nurses mobilize their resources and coping strategies to protect the relationship and are frustrated when they are unable to do so. Consequently, nurses may be most satisfied with their job and career when the care environment is supportive of their relationship-focused goals.

Value of Relationship: Implications of Findings

In many different ways, this sample of successful long-term dementia care nurses communicated their investment in and commitment to their relationships with others, including residents, residents' families, and coworkers. Frequently, nurses' interviews contained the word "love." For example, nurses talked about loving residents like grandparents as well as loving the work. Some of the participants also described their work setting as a second home, and the people at that home as an extended family. Given these family-like feelings and commitment, many of these nurses were committed to a career in dementia care and had a strong, proud identity as a professional dementia caregiver.

If these nurses are an indicator, nurses who value relationships may be said to be a good fit for dementia care and would be good hires. This fit may help administrators in several ways. Nurses who value relationship seek relationship with residents, even if evidence of these relationships is slight. Nurses who value relationships will work hard to provide quality care to residents, and will be involved in the development of teams that can help them perform their work. When these relationships can be sustained, nurses are more satisfied with their work experience.

Subsequently, when nurses are satisfied, they may be more inclined to remain committed to their jobs. Job commitment may allow for a more consistent care team. As some of the nurses pointed out, consistency of a care team is essential, as residents often react to unfamiliar faces in negative ways. This type of resident reactivity tends to shift responsibilities to regular staff, even if temporary staff is present. If staff is more consistent, nurses

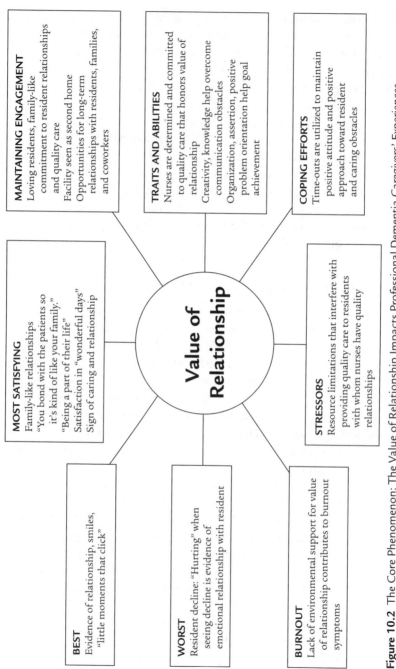

Figure 10.2 The Core Phenomenon: The Value of Relationship Impacts Professional Dementia Caregivers' Experiences

MAINTAINING ENGAGEMENT
Loving residents, family-like commitment to resident relationships and quality care
Facility seen as second home
Opportunities for long-term relationships with residents, families, and coworkers

TRAITS AND ABILITIES
Nurses are determined and committed to quality care that honors value of relationship
Creativity, knowledge help overcome communication obstacles
Organization, assertion, positive problem orientation help goal achievement

COPING EFFORTS
Time-outs are utilized to maintain positive attitude and positive approach toward resident and caring obstacles

MOST SATISFYING
Family-like relationships
"You bond with the patients so it's kind of like your family."
"Being a part of their life"
Satisfaction in "wonderful days"
Sign of caring and relationship

Value of Relationship

STRESSORS
Resource limitations that interfere with providing quality care to residents with whom nurses have quality relationships

BEST
Evidence of relationship, smiles, "little moments that click"

WORST
Resident decline: "Hurting" when seeing decline is evidence of emotional relationship with resident

BURNOUT
Lack of environmental support for value of relationship contributes to burnout symptoms

may experience less distress. Therefore, hiring, supporting, and retaining relationship-oriented nurses may reduce stress in the caring system.

Yet, hiring a relationship-oriented nurse is only the first step. The experienced nurses who were interviewed for this research study have had an average of 15 years of experience and knowledge to help them navigate the challenges of relationships and demands. New dementia care providers will likely need training and support to help them reach a comfortable place at negotiating relationships and demands. According to Zimmerman et al. (2005), professional caregivers are more likely to report stress and job dissatisfaction if they have worked in dementia care for 2 years or less.

To ready nurses for the long-term dementia care environment, nurses should be trained in ways to navigate the demands of the environment in addition to being educated about the medical aspects of dementia and the dementia disease process. To prevent or reduce stress, both new and seasoned dementia care providers may benefit from trainings related to team-building skills, social problem-solving skills, and time and stress management skills. Nurses should also be encouraged to maintain their personal family relationships and leisure activity schedules, as these may be important sources of support and stress reduction. In addition to a broad range of activities, many of the nurses in this study reported relying on time with their children or grandchildren to provide them with a playful counterpoint to end-of-life care.

Further, nurses would benefit from training or mentoring in ways to relate to people experiencing the symptoms of dementia. Participants in this study often described communication strategies that seemed to fall under the category of validation, an emotion-focused approach to negotiating relationships with residents. Validation therapy is an approach developed by Naomi Fell that aims to restore self-worth and reduce stress by validating the person's ties to the past (Cotelli, Calabria, & Zanetti, 2006). Verkaik, van Weert, and Francke (2005) suggested that there has been insufficient research to confirm validation as effective in reducing depressed, aggressive, and apathetic behaviors of dementia. They further stated that psychosocial methods for reducing behavioral symptoms in people with dementia have a very modest impact. Yet, nurses in this study frequently endorsed joining residents in reminiscing about their past to calm and engage them in a few moments of pleasure. If the validation intervention does not reduce symptoms, at least it does help the nurse find some way to relate to residents. This relating may help sustain the nurses' engagement and perhaps reduces nurse stress.

When administrators of a long-term care facility invest in hiring and retaining relationship-oriented staff, they begin to develop a supportive work environment. Yet, there are other factors that require attention as well. For example, nurses may feel more satisfied if environmental resources are in balance with their demands, or, at minimum, sufficient. Excessive tasks and care demands increase stress of nurses, because they cause nurses to struggle to achieve the high quality of care they expect to provide. Administration can foster a supportive environment by being sensitive to caring requirements and by fostering a supportive care team that will assist with problem solving and prioritizing when resources are low. In addition, a supportive care team can support nurses emotionally when they inevitably experience distress or grief over the decline or loss of a resident they have loved.

What is a supportive environment? While participants in this study were not asked to define a supportive work environment, they did provide some possible indicators for review. Eighty-one percent of the private care facility nurses endorsed that they experienced a supportive work environment. In addition, these nurses endorsed availability of other resources, such as required in-service trainings, an employee assistance plan, options for flex-time hours, benefit package choices, specialized environments, and availability of mentors and preceptors. In contrast, 100% of the county nurses did not perceive their work environment as supportive in terms of resources. The resources these nurses noted having available included only the required in-service trainings and benefit package choices. While administrators may not be able to provide some of these resources, they may be able to provide some key ingredients that will help build their caring team and a supportive environment for them.

In conclusion, participants in this study described the experience of dementia care as a process bound in the value of relationship. Satisfying aspects of dementia care were often detailed as connecting with and loving residents, or connecting with families and coworkers. Stressful aspects of dementia care often related to nurses' feeling that they could not protect residents from harm, reduce suffering, or engage them at the level of quality they desired. Nurses also noted that seeing residents decline, and ultimately losing them, was a very difficult part of the caring process.

One the whole, when nurses were distressed, they fought burnout valiantly. They relied on time-outs to help them stop and think. Stopping and thinking helped them rationally determine their next approach or intervention. In the work setting, nurses were creative problem solvers who worked hard to remain positive and organized in the face of multiple demands. Additionally, nurses found support or positive distraction from others at work or at home. Yet, most consistently, nurses attributed their continued interest and engagement in dementia care to having a deep family-like commitment to their residents.

CARE ALTERNATIVES THAT ENHANCE RELATIONSHIP AND QUALITY OF LIFE

Eden Alternative

Thus far, the focus of this chapter has been on the value of relationship for nurses in the long-term dementia care environment. What has not been discussed is the care environment itself. How do components of the care environment influence care engagement, care relationships, quality of care, and resident quality of life? One complaint often heard about long-term care settings is that care centers appear institutional and not homelike, and that institutional settings foster dehumanization and despair in the elderly clients. Thomas (1994) has been an advocate of changing the long-term care environment to a more homelike environment. His model of care is called the Eden Alternative. His goal was to "transform the nursing home from an institutionalized environment where older adults went to die into a human habitat where older people want to live" (Hinman & Heyl, 2002, p. 2). Hinman and Heyl described a process of "Edenizing" the care setting. This "Edenizing" process included introducing plants, animals, and children to the care environment with the hopes of bringing the elderly companionship to combat loneliness, as well as variety and spontaneity to counter boredom. The acts of giving care to plants, pets, and children were said to be a way to help elders counter feelings of helplessness.

Several studies have been conducted to determine the impact of the Eden Alternative on the long-term care environment (Coleman et al., 2002; Drew, 2005; Hinman & Heyl, 2002; Rosher & Robinson, 2005). Findings have demonstrated mixed results depending on the quantitative or qualitative measures and focus of the research. Coleman et al. (2002) did not find any positive effects of the Eden Alternative related to survival, infection rates, functional status, cognition, or nutritional status based on Minimum Data Set (MDS) measures. They also noted more termination of staff during the initial year of Eden Alternative implementation when compared to a control group traditional long-term care site. Given that many staff may have had difficulty with transition to a new model, the authors suggested that it may take more than 1 year to demonstrate improvements in functional status and employee retention. In terms of qualitative data, Coleman et al. noted that observations and staff comments in the Eden Alternative settings were positive. The authors quoted one worker who said, "The atmosphere here changed the day the animals came into the facility. . . . It has certainly changed the attitudes of the workers as well as the residents" (p. M426).

In contrast, Hinman and Heyl (2002) conducted a descriptive study based on grounded theory and a quasi-experimental study comparing functional ratings provided by the MDS related to physical, social, mental, and emotional domains before and after the implementation of the Eden Alternative approach. Additionally, the research investigators engaged in direct observation for 15 separate visits to log interactions between the residents and plants, animals, and children in the environment once they were incorporated into the environment. In this case, the research was also conducted 1 year after Eden Alternative implementation. The researchers observational and staff interview–based findings showed that the Eden-based environment stimulated function among residents particularly in the physical and social domains. However, MDS measures showed no significant functional changes in the selected areas within the 1-year timespan. It is important to note that this research does not approach the issue of how more positive social and physical engagement impacts staff morale and engagement. More research is needed to address this topic.

Fortunately, Rosher and Robinson (2005) have examined the impact of Eden Alternatives on those who may potentially work in long-term care with the elderly. These authors asked the question, "Does experience in a care center that operates with an Eden Alternative model improve nursing and medical students' attitudes regarding work with the geriatric population in long-term care?" Two groups of students, each including students of internal medicine, RN students, and LPN students were asked to complete the Health Professionals Beliefs and Opinions about Elders-Part A (HPBOE-Part A), a measure which specifically addresses attitudes toward elders receiving nursing home care. The research took place at a 150-bed nursing home in the Midwest. The first group of students completed the survey prior to the nursing home's implementation of the Eden Alternative. The second group of students who completed the survey was involved in the nursing home setting after nursing home staff had been trained and implemented Eden Alternative strategies. Results of the surveys indicated that the second group had significantly more positive attitudes toward elders in nursing homes. Additionally, the second group's exposure to the Eden Alternative implementation in the nursing home resulted in more nurses stating they would select a career with the elder population.

Finally, Rosher and Robinson (2005) noted that instructors of the students also seemed to have more positive attitudes about the care center when the Eden Alternative was applied:

> The instructors indicated that students had commented that the nursing-home environment was more homelike and much more pleasant than they had anticipated. The presence of the animals seemed to reduce the

students' stress level. The instructors themselves stated they felt more positive about this nursing home as a clinical site since the implementation of the Eden Alternative. They felt that the biggest factor was that staff were treating elders with much greater respect (p. 280).

Green House Concept

The Green House Concept (Rabig, Thomas, Kane, Cutler, & McAlilly, 2006) takes changing the environment to enhance quality of life in elder care to another level. Rabig et al. describe a Green House as "a purposely built residence ordinarily for 10 or fewer elders needing nursing home–level care" (p. 533). Green Houses are designed to meet nursing facility and licensure requirements and to make care provision within Medicaid rates possible. However, the physical plant and staffing culture are "radically transformed" to reduce the medical model/institutional feeling of the care setting. When placed in a neighborhood, the Green House is designed to blend into the neighborhood environment. Inside the home, the house resembles a living space for a large family, including a living room, large kitchen and dining room, and laundry area. All residents have private rooms with full baths. Health-monitoring systems were to be imbedded in each room and a larger "smart" house infrastructure with signals sent to workers on silent pagers regarding resident needs to reduce any institutional character.

Other characteristics of the Green House setting relate to organizational components. Key staff members are called Shahbazim, certified nurse assistants that receive 120 hours of additional training so they may take on additional responsibilities such as grocery shopping, cooking, cleaning, and personal care, and to serve as a resource person to the residents to assure their quality of life (Rabig et al., 2006). The supervising administrator role in this environment is known as a guide. The guide supervises the Shahbazim and the interdisciplinary clinical support team that visits, not resides in, the Green House environment. Physical structure, organizational structure, technology, and language all serve to inspire people to engage in more humane, family-like relationships instead of depersonalized professional ones. The expected outcomes of the Green House concept included a "measurably better quality of life, social involvement, and emotional well-being for residents, with no decline in outcomes" (p. 535). Residents' family members were also expected to feel less burdened and more pleased with care. Finally, Shahbazim were expected to know residents better than they may have known residents in traditional care settings, feel more empowered to impact positive change in the lives of residents, and to be more engaged and satisfied with work. A reduced rate of employee absenteeism and turnover was anticipated.

The Green House is more than an abstract concept. For example, four Green Houses were built in Tupelo, Mississippi in 2003. Rabig et al. (2006) have reported on some of the initial findings in regard to those houses. As the model came to life, the authors unexpectedly found that professional staff on the clinical team initially expressed resistance to the organizational model. However, training and engagement in the model appeared to alleviate early fears, and enthusiasm developed. When the authors compared staff absenteeism and turnover in the Green House to the same system's traditional nursing facilities, lower rates of absenteeism and turnover were found in the Green Houses. Given that Green House systems require radically different staff roles and responsibilities, the authors asserted that training to aid communication and team formation was an essential component of successful implementation. A longer term study to assess a variety of Green House outcomes has been initiated. Preliminary results seem to indicate that fostering authentic relationships between staff and residents in a more homelike setting brings value and comfort to elders' and workers' daily lives without risk of increased injury or cost.

SUMMARY

A long-term care culture that values relationships among nurses, residents, family members, professionals, paraprofessionals, other workers, and administrators of the care team supports quality care and quality of life. In the study reviewed, nurses consistently described the most satisfying aspects of their work as honoring their relationships with residents through quality care. Alternatively, nurses experienced the most frustration and distress when demands exceeded resources and they were unable to provide the person-centered quality care that they desired. This type of nurse distress can lead to job dissatisfaction, burnout, turnover, and diminished quality of care. Because the cost of ignoring the value of relationship is great, it behooves administrators to understand, validate, and support relationships as a key to achieving quality of care and quality of life goals.

Case Study

To highlight the learning concepts addressed in this chapter information, the Director of Nursing of a private long-term care center, Nurse M., was interviewed. Nurse M. has served as Director of Nursing for over 12 years at a privately owned, 180-bed care center with many units, including one specialized dementia unit. Units are called neighborhoods, and residents are involved in determining how their neighborhoods run. Pets and children are welcome at the care center. Day-to-day operations feature some elements of Eden Alternative philosophies, as well as other patient-centered philosophies of care. Nurse M.'s viewpoints mirror the research results that emphasize the importance of relationship in enhancing the quality of life for both workers and residents. The following information includes a summary and excerpts of this discussion. Key topics include interview techniques and management techniques that support hiring and maintaining nurse employees who are well suited for long-term gerontology care.

Interviewer: What questions do you ask prospective employees [nurses]?

Nurse M.:
1. What attracted you to this care center?
2. What is it about elders and geriatrics that makes you do this kind of work?
3. What is it that you find most rewarding when you are out in the trenches taking care of the elderly on a day-to-day basis?
4. What do you find most frustrating about working with the elderly on a day-to-day basis?
5. If there is one thing that you could change in the delivery of care, what would that be?
6. What are your two greatest qualities?
7. What are two areas that you would like to change or improve on?
8. What are your goals?

Interviewer: What are you looking for in potential employees?

Nurse M.: I am looking for a passion to serve. I believe life is based on relationships and I think that the value of life is found in the blessings of that relationship. The answer I am looking for is a story, a story of a relationship that they had with an elder, and how that relationship with the elder made a difference in the elder *and* how it made a difference to them. How did that relationship with the elder change [their] life and make [them] want to do this kind of work?

Interviewer: What do you feel it is important to tell potential employees [nurses]?

Nurse M.: We certainly aren't offering the highest salary and we certainly aren't offering the most glamorous job. I [tell] them right there that there are many other things that they could be doing in life that will give [them] better financial blessings that are not as demanding physically and emotionally. So, if you are not passionate and don't feel called to do this work and do not get rewarded by one smile, then it's not the place you want to be.

Interviewer: What do nurses find most rewarding?

Nurse M.: Eighty to ninety percent of the time, it would be just making a difference in one person's life. Seeing that smile and [receiving] that thank you gives them the intrinsic reward and allows them to grow deeper in their passion and [desire] to come back the next day.

Interviewer: What do nurses find most frustrating?

Nurse M.: When the nurse has a calling and passion to serve the elderly, usually the answer is not having enough time to [do] all that they need to do, or leaving and knowing that there was a lot more that could have done and didn't because there wasn't the time, or working with people who are not willing to help. Those are the answers I am looking for.

Interviewer: Why do you look for a sense of frustration related to time limitations?

Nurse M.: When you are caring for someone and when you are nurturing them, it is a very intimate experience. So, you are using all of your senses, and by doing that you are not only giving, but you are receiving. When you are pressured you start labeling people, "The hip down the hall needs this, the dementia person over there is going off again." We start to label and dehumanize the residents or patients. Once we do that, we have lost the relationship. We lost the part that was rewarding to us. So those are the answers I am looking for.

Interviewer: What positive qualities are you looking for potential employees to highlight and talk about?

Nurse M.: These are things I look for people to say: "I am compassionate. I am willing to learn. I am a very personable person. I don't get upset easily. I don't take it personally when a patient is having a difficult day. I realize my role is to help to change that, not to personalize that and take offense."

Interviewer: What areas of improvement are you looking for potential employees to speak about and why?

Nurse M.: Usually they will say, "Well, I wish I did not take things personally, I wish I didn't always feel like I had to please so that I could be a little firmer in my stand." Although it's something they would like to improve, in my eyes, it is certainly the quality of a caregiver to maybe be overly passionate, to be overly concerned, because it's the intimacy that creates a beautiful trusting relationship. I also look for a desire to advance their knowledge. If I hear that they think they know everything there is to know, then that's the time for them to go somewhere else. With fresh knowledge, experience, and wisdom, great things happen. I look for people with minds and hearts open to new knowledge.

Interviewer: Why is fostering a relationship with your potential employees important to you as director?

Nurse M.: Everyone comes from a story. Everyone comes with gifts and talents based on that story, as well as areas that might not be as positive as we would like. I believe in understanding that individual's story. When I am interviewing, that's my intimate time with this person. That's where I am learning who they are, as best I can. So that I, as their manager, can allow their gifts and talents to soar . . . but I will also know how to manage areas that may need to be improved upon.

You feel good when you are surrounded by the people who care about you and want you to do well, so that is my commitment to them [employees]. If I chose them to work here, then I feel a responsibility and obligation to make it the best experience I possibly can. It's like a mothering relationship. Just like we do for our children, we recognize gifts, talents. It is our responsibility to allow them to soar and to set the pathway so that they can move in the direction that they so choose. But, it's our encouragement and recognition of their gifts that allows them to be successful.

Interviewer: How do you facilitate the process of new employees becoming invested in relationships with you, coworkers, and residents?

Nurse M.: It begins at the beginning. You set the employee up to succeed. So, once you ask the right questions when you interview and find the passion to serve, the orientation process is very important. What a lot of centers do (healthcare centers, hospitals, nursing homes, assisted living centers) is throw the people on the floor because they need the body. Even if they are good, that's setting someone up for failure. You have an obligation to set this individual up to succeed, and to use the finances you are investing in this person wisely.

With the new employee, you start with mandatory orientation, but you also teach them about your culture. You talk about community. You talk about mushy stuff that they stay away from: gifts, talents, and relationships. [I provide] an open-door policy [and communicate] that there is nothing we can't talk about and work out together.

Interviewer: How does an administrator foster an overall culture of positive regard and excellent care?

Nurse M.: Nurses are inherently very altruistic. They will take on any responsibility you give them, but the worst thing you can do is give them all the responsibilities and no authority. I've been in my position for 12 years. That is unusual. But it is because of them [the nurses] that I am here. I want to be here. And because of me that [the nurses] are [working at the care center] and want to be there. There is that constant exchange; investing in education, setting someone up to succeed at the get-go, and truly not throwing them to the wolves allows them to be successful.

[Administrators] are often bottom-line driven. And what they don't get is, this is so key—that care drives dollars. If you provide the highest quality of care [you will be successful]. I am committed to care, to being a leader, because everyone in their interview told me that they want to do the very best they can. So I have the tools that they need: the right instruments, equipment, and support to provide the best care possible, and by doing, that you create a culture of excellence.

Every time I am presented with a situation where there's a conflict, I stop myself and say, what is the right thing for this resident? That is what I tell [the nurses] to do. The rest will fall into place. Administrators are afraid because, well, we don't have the money for that or we don't have this. You've got to stop that cycle because you are never going to move forward. You are always putting out fires. You have to make a commitment to provide the best care and do what's right for the employee. Do what's right for the residents. Do what is right for the center. [It establishes] the reputation of the care and the caregivers.

Interviewer: How do you address an employee who may be faltering or falling away from their original passion to serve?

Nurse M.: Well, it's like any relationship. You need a deeper understanding as to why you are witnessing what you are witnessing. Take them on the side quietly, and say, "you know, Mary, I noticed that you just don't seem like yourself. You've been short with some of the residents. Your peers say you have been very quiet, and that you have received several calls. Is everything all right?" That's when the story or tears flow. If I help her through this now, by providing support in ways that are needed, in 2 years when everyone is sick and no one can come in, and I call her, she will come. Understanding what it is [that is the problem] is at the core. So, everyone [new employees] is on a minimum of 1 month of orientation with a preceptor.

Interviewer: Why is fostering a relationship between employees and residents important to you as a director?

Nurse M.: The individual you are caring for has a story. If you don't become intimate with them [know their story] you can't provide the best care. So, I believe you need to be familiar. Employees may share some of their own stories and challenges with a resident. In response, a resident may give advice, and that intimacy gives them a purpose in life. It is a different style, but I learned that it is important for both the resident and the employee.

Interviewer: How do you help nurses get to know the residents (especially those with dementia)?

Nurse M.: We used to do a resident biography on admission. Now we discharge 70% of the residents, so getting the biography often times does not happen. When we have someone with dementia, stories are told and they are documented so that the caregivers don't have to wait for the obituary and say, "Wow, what an accomplished person, had I only known." So, we like to know their story.

An administrator may talk person-centered care, but if the administration is saying it's not important to get the story; it's not important to share the story; it's not important to implement the measures that have value and meaning to the story, then [person-centered care] isn't going to happen. It is going to bath, meals, and changing.

Interviewer: What final recommendations do you have for other nurse managers or administrators related to hiring or maintaining staff?

Nurse M.: Always take time to do the interview yourself and look for the passion to serve. Always make certain that there is an orientation and education process that begins with the hire and continues through the life of the employee working for you in a way that sets them up to succeed. So, you must have a strong orientation and education program with mentor or preceptors, whatever you choose to call them. Get to know the gifts and talents that individuals bring to the residents and to the center and then use those talents and gifts where they are best served.

Discussion Questions

1. What are the key values that motivate nurses to sustain positive engagement in their work with elders and others who experience symptoms of dementia?
2. What are some of the most significant obstacles to job-satisfaction for nurses working in dementia care?
3. How does job satisfaction impact burnout, turnover, and quality of care?
4. What are some of the ways administrators can create an environment of support that fosters relationships between residents, staff, and administration?

ADDITIONAL RESOURCES

Bauer, J. (2009). Green house concept combines best new thinking for elderly. *The Grand Rapids Press*. Retrieved March 25, 2012, from http://www. globalaging.org/elderrights/us/2009/green.htm.

Eden Alternative website: www.edenalt.org

Green House Concept website: www.ncbdc.org

REFERENCES

Accorinti, K. L., Gilster, S. D., & Dalessandro, J. L. (2000). Staff programs focus on reducing turnover. *Balance, 4,* 12–14, 28.

Alspaugh, M., Stephens, M., Townsend, A., Zarit, S., & Greene, R. (1999). Longitudinal patterns of risk for depression in dementia caregivers: Objective and subjective primary stress as predictors. *Psychology and Aging, 14,* 34–43.

American Health Care Association (AHCA). (2010). Results of the 2008 AHCA survey of nursing staff vacancy, retention and turnover in nursing homes. Retrieved March 24, 2012, from http://www.ahcancal.org/research_data/staffing/Documents/Retention_Vacancy_Turnover_Survey2008.pdf.

American Psychiatric Association (APA). (1989). *Nursing homes and the mentally ill: A report of the task force on nursing homes and the mentally ill elderly.* Washington, DC: Author.

American Psychiatric Association (APA). (2000). *Diagnostic and statistical manual of mental disorders (text revision).* Washington DC: Author.

Angelelli, J., Gifford, D., Shah, A., & Mor, V. (2001). External threats and nursing home administrator turnover. *Health Care Management Review, 26,* 52–62.

Astrom, S., Norberg, A., Sandman, P., & Winblad, B. (1991). Staff burnout in dementia care–relations to empathy and attitudes. *International Journal of Nursing Studies, 28,* 65–75.

Berg, A., & Welander Hansson, U. (2000). Dementia care nurses' experiences of systematic clinical group supervision and supervised planned nursing care. *Journal of Nursing Management, 8,* 357–368.

Billings, A., & Moos, R. H. (1981). The role of coping responses and social resources in attenuating the stress of life events. *Journal of Behavioral Medicine, 4,* 139–157.

Boise, L., Heagerty, B., & Eskenazi, L. (1996). Facing chronic illness: The family support model and its benefits. *Patient Education and Counseling, 27,* 75–84.

Brodaty, H., Draper, B., & Low, L. (2003). Nursing staff attitudes towards residents with dementia: Strain and satisfaction with work. *Journal of Advanced Nursing, 44,* 583–590.

Castle, N., & Engberg, J. (2005). Staff turnover and quality of care in nursing homes. *Medical Care, 43,* 616–626.

Chemers, M., Hays, R., Rhodewalt, F., & Wysocki, J. (1985). A person-environment analysis of job stress: A contingency model explanation. *Journal of Personality and Social Psychology, 49*, 628-635.

Cohen-Mansfield, J., & Wirtz, P. (2007). Characteristics of adult day care participants who enter a nursing home. *Psychology and Aging, 22*, 354-360.

Coleman, M. T., Looney, S., O'Brien, J., Ziegler, C., Pastorino, C., & Turner, C. (2002). The Eden alternative: Findings after 1 year of implementation. *Journal of Gerontology: Medical Sciences, 57a*, M422-M427.

Corey-Bloom, J. (2004). Alzheimer's disease. *Continuum, 10*, 29-57.

Cotelli, M., Calabria, M., & Zenetti, O. (2006). Cognitive rehabilitation in Alzheimer's disease. *Aging Clinical and Experimental Research, 18*, 141-143

Debring, C., McCarty, E., & Lombardo, N. (2002). Professional caregivers for patients with dementia: Predictors of job and career commitment. *American Journal of Alzheimer's Disease and Other Dementias, 17*, 357-366.

Decker, F. H. (2005). *Nursing homes, 1977-99: What has changed, what has not?* Hyattsville, MD: National Center for Health Statistics.

Drew, J. (2005). Making the long-term care environment more like home. The Eden Alternative: What families want and why. In J. E. Gaugler (Ed.), *Promoting family involvement in long-term care settings: A guide to programs that work* (pp. 71-89). Baltimore, MD: Health Professions Press.

Edwards, J. (1996). An examination of competing versions of the person-environment fit approach to stress. *Academy of Management Journal, 39*, 292-339.

Edwards, D., & Burnard, P. (2003). A systematic review of stress and stress management intervention for mental health nurses. *Journal of Advanced Nursing, 42*, 169-200.

Eisdorfer, C., Czaj, S., Loewenstein, D., Ruber, M., Arguelles, S., Mitrani, V., & Szapocznik, J. (2003). The effect of a family therapy and technology-based intervention on caregiver depression. *The Gerontologist, 43*, 521-531.

Elliot, T., Shewchuk, R., & Richards, J. S. (2001). Family caregiver social problem-solving abilities and role adjustment during the initial year of the caregiving role. *Journal of Counseling Psychology, 48*, 223-232.

Feldman, H., & Woodward, M. (2005). The staging and assessment of moderate to severe Alzheimer Disease. *Neurology, 65*, S10-S17.

Fillion, L., Tremblay, M., Truchon, M., & Cote, D. (2007). Job satisfaction and emotional distress among nurses providing palliative care: Empirical evidence for an integrative occupational stress model. *International Journal of Stress Management, 14*, 1-25.

Folkman, S., & Moskowitz, J. (2000). Coping: Pitfalls and promise. *Annual Review of Psychology, 55*, 745-774.

Golant, M. (2004). Do impaired older persons with health care needs occupy U.S. assisted living facilities? An analysis of six national studies. *Journal of Gerontology, 59*, 569-579.

Goode, K., Haley, W., Roth, D., & Ford, G. (1998). Predicting longitudinal changes in caregiver physical and mental health a stress process model. *Health Psychology, 17,* 190–198.

Goergen, T. (2001). Stress, conflict, elder abuse and neglect in German nursing homes: A pilot study among professional caregivers. *Journal of Elder Abuse & Neglect, 13,* 1–26.

Gottlieb, B., & Gignac, M. (1996). Content and domain specificity of coping among family caregivers of persons with dementia. *Journal of Aging Studies, 10,* 137–155.

Gruss, V., McCann, J., Edelman, P., & Farran, C. (2004). Job stress among nursing home certified nursing assistants: Comparison of empowered and nonempowered work environments. *Alzheimer's Care Quarterly, 5,* 207–216.

Hall, D. (2004). Work-related stress of registered nurses in a hospital setting. *Journal for Nurses in Staff Development, 20,* 6–14.

Hallberg, I., Welander Hansson, U., & Axelsson, K. (1994). Satisfaction with nursing care and work during a year of clinical supervision and individualized care: Comparison between two wards for the care of severely demented patients. *Journal of Nursing Management, 1,* 297–307.

Hayhurst, A., Saylor, C., & Stuenkel, D. (2005). Work environmental factors and retention of nurses. *Journal of Nursing Care Quality, 20,* 283–288.

Hinman, M., & Heyl, D. (2002). Influence of the Eden alternative on the functional status of nursing home residents. *Physical & Occupational Therapy in Geriatrics, 20,* 1–12.

Hobfoll, S. (2001). The influence of culture, community, and the nested-self in the stress process: Advancing conservation of resources theory. *Applied Psychology: An International Review, 50,* 337–421.

Hobfoll, S., & Lilly, R. S. (1993). Resource conservation as a strategy for community psychology. *Journal of Community Psychology, 21,* 128–148.

Houts, P., Nezu, A., Nezu, C., & Bucher, J. (1996). The prepared family caregiver: A problem-solving approach to family caregiver education. *Patient Education and Counseling, 27,* 63–73.

Jeste, D., Blacker, D., Blazer, D., Gangui, M., Grant, I., Paulsen, J., Peterson, R., & Sachdeve, P. (2010). Neurocognitive disorders: A proposal from the DSM-5 work group. American Psychiatric Association. Retrieved March 26, 2012, from http://www.dsm5.org/Proposed%20Revision%20Attachments/APA%20 Neurocognitive%20Disorders%20Proposal%20for%20DSM-5.pdf.

Knapp, M., & Missiakoulis, S. (1983). Predicting turnover rates among the staff of English and Welsh old people's homes. *Social Science Medicine, 17,* 29–36.

Lintern, T., Woods, B., & Phair, L. (2000). Training is not enough to change care practice. *Journal of Dementia Care, 8,* 15–17.

Maslach, C., & Jackson, S. E. (1986). *The Maslach burnout inventory* (Research ed.). Palo Alto, CA: Consulting Psychologists Press.

Maslach, C., & Leiter, M. P. (1997). *The truth about burnout: How organizations cause personal stress and what to do about it.* San Francisco: Jossey-Bass.

Maslach, C., Schaufeli, W., & Leiter, P. (2001). Job burnout. *Annual Reviews, 52,* 397–422.

Parker-Bell, B. (2008). Exploring professional dementia caregivers' experiences. (Unpublished doctoral dissertation). Philadelphia College of Osteopathic Medicine, Philadelphia, PA.

Patterson, T., & Grant, I. (2003). Interventions for caregiving in dementia: Physical outcomes. *Current Opinion in Psychiatry, 16,* 629–633.

Pinquart, M., & Sorenson, S. (2003). Differences between caregivers and noncaregivers in psychological health and physical health: A meta-analysis. *Psychology and Aging, 18,* 250–267.

Rabig, J., Thomas, W., Kane, R. A., Cutler, L. J., & McAlilly, S. (2006). Radical redesign of nursing homes: Applying the green house concept in Tupelo, Mississippi. *The Gerontologist, 46,* 533–539.

Robison, J., Porter, M., Wong, M., & Wild-Wesley, R. (2004). Frontline staff job satisfaction in nursing home dementia care units. *The Gerontologist, 44,* 461.

Rodney, V. (2000). Nurse stress associated with aggression in people with dementia: Its relationship to hardiness, cognitive appraisal and coping. *Journal of Advanced Nursing, 31,* 172–180.

Rosher, R. B., & Robinson, S. (2005). The Eden alternative: Impact on student attitudes. *Educational Gerontology, 31,* 273–282.

Schaefer, J. A., & Moos, R. H. (1993). Relationship, tasks, stressors and work climate on long-term care staff's morale and functioning. *Research in Nursing & Health, 19,* 63–73.

Shader, K., Broome, M., Broome, C., West, M., & Nash, M. (2001). Factors influencing satisfaction and anticipated turnover for nurses in an academic medical center. *Journal of Nursing Administration, 31,* 210–216.

Staw, B. (1980). The consequences of turnover. *Journal of Occupational Behavior, 1,* 253–273.

Strauss, A., & Corbin, J. (1998). *Basics of qualitative research: Techniques and procedures for developing grounded theory* (2nd ed.). Thousand Oaks, CA: Sage.

Schulz, R., & Beach, S. (1999). Caregiving as a risk factor for mortality. The Caregiver Health Effects Study. *Journal of the American Medical Association, 282,* 2215–2219.

Streim, J. (2005). Unique tools of the trade: Nursing homes and research in geriatric psychiatry. *American Journal of Geriatric Psychiatry, 13,* 437–440.

Takase, M., Maude, P., & Manias, E. (2005). Nurses' job dissatisfaction and turnover intention: Methodological myths and an alternative approach. *Nursing and Health Sciences, 7,* 209–217.

Thomas, W. (1994). *The Eden Alternative: Nature, hope, and nursing homes.* Sherburne, NY: Eden Alternatives Foundation.

Verkaik, R., van Weert, J. C., & Francke, A. (2005). The effects of psychosocial methods on depressed aggressive and apathetic behaviors of people with dementia: A systematic review. *Journal of Geriatric Psychiatry, 20,* 301–314.

Watson, D., Clark, L., & Tellegen, A. (1988). Development and validation of brief measures of positive and negative affect. *Journal of Personality and Social Psychology, 54,* 1063–1070.

Wilson, R., McCann, J. J., Li, Y., Aggarwal, N. T., Gilley, D. W., & Evans, D. A. (2007). Nursing home placement, day care use, and cognitive decline in Alzheimer's disease. *American Journal of Psychiatry, 164,* 910–915.

Wisniewski, S., Belle, S., Coon, D., Marcus, S., Ory, M., Burgio, L., & Burns, R. (2003). The resources for enhancing Alzheimer's caregiver health (REACH): Project design and baseline characteristics. *Psychology and Aging, 18,* 375–384.

Wright, L., Litaker, M., Laraia, M., & DeAndrade, S. (2001). Continuum of care for Alzheimer's disease: A nurse education and counseling program. *Issues in Mental Health Nursing, 22,* 231–252.

Yaffe, K., Fox, P., Newcomer, R., Sands, L., Lindquist, K., Dane, K., & Covinsky, K. (2002). Patient and caregiver characteristics and nursing home placement in patients with dementia. *Journal of the American Medical Association, 287,* 2090–2097.

Zarit, S. H., Gaugler, J. E., & Jarrot, S. E. (1999). Useful services for families: Research findings and directions. *International Journal of Geriatric Psychiatry, 14,* 165–181.

Zellars, K., Perrewe, P., Hochwarter, W., & Anderson, K. (2006). The interactive effects of positive affect and conscientiousness on strain. *Journal of Occupational Health Psychology, 11,* 281–289.

Zimmerman, S., Williams, C., Reed, P., Boustani, M., Presser, J., Heck, E., & Sloane, P. (2005). Attitudes, stress, and satisfaction of staff who care for residents with dementia. *The Gerontologist, 45,* 96–104.

Chapter 11

Quality of Care in Geriatric Health Services

Joseph P. Lyons, ScD
Assisted by Kathleen Healy-Karabell, DNP, MSN, CNS, RN

LEARNING OBJECTIVES

1. To understand the role of the administrator and the facility administration in creating a quality-oriented culture

2. To understand the role of the therapists and support staff in bringing about improvements in the quality of care delivered to the clients and residents

3. To gain knowledge about quality measures currently used in the field of gerontology

4. To understand the role of state, local, and federal governments and private industry in developing and enforcing quality regulations in the gerontology field

5. To discuss the role of the consumer and consumer advocates in assisting administrators and therapists in evaluating the quality of care and in choosing the appropriate facility for the client or patient

6. To gain knowledge about the decision-making process of the consumer and consumer advocates and the implications of their involvement in the provision of therapy

KEY TERMS

Patient Level of Need: The categorization of the patient so that care and treatment given to like patients can be compared to the level of quality care being provided

Activities of Daily Living: A set of common, everyday tasks, performance of which is required for personal self-care and independent living; in order to measure the quality of care provided to an individual, one must assess the individual level of function and then how appropriate the services are to improve that individual's quality of life

Quality Improvement: Involves providing customer satisfaction, measuring quality and performance data to set priorities for improvement efforts, sanctioning and monitoring cross-functional quality improvement teams (QITs), reviewing performance and resident satisfaction data, and setting staff involvement and education goals

Quality Culture: An attitude and set of values employed by a company to improve the levels of quality in its service—to improve the quality of relationships with customers, to improve communication between employees, or to improve the attitude of employees; the best way to establish and maintain a positive quality culture is through regular training and educational sessions

Cause-and-Effect Diagram: A diagram used to help identify the various major causes and secondary causes leading to a specific problem or effect

Process Control: Application of statistical methods to the monitoring and control of a process to ensure that it operates at its full potential to produce conforming products; using these methods, process variation is measured and then further separated into common cause variation and assignable cause variation

Common Cause Variation: Variation that is expected and acceptable

Assignable Cause Variation: Process variation that is important to identify and remove; it is not acceptable and must be removed in order to improve the output quality of the process

Quality-Adjusted Life Years: A measurement tool that brings together the effects of life expectancy with the effects on quality of life into one single measure

Six Sigma: A quality measure; it is 3.4 defects per million opportunities for defects; a far superior level of quality than the traditional three sigma level of 27 defects per 10,000 opportunities

INTRODUCTION

This chapter introduces the concept of quality care and provides strategies and examples for implementing such procedures in a long-term care environment. The major sections of discussion are:

1. Methods to measure patient level of need
2. Online tools for evaluating the quality of each facility
3. Steps involved in undertaking process improvement

4. Short survey of tools used in quality improvement
5. Is Six Sigma worth the effort?
6. The use of quality-adjusted life years
7. Conclusions

Further explanation and examples as to how these concepts are integrated with the care of the elderly are included.

Improving health care in the United States has been the goal of federal and professional organizations since the 1970s. In recognition of identified healthcare disparities, the U.S. federal government responded with long-range plans to reduce mortality, increase quality of life, provide greater access to health care, and intervene in health risks. These nationwide goals, expressed as "Healthy People Objectives," were set to be accomplished by the years 2000 and 2010 (U.S. Department of Health and Human Services, 2006).

At approximately the same time as findings from the U.S. Department of Health and Human Services (DHHS) became public in 2000, the Institute of Medicine (IOM; 2001) reported concerns that reflected risks to the well-being of the nation's healthcare delivery system. The IOM publication, "Crossing the Quality Chasm," described a gap in health care between present conditions and previously proposed federal mandates (IOM, 2001). Discrepancies in health care have been attributed to the numerous factors responsible for creating an overburdened healthcare system in desperate need of change.

The most serious implication in the IOM statement relates to patient safety issues. In 2003, it was estimated that at least 98,000 deaths per year were occurring as a result of healthcare errors. Years later the safety crisis lacks evidence of abating. According to a more recent report, federal analysts document an ever-increasing preventable medical error rate (Crowley & Nalder, 2009). The impact of such risks is predominantly felt by the elderly. Falls and medication errors alone account for an increase in trauma among the elderly hospitalized patient (Centers for Disease Control and Prevention [CDC], 2009).

Rationale for declining quality of care in the aging population has been attributed to the rise in individuals plagued by chronic conditions within a healthcare system that attends to acute health crises, while neglecting comorbid conditions resulting from increased longevity. The aging population worldwide is expanding. It is estimated that by the year 2030, the number of elder adults will increase to 71.5 million, as compared to 35 million in 2002 (National Center for Health Statistics, 2007). Life expectancy of elders living to 85 years or older will rise to 21 million by 2050, creating a larger older adult population than that of children age 0–14 years (DHHS, 2008).

A growing aging population will increase healthcare demands. Declining strength and health will mean added risks. The slowing of physiological processes and cognitive impairments potentiate mobility problems and sleep disorders, thereby enhancing the risk of falls with consequent fatal trauma. Medication administration, often comprising polypharmacy, compounds these concerns and increases the potential for overdose and confusion. Living longer will require diet modifications and pain management secondary to the constraints of chronic illness. Weakened immune systems will be further threatened by acute illness, requiring longer hospital stays.

These factors additionally impact other areas of life for the elderly individual. The need to modify lifestyles, survive the demise of friends and family, manage finances, access health care, provide self-care, and enjoy social and spiritual activities, will all become challenges to quality of life and produce special needs in this unique population. The manner in which these needs are met is dependent upon the responsiveness of the healthcare system.

According to Draye, Acker, and Zimmer (2006), changing population demographics produce growing complexities of care, which increase the demand for services. Clearly, the present method of delivering health care in the United States has not responded adaptively, as system demands have increased and patients' needs have changed. As older Americans live longer, the strain on the healthcare system will only increase unless proactive measures are implemented to deal with growing concerns. The predicted shortage of sufficient numbers of healthcare practitioners to meet the needs of the elderly adds to the dilemma.

As a result, the IOM recommends that stakeholders (professional organizations, policy makers, administrators, educators) begin to revise the present healthcare system. One method of doing so entails compliance with the IOM's (2008) call for reevaluating the methods by which health care is delivered. The quality of care administered has a direct impact on practice outcomes. To protect the needs of vulnerable populations such as the elderly, it has been recommended that evidence-based practice initiatives drive quality improvement measures.

Quality improvement (QI) has been defined as sustained methods to enable change in a systematic way, measuring and assessing the effects of change, feeding the information back into the clinical setting, and making adjustments until desired results are satisfied (Baily, 2008). For this endeavor to be successful, total quality management must be dedicated to creating a culture of quality as a central theme of the healthcare system.

Deming (2000), a theorist, educator, and practitioner of quality, defined the concept broadly: "A product or service possesses quality if it helps somebody and enjoys a good and sustainable market" (p. 198). According to Deming (1986), development of a culture of quality is necessary to improve the system in which excellence is valued. Doing so requires utilizing a well-defined and written strategic practice plan that is continuously reviewed and evaluated for alignment with quality initiative visions and goals.

Evidence-based practice aligns with the IOM (2008) mandates that health care should be patient centered and based on the best available scientific knowledge. Finding ways to improve quality assures that knowledge gets transferred to everyday clinical practice. Since outcomes are dependent upon the effectiveness of implementation measures, those measures must also be driven by a spirit to improve care sufficiently enough to guide future clinical decision making.

Globalization has led to rapid changes in health care and culminated in a system that demands accountability. Stakeholders are becoming increasingly concerned about quality care issues. The present change movement is focused on standardization of measurements to promote continuous quality improvement. A review of significant practice research promotes quality change through methods that address relevancy, efficacy, and cost effectiveness, while at the same time considers responsiveness to the needs of the public (Wilson & DiIulio, 2007).

Chism (2010) concurs that "the overall goal of evidence-based practice is to promote optimal healthcare outcomes, which are based on critically reviewed clinical evidence, for individual patients, families, and communities" (p. 67). Outcomes then become dependent upon patient preferences, the effectiveness of implementation measures, and the expertise of application. Consequently, the pursuit of quality informs evidence-based practice, and evidence-based practice informs quality.

Healthcare providers are presently struggling to meet the needs of an overburdened, defective system. Developing proactive approaches to reverse this trend and improve care is necessary to assess problem areas and to promote change. In order to do that, the current healthcare system requires the transformation of the best available knowledge into safe, innovative, effective outcomes. Accomplishing this goal depends on a range of evaluation options. The increasing needs of the elderly population have prompted the development of various tools to evaluate the quality of care in gerontology facilities. The following tools, rigorously applied and evaluated, will eliminate care based on intuition and tradition by giving way to evidence-based protocols.

The Agency for Healthcare Research and Quality (2007) defines quality health care as "doing the right thing, at the right time, in the right way, for the right person—and having the best possible results." Measurement of defects is integral to quality improvement. A systematic measurement of quality demonstrates whether improvement efforts: (1) lead to change in the primary endpoint in the desired direction, (2) contribute to unintended results in different parts of the system, and (3) require additional efforts to bring a process back into acceptable ranges.

Donabedian (1997), often considered the father of quality measurement, described quality design in relationship to structure, process, and outcomes. Structural measures assess the availability and quality of resources, management systems, and policy guidelines, and are often critical to sustaining processes over time. This type of assessment is used primarily for licensing and for hospital accreditation. An example of a healthcare structural component is the decision to use intensivists in the intensive care unit to decrease mortality.

Process measures use the actual process of healthcare delivery as the indicator of quality by analyzing the activities of physicians or other healthcare professionals to determine whether medicine is practiced according to guidelines. An example of a process measure is the proportion of diabetic patients who undergo an annual retinal examination.

Outcome indicators measure the end result of health care and often depend not only on medical care, but also on genetic, environmental, and behavioral factors. They are usually based on group results rather than individual cases, and thus do not indicate the quality of care delivered to an individual patient. Examples of outcome measures include mortality and patient satisfaction data.

Quality in health care and especially in the provision of gerontology services has two dimensions: (1) technical excellence, and (2) patient's perception, or "through a patient's eyes." Technical excellence is the skill and competence of health professionals and the ability of diagnostic or therapeutic equipment, procedures, and systems to accomplish what they are meant to accomplish reliably and effectively. The second dimension is the patient's perception, which is a subjective experience. Healthcare professionals are often uneasy with addressing this second dimension since it is difficult to measure. Patients, on the other hand, are very interested in enhancement of their sense of well-being and relief from their suffering.

In 1987, the Picker/Commonwealth Program for Patient-Centered Care defined eight dimensions of patient-centered care that could be measured. These dimensions ranged from access to care and respect for patient values, to physical comfort, involvement of family and friends, and transition and continuity, as well as coordination and integration of services, information, communication, and education. All of these dimensions are important to elderly patients who will receive care in gerontology facilities. Care that meets these requirements at a high level would be considered quality care (Silow-Corroll, Alteras, & Stepnick, 2006). These dimensions were furthered emphasized in the 2001 IOM report, "Crossing the Quality Chasm."

Most aging individuals have spent their entire lives in their homes and would prefer to live out their lives at home. This raised the first question faced by most individuals and their families: Can Mom or Dad live at home safely, or is it better for her or him to enter an assisted living facility or a gerontology facility better suited to meet her or his immediate and long-term needs?

METHODS TO MEASURE THE PATIENT'S OR CLIENT'S LEVEL OF NEED

In order to assess the quality of care delivered to patients, one must first categorize the patient so that care and treatment given to like patients can be compared as to the level of quality care being provided. In each county in the United States, an Office on Aging assists individuals and home care agents in the assessment of a person's ability to handle activities of daily living (ADLs). The term *activities of daily living* refers to a set of common, everyday tasks, performance of which is required for personal self-care and independent living. In order to measure the quality of care provided to an individual, one must assess the individual level of function, and then how appropriate the services are for improving that individual's quality of life.

The most often used measure of functional ability is the Katz Activities of Daily Living Scale (Katz, 1983). In this scale, the set of tasks assessed are bathing, dressing, transferring, using the toilet, continence, and eating. A theoretical basis for selecting these functions is that they represent milestones in the sociobiological development of self-care independence in children (Katz & Akpom, 1976). Its original purpose was to differentiate physical functional abilities among rehabilitating and recuperating patients. General measures of health status, such as diagnoses or medical conditions, are limited indicators of the independence and functional capabilities of an individual (Fillenbaum, 1984; Kane & Kane, 1981). Therefore, researchers have devoted considerable attention to developing measures that tap practical dimensions of everyday life as a way of measuring a person's functional status.

ADLs are used to measure disability. They are key elements in efforts to measure quality of life and functional status (Spitzer, 1987). Measurement of ADLs is critical because they have been found to be significant predictors of admission to nursing homes (Branch & Jette, 1982), use of paid home care (Katz, Ford, & Garber, 1989; Soldo & Manton, 1985), use of hospital services (Branch, Jette, & Evashwick, 1981; Wan & Odell, 1981), living arrangements (Bishop, 1986), use of physician services (Wan & Odell, 1981), insurance coverage (Dunlop, Wells, & Wilensky, 1989), and mortality (Manton, 1988). For research on the elderly, the ability to perform the ADLs has become a standard variable to include in analyses, just like age, sex, marital status, and income. ADLs are used by nursing homes and hospitals, rehabilitation facilities, homecare agencies, and local offices of aging to assess an individual's ability to function in the home on an independent and semi-independent basis.

In order to further determine one's capacity to remain in his or her own home with or without the assistance of a caretaker, the application of additional tools is necessary. Home care is compared here with various residential facilities, such as assisted living and long-term care nursing facilities, since the best care is that which is least restrictive and the most appropriate level for a particular patient. In addition to ADLs, another assessment tool, the Outcome and Assessment Information Set (OASIS), was developed by the University of Colorado Center for Health Services and Policy Research (Shaughnessy, 1996) for the purpose of measuring home healthcare outcomes. OASIS is a tool that measures 41 different areas. The development of OASIS began with an evaluation of quality measurement approaches for home health care and included an ongoing literature review, provider surveys, and consumer and provider input. The investigators considered measuring quality through outcomes, process, and structure. However, they reached a consensus that outcome measures are most appropriate for home care, primarily because the purpose of this care is to effect patient well-being. Measuring outcomes provides information on the degree to which the system's purpose has been achieved. The researchers initially considered an expansive set of 500–700 different outcome measures and narrowed these down based on the criteria of usefulness and practicality for clinicians, benefits to patients, measurability, and scientific issues. Several evaluation projects used these measures, for example, to study outcomes of care under fee-for-service versus health maintenance organization (HMO) plans.

Patient outcome was defined as a change in health status between two or more time points. As a result, it is necessary for the clinician to perform multiple OASIS assessments, generally at the start of care and at discharge from care at a minimum. Because a great deal can happen between these two time points, Shaughnessy (1996) and his colleagues from the University of Colorado Center for Health Services and Policy Research who developed OASIS collected data at more frequent intervals. They found that very little is lost by focusing only on the endpoints. The researchers tested several kinds of outcome measures.

In 2008, there were more than 9,000 Medicare-certified home health agencies throughout the United States. In 2006, more than 3 million beneficiaries were served, and 103,931,188 visits made. Home health is covered under the Part A Medicare benefit. It consists of part-time, medically necessary skilled care (nursing, physical therapy, occupational therapy, and speech-language therapy) that is ordered by a physician. Since fall 2003, the Centers for Medicare and Medicaid Services (CMS) has posted a subset of OASIS-based quality performance information showing how well home health agencies assist their patients in regaining or maintaining their ability to function (www.medicare.gov/homehealthcompare/ (S(nkz4x4455wefwsifxscvm545))/about/overview.aspx). Based on the 2005 National Quality Forum (NQF) endorsement, as of 2007, 12 of these measures have been posted to Home Health Compare (a website supported by CMS to provide information about the quality of care provided by "Medicare-certified" home health agencies throughout the nation):

1. Improvement in ambulation/locomotion
2. Improvement in bathing
3. Improvement in transferring
4. Improvement in management of oral medication
5. Improvement in pain interfering with activity
6. Acute care hospitalization
7. Emergent care
8. Discharge to community
9. Improvement in dyspnea (shortness of breath)
10. Improvement in urinary incontinence
11. Improvement in surgical wound status
12. Emergent care for wound deterioration

At the request of the CMS, the NQF reviewed for potential endorsement a set of refined and newly developed home health measures—in particular, process measures for immunization, medication management, pain management, fall prevention, depression screening/intervention, care coordination, risk assessment, heart failure, and diabetes. These measures were tested in the revised OASIS C tool.

In 1999, Medicare began requiring an OASIS assessment by homecare agencies. The use of ADLs and OASIS is important in terms of quality evaluations, since it provides a mechanism to classify patients into a specific level of need, and therefore, different treatments and services can be provided to meet the specific needs of each type of patient, and programs can then be compared appropriately. These same OASIS measures can be used to determine, with the help and approval of the family, that the patient is in need of a more supportive environment, such as an assisted living facility or a nursing home.

ONLINE TOOLS FOR EVALUATING THE QUALITY OF EACH GERONTOLOGY FACILITY

Periodically, the individual and the family may want to evaluate the alternative facilities that are available in the community. Medicare.gov has developed a very useful website that can be used by the professionals, the individual, and the family to make this assessment. The website is called Nursing Home Compare (see www.medicare.gov/NHCompare). Once the user has accessed the website, he or she is asked a few basic questions, such as zip code and a search radius. The Nursing Home Compare system uses Five-Star Quality Ratings. Nursing homes are rated overall, and then on specifics, including health inspections, nursing home staffing, fire safety, and quality measures. By choosing a range of 25 miles, at least 35 nursing homes will be located in a small city area. The example shown in **Table 11.1** is based on a 5-mile radius, and is illustrative of the results. The Nursing Home Compare website can be used by the family and the individual, as well as representatives of the local Office on Aging and other helping agencies to assist the family in evaluating which facility will provide the highest quality services for the individual.

Table 11.1 Sample Search Using Nursing Home Compare

Nursing Home Name	Overall Rating	Health Inspection	Nursing Home Staffing	Quality Measure	Program Partici-pation	Number of Certified Beds	Ownership
Option #1	* 1 out of 5 stars	* 1 out of 5 stars	** 2 out of 5 stars	**** 4 out of 5 stars	Medicare and Medicaid	145	Nonprofit
Option #2	** 2 out of 5 stars	* 1 out of 5 stars	**** 4 out of 5 stars	*** 3 out of 5 stars	Medicare and Medicaid	65	Nonprofit
Option #3	* 1 out of 5 stars	* 1 out of 5 stars	** 2 out of 5 stars	**** 4 out of 5 stars	Medicare and Medicaid	176	Nonprofit

This example search resulted in three nursing homes available within 5 miles of a random ZIP code. The names of the facilities have been changed here since the purpose is to illustrate the concept and not provide a real-life case for review. The results are sorted by nursing home name.

Source: Department of Health and Human Services. (2011). Nursing Home Compare. Retrieved March 1, 2012, from http://www.medicare.gov/NHCompare.

Many different organizations, both government and private, have a need to evaluate the quality of the service being provided by each agency in the system. Evidence-based quality assessment and resulting improvement in nursing homes relies heavily on administrative data, which is a structure measure, and resident assessment data, which provides an opportunity to measure both process and outcome. There are two major national systems that routinely collect nursing home quality information required by the CMS based on the Omnibus Budget Reconciliation Act of 1987: (1) the Minimum Data Set (MDS), and (2) the Online Survey Certification and Reporting (OSCAR) systems. MDS uses similar data to OASIS, but includes a number of additional administrative and facility-based items that measure structure. The Nursing Home Compare website uses MDS to produce its quality ranking system. MDS collects nursing home quality information at the resident level, while OSCAR collects information at the facility level. Federal and state governments rely on these systems to regulate nursing home compliance with quality standards and to reimburse their operations.

MDS is a powerful tool for implementing standardized assessment and for facilitating care management in nursing homes and noncritical access hospital swing beds. Its content has implications for residents, families, providers, researchers, and policymakers, all of whom have expressed concerns about the reliability, validity, and relevance of MDS 2.0. Some argue that because MDS 2.0 fails to include items that rely on direct resident interviews, it fails to obtain critical information and effectively disenfranchises many residents from the assessment process. In addition, many users and government agencies have expressed concerns about MDS 2.0 data quality and validity. Other stakeholders contend that items used in other care settings should be included to improve communication across providers.

MDS 3.0 has been designed to improve the reliability, accuracy, and usefulness of the MDS; to include the resident in the assessment process; and to use standard protocols used in other settings. These improvements have profound implications for nursing home and swing-bed care, and public policy. Enhanced accuracy supports the primary legislative intent that MDS be a tool to improve clinical assessment, and supports the credibility of programs that rely on MDS.

Both MDS and OSCAR were mandated as government endeavors to improve the quality of care in nursing homes. MDS includes not only demographic and health condition variables, but also a broad array of clinical measures that are collected through resident assessments by nurses at admission, quarterly, and yearly assessments. Some important categories of measures include cognitive patterns, psychosocial well-being, physical functioning, disease diagnoses, medications, and special treatment. MDS and OSCAR have also been increasingly used in a number of government and public reports. Most importantly, based on these two administrative databases, the CMS has launched three public reporting systems to guide the public in selecting nursing homes:

1. Nursing Home Compare: http://www.Medicare.gov/NHCompare
2. Five-Star Quality Rating: http://www.cms.hhs.gov/ Certificationandcomplianc/13_FSQRS.asp
3. Special Focus Facility: http://www.cms.hhs.gov/ CertificationandComplianc/Downloads/SFFList.pdf

Nursing Home Compare represents a newer generation of quality measurement for nursing home care, since it uses a multi-dimensional and multi-level measurement system that incorporates CMS outcome measures, nurse staffing, and inspection deficiency measures at both resident and facility levels. The latter two measures are derived from OSCAR data. Nursing Home Compare contains the most comprehensive nursing home quality measures and includes facility structure (staffing), process (deficiencies), and outcome measures. It has become the foundation for the CMS Five-Star Rating System. Although Nursing Home Compare and the Five-Star Rating System are associated with nursing home quality, they have not been systemically evaluated in terms of reliability and validity. In an effort to formulate a single dimension scorecard based on Nursing Home Compare, the Five-Star Quality Rating system was developed to represent a comprehensive ranking for nursing homes similar to that used by the hotel business. Special Focus Facility, on the other hand, annually publishes a list of facilities with persistent deficiencies and life-threatening citations documented in OSCAR data. In recent years, consumers have been able to choose desirable nursing homes for themselves or family members as a result of the public information available online derived from these two data systems. In addition, policymakers and nursing home advocates have made decisions and influenced policies in light of the evidence presented in these data systems.

STEPS INVOLVED IN UNDERTAKING PROCESS IMPROVEMENT

Gerontology facility administrators may be interested in improving their overall scores in one or all three of these systems. In order to get started, the senior management of a gerontology facility can begin by forming a facility-wide Quality Improvement Council (QIC) made up of 10 to 12 leaders from nursing, management, housekeeping, dietary, and social services. The QIC should solicit suggestions for quality improvement projects through staff surveys and reward-based suggestion boxes. The QIC will then prioritize the quality improvement projects and allocate appropriate resources and time to complete the projects chosen. They will also publicize the efforts and add credibility to all quality improvement projects. The QIC's important roles include using customer satisfaction, quality, and performance data to set priorities for improvement efforts; sanctioning and monitoring cross-functional quality improvement teams (QITs); reviewing performance and resident satisfaction data; and setting staff involvement and education goals.

Quality improvement begins with selecting a process to improve and choosing the members of the QIT. Improving quality consumes significant staff time for regular staff members and those who provide support. This means that the nursing facility is best served if highly valued processes are improved first. The QIT can achieve success by improving the simple, but important processes. This produces results quickly, demonstrates the value of quality improvement, and helps convince skeptical staff of the value of the improvement efforts. The steps of this process are summarized in **Table 11.2**.

SHORT SURVEY OF TOOLS FOR IMPROVEMENT

Tools for improvement include ISO 9000, control charts, cause-and-effect diagrams, Pareto analysis, failure modes effects analysis, and Six Sigma. These tools are sometimes difficult to learn and use. The staff and the members of the quality improvement council may find their use overwhelming. The QIC should consider hiring a quality consultant to help train staff and the council on the importance and use of each of these methods. The local

Table 11.2 Steps Involved in Undertaking Process Improvement

Step 0	Form a quality improvement council (QIC)
Step 1	Form quality improvement teams (QITs)
Step 2	Establish the focus for each team
Step 3	Each team examines the current situation
Step 4	Analyze the causes of problems
Step 5	Act on the causes and change the system
Step 6	Study the results
Step 7	Analyze the changes
Step 8	Draw conclusions

chapter of the American Society for Quality (ASQ) can provide a list of quality consultants through their website (www.asq.org) who have experience in healthcare quality improvement.

Implementing a Quality Assessment Standard—ISO 9000

MDS and OSCAR are appropriate instruments to evaluate the quality of nursing facilities. Once a nursing facility has identified that it has certain deficiencies, it should proceed with improving the system and eliminating these deficiencies. A measure that is heavily used in industry and is becoming more prevalent in healthcare delivery was developed by the International Organization for Standardization (ISO) and is called ISO 9000. ISO is a nongovernmental organization that was established in 1947 in Switzerland to develop common international standards for quality management and quality assurance. ISO derives its name from the Greek word *isos* meaning "equal," which can be thought of as "standard" in quality assurance terminology. The ISO 9000 series is currently used in more than 90 countries. The standards that it provides apply to a variety of areas of service organizations. ISO 9000 is a series of standards that document, structure, account for, and trace services produced by an organization. The standards developed by ISO and the implementation of these standards are voluntary. ISO does not have any legislative power and is not a part of any government or the United Nations. Governments, as well as individual companies, make the decision to voluntarily integrate ISO standards into their systems on a voluntary basis. Many companies choose to become ISO 9000 certified because customers expect quality services. Many companies consider ISO 9000 more than a marketing tool and a minimum standard. By working through the ISO 9000 process, they have been able to compete for, and satisfy their customers more effectively. In nursing care and long-term facilities, residents are often viewed as customers and not patients. Therefore, an instrument such as ISO 9000 that is used to improve customer satisfaction has been shown to be very useful in improving service-delivery quality (ISO, 2011).

Use of Control Charts to Identify and Reduce Defects

The following application of control charting in healthcare delivery is provided here in order to encourage the reader to learn more about how quality control technology is used to identify and reduce defects in health service delivery systems. A central tool used to improve quality is called a control chart. The control chart is used to chart the variation of a process over time. Process variation bounds representing a 99% quality level (typically at ± 2 or

3 standard deviations) are also marked on the chart according to the time sequence of a chart. These bounds are referred to as upper and lower control limits (Pyzdek, 2003).

Process variation is then further separated into common cause variation, which is expected and acceptable, and assignable cause variation, which is important to identify and remove. Assignable cause variation is not acceptable and must be removed in order to improve the output quality of the process.

As an approach, statistical process control uses control charts to identify potential for process improvement (eliminating assignable causes) and to monitor a process in real time in order to detect deteriorating performance (importantly seeking to identify trends and so preempt unacceptable, "out-of-control" performance). All processes vary to some degree. An aspirin, for example, may be given to an acute myocardial infarction (heart attack) patient a few minutes earlier or later than to another patient. The National Database of Nursing Quality Indicators (NDNQI) collects data about nursing quality. One problem the NDNQI is addressing using control charts is patient falls. As shown in **Figure 11.1**, measures such as falls per 1,000 patient days can be plotted using control charts. The average is 5.5 falls per 1,000 days, with an upper control limit (UCL) of 9.1 falls and lower control

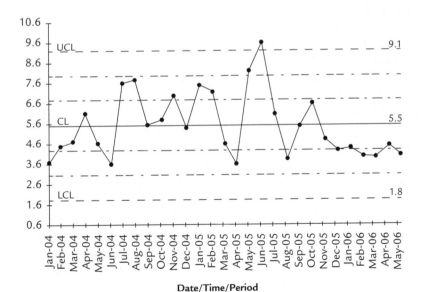

Figure 11.1 Falls per 1,000 Patient Days

Source: Arthur, J. (2008). Statistical process control for health care. *Quality Digest.* Retrieved March 25, 2012, from http://www.qualitydigest.com/june08/articles/03_article.shtml. XmR chart created with QI macros for Excel (www.qimacros.com). © 2008 QCI International.

limit (LCL) of 1.8 falls. Special assignable causes occured in May and June 2005.

The quality improvement team can then use this data and the control chart to investigate why falls increased in May and June 2005 (Arthur, 2008). The statistics here indicate that in May and June 2005, the number of falls was significantly higher than the rest of the year. This is a signal to the QIT to focus on these dates and determine the cause of the number of falls being so high in May and June 2005. The QIT can then identify the cause and eliminate the assignable cause variation so that only common cause or acceptable variation will remain. One tool that is often used by quality improvement teams to identify the reason for falls being so high in May and June 2005 is the cause-and-effect diagram. An example of a cause-and-effect diagram is presented in the next section.

IS SIX SIGMA WORTH THE EFFORT IN HEALTHCARE DELIVERY?

The pursuit of zero defects began when Japanese manufacturers took over a television-manufacturing unit of Motorola in 1970. The new management decided to change the way the operations were conducted. The Japanese management made sure to place a high emphasis on all the activities leading to production. Finally, because of their zealous approach, they started manufacturing TV sets with a much higher level of quality—far superior to the original Motorola standard. The discussion regarding the evolution of Six Sigma would be incomplete without mentioning the valuable contribution from Motorola. Bill Smith, along with Mikel Harry, had written and codified a research report on the new quality management system that emphasized the interdependence between a product's performance in the market and the adjustments required at the manufacturing point (Harry & Schroeder, 1999). The report clearly indicated that the lesser the number of nonconformities at each stage of production, the better the performance. This report was no less than a revolution, because it paved the way for the implementation of the "logical filters" as a key tool to solve problems. Bob Galvin, then the CEO of Motorola, became a leader in this system, and with his help this four-stage logical filter, became the skeleton of the present-day Six Sigma. The four stages were known as measure, analyze, improve, and control.

In medicine, 99% quality, measured using control chart methodology, may not be good enough. A much higher level of quality is needed, and it is known as Six Sigma. The control chart is based on the controlling data within plus or minus three standard deviations (sigma) from the average or mean value. The control chart will determine if greater than 27 defects exist in a sample of 10,000, or 99%. However, in medicine, 99% quality may not be good enough. For example:

1. If a surgeon removes 99% of the tumor, the cancer is still there. If the antibiotic prescribed is 99% effective against the bacteria, the infection can recur.
2. If a sterilization technique for cystoscopy is 99% effective, 2 people per year will be infected, and a busy urology group will infect 10–20 per year, potentially, with an infectious disease!
3. If a specimen labeling process is 99% effective, specimens will be mixed up at least 26 times per year.
4. If a busy internist is given the correct chart with 99% accuracy, the intern will make his or her notation in the wrong chart on 52 patients per year, on average.
5. If a lab's filing system is 99% accurate, labs will be misfiled 100 times per year, on average, in a moderately busy doctors' office.

Ninety-nine percent sounds great, but in actuality, it is only good if you are taking a college final exam. In medicine, 99% is not very good at all. So how do we approach zero defects?

In doctors' offices, hospitals, and clinics, the uses of Six Sigma in health care include shortening wait times, decreasing mortality rates, reducing costs, and increasing efficiency. But is Six Sigma worth the effort? The impact of implementing Six Sigma methodologies has provided many benefits and success stories, such as:

· St. Joseph's Hospital changed the emergency department patient flow, allowing the hospital to treat at least 10,000 more patients annually and adding nearly $8 million annually in incremental margin. —*Tampa Bay Business Journal*, 9/28/2009
· The Pittsburgh Regional Healthcare Initiative cut the amount of reported central line–associated bloodstream infections by more than 50%. The rate per 1,000 line days (the measure hospitals use) plummeted from 4.2 to 1.9. —*asq.org*, 3/15/2010
· H. Lee Moffitt Cancer Center and Research Institute is expected to increase procedural volume by 12%, which will add nearly $8 million annually in incremental margin. —*Tampa Bay Business Journal*, 9/28/2009
· A major hospital in the United States was able to reduce inpatient mortality rates by 47.8%. —*iSixSigma.com*, 3/15/2010
· Mercy Medical Center decreased in-hospital mortality rates from 6.7% to 3.5%, a 47.8% reduction. —*Medical News Today*, 12/3/2007

Six Sigma means 3.4 defects per million opportunities for defects. This is a far superior level of quality than the traditional three sigma level of 27 defects per 10,000 opportunities. The mathematics of Six Sigma is beyond the scope of this chapter. However, with the help of an ASQ consultant, Six Sigma studies of crucial processes in gerontology facilities can be designed and implemented.

A first step in applying Six Sigma is to create a flowchart for the process. In healthcare facilities, this is known as the creation of a clinical process flow map (see **Figure 11.2**).

Once the process has been mapped, members of the QIT will be asked to use the clinical process flow map to identify bottlenecks in the process. One such bottleneck is extensive lengths of stay. The QIT is then asked

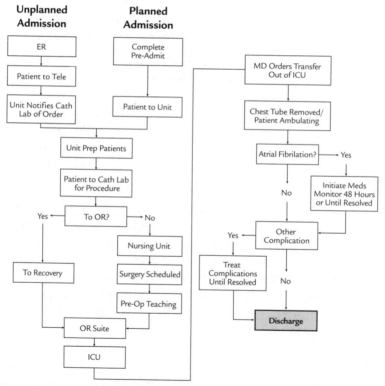

Figure 11.2 Example of a Clinical Process Flow Map

Source: Used with permission from Luchsinger, J., Taylor, C., & Weissman, M. (2010). Six Sigma catapults hospitals to next level of quality. Retrieved March 13, 2012, from http://isixsigma.com/new-to-six-sigma/dmaic/six-sigma-catapults-hospitals-next-level-quality/.

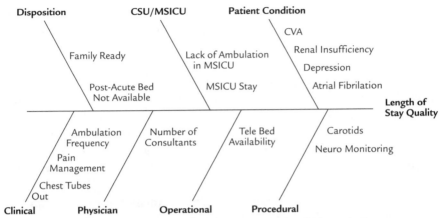

Figure 11.3 Cause-and-Effect Diagram: Length of Stay—Identifying Root Causes

Source: Used with permission from Luchsinger, J., Taylor, C., & Weissman, M. (2010). Six Sigma catapults hospitals to next level of quality. Retrieved March 13, 2012, from http://isixsigma.com/new-to-six-sigma/dmaic/six-sigma-catapults-hospitals-next-level-quality/.

to identify and brainstorm what the root causes of the bottleneck are by working as a team and creating a cause-and-effect diagram (illustrated in **Figure 11.3**). The cause-and-effect diagram is used by the QIT to focus on the root causes of extensive length of stay in order to improve the clinical process.

Once the root causes are identified, members of the QIT can take steps to eliminate the problems identified. There are many other tools used in quality improvement. The reader is encouraged to read about Six Sigma in each reference provided and to use the services of a consultant trained in quality improvement.

QUALITY-ADJUSTED LIFE YEARS (QALY)

Once an individual has entered into a mode of treatment, such as home care, assisted living, or institutional care (e.g., a gerontology facility), his or her condition may require medical treatment. As clinicians attempt to provide care and treatment to individuals, they must first assess what the patient wants. The individual has two goals: (1) he or she would like to live longer, and (2) he or she would prefer to have the highest quality of life possible. Therefore, the question presented to the patient or significant others is: Will this treatment have a significant impact upon either of these two goals? Most people are willing to sacrifice some additional gain in life expectancy for a better quality of life and vice versa. The measurement tool, called quality-adjusted life years (QALY), was developed to bring together the effects of life expectancy with the effects on quality of life into one single measure: If some health activity would give someone an extra year of healthy life expectancy, then that would count as QALY = 1. If a treatment could provide an additional year of life in a rather poor state of health, then that would be counted as less than 1 QALY and would be the lower health state. Death is scored as QALY = 0. QALYs represent the years of life following the implementation of a medical technology that are measured and adjusted for the quality of life experienced by the patient during those years (Torrance & Feeny, 1989). According to Goodman (2004), they provide the ability to: (1) estimate the overall burden of disease; (2) compare the relevant impact of specific diseases, conditions, and syndromes as they relate to medical technology intervention; and (3) conceive economic correlations, such as the deemed cost effectiveness, and cost utility in particular, of different medical technologies. See **Table 11.3** for a visual representation of capabilities QALY applies to outcome analysis. The table indicates that although the cost of conventional medical treatment is the lowest, its cost per QALY is the highest, as the life-years gained and the patient utility of those years are low compared to the alternatives. The costs of heart transplantation and total artificial heart are of similar magnitude, but the cost per QALY is much lower for heart transplantation, as the life-years gained and the patient utility of those years are higher compared to the total artificial heart.

Table 11.3 Cost Utilities for Alternative Therapies for End-Stage Heart Disease

Therapy	Life-years gained (yr)	Mean utility	QALY (yr)	Aggregate cost ($)	Cost per QALY ($/yr)
Conventional medical treatment	0.50	0.05	**0.03**	$28,500	$950,000
Heart transplantation	11.30	0.75	**8.45**	$298,200	$35,290
Total artificial heart	4.42	0.65	**2.88**	$327,600	$113,750

Note: Costs and outcomes discounted at 3% per year; 20-year horizon. Mean utilities derived using time-tradeoff method on scale for which 1.0 was well, 0.0 was death, and states worse than death were valued between 0.0 and 1.0.

Source: Data from Goodman, C. (2004). HTA 101: Introduction to health technology assessment. Retrieved March 26, 2012, from http://www.nlm.nih.gov/nichsr/hta101/hta101.pdf.

SUMMARY

In order to determine the quality of care provided to a patient, one must assess the level of treatment needed first by using ADLs and OASIS. Once an OASIS is performed, the therapist, the individual, and the family can determine if home care is appropriate for the individual or if assisted living or nursing home is more appropriate. Individuals, family, and treatment professionals can evaluate the various treatment options using Nursing Home Compare. Government agencies have developed two sophisticated data sets based on OASIS studies called MDS and OSCAR. These two databases are used by state, federal, and private quality assessment agencies to develop Nursing Home Compare and other similar online tools. Once a home care, assisted living agency, or nursing facility is designated as below an acceptable level of quality on any one of several measures, the organization can use standard quality improvement methodologies to improve the quality of care available at the facility, such as ISO 9000, control charts, cause-and-effect diagrams, or other quality improvement tools. An administrator of a gerontology facility is encouraged to create and designate a quality council and several quality improvement teams, which will focus attention on quality problems in the facility and direct staff to improve treatment processes. The administrator is also encouraged to explore the use of Six Sigma tools and processes. This will most likely require employing outside consultants, but the long-term improvements have been demonstrated to be well worth the expenditures. The individual, the family, and the clinician are encouraged to explore the use of quality-adjusted life years when faced with critical treatment decisions. A detailed example has been presented along with several references for further inquiry.

Discussion Questions

1. Visit an elderly relative (or acquaintance) who is receiving care in a long-term care facility.
2. How does the staff of the long-term facility measure what level of care your relative (or acquaintance) should receive?
3. How do you know if he or she is receiving the best care possible?
4. Assume that your relative (or acquaintance) must be moved to a new facility: What tool would you use to help yourself, the patient, and other relatives and friends? Try the tool mentioned in the chapter text. Did it provide useful information?

5. Next, assume that you are the facility administrator: How do you go about measuring the quality of the care provided in your facility? How do you go about getting your staff involved in improving the level of care provided in your facility?
6. What are the measures used by state and federal governments and other regulatory accrediting agencies?
7. Assume you or your relative must decide which treatment is best.
8. What criteria should you use? Cost, quality of treatment, or years of quality life expected?
9. How do you put these measures together into one table that can be discussed rationally with your doctor and family members in order to arrive at the best solution?

REFERENCES

Agency for Healthcare Research and Quality, U.S. Department of Health & Human Services. (2007). A quick look at quality. Retrieved March 25, 2012, from http://archive.ahrq.gov/consumer/qnt/qntqlook.htm.

Arthur, J. (2008). Statistical process control for health care. *Quality Digest*. Retrieved March 25, 2012, from http://www.qualitydigest.com/june08/articles/03_article.shtml.

Baily, M. A. (2008). Harming through protection? *New England Journal of Medicine, 358*(8), 768–769.

Bishop, C. (1986). Living arrangement choices of elderly singles. *Health Care Financing Review, 7*, 65–73.

Branch, L. G., & Jette, A. M. (1982). A prospective study of long-term care institutionalization among the aged. *American Journal of Public Health, 72*, 1373–1379.

Branch, L. G., Jette, A. M., & Evashwick, C. (1981). Toward understanding elders' health service utilization. *Journal of Community Health, 7*, 80–92.

Centers for Disease Control and Prevention (CDC). (2009). *CDC promotes public health approach to address depression among older adults.* Retrieved March 26, 2012, from http://www.cdc.gov/aging/pdf/CIB_mental_health.pdf.

Chism, L. A. (2010). *The doctor of nursing practice: A guidebook for role development and professional issues.* Sudbury, MA: Jones & Bartlett Learning.

Crowley, C. F., & Nalder, E. (2009). Within health care hides massive, avoidable death toll *Hearst Newspapers.* Retrieved May 3, 2012, from http://www.seattlepi.com/national/article/Dead-by-Mistake-Within-health-care-hides-1305620.php

Donabedian, A. (1997). The quality of care, how can it be assessed? *Archives of Pathology & Laboratory Medicine, 121*(11), 1145–1150.

Deming, W. E. (1986). *Out of the crisis.* Boston, MA: MIT Press.

Deming, W. E. (2000). *Out of the crisis.* Boston, MA: MIT Press.

Dunlop, B., Wells, J., & Wilensky, G. (1989). The influence of insurance coverage on the health care utilization patterns of the elderly. *Journal of Health and Human Resources Administration, 11*(285–310).

Draye, M., Acker, M., & Zimmer, P. (2006). The practice doctorate in nursing: Approaches to transform nurse practitioner education and practice. *Nursing Outlook, 54*(3), 123–129.

Fillenbaum, G. G. (1984). *The wellbeing of the elderly: Approaches to multidimensional assessment.* Geneva, Switzerland: World Health Organization.

Goodman, C. (2004). HTA 101: Introduction to health technology assessment. Retrieved March 26, 2012, from www.nlm.nih.gov/nichsr/hta101/hta101.pdf.

Harry, M., & Schroeder, R. (1999). *Six Sigma: The breakthrough management strategy revolutionizing the world's top corporations.* New York: Doubleday.

Institute of Medicine (IOM). (2001). *Crossing the quality chasm.* Washington, DC: National Academies Press.

Institute of Medicine. (2008). *Report brief: knowing what works in health care: A road map for the nation.* Washington, DC: National Academies Press.

International Organization for Standardization (ISO). (2011). ISO 9000 guidelines for health care sector. Retrieved March 26, 2012, from http://www.iso.org/iso/pressrelease.htm?refid=Ref802.

Kane, R. A., & Kane, R. L. (1981). *Assessing the elderly: A practical guide to measurement.* Lexington, MA: D.C. Health and Company.

Katz, S. (1983). Assessing self-maintenance: Activities of daily living, mobility, and instrumental activities of daily living. *Journal of the American Geriatrics Association, 31*, 721–727.

Katz, S., & Akpom, C. A. (1976). A measure of primary sociobiological functions. *International Journal of Health Services, 6*, 493–507.

Katz, S., Ford, A. B., & Garber, A. M. (1989). Long-term care, welfare, and health of the disabled elderly living in the community. In David A. Wise (Ed.), *The economics of aging* (p. 35). Chicago: The University of Chicago Press.

Manton, K. G. (1988). A longitudinal study of functional change and mortality in the United States. *Journal of Gerontology, 43*, S153–S161.

Medicare.gov, the Official U.S. Government Site for Medicare. (n.d.). *Medicare.gov: The Official U.S. Government Site for Medicare.* Retrieved January 27, 2011, from http://www.medicare.gov/homehealthcompare/%28S%280xq5nwaoeymdme455bcju245%29%29/Data/Measures/List.aspx.

National Center for Health Statistics, U.S. Department of Health and Human Services. (2007). *Health: United States, 2007.* Hyattsville, MD: Author.

Pyzdek, T. (2003). *The Six Sigma handbook: A complete guide for green belts, black belts, and managers at all levels* (Rev. and expanded ed.). New York: McGraw-Hill.

Shaughnessy, P. (1996). *Quality of long term care services in home and community based settings.* Washington, DC: Institute of Medicine, National Academies Press.

Silow-Corroll, S., Alteras, T., & Stepnick, L. (2006). *Patient-centered care for underserved populations: Definition and best practices.* Washington, DC: Economic and Social Research Institute, pp. 1–43.

Soldo, B., & Manton, K. G. (1985). Health status and service needs of the oldest old: Current patterns and future trends. *Milbank Quarterly, 63,* 286–323.

Spitzer, W. O. (1987). State of science 1986: Quality of life and functional status as target variables for research. *Journal of Chronic Disease, 40,* 465–471.

Torrance, G., & Feeny, D. (1989). Utilities and quality-adjusted life years. *International Journal of Technology Assessment in Health Care, 5*(4), 559–575.

U.S. Department of Health and Human Services (DHHS). (2000). *Midcourse review: Healthy people 2000.* Washington, DC: National Institutes of Health.

U.S. Department of Health and Human Services. (2006). *Understanding and improving health.* Washington, DC: National Institutes of Health.

U.S. Department of Health and Human Services. (2008). *Adverse events in hospitals: Public disclosure information.* Retrieved March 26, 2012, from http://www.oig.hhs.gov/oei/reports/oei-06-09-00360.pdf.

Wan, T. T. H., & Odell, B. G. (1981). Factors affecting the use of social and health services for the elderly. *Ageing and Society, 1,* 95–115.

Wilson, J. Q., & DiIulio, J. J. (2007). *American government: Institutions and policies* (10th ed.). Boston, MA: Houghton Mifflin Company.

Chapter 12

Oral History

Kathleen P. Munley, PhD

LEARNING OBJECTIVES

1. To understand a brief history of the development of oral history studies, development of the field of gerontology, and the relationship between the two disciplines

2. To discuss literature supporting life review/oral history projects with senior citizens

3. To identify two oral history approaches, formal and informal, appropriate to a gerontological setting

4. To understand explanations, planning, implementation, and other important elements essential to the undertaking of a formal oral history study with a geriatric population

5. To identify and discuss issues and concerns that should be taken into account prior to, during, and following the undertaking of an oral history project with this population

KEY TERMS

Oral History: A method of collecting historical information through the use of oral interviews with selected subjects

Formal and Informal Oral History Project: Two approaches to oral history studies

Project Director: Person responsible for the oral history project; oversees all aspects

Interviewer: The person who interviews the subjects of the oral history project

Interviewee: The person who is interviewed for the oral history project

Self-Directed Autobiographical Oral History Study: Subjects are directed to write autobiographies

Reminiscence and Life Review: Studies or conversations involving review of one's life and memories

INTRODUCTION: WHAT IS ORAL HISTORY AND HOW IS IT RELEVANT TO GERONTOLOGY?

This chapter is a succinct presentation of the use of oral history in a gerontological setting. It is directed in particular to administrators of facilities for gerontology health services and explores some basic oral history techniques and planning, organization, and implementation of oral history projects with particular attention to the gerontological population.

Oral history is essentially the study of history using a methodology in which historians, professional and nonprofessional, collect historical information about a subject through interviews of significant persons related to the topic under study. (See the Oral History Association website for more information: www.oralhistory.org.)

Given the technological explosion of the past 20 or so years, there are currently a number of technologies that are used for the collection of this information, including tape recorders, digital recorders, and audio/video recorders. While historians have been using this approach to historical research since ancient times, recording interviews in longhand, oral history, as a subset of professional historical research and study in the United States, began gaining prominence in the mid-20th century with the creation of several now nationally famous oral history projects, such as the 1930s New Deal Federal Writers' Project and various World War II studies. Gradually, as more and more prominent American historians became interested in this methodology, American universities began to show interest in establishing centers for the study and collection of oral history and included oral history studies in their curricular offerings. Columbia University in New York City and the University of California led the way. Other universities soon followed suit, and by the 1960s, oral history was recognized as a legitimate and scholarly area of historical research and study, generally tied to the newly emerging field of social history, which focused on history of ordinary people and events (sometimes referred to as history "from the bottom up"). As a testimony to growing interest in this form of historical study in the United States and elsewhere, by the mid-1960s historians and others (now referred to as "oral historians") began gathering in scholarly groups and sharing research. In the United States, an outcome of this interest was the creation of the Oral History Association (OHA) in 1966, which was chartered in

1967 and began publication of the *Oral History Review* in 1973. Today, the Oral History Association is an established and highly respected professional organization—one of many internationally—devoted to advancing the field of oral history in the United States and globally (Sharpless, 2007).

Although oral history and gerontology have not had a particularly strong connection, there is evidence today that this is changing, as these two areas have begun to meld together in their common interest in people. While gerontology is intrinsically focused on the senior population, oral history, which is not exclusively limited to the aging population, is nonetheless interested in the past, and as a result, frequently seeks formation that is best provided by seniors in the population. Bornat and Tetley (2010) of the Centre for Ageing and Biographical Studies at The Open University in the United Kingdom, noted that "oral history and gerontology have had a rarely spoken relationship over the years." In the United Kingdom, they continued, "the Oral History Society and the British Society of gerontology have shared almost the same 40 years since they originated," but that there have been few acknowledgments of each other's existence. In the United States, the field of gerontology began to emerge in the 1940s, in particular with the creation of the Gerontological Society of America (GSA), which celebrated 65 years in 2010, as the "oldest and largest interdisciplinary organization in the United States," whose mission is "devoted to research, education, and practice in the field of aging." The "idea" of bringing scientists, physicians, and others together to focus on the aging population had resulted in the formation of the Club for Research on Ageing, formed in 1939, which in 1945 formally established the Gerontological Society of America to "promote scientific study of aging." It held its first annual meeting in New York City in 1946, and the same year began publication of the *Journal of Gerontology*. Thereafter, the GSA divided into four groupings: two devoted to science (biology, psychology, and the social sciences), and two devoted to applied areas (social work, administration, and health science) (GSA, 2008).

The links between the oral history and gerontology "should be obvious primarily because each has an interest in older people" (Bornat & Tetley, 2010). Yet, that is not the case. Each tends to remain distinct and even unaware of the other. In their 2010 article in the British Society of Gerontology's newsletter, *Generations Review*, Bornat and Tetley addressed this "parallel existence" (a phrase used by Bornat in a 2001 study) of oral history and gerontology. They said that this parallel existence appears to be similar in the United States, although there are exceptions. At Marywood University, an oral history course is offered as part of the gerontology certificate and masters of science (MS) in gerontology programs. On occasion, Marywood has conducted campus seminars in which oral history and its connection to gerontology were highlighted. Likewise, the OHA has frequently included studies that target concerns and issues of the aging population, as well as generally welcomed studies from local and regional historians that "place" ordinary people living in very ordinary circumstances in larger, national and world situations. Bornat and Tetley make an excellent point for the argument of connectivity of these two disciplines that share a common ground in working with the aging persons. Both employ the interview as a "key research [method], both focus on remembering and both show concern for issues raised by participation, ownership and the presentation of the outcomes of their engagement with the lives of older people" (Bornat & Tetley, 2010).

The literature suggests that the inspiration for connecting gerontological studies with oral history was the American psychiatrist Robert Butler, who recently passed away. As most persons in gerontology know, Dr. Butler was the president and CEO of the International Longevity Center of New York City and founding director of the National Institute on Aging, where he served as director for 6 years. Dr. Butler will ever be remembered as a pioneer in the field of gerontology for developing the concept of "life review"—something that he maintained was healthy and essential to the aging process. In Butler's view, when aging persons talk of their memories, this is not "living in the past," something that earlier persons involved with this population viewed as evidence of senility. He coined the term *ageism* and, as noted in his *New York Times* obituary, he "challenged long-held conceptions about aging," and "helped establish . . . that senility is not inevitable with aging" (Martin, 2010). He brought together these ideas in his seminal work, *Why Survive? Being Old in America*, for which he was awarded the Pulitzer Prize in 1975. Martin (2010), citing Dr. Christine Cassel, president of the American Board of Internal Medicine, said that Dr. Butler's work had "created an entire field of medicine" and before Dr. Butler, "nobody thought research on aging was a legitimate field." Bornat and Tetley (2010) attest to Dr. Butler's worldwide influence in this area, stating that "Butler's focus on inequalities and the positive contribution of encouraging people to remember fed into developments in the UK which were to bring oral historians and gerontologists together working on practical projects," which ultimately led to a reversal of long-held positions and the onset of a number of "community-based oral history projects." As Bornat and Tetley and others indicate, changing views in the field of gerontology helped advance the field of oral history as well (Adams, 1986; Bornat & Tetley, 2010).

Today, reminiscence and life review are considered not only normal, but also valuable experiences for the geriatric population. According to

Kirshenblatt-Gimblett, Hufford, Hunt, and Zeitlin (2006), "reviewing one's life in old age is both therapeutic and culturally important, it can reveal coping and adaptive strategies helpful in successful aging." As an essential activity for aging people, "telling stories and repeating parts that hold significance is part of the creative process of passing on one's legacy" (Zablotny, 2006). Others emphasize that reminiscence, in addition to being a "part of a normal life review process," is the result of "realization of mortality," and, as such, the processes of remembering "can be focused or guided, and are often therapeutic" (Quigley, 1981). Others emphasize that "thinking or talking about the past can be especially comforting for individuals with Alzheimer's disease," in that it can spark particular memories or serve as a vehicle for bringing people together to "share special moments" (Forest Pharmaceuticals, 2005).

By combining the importance of reminiscence therapy as a method for caring for the geriatric population with the mission of oral history and projects undertaken with the aging population to connect memories and shared life experiences of seniors with younger people, we allow for the flow of information, perceptions, and values about the past to a new generation with its own perceptions and values. In this way, both areas of endeavor—gerontology and history—are served and enhanced. At the same time, the people participating are individually and collectively affected and, as a result, grow in understanding and sensitivity, and acceptance of life's lessons about humanity and mortality.

FORMAL AND INFORMAL ORAL HISTORY WITH THE GERIATRIC POPULATION

There are two possible approaches for one to employ in conducting a study in the gerontological setting: a formal approach, and an informal approach. What are the differences? The formal approach, which is expanded on in this chapter, is by its overall nature "formal," meaning that in this type of study, one undertakes a well thought-out project, complete with identified goals and objectives. The project is formally planned, organized, and implemented, and uses accepted oral history methodology that is designed to collect significant data about the subjects that are directly related to the overall objective(s), and it does so in an ethical, legally correct, and sensitive manner. Uniform techniques and materials are employed throughout the life of the project. This means that in order to undertake the project, the person in charge would bring the proposed project to persons in authority, provide full and complete information about said project to these persons, and receive documented permission to undertake the project. Next, the project director, often in conjunction with persons in charge of facilities, carefully identifies a target population; prepares information for that population, including a questionnaire; meets with this population to discuss the overall project; and receives signed permissions from individuals in that population to be interviewed for the project. Sometimes, in the case of aging persons, this involves including others connected to their care who have responsibility of these persons, such as family members or legal representatives. The interview process with the persons selected follows tried and true oral history guidelines, and great care is taken for approaching questions with clarity and honestly. Collection of the information provided by the persons interviewed is treated as historical research and is subject to strict rules of identification and recognition. Interviews are recorded and ultimately transcribed or used for information by the project director. A formal project is undertaken with its purpose related to the collection of useful and reliable data that can be used to advance the study and understanding of the geriatric person. Later in this chapter, specific steps are given for implementation and completion of the formal project.

The informal approach, as this appellation suggests, is the use of oral history in the daily care and treatment of the geriatric individual. Individual caregivers may incorporate this approach in everyday care efforts with an aging population, although it is strongly recommended that such persons secure permission to do so from various parties charged with the care and well-being of this population. An informal approach can happen as simply and easily as asking aging persons to tell something of their childhood or some other such memory, or by listening to an aging person recount a story about something from the past. Many caregivers use this technique to relax or calm aging persons in order to more easily and effectively provide care. Informally using reminiscence therapy may reflect some serious intent on the part of the caregiver to collect meaningful data for a study, but if that is the case, some of the formal methodology should be honored, such as permission to use information for a study. Usually, this approach does not make use of any recording device or questionnaire. Even so, this approach still demands that those involved have a plan and be organized in their approach to the degree that the geriatric persons will benefit from this use as a therapy. In general, as the literature suggests, reminiscence therapy is widely recognized to assist in the overall care of the patient or subject (Weiss & Subak-Sharpe, 1988).

One particular type of oral history is called the "self-directed autobiographical" study. As the name implies, this type of project is designed to encourage subjects to write their autobiographies with a minimum of out-side direction and involvement. This type of oral history project can be organized and implemented either formally or informally, but the emphasis is on self-direction. Depending on the geriatric population, this form could be interesting and helpful to use with seniors. Not only might it trigger memories and encourage various intellectual skills, but it could also be used to stimulate follow-up conversations and even to generate social activities. The autobiographical study results in the collection of various forms of information that differ from one person to another, and, as such, may or may not be limited in helping geriatric care persons.

GETTING STARTED WITH THE FORMAL ORAL HISTORY PROJECT

Step One: Goals and Objectives

Given the supporting literature on the importance of reminiscence therapy in the care and treatment of an aging population, you, as an administrator, determine that you want to undertake a formal project in your facility. The first thing you should do is determine at the onset the overall goal or goals that you are interested in achieving and the various objectives necessary to accomplish these goals. It may be that you have read about a study undertaken in another facility—one that could be replicated or modified for use in your care area. The goal may be a relatively simple one: to attain more social interaction among or within a certain group of persons under your care. How to measure this would be revealed in the objectives, such as: Enable or encourage residents or day care persons to express views about some particular subjects and/or time periods in their lives (marriage, children, living through war, etc.). In any case, this step should be thoroughly explored and documented in such a way that assessment is tied to the various objectives as outcomes. This step should also include identification of someone in your facility as a program director, or, if you are serving in this capacity, as an assistant.

Step Two: Meetings with Significant Parties

This step varies in relation to the gerontological setting and the persons of authority and with responsibility for this facility. As an administrator, you present your proposal and its rationale to persons of authority. This should include any legal personnel connected with the facility. If you are not the top administrator, then you would follow through with meetings with those in the hierarchy above your level. At these meetings, you should be prepared to outline clearly the goals and objectives of your study, the methodology, factors involved with implementation, techniques, and the like. You should also be prepared to discuss the advantages of undertaking such a project, costs (if any) involved, other persons involved, the antici-pated population to be targeted, and the results you hope to attain. This information should be written and well organized and contain a list of scholarly sources related to studies relevant to the one you are proposing.

Step Three: Record Keeping

Before going any further, set up a plan for keeping all records of this proj-ect, from the earliest proposal that you presented to superiors, to signed permissions, to the interview materials—names of persons participating, permissions, recordings of interviews, notes taken at the interviews, and so on. This author usually develops a filing system for this information with separate file folders for each item and separate file folders for each person interviewed. Whatever system you choose, select one that is easy for you to retain, access, and, as necessary, make available should questions arise concerning the project. The file, of course, will be very important if you are planning on presenting your project at professional seminars, for example. A file of the records of the project should be retained by the geriatric facil-ity as well.

Step Four: Permissions

There are two types of permission forms necessary for conducting an oral history project. **Figures 12.1** and **12.2** are samples of these permission forms, created by the author. The first is a permission form that signi-fies permission to conduct an oral history project. This form would be prepared for the signature(s) of the persons whom you have contacted in Step Two. This form should clearly indicate that this person has, or these persons have, granted you power to conduct this project. The form should also contain pertinent information about the project, such as: title; a brief description; the dates on which the project will be conducted, including the expected conclusion date; the population with whom the project is concerned; and any other information that those in authority desire. You should sign this form as well, and it should be dated. *This form or forms, if there are multiple persons involved in granting you permission, must be completed before you proceed with the project.*

I. Permission Form for Administrator of Nursing Home/ Care Facility, Etc.

Permission of Administrator/etc. of _____
                                          (nursing home, etc.)

Oral History Project _____

Title _____

Brief Description (includes goals, objectives, rationale, implementation, etc.)

_____

_____

_____

Project Director _____

Affiliation _____

Dates of Project _____

Name of Administrator _____

Geriatric Facility _____

I, _____, in my capacity as _____ of this facility, grant permission for the director of the oral history project named above to conduct oral interviews of selected persons in this facility on the dates indicated. (May add or adjust this statement as necessary for the person's title depending on the facility.)

Exceptions (any particular exceptions/restrictions, requirements, etc. that administrator feels necessary to include) _____

_____

_____

_____

Signed _____
                (administrator—full title, credentials, etc.)

Signed Project Director _____

Date _____

Figure 12.1 Sample Permission Form #1

II. Permission of Interviewee

Name of Nursing Home/Care Facility, etc. _____

Oral History Project _____

Brief Description of Project (include purpose of project) _____

_____

_____

_____

Project Director _____

Affiliation _____

Dates of Project _____

Name of Interviewee _____

Address _____

I, _____ (the above-named interviewee), state that I agree to participate in the above-named oral history project, that the purpose and nature of the project has been explained to me to my satisfaction and that I agree to be interviewed by _____

(name of interviewer) at the (place) _____

on (date) _____. I grant the project director the right to use the material from my interview for purposes related to the project, as described above, subject to the following exceptions. Exceptions (e.g., "my name may not be identified in any presentation and/or publication related to this project, or the content of my interview [or a particular part of it, note what part] may not be used in any way for 50 years," etc.). _____

_____

_____

_____

Signed _____

Witness, if needed _____

Signed Project Director _____

Date of Signing _____

Figure 12.2 Sample Permission Form #2

The second is a permission form that each person you are going to interview will sign. In a gerontological setting, this form may have to be signed, cosigned, or witnessed by caregivers or family members, depending on the particular situation. This form, like the first, should contain all pertinent information about the project; it should include identification information about the person to be interviewed (the interviewee), and it should provide space for "exceptions"—that is, particular elements about the interview that the interviewee wants done, such as not to publish certain information given in the interview before a certain due date, or during his or her lifetime. This form should also contain your signature, and it should be dated. *This form must be completed with each individual interviewee before you conduct your interview.* This being the case, and in consideration of the population involved, you may want to arrange separate meetings with your interviewees for the signing of their forms. Interviewees may want other persons present at these meetings before signing, and, in such cases, it may be helpful and judicious for you to ask these persons to cosign the permission form. The rule to follow here is to do everything in your power to make the experience a worthwhile, positive, and therapeutic one for the interviewee—one that is in line with the objectives of reminiscence therapy. This, after all, is your primary motivation in conducting the project. If in the course of the project you gain useful information that can be applied to your facility or service, or used for scholarly presentations, then that is a bonus benefit.

Step Five: Ethical/Legal Considerations

A person's unpublished words are his or her property and must not be used without his or her consent or the consent of someone who has been designated as his or her guardian or responsible party. This is the reason for obtaining permission from persons in authority in your facility or service and from those persons whom you propose to interview.

Although some oral history publications may tell you that permissions (sometimes called releases) can be obtained either *before or after the interview*—if after, immediately following the recording of the interview—this author prefers to have *all* permission forms completed and in hand *before* taking the project to the interview phase. This makes for greater clarity of the project and protects all parties involved from misunderstandings about the project as a whole, its rationale, and the information that you are seeking by way of the interviews. If you intend to present and/or publish any data secured by the project, you should, at the time of signing the permissions, make that clear. Knowing this, for example, may make a great difference for the parties involved, and may necessitate your making some adjustments to your project. Interviewees, for example, are often sensitive about particular information or verbal expressions, and may request that you honor their wishes in your writing about their interviews—such things would become "exceptions" on your permission forms. Likewise, those in charge of your facility may have some legal or ethical concerns about the public if you were to present or publish information gained from the project. These would also have to be addressed and clarified to the satisfaction of all parties during your preliminary meetings with those in authority at your facility.

This author cannot stress enough the necessity of securing permissions from all participants in an oral history project. In a project undertaken in a gerontological setting, this means both the responsible caregivers'/agency's permission to implement the project in your facility and interview persons for whom they are responsible, and those persons living in, or associated with, the facility, whom you are going to interview. If your project has been undertaken with the intent to use the content of the interviews in any way, whether for a scholarly research study or for everyday planning for the administration of your facility and its programs, you must hold to the highest ethical and moral standards of your field and for those of historical and other scholarly research. An oral history study is the same as any research project you would undertake—that is, you have a responsibility as a researcher and scholar to identify your research sources and give them credit for information in anything that you write and publish from your study. While you are often dealing with a research-focused population for typical research projects, in the case of oral histories, the population likely has some other significant persons involved with them, including professional healthcare people who are responsible for their care and good health, and/or family members. Legal representatives may also be involved, as would be the case, for example, with persons to be interviewed who may not be able to make judgments about participating in your project, or who feel uncertain about making such judgments. In such cases, they may signify that they want another person or persons, such as a relative, agency, and/or lawyer involved before they will give permission to participate in your project. Of course, it is understood that if a person does not want to be interviewed or is deemed incompetent to be interviewed, you should not pursue it further.

When you have secured the necessary permissions to proceed with the project, you have the right to use the content of the interviews, unless prohibited by the agency, an interviewee, or some other significant party; the right to use the name of the person as related to the material from his or her interview, unless prohibited by the agency, the interviewee, or some other significant party; and the right to publish data related to the information you have gained by the interview(s), unless prohibited by the agency, the interviewee, or some other significant party. When writing about your project, you should adhere to the same research rules for citations and the like that govern scholarly work in your field—in this case, citing the interviewee(s) whose information you are using and the date of the interview.

Signed permission forms or releases do not absolve you of all legal responsibility, especially for publishing libel. If someone is hurt by the publication, you, as well as the interviewee, may be held accountable. Note: The legal definition of libel varies from state to state, but in general, libel is usually written, printed, or pictorial statements that damage a person by defaming character or exposing a person to ridicule. Consequently, you have a responsibility to avoid publishing anything that may damage the reputation of a living person. This would include the interviewee or any other person mentioned or alluded to in the interview.

Finally, there are a number of subtle ethical issues that project leaders should be aware of and avoid at all costs. No one should be pressured to participate. Interviewees should not be promised something for participating in the project.

Even though it is useful to know something about potential interviewees in order to frame questions in a certain way, intensive background checks should not be requested or attempted by those responsible for the project. This would include such things as bank records; school records; or interviews with friends, colleagues, or neighbors of the interviewees.

Do not play the role of a psychological therapist for the interviewee by exploring "bad memories," for example.

If you feel guilty or discontented with certain questions, it is better not to ask these questions. Always maintain the highest standards of integrity at all times during the project. If you have a particular legal or ethical concern, you should seek the advice and counsel of a person of authority.

A neutral position is required of the oral historian. This helps increase objectivity and makes for better communication with the interviewee and understanding of the content of the interview. A neutral stance may seem cold and insensitive.

Permission forms may be tailored to the particular project and to the care facility. They can include any additional information that is pertinent. It is important to remember that these forms are necessary for the project director to retain, and in some cases, for the care facility to keep as well. These forms must be available should any questions arise about the project, the interview(s), or interviewee(s). In some instances, healthcare administrators and others may ask for a legal representation of their facility to review the permission forms. That person may make suggestions for revision of your form or forms. Such advice must be accepted.

THE INTERVIEW

Step One: Preparation

After you have received permission to undertake an oral history project and you have the permission form(s) signed by those persons in authority, it is time to identify the persons to be interviewed and meet with them in order to explain the project and secure from them the necessary signed permission forms. Identification of persons to be interviewed depends on a number of factors and might require some discussion with various staff persons and other care providers. In a senior day care center, for example, to get word of the project out, you might begin with the posting of a message announcing the project, its purposes, and inviting persons to come to a meeting to learn more about the project and the possibility of participating in it. It is helpful to arrange this meeting with a social cast to it: including refreshments and stressing that attendance is voluntary. This message should contain clear, specific information about this meeting, such as when and where it will be held. Your announcement should also include some specifics about your study and how it will be undertaken. You should include some identifying information about yourself as the project director.

It is quite common to use the informal information session technique to interest persons in participating. This gives persons you are interested in interviewing the opportunity to learn about the project, ask questions about it, and receive answers for concerns they might have about participation. It will also give people the opportunity to meet you, and you, them. Depending on the situation and various circumstances, if you feel it is opportune, you might use this session to begin signing up interested persons.

If your project is to be in a nursing home, the administrator or other personnel may be able to assist with identifying those persons who would be most apt or able to participate. In such circumstances, it may not be possible or useful to conduct a general information meeting. Determination of this is up to you and those with whom you are working on the oral history project. Whatever the case, the guiding principle should be successful completion of the goal of the project within the confines of the geriatric world in which you are working.

Step Two: Meeting the Interviewees

The purpose of this meeting is to explain the project, answer questions, and deal with issues and concerns of the targeted population. If this first meeting with likely interviewees is a group meeting, here are some useful techniques to follow:

· *Introductions.* Introduce yourself and any others who will be involved with the project.

· *Explain the purpose for the meeting.* Provide clear, specific information about the project and how it will be undertaken. It might be helpful to outline this information on paper and hand it out at the meeting. Provide some sample questions to give people an idea of the kind of information you will be seeking.

· *Group introductions.* Ask the persons attending to introduce themselves, and, depending on the population's health and mental capacity, ask each attendee to tell a little something about themselves.

· *Permission forms.* Pass out the participant permission forms and review with the attendees.

· *Project participation forms.* Ask the attendees to participate, and, if they are interested in so doing, ask them to add their names to a project participation form that you are passing out. On this form, ask them to include information about their availability for an individual meeting, at which time you will go over the project again and answer any questions or concerns they might have about it. It is a good idea to try to make these individual meetings soon after the initial contact. Most persons conducting projects with aging persons and others do not provide interviewee permission forms at this initial meeting, but, rather, plan to do this at the next, individual meetings. You should, however, tell the group or person at this point that permission forms are required for them to sign in order to participate in the project. You might pass out a sample form for them to look over. Some persons may require others to be involved in the signing. If this is the case, it is best to be aware of this as soon as possible and plan to make arrangements for such persons to attend the next meeting with the prospective interviewee. Information concerning additional responsible parties involved with the care and treatment of an aging population as this relates to the project should be included at the initial stages of selecting interviewees. Additional meetings with these persons to review the project may be necessary before you can move ahead with the interview process.

· *Questionnaires.* Most oral historians develop a questionnaire for the oral history project that includes all the particular questions that they are seeking to have answered by interviewees. The initial meeting is not usually a good time to present this, but the project director should have it ready for this meeting and plan to pass out copies for persons to take with them and study after the meeting. Let the persons keep the questionnaires and ask them to review the questionnaire prior to the next meeting. Interview questions are targeted to your particular goal and the objectives of the project, but also must include basic personal identification/information questions, such as name, address, date, age, marital status, whether they have children (yes or no; number), and so on. Questions involving religion, race and or ethnicity, political affiliation, and the like should not be included. Some questions on the questionnaire will not be relevant to every interviewee. Explain this and reassure the prospective interviewees.

Distribution of the questionnaire should occur sometime before the interview, at either this initial meeting—even if this is a meeting in a group setting—or later at individual meetings with those who have agreed to be interviewed. Passing out the questionnaire at either point in the pre-interview stage affords you the opportunity of going over it with likely or actual project participants and answering any questions that might come up. More about the questionnaire is covered later in this chapter.

· *Conclusion of meeting.* Conclude the meeting and set a time for the next meeting, which will most often be individual meetings with interested parties.

· *Social.* Including some refreshments, either before or after this meeting, tends to relax prospective interviewees (and you) and enables easier exchange of information. It is important that the persons you are hoping to interview get to know you and feel comfortable with you, which is what makes a social gathering a good approach. It is also an excellent opportunity for you as the project director to become better acquainted with your prospective subjects.

If the population you have targeted for the project cannot attend the meeting or prefers to meet with you separately, you would meet with this person or persons as necessary and go over the project along these same lines.

A final word about the choice of interviewees: If the goal of your project is to enhance the life experiences of the aging population, then the choice of interviewees must be persons who can be identified as likely to gain from the experience of participating in this project and who can provide information that will help you realize this goal.

Step Three: Arranging the Interview

Individual Meetings with Prospective Interviewees Prior to the Interview

Arrangements to interview persons chosen for the project require careful advance planning. Letters or phone calls are the usual methods of contact with interviewees at this point. Or, in the case of residents of a nursing facility or a person visiting a senior living/care facility, some other form of communication is required, such as a scheduled meeting at the facility. Whatever approach you use, be brief and to the point. Agree on a time and place for this meeting, and contact any additional persons that should be present at this meeting, such as family, friends, or nursing facility assistants.

Individual Meeting Prior to Interview

This contact is primarily for the purpose of discussing the project with likely interviewees and answering any individual questions or concerns they, or others responsible for their care and well-being, may have. The person(s) and their particular situation will determine whatever contact method you employ. The most important objective of this meeting is to make likely interviewees aware of the purpose of the project and to explain it clearly and simply to avoid any confusion or concern, as this could be counterproductive. Consequently, at this meeting you should discuss:

- *Details.* Review your purpose in undertaking the project and include particulars concerning it, including the recording methodology you will be using (tape or digital recorder; video recorder, etc.).
- *Timeframe.* Indicate the time period you purpose to follow for the interview (e.g., 1 hour), taking into consideration the health of the interviewee. (If the interviewee is particularly health challenged, it may be necessary to schedule interviews in short sessions.)
- *Review interviewee permission form.* Read through the interviewee permission forms and explain again the particulars, including the possibility of adding exceptions to the form. Review with the interviewee the guarantee of privacy (as provided in the permission form).
- *Review questionnaire.* Bring questionnaire containing the questions you will be using in the interview to this meeting, and go over the questions. If you have already given persons this questionnaire at an earlier meeting, ask if there are any questions about it. Review questions with the interviewee. Reassure them that it is not necessary for

them to answer every question—that, in fact, some questions may not be relevant to them. Tell them that they may refer to the questionnaire at the time of the interview, but discourage them from simply reciting answers to questions at the interview.

- *Answer questions.* Be prepared to answer any and all questions the prospective interviewee or others at this meeting may have about the project, interview methodology, the questions, and so on in a friendly, open manner.
- *Sensitivity.* Be sensitive to individual concerns and strive to reassure and adjust to the wishes of the parties involved as much as possible.
- *Setting date and time for interview.* Finally, at this meeting, you and the prospective interviewee should set a particular date/time/place for the interview. The selection of a place for the interview should be somewhere that is quiet and private, although in some cases, sites may be limited by the geriatric person's condition and/or needs. The interview should occur soon after this meeting—no later than 2 weeks afterward, if possible.

The approach to gaining information from interviewees is similar for both the formal and informal approach. The difference is that in the informal approach, interviews most often take the form of spontaneous conversations or brief questions to the geriatric person to stimulate interest or memory, and are usually relatively brief and do not include questionnaires. However, if you are seriously collecting data from the informal approach, you may develop a questionnaire that contains the particular areas you feel are important to cover with the population you have targeted, and you may want to record responses. Although informal, this approach still requires that you receive permission of the care facility and/or other parties for whom it is responsible in order to conduct this project, and requires this facility to support this approach in the care and treatment of its geriatric population. In addition, you should seek some signed permission form either from the patient or from those responsible for her or him. Files of this sort of activity should be retained by the facility and you.

Maintaining the integrity of the interview is most important. With both the formal and informal approaches, interviews are conducted with individuals (interviewees) separately, not in group settings. The exception to this is that persons responsible for the well-being of the interviewee (relative, etc.) may wish to be present, or, depending on the health of the interviewee, are required to be present. This is permitted, but the interview must be with the interviewee, not the outside party. Special effort must be made to make this clear to the outside party as well as to the interviewee. The reasons for this are fairly obvious: a one-on-one interview is more focused, less subject to distractions, and the information given by the interviewee is his or her own, not someone else's. Reassure the interviewee that issues involving memory lapses or inability to respond are common in all oral history projects, and if this occurs, the interviewer will go to the next area. Another reason for the interview to be with only the interviewee is that the quality of the recording of the interview, including the sound and the information collected, is not compromised by outside noises or comment.

Step Four: Preparing for the Interview

Overview

An oral history project is really the collection of pertinent information and, as such, is a "life history" of the interviewee(s). This means that in your interviews you will be seeking information about various segments of the life of your interviewee—early life, community, education, family and relationships, work history, as well as information that is more current. Life history requires that you view this information against a social situation, such as:

> What kind of family, neighborhood, and economic class are part of the interviewee's life?
> What schools did he or she attend?
> What friends does or did he or she have?
> What types of entertainment does or did the interviewee enjoy?
> Whom did the interviewee marry? Did they have children?
> What type of work did the interviewee do, and did he or she work during a time of prosperity or otherwise?
> What was the interviewee's life like during the various segments of time?
> How does the subject feel about important events that occurred during his or her lifetime (war, economic distress, etc.)? Has the view of the interviewee changed about these things over time?

Your questions will reflect the particular goal and objectives of your project. If, for example, you are interested in discovering interviewees' views about life in current times or current concerns, you would construct questions related to these subjects. If your goal is to encourage or stimulate enhanced cognitive awareness or activity, your questions should be geared to subjects that might arouse interviewees' thoughts, memories, observations, and the like.

Research the backgrounds of the interviewees. Do some homework! Gather information on the periods that occurred during the interviewees' lives and study significant historical events that your interviewees have lived through. Thorough background research of the interviewees and these periods makes it possible to recognize bad answers, dishonesty, or poor memory, while, at the same time, your knowledge of this information will serve to stimulate interviewees' memories and provide good content.

How does one gather information about prospective interviewees? This will depend on their circumstances. If, for example, they are living in an assisted care situation, background data may be available—if it is not restricted for privacy reasons. Persons in authority in a senior care facility will usually have general information about the subjects in the facility, but are subject to laws related to confidentiality. If no background information can be obtained from the facility, the interviewees themselves may be able or willing to provide this information to you. Sometimes relatives or friends of the interviewee will provide some general information, but you must obtain the permission of the facility or service and the interviewee before you seek information from this source. Most often, however, the interviewee him- or herself will provide some basic information. After all, you must have had some reason to ask the person for an interview in the first place. If all else fails, the interviewer may look to the person's circumstances for a few clues.

Step Five: Preparation of Questions

To be well prepared for the interview, it is necessary to think: How can I relate the information I have about the interviewee to the interview? An essential part of conducting a successful oral history project is the preparation of specific questions to be used in the interview. The basic questionnaire is prepared in advance of the interview, as noted earlier, and you have already made it available to prospective interviewees. This questionnaire, in addition to containing identification information, contains particular questions related to the project, its objectives, its overall goal, and to the interviewees themselves. Yet, you as the interviewer should not feel confined to these basic areas. Many times interviewees will go further than a question on the questionnaire, or you may decide to probe for further information or details. A good rule to adopt is: Be flexible at all times during the interview.

Now that you are set to begin interviewing, you should review the questions you have constructed on the questionnaire. You have by this time already met the interviewees, so it may be possible to ascertain certain areas in which this or that interviewee might provide additional or more specific information. Be prepared for such times. Outside of purely identifying questions (e.g., how many children do you have?), develop "open-ended" questions. These are questions that are designed to allow the interviewee to respond more fully and in more detail. An example of an open-ended question is: How did you feel about this? Or, tell me something about your life in that community. As already noted, it is common to distribute this questionnaire to the interviewees sometime before the interview. This is done in order to allow them time to think about and to recall the subject of the questionnaire. Experienced oral historians believe that early reading/review of the questionnaire also relaxes the interviewee and makes him or her less fearful, anxious, or stressed, so that at the time of the actual interview, the situation is comfortable and unstrained. This makes for a good interview and a satisfying experience for both parties: interviewee and interviewer.

Some interviewers prepare a written interview guide containing notes, possible questions, and the order in which to ask questions related to the persons they will be interviewing. Interviewers should not attempt to rely on memory during an interview, nor should they glue themselves to a questionnaire—this may result in a robot-like interview and actually discourage interviewees from adding interesting or important details to an answer. Instead, it is advisable for the interviewer to think of some key words to stir the memory. Note cards or books are often used with a key word on top, and interviewers use space below to take notes during, or immediately after, the interview.

Bear in mind that no interview will (or should) run according to some exactly planned script—spontaneity is a good thing—especially if the interviewee moves beyond a particular question or questions to tell you a special story or relate a particular memory! For the interviewer, this might become the best part of the interview and, if your objectives for the project include enhancement of the interviewees' lives and stimulation of memories, such spontaneity would serve to advance this purpose.

With a geriatric subject, the actual site for the implementation of this type of project may be an elder care facility (senior citizen center or nursing home), or, if preferred by the interviewee, a private residence or another site of the interviewee's choosing, agreeable to the interviewer. The one necessity is that, whatever the site, it must be comfortable, quiet, have access for the technology to be used in the interview, and, given the geriatric factor, contain whatever else is necessary for the interviewee to be able to participate in the project.

The following are some factors you should consider before preparing your questions/questionnaire to implement the formal approach.

1. *Goal(s) and objectives of project.* Going back to your initial goal(s) and objectives for this project, ask: What is it that I would like to learn from this study? How is this related to my goal(s) and objectives? Develop questions that are clearly stated and measurable in relation to the objectives.

2. *Questions/questionnaire.* Develop questions that are simple and clear, use basic vocabulary, and are brief. Do not embellish your questions with unnecessary adjectives/adverbs and other modifiers. Do not try to "impress" the interviewee with use of scholarly terminology. Remember: "Know your interviewee" is an excellent axiom to follow, as is also, "show some sensitivity to the person you will be interviewing." As noted earlier, compose open-ended questions that encourage the interviewee to recall events and give you their thoughts and ideas.

3. *Pertinent information on questionnaire.* Include identification information about the interviewee on the first page of questionnaire, such as name, age, occupation, and any other basic information that is pertinent to your study. The date on the questionnaire should be the date of the actual interview.

4. *Questions in logical order.* Be sure to develop questions in a logical order, asking questions that have a relationship with the previous questions. Do not jump from subject to subject.

5. *Ordering of questions.* Ordering questions is important. It is a good idea to start out with basic questions and advance to the more complex, saving the more difficult questions for later in the interview.

6. *Do not rely on your memory.* There is much to think about during an interview, so do not rely on your memory—ask your questions from the questionnaire. Allow the interviewee to have his or her copy of the questionnaire there as well. Some interviewees will prepare to write out the answers on the questionnaire and answer the oral questions directly from the questionnaire. This means that the interviewer cannot skip around the questionnaire, but will have to ask his or her questions directly from the questionnaire.

Some oral historians believe it is a mistake to use a written questionnaire or to have any prepared questions—that this creates a robot-like interview and discourages spontaneity. This could happen, but the author prefers to plan the project with a primary focus on the interviewee as related to the overall goal(s) and objectives of the project. If you are conducting interviews with a population that is challenged or particular in any way, this must be your overriding consideration. In the case of an aging population who may have some difficulties with memory and anxiety, have health issues, and so on, it is essential to provide an interview vehicle that is doable.

Some interviewers prefer to use a notepad with a keyword on top and take notes during the interview, rather than have and use the questionnaire. If this is something that seems to work with you, then follow this technique. The problem with this technique, in my opinion, is that it puts a great deal of stress on the interviewer to recall particular questions that he or she wants to ask. It also opens up the possibility for questions to be asked for which the interviewee may feel unprepared or uncomfortable.

If taking notes during the interview helps you concentrate on your project and remember certain points, then do this, but do not take extensive notes. Write brief summaries of responses, or take notes on a particular point or a quotable comment. Many oral historians like to think of their interviews as conversations. Maintaining a conversational style during the interview makes for a more relaxing, pleasant experience for the interviewee as well.

If you do use notes, remember: No interview will follow exactly prearranged notes. There is always something new that will come up which will give the interview a unique and interesting quality. Sometimes the particular information that is a response to a scripted question will suggest an unplanned follow-up question. In such an instance, the interviewer should go ahead and include this follow-up question.

A final word about the questions: If you feel guilty or discontented with certain questions, it is better not to ask these questions. Likewise, if the interviewee volunteers personal information which is either outside the focus of your project or which you know or feel to be inappropriate and unnecessary, use your skilled training to move the interview away from such topics. When transcribing and using this interview in relation to your project's goal, this information should not be used. If you have any doubts about the ethical way to proceed in such a circumstance, you should consult someone in authority. The rule to follow here is that in all things related to the project, you will always maintain the highest standards of integrity.

Step Six: Equipment

As you prepare for the interview, make a point of checking out your equipment. Depending on the equipment you will be using, be prepared for any eventuality. Carry extra SIM cards, batteries, electric plugs, extension cords (do not rely on batteries), tapes, and so on. If you feel more confident plugging your recorder into an electrical outlet, do so, but if this is your plan, be sure to take an extension cord along to the interview.

Today, there are a number of choices available for conducting an oral history project. Many oral historians still use a tape or a cassette recorder. However, these devices are declining in use, as better and easier-to-use technologies have come on the market, such as the digital recorder and the video recorder. Whatever equipment you choose, it is vital to the success of the project to use a recording device that is comfortable for you, and that you are skilled in using. As such, it is a good idea to do a brief run through before the interview. You might start recording the name of the person, place, date, and your name in advance of that interview. Play it back to be certain it is clear. Some of the newer technology may seem complicated to you. If that is the case, consult a technician for expert advice and run through a mock recording with him or her.

Practice operating the recorder in advance of the interview. Before each interview, record the project name and your name as an introduction to the interview. Record also the full name of the interviewee, place of the interview, and date of the interview.

A number of oral historical projects are currently using video cameras. There are both pros and cons to video use. Much depends on the project and the interviewees. In the case of a life history project such as you would be undertaking in a senior facility, video may not work as well as conducting oral interviews using recording devices—unless your objective is to study visual responses, for example. It is known that video cameras may cause interviewees stress and anxiety—subjects tend to be distracted by the fact that they are being filmed and get off point or get nervous with the result that they are paying more attention to the camera, and their thought process suffers. In the case of an aging population, this form could appear intrusive and discomforting, and could cause potential subjects to decline participation in the project. On the other hand, we have all seen documentaries that make use of an aging population telling something of their lives, or parts they played in important events. Such material can be particularly revealing as we look into their faces, see their expressions, and hear their thoughts. Some projects today that are connected to various grants mandate use of video. As you consider undertaking your project you must weigh these pros and cons and decide on equipment that is in the best interests of all involved. If you do decide to use a video recorder, be mindful that its use would have to be included in your initial discussions with those in authority, and permission to use this type of device must be included on all permission forms. This would also be the case as you begin to meet with prospective interviewees. Yet another factor to be aware of with the use of video is that it may be necessary for you to employ a person who is adept at the use of a video camera to assist you. Some small, user-friendly video equipment is available, but focusing and other concerns relative to recording the interview with this equipment may make it difficult for you, the interviewer, to concentrate on the interview.

Step Seven: Conducting the Interview

Interviews Are Conducted on an Individual Basis

Arrangement to Conduct an Interview is Made by Appointment

Arriving at the Interview

Arrive at the time set for the interview. Set the stage for a pleasant experience. After social informalities, spend a few minutes explaining the project again and the interviewee's part in it. Ask if the interviewee has any questions and respond fully to these. You might include some information you have found about the interviewee during your preliminary research. This helps eliminate dishonest or incorrect information, or it may simply help jog memory. Ask the interviewee how he or she would like to be addressed during the interview: formally, as in Mr. Smith or Mrs. Smith, by first name, or a shortened form of first name. If there are other persons to be present during the interview, it is a good time to review the basic interview format and to request that such persons refrain from responding or assisting the interviewees in their responses. Mention again, the need to maintain a level of quiet during the interview. Answer any questions the interviewee might have and go over any aspect of the interview or project that the interviewee wants to discuss. Ask that water be provided at the site of the interview.

Set Up Your Equipment

Survey the Environment

Watch out for noise, other persons in the area, television, radio, or anything that would distract you from the interview or interfere with the interview. Make every effort to establish a relaxed atmosphere during the interview. Be friendly and relaxed. Be sensitive to the interviewees and their concerns, fears, questions, and the like. Under no circumstances should you be argumentative or judgmental. As a scholar, your job is to faithfully record the information provided by the interviewees. If the interviewee requests that you turn off the recorder, do so. If you notice the interviewee getting tired, suggest ending the interview for the day and make arrangements to go on later.

Try Not to Focus on the Recording Device

If the subject is concerned about it, allow time for her or him to get used to it. You might play back some of the interview, for example. Go slowly, minimize the recorder's presence, but make sure you have easy access to it and can check it at various points during the interview to determine that it is working properly. An advantage of newer digital recorders is that they are small and compact and not so noticeable, while at the same time offering excellent quality. Moreover, the recordings can be transferred to a CD or other media for listening and preservation.

Most Interviewers Take Some Notes During the Interview

This helps you concentrate on your topic and remember certain key points. These notes should not be extensive—more like summaries to responses. If it is not appropriate or you do not feel comfortable taking notes during the interview, plan to do so immediately afterward. Note taking gives you the opportunity to register your own thoughts and perceptions during the interview.

If Other Persons Are Present During the Interview

As noted already, it is not unusual for interviewees to want another person present during an interview (a family member, friend, representative). Likewise, as also noted, that person should not contribute to the interview and you should have made this clear earlier. However, sometimes this does become a problem with the outsider making a comment or trying to assist the interviewee with an answer. If this happens, turn off the recorder and ask this person to refrain from participating. If this continues, you will have to end the interview. Explain the reason for doing this. You are interested in gaining information from the interviewee, not from some other person. Including the responses or comments of other parties compromises the scholarly integrity of the interview. A confidential discussion of this with these persons in advance of the interview is usually sufficient to correct this situation.

Listen

More so than anything else during the interview, listen. Notice the demeanor of the interviewee. Note his or her language and expression. During the interview, be alert to interviewee's mannerisms, gestures, facial expressions, and the like. Such things may indicate that the interviewee is tiring or not focusing, or unable to continue. If that is the case, it may be better to conclude the interview and suggest meeting another day. It is up to you to control the interview and its direction.

Maintain the Integrity of the Surroundings

There should be no background noise, so planning as to the site of the interview is important. If there is unexpected noise or interrupting sounds, stop the interview and try to correct the problem. If another person is involved, such as a family member who makes certain sounds or contributes comments, be diplomatic but firm, and always courteous and polite.

How Do You Deal with Silence?

The interviewee may not answer immediately or some time may elapse between the question and the answer. Remembering takes time. Allow the interviewee time. Do not rush the interviewee. Sometimes you may want to contribute a thought on the topic, or a comment on the subject from your own experience. This can help move the interview along, jog memory, and elicit information or a feeling from the interviewee that he did not know he had.

Some Common-Sense Directives

When asking questions, these are the hard and fast rules to live by: Be courteous, show empathy, seek detail, ask open-ended and probing questions, and always follow up on answers so that you have a thorough response to the subject.

Completing the Interview

When you have come to the end of your questions, thank the interviewee and tell her or him something of your schedule with the project. It is not unusual for interviewees to ask if they can have a copy of their interview for themselves or family members. If there are not legal or other concerns about this, you may agree to this. An interview with a beloved relative or friend often becomes a cherished possession as time goes on. A day or so after an interview, it is a thoughtful gesture to send the interviewee a note thanking them for allowing you to interview them.

Completing the Project

When you have completed your interviews, it is time to transcribe the interviews, or if your objective was to use the interviews to gain information and simply take or make notes from the interviews, then this is the next step. Transcribing interviews is a project in itself, and requires a professional transcriber. This can be costly, but it is necessary if your goal is publication of a book or article using the *exact* words of the interviewees in response to your questions. If your purpose is publication of your findings based on information collected from your interviews, you must make it clear that you are interpreting the responses in your own words. In both instances, the interviewees are cited as sources.

If your goal, on the other hand, is to gain insight and data concerning the aging population in certain life situations and/or with regard to certain issues for the purpose of applying this information to enhance the services you provide, then you would, most likely, take notes from the recorded interviews and develop an overall plan for implementation at your facility.

At this point in the project, it is important to organize carefully all your information and records, including transferring your interviews to a CD, for safekeeping. It is advisable to make a duplicate file in case records become lost or misplaced over time (Baum, 1995).

SUMMARY

This chapter provides a guide for administrators of geriatric facilities who might be interested in undertaking oral history projects. Although there are numerous works available detailing oral history methodologies, this author has fashioned a concise, but specific, detailed, and sensitive approach for doing an oral history study with the aging population. Beginning with a brief history of oral history and gerontology and the relationship between the two disciplines; then providing an analysis of the growing body of literature in gerontology and oral history, emphasizing connections between the two fields; laying out the "nuts and bolts" of an oral history project that includes planning, implementation, and consideration of issues and concerns; we have come full circle to the initial question: Why undertake this approach in the first place? Research tells us that that there are a number of possible benefits to be gained for aging people from reminiscence or thinking about their lives. Perhaps the most important therapeutic outcome seen by theorists in the field of gerontology is that it can enhance memory; even in the simplest form, a conversation between a nurse or geriatric aid and an aging person about the past, can stir or improve memory.

This author suggests that additional benefits to the aging population may be forthcoming as well. First and foremost may be a sense of pride in one's life story. This can also be combined with a renewed sense of self-esteem and worth for a population that may have come to the point in their lives when they feel or believe that their accomplishments are in the past and are no longer of any importance. Depression, often associated with the aging, may be helped by participating in an oral history project that is designed to emphasize lives well lived and contributions made to the community and to the nation.

Another benefit to be gained for an aging population who are part of an oral history project is simply, socialization. In a group project, this may be gained by including some autobiographical reading of the interviewees' work or by participation in project meetings to talk and share information. Even the preparatory meeting and individual interview itself can become an opportunity for greater socialization for the interviewees—periods for interaction and opportunities for conversation and, in some instances, amusement. Interview sessions can be enhancing and therapeutic for interviewees, and for caregivers and healthcare professionals alike.

Certain projects can be designed to target particular concerns and issues of geriatric healthcare professionals, such as identification of patients' anxieties about a facility, their family, personal problems, or their futures. Identification of such issues offers healthcare persons and the facility an opportunity to address problems before they can become debilitating or counterproductive to persons' overall health.

As healthcare professionals considering the possibility of undertaking oral history projects in geriatric settings, there are many possible therapeutic benefits that you may envision based on your personal expertise in the field and particular area of focus. Merging the field of gerontology and oral history and developing oral history projects in geriatric settings offers healthcare professionals a proven method and the opportunity for original thinking to achieve positive results for those persons to whom they are dedicated, and to contribute to the field in which they have chosen to serve.

Discussion Questions

1. What are some reasons (goals and objectives) I should consider for creating an oral history project at the facility where I work?

2. What are some issues or concerns relative to my facility and the geriatric population in my care that I should confront before I make a final decision on using oral history at my facility?

3. Should I consult with any healthcare professionals before I undertake an oral history project? If so, whom?

4. Given my particular facility and as administrator (or professional in some other capacity), who are some persons in management or other areas above my level in the chain of command to whom I report, to whom I am responsible, and with whom I would (or should) review the project and receive permission to go ahead with its implementation?

5. If I decide to implement a project, should I include staff persons and, if so, who and how many?

6. Should I consider conducting a formal or informal oral history project? What would be the benefits of each? The drawbacks?

7. What are the cost factors involved with conducting an oral history project at my facility? Example: a recording device.

8. What facilities and necessary items are available at my facility for this project (rooms, etc.)?

9. How would I measure success of such a project?

10. What are the long-range potentials for an oral history project at my facility?

FURTHER READING

Bogart, B. A., & Montell, W. L. (1981). *From memory to history: Using oral sources for historical research.* Nashville, TN: American Association for State and Local History.

Davis, C., Black, K., & McLean, K. (1997). *Oral history: From tape to type.* Chicago, IL: American Library Association.

Dunaway, D. K., & Baum, W. K. (Eds). (1996). *Oral history: An interdisciplinary anthology* (2nd ed.). Walnut Creek, CA: AltaMira Press.

Fletcher, W. (1986). *Recording your family history: A guide to preserving oral history with video tape, audio tape, suggested topics and questions.* New York: Dodd, Mead and Co.

Havlice, P. P. (1985). *Oral history: A reference guide and annotated bibliography.* Jefferson, NC: McFarland.

Hoopes, J. (1979). *Oral history: An introduction for students.* Chapel Hill, NC: University of North Carolina Press.

Ives, E. (1980). *The tape recorded interview.* Knoxville, TN: University of Tennessee.

Jackson, B. (1987). *Fieldwork.* Urbana, IL: University of Illinois Press.

Lance, D. (1978). *An archive approach to oral history.* London: Imperial War Museum.

Matters, M. (1995). *Oral history cataloging manual.* Chicago, IL: Society of American Archivists.

Moss, W. (1974). *Oral history program manual.* New York: Praeger.

Neuenschwander, J. A. (1993). *Oral history and the law* (2nd ed., rev.) Denton, TX: Oral History Association.

Oral History Association. (1989). *Oral history evaluation guidelines.* Carlisle, PA: Dickinson College. Available online at http://omega.dickinson.edu/organizations/oha/pub_eg.html.

Ritchie, D. A. (1995). *Doing oral history,* New York: Twayne Publishers.

Sitton, T., Mehaffy, G. L., & Davis, O. L. (1983). *Oral history: A guide for teachers (and others).* Austin, TX: University of Texas Press.

Sommer, B. W., & Quinlan, M. K. (2002). A guide to oral history interviews. Technical Leaflet #210. American Association for State and Local History. Included in *History News, Vol. 55, No.3, Summer 2000. The Oral History Manual.* Walnut Creek, CA: AltaMira Press.

Stielow, F. J. (1986). *The management of oral history sound archives.* New York: Greenwood Press.

Thompson, P. (1978). *The voice of the past: Oral history*. New York: Oxford University Press.

United States Holocaust Memorial Museum. (1998). *Oral history interview guidelines*. Washington, DC: The Museum. Available online at http://www.ushmm.org/archives/oralhist.pdf.

Ward, A. (1990). *A manual of sound archive administration*. Brookfield, VT: Gower Publishing Co.

Whitman, G. (2004). *Dialogue with the past: Engaging students and meeting standards through oral history*. Walnut Creek, CA: AltaMira Press.

Yow, V. R. (1994). *Recording oral history: A practical guide for social scientists*. Thousand Oaks: SAGE Publications.

REFERENCES

Adams, J. (1986, September/October). Anamnesis in dementia: Restoring a personal history. *Geriatric Nursing, 6*(5), 25–27.

Baum, W. K. (1995). *Oral history for the local historical society* (3rd ed.). Walnut creek, CA: AltaMira Press.

Bornat, J., & Tetley, J. (2010). Oral history and ageing. *Generations Review: Newsletter of the British Society of Gerontology*. Retrieved March 26, 2012, from http://www.britishgerontology.org/DB/gr-editions-2/generations-review/oral-history-and-ageing.html.

Butler, R. N. (1975). *Why survive? Being old in America*. Baltimore, MD: The Johns Hopkins University Press.

Forest Pharmaceuticals. (2005). *The Alzheimer's activities guide: A caregiver's guide of daily activities for people with Alzheimer's disease*. St. Louis, MO: Author.

Frank, B. M. (1982). *A "do-it-yourself" oral history primer*. Washington, DC: History and Museums Divisions, Headquarters, U.S. Marine Corps.

Gerontological Society of America (GSA). (2008). History. Retrieved March 25, 2012, from http://www.geron.org/About%20Us/history.

Kirshenblatt-Gimblett, B., Hufford, M., Hunt, M., & Zeitlin, S. (2006). The grand generation: Forklore and the culture of aging. *Generations, 30*(1), 32–37.

Martin, D. (2010, July 7). Robert Butler, 83, aging expert, dies: Inspired new approaches for aging population. *New York Times*, p. A13.

Quigley, P. (1981). *Those were the days: Life review therapy for aging population residents in long term care facilities*. Buffalo, NY: Health & Aging Services, Inc.

Sharpless, R. (2007). The history of oral history. In L. E. Thomas & L. Carlaton (Eds.), *History of oral history: Foundations and methodology* (pp. 9–12). Lanham, MD: AltaMira Press, Rowman and Littlefield.

Weiss, R. J., & Subak-Sharpe, G. J. (1988). *Complete guide to health and well-being after 50*. New York: Times Books.

Zablotny, C. (2006). Elders share the arts: Transforming memory into art. *Generations, 30*(1), 57–58.

Chapter 13

Ethics in Long-Term Care

Christina A. Hasemann, PhD, RD, L/CDN, CNSD

LEARNING OBJECTIVES

1. To increase knowledge and understanding of ethical principles and theories
2. To heighten awareness of modern ethical theory
3. To gain greater awareness of ethical concerns in health care today
4. To create awareness of the role of leadership in creating an ethical organization
5. To understand the importance of an ethical organization in providing quality care

KEY TERMS

Ethics: The rules or standards governing the conduct of an individual, or the members of a society

Ethical Issues: Pertaining to, or dealing with, morals and values

Teleology: The study of goals, ends, and purposes

Analytical Principlism: An ethical framework that applies the four moral principles: autonomy, beneficence, nonmaleficence, and justice to contemporary ethical dilemmas

INTRODUCTION

Ethics is a topic that often elicits a level of discomfort, even in the most confident. As professionals, we like answers to our questions and critical pathways and protocols that give us concrete guidance. The realm of ethics is lacking these comforts. Ethics is a systematic process of reflection in which issues of what one morally ought to do are analyzed, decided, and evaluated through moral reasoning (Silva, 1990). It is the vagueness that leaves us unsettled, especially when it involves life-and-death decisions.

In the broad sense, ethics deals with the evaluation of human actions in everyday situations. It refers to how individuals conduct themselves in their personal and professional endeavors (Scott, 2009). Ethics encompasses a process of determining what is morally right versus wrong—the same right versus wrong we learned as children. Individual ethics are formulated from a variety of factors: family orientation, life experiences, societal norms, and the influences of religion, education, and environment.

Ethical issues no longer are limited to concerns with human experimentation and laboratory research. Human value issues have assumed increasing importance in recent decades. These issues have expanded to encompass the growing spectrum of health-related decisions throughout the lifecycle, and the economic impacts of allocation of healthcare resources. Ethical issues in today's health care have expanded to well beyond the scope of the Hippocratic oath, which focuses on the responsibilities of the medical practitioner to his patient.

REVIEW OF ETHICAL PRINCIPLES AND FRAMEWORKS

The word "ethics" is derived from the Greek words *ethikos*, which means character, and *ethos*, which means character, customs, or habitual uses (Guido, 2009). Healthcare professionals are guided by four ethical principles in caring for patients and when conducting clinical research. These four principles are autonomy, beneficence, nonmaleficence, and justice (Beauchamp & Childress, 2001).

The ethical principle of autonomy refers to self-governance, personal freedom, and self-determination. The legal doctrine of informed consent is a direct result of this ethical principle. Autonomy is not a legal right, and thus restrictions can be placed on a person's right to endanger others. An example of this would be knowingly spreading the HIV virus through unprotected sexual contact. Respect for autonomy is based in the respect for self-determination. In the healthcare delivery system, the patient self-determination act allows patients the right to control what is done for or to them. Patients have autonomy regardless of their ability to pay for care. Healthcare professionals exercise autonomy within the scope of their professional practice and through professional codes of ethics (Scott, 2009).

The ethical principle of beneficence states that the actions one takes should promote good. In health care, good can be defined in a variety of ways—from donation of blood or solid organs, to allowing one to die without aggressive measures. Conversely, good can prompt healthcare professionals to persuade patients to undergo painful treatments if the treatment will extend the long-term quantity and quality of life—such as surgery, chemotherapy, and radiation for cancers. Thus, the difficulty lies in how "good" is defined.

The ethical principle of nonmaleficence means do no harm. Interventions carried out by healthcare professionals can cause pain, or even injury. This principle requires that healthcare professionals not intentionally or maliciously cause harm or injury. As with other ethical principles, the ethical duty of nonmaleficence applies to omissions, or the failure to act when one should act, such as not calling 911 after seeing an accident occur (Scott, 2009).

A classic illustration of the principle of nonmaleficence is assisted suicide. In the 1990s, the right-to-die activist, Dr. Jack Kevorkian, assisted at least 130 clients to die. He confidently declared that he did not violate the principle of nonmaleficence because his purpose in intervening was to alleviate their suffering: "My aim in helping the patient was not to cause death. My aim was to end suffering" (Kevorkian as cited in Colavecchio-VanSickler, 2008, p. B1). The principle of beneficence also is involved in the situation highlighting the intricacy of defining good.

The ethical principle of justice states that people should be treated equally and fairly. Justice is defined as giving a person what he or she deserves following a standard of rightness. Fairness refers to the ability to judge without reference to one's feelings or interests, thereby allowing each person to be treated equally. Where people can differ significantly is when decisions must be made with respect to how benefits and burdens will be distributed. This principle generally arises in times of shortages or where there is competition for benefits or resources—such as when there are two equally qualified individuals awaiting a heart transplant (Guido, 2009).

CLASSICAL ETHICAL THEORIES

Clearly there is a need for a framework in healthcare ethics that allows for the establishment of broad principles on the basis of which individual ethical conflicts can be assessed. Traditional frameworks rely heavily on philosophical roots. According to Frankena (1963), ethical theories are often divided into two classifications: teleological and deontological. The main distinction between these two theories is in the relationship of the central concepts of ethics: the good and the right. The concept of good concerns itself with the morally good properties of human beings. The concept of right concerns itself with duty: actions we ought to perform and those that it would be wrong to perform. Different frameworks hold different approaches to the concepts of good and right. Each ethical theory must define how these concepts relate to one another. There are two ways in which the value of good relates to the value of right: teleological theory and deontological theory.

The Greek word *telos* means end or goal. Teleology is the study of goals, ends, and purposes. A teleological connection would therefore emphasize that morality is oriented toward a certain goal. Classic utilitarianism—the tailoring of one's conduct so as to effect the greatest social good with a minimum of adverse consequences—is an example of teleological theory. The moral quality of conduct is assessed by focusing on its effects or consequences. Thus, from a teleological perspective, a morally right act, or omission, is one that will produce a good outcome. From this framework came the aphorism, "the end justifies the means" (Frankena, 1963).

The Greek word *deon* means duty. The nature of one's conduct is prospectively assessed using universally accepted standards for behavior, such as professional ethics codes, laws, and rules. One fulfills duties based on laws and rules without regard for adverse consequences, independent of the good or evil generated. This framework derives the rightness or wrongness of the conduct from the behavior, not the character. Deontological theories are seen as the opposite of teleological theories.

However, the relation between the theory of good and the theory of right is not as clear as initially proposed. There are some issues with this traditional philosophical classification. Ancient Greek theories are usually considered to be teleological theories, but they do not all easily fit into the traditional classification (Frankena, 1963). Teleological theories define the right in terms of the good. Aristotle's virtue theory focuses on character and judgment as related to other persons, rather than specifically on rules and laws or adverse consequences. According to Aristotle, the goal of ethics is to explain how one achieves the good life for humans. He defined good as eudaimonia, or happiness, and this was attained through virtuous living. He stated that by possessing certain characteristics and good judgment, human beings would have the proper skills to live a happy life. Because Aristotle's virtue theory does not define right in terms of good, it does not fit the schema of a classical teleological theory (Frankena, 1963).

Modern ethics is a blend of theories. The true differences lie in the way moral dilemmas are approached rather than in the conclusions reached. While teleological and deontological theories seem to oppose, they complement each other in practice. In the challenge of identifying and resolving ethical dilemmas, neither should be discounted. To simplify: for deontology, think duty driven, means count; for teleology, think goal driven, ends count. The deonutility theory combines the ethical theories of teleology and deontology. This modern framework brings together good principles and good guidance for good results. It allows for a respect for rules as well as a concern with outcomes/consequences. Early deontological focus was on strict compliance with duties and oaths. Early teleological focus had little regard for the means. Like all things, ethics continues to evolve. Healthcare ethics has undergone a metamorphosis over time from an early deontological focus to analytical principlism (Pellegrino, 1993).

Analytical principlism emerges from modern or analytical ethics. Developed in the 1970s by Beauchamp and Childress (2001), this framework applies the four moral principles: autonomy, beneficence, nonmaleficence, and justice to contemporary ethical dilemmas. Despite criticism for its lack of foundational theory and its modern methodology, the practicality of this approach over the traditional philosophical approaches is widely accepted in education, health care, and even in religious and cultural concerns.

In clinical practice, healthcare professionals rely on multiple ethical principles when caring for patients. Often, imbalances and conflicts between principles arise. For example, consider a homecare nurse caring for an elderly client who is having progressive difficulty with independence in activities of daily living. The homecare nurse must balance the client's need for independence (autonomy) while still addressing (with family) the need for a higher level of care (beneficence). It is a matter of finding that balance. Ethical decision making is always a process. Many healthcare facilities have ethics committees in place to assist in providing a framework or model by which decisions can be made.

PATIENT SELF-DETERMINATION ACT

The Patient Self-Determination Act of 1990 codifies the rights of hospitalized patients and nursing home residents to participate in decisions related to their care and to control the use of extraordinary treatment measures to extend life. This act binds all healthcare facilities that receive government funding—that is, Medicare and Medicaid—to inform patients about their rights under the state laws with respect to their treatment. Usually, the right of self-determination is addressed in issues surrounding death and dying, but self-determination concerns all aspects of consent to medical treatment, or its refusal.

The change in long-term care to a more resident-centered culture further expands the interpretation of the patient self-determination act.

Person-centered care is a philosophical approach to health care that honors the choices of consumers. This culture-change movement is a broad-based effort to individualize care and transform nursing homes from institutions to homelike environments. In the nursing home setting, resident-centered care is not only driven by regulations, but also by quality. This philosophy is the Eden Alternative of the 21st century. With this movement, patient self-determination continues throughout the lifecycle, especially as life expectancy continues to increase and medical technology breakthroughs have us making healthcare decisions well into our 80s and 90s. Prior to this, those decisions were much easier.

CREATING AN ETHICAL ORGANIZATION

Ethical behavior, decision making, and leadership are becoming increasingly important in the healthcare environment. The fixation on the profit-oriented business model has ominous implications for the ethical provision of healthcare services (Rolland, 2009).

Often, it is individuals who are identified as the source of ethical failures. However, one of the most important aspects of creating ethical behavior is the culture and environment of the organization in which these individuals function. Ethical failures are not individual failures, but organizational failures: Managerial ethics assume a position of profound consequence here in the form of organizational policies and processes, culture, espoused versus enacted values, leadership behavior, rewards and punishments, social networks, and treatment of employees (Taft, Hawn, Barber, & Bidwell, 1999). Organizational cultures create in employees a perception of the levels and limits of trust and integrity, two domains nearly synonymous with ethics (Becker, 1998). Ethical frameworks are a necessity, not an option. Through organizational socialization, employees learn what constitutes acceptable behavior (Covey, 1990). The ethical conduct of leaders, or lack thereof, has subtle but profound influence on the behaviors of all employees (Payne, 1997). Healthcare administration is an important leadership role that cannot be minimized if an organization is to maintain its integrity and foster a culture based on ethical behavior and moral values. An administrator's leadership and morals help to solidify the ethical framework on which a facility's staff will make ethical judgments. This ethical behavior is especially critical in the healthcare environment, where profit motive does not excuse illegal, immoral, or unethical behavior (Rolland, 2009).

A failure in ethics may underlie an organizational failure in leadership. This is an unnecessary tragedy, because with minimal effort, any organization can create, define, implement, and maintain a coherent, intelligent, logical, and ethically and morally defensible code of ethics (Rolland, 2009). According to the preamble of the American College of Healthcare Executives (ACHE),

> The Code of Ethics incorporates standards of ethical behavior governing individual behavior, particularly when that conduct directly relates to the role and identity of healthcare executives . . . being a model means that decisions and actions will reflect personal integrity and ethical leadership that others will seek to emulate (ACHE, 2011).

The administrator is ultimately responsible for putting into effect, and maintaining, the governing body's ethical, legal, and moral behavior that exists within the organization. According to the ACHE Code of Ethics, there are six areas of a healthcare executive's responsibilities with regard to the profession. Of all of the individuals within the facility, the administrator is the identity of the organization more than any other individual. The person in this role must solidly project the ethical, legal, and moral values of the organization. If this person is seen as ethical and moral, then the facility will be seen this way as well. The next level of ethical responsibility rests with the department directors (Rolland, 2009). The department directors are individual healthcare professionals who need to uphold codes of ethics from their respective disciplines.

Creating an ethical organization—a true culture of ethical behavior—within a healthcare facility takes time and effort. There are several models that can provide guidance. According to Rest (1986), there is a four-step process for ethical decision making. The steps include (1) recognizing the moral issue, (2) making a moral judgment, (3) resolving to place moral concerns ahead of other concerns, and (4) acting promptly on the moral concern. This is such a simplistic model that it would seem that an organization would not have any ethical failures if all individuals acted according to this model (Rolland, 2009). Another model for creating an ethical organizational culture, from Renz and Eddy (1996), is also a four-step process. The steps include (1) conducting a formal process to clarify and articulate the organization's values and link them to the mission and vision statements; (2) facilitating communication and learning about ethics and ethical issues, including values clarification and reflection and their link to practice; (3) creating structures that encourage and support ethical culture; and (4) creating processes that monitor and offer feedback on ethical performance. Regardless of what pathway is undertaken, creating an ethical culture is critical to a healthcare facility's success. Consumers equate successful leadership with ethics and good quality of care.

Despite the growing interest in ethics, there has been very little information published about organizational and administrative ethics in the healthcare literature. This may be due, in part, to the fact that organizational ethics are much broader than clinical ethics, and the number of stakeholders involved makes it a very unwieldy process (Brodeur, 1998).

ETHICS AND QUALITY OF CARE

Healthcare ethics are unique. In health care, we deal with situations where people are injured and in pain. There are multiple stresses, and people are likely to be more vulnerable to exploitation. Under these circumstances, the consequences of a bad decision are likely to harm or kill. Ethics in health care are more demanding than general ethics, and they demand more of healthcare professionals. It is a primary responsibility that healthcare professionals have knowledge and appreciation of ethical principles. Strict adherence to ethical standards is an important aspect of healthcare quality. We may not realize it, but consumers of health care are aware of ethics, and they identify with healthcare providers who keep their sensitive medical information private, trust in the advocacy of healthcare professionals, and participate in informed decision making. While consumers may not understand healthcare performance data, they do grasp ethical norms and seek quality care based on those standards. Ethics is an integral component of quality of care.

Avedis Donabedian, the father of quality assurance in modern health care, spoke of seven components of quality of care: efficacy, effectiveness, efficiency, optimality, acceptability, legitimacy, and equity. These seven components, when taken collectively, "constitute a definition of quality and when measured in one way or another will signify its magnitude" (Donabedian, 2003). The first four components are concerned with quality assurance, and the latter three components are concerned with the conformity to the wishes, desires, and expectations of healthcare consumers. Donabedian's work confirms the relationship of quality of care to ethics. Quality care is ethical care.

ETHICS AND QUALITY IMPROVEMENT IN HEALTH CARE

As Americans, we have come to expect high quality health care. It is seen as an American right, and just as important to individuals as our constitutional freedoms. A nearly unanimous definition of quality with respect to health care includes the adjectives such as timely, equitable, safe, efficient, and patient centered (Institute of Medicine, 2001). In order to assure that quality health care is delivered, healthcare institutions must have quality improvement programs. Quality improvement can easily be defined as the cumulative efforts of healthcare professionals, educators, researchers, healthcare payors (such as Medicare, Medicaid, and private insurances), and patients to make changes that will lead to improved healthcare outcomes. In healthcare institutions, there are tools to collect data that can be used for quality improvement purposes. Examples of such tools include the Outcome and Assessment Information Set (OASIS) in home care, and the Minimum Data Set (MDS 3.0) in nursing homes. Ethical issues can arise from quality improvement efforts. Although improvement efforts require change, not all changes lead to improvement. Some quality improvement efforts may inadvertently cause harm, affect some individuals unfairly, or may dwindle already scarce medical resources. Some quality improvement requires the use of patient data or patients themselves. This brings quality improvement activities into a new light under ethical and regulatory requirements (Lynn et al., 2007). Quality improvement is a fine line between maintaining the status quo and making it better without causing ethical issues. Thus, ethical oversight of quality improvement activities should be part of an already existing accountability system inherent in clinical care.

ETHICS, HEALTHCARE COSTS, AND FUTILITY OF CARE

The United States leads the world in medical technology and research. The same technology and research that are contributing to an increasing life expectancy bring high costs and increased demands on our healthcare system from an aging population. Advances in technology are sustaining lives, but not all persons have access to basic health care or the latest technology. Developing technologies present moral and ethical questions for healthcare providers and healthcare payers. Competition for healthcare resources is growing beyond the system's ability to provide services to everyone. Costs are spiraling out of control. There are physician and nursing shortages. As a consequence, ethicists and healthcare professionals are beginning to raise concerns about when and to whom treatments should be withheld. This poses difficult moral questions for society in general.

Futile medical care refers to situations in which there is no hope of improvement or no course of treatment is called for. There is no universal agreement about the point at which care becomes futile. In most circumstances, it is a decision between patient and physician. Healthcare decisions of our elders for not prolonging a life without quality should be respected. As the situation of limited healthcare resources and access to health care becomes more challenged, futile care involves the utilization of resources that could potentially be used by another. Although most illustrations of the futility of care are concerned with serious acute medical crises, in nursing homes, end-of-life care is a frequent circumstance, raising questions of ethics. Healthcare administrators need to have ethical frameworks in place to allow for proper decision making and the best allocation of healthcare resources.

Healthcare professionals focus their attention on patients who are at the end of their lives. About 25% of Medicare expenditures are for the last year of life. (Hogan, Lunney, & Gabel, 2001). With an aging society, these costs are expected to increase dramatically. Healthcare professionals need to be aware of the ethical dilemmas and also be responsible fiduciary stewards. While life-and-death decisions are made largely by patients in tandem with their physicians, all healthcare professional codes of ethics address professional responsibilities related to life-and-death decisions, at least indirectly, through provisions requiring professionals to respect patient autonomy, maintain confidentiality, and keep the patient's best interests in mind (Scott, 2009).

ETHICS AND CAREGIVING

As life expectancies continue to increase, so does the likelihood that many adults will spend a significant portion of their lives caring for an aging family member. Although many seniors will spend their final season of life in a nursing home, many dying people are cared for at home by family members. Family caregiving has always been an important kinship obligation (Levine, 2008).

The general moral principles of autonomy, beneficence, nonmaleficence, and justice apply to caregiving. The duty to care remains even when medical efforts to prolong life cease. The respect for the person and his or her best interests must be kept in mind, and all efforts to prevent abuse are important. Justice may be a waxing concern if caregiver resources are limited. Since the act of caregiving is generally long term, the ethics of character may play a larger role. The ethics of character are the formative impact of our actions defining the type of person we are, for better or for worse.

Family members' obligations are moral rather than legal. Our healthcare system's values are legal and moral. Public policy that supports family caregiving embodies the accepted view that the family unit is important because of the meaning and depth of blood relationships. Therefore, a family member will approach caregiving with a different set of priorities than a paid caregiver or policymaker (Levine, 2008). Proper resources are necessary for caregivers to diminish any likelihood of caregiver burnout and abuse.

SUMMARY

Ethical concerns will continue to be tantamount to quality health care at all levels and for all stages of the lifecycle. Central to a healthcare administrator's success will be exercising the knowledge of ethical principles and frameworks in a meaningful way to create an ethical organizational culture.

Discussion Questions

1. How is the role of ethics in health care changing to meet our needs related to a longer lifespan and greater usage of medical technology to prolong life?
2. What was the role of ancient philosophers in forming modern ethical theories?
3. What are some of the hallmarks of an ethical organization?
4. How does leadership affect ethical culture in an organization?
5. Are ethics and quality of care in health care one and the same?

REFERENCES

American College of Healthcare Executives (ACHE). (2011). *Code of ethics*. Retrieved March 25, 2012, from http://ache.org/abt_ache/code.cfm.

Beauchamp, T., & Childress, J. (2001). *Principles of biomedical ethics*. New York: Oxford University Press.

Becker, T. (1998). Integrity in organizations: Beyond honesty and conscientiousness. *Academy of Management Review, 23*(1), 154–161.

Brodeur, D. (1998). Healthcare institutional ethics: Broader than clinical ethics. In J. Monagle, & D. Thomasma (Eds.), *Healthcare ethics: Critical issues for the 21st century* (pp. 497–504). Gaithersburg, MD: Aspen.

Colavecchio-VanSickler, S. (2008, January 16). Dignity for Dr. Death. *The St. Petersburg Times*, p. B1.

Covey, S. (1990). *The seven habits of highly effective people: Restoring the character of ethic*. New York: Simon & Shuster.

Donabedian, A. (2003). *An introduction to quality assurance in health care*. New York: Oxford University Press.

Frankena, W. (1963). *Ethics: Foundations of philosophy series*. Englewood Cliffs, NJ: Prentice Hall.

Guido, G. W. (2009). *Legal and ethical issues in nursing* (5th ed.). Upper Saddle River, NJ: Pearson Health Science.

Hogan, C., Lunney, J., & Gabel, J. (2001). Medicare beneficiaries' costs of care in the last year of life. *Health Affairs, 20*(4), 188–195.

Institute of Medicine. (2001). *Crossing the quality chasm.* Washington, DC: National Academies Press.

Levine, C. (2008). Family caregiving. In M. Crowley (Ed.), *From birth to death and bench to clinic: The Hastings Center bioethics briefing book for journalists, policymakers, and campaigns* (pp. 63–68). Garrison, NY: The Hastings Center.

Lynn, J., Baily, M. A., Bottrell, M., Jennings, B., Levine, R. J., Davidoff, F., et al. (2007). The ethics of using quality improvement methods in health care. *Annals of Internal Medicine, 146,* 666–673.

Patient Self-Determination Act of 1990, 42 United States Code Sections 1395, 1396.

Payne, L. (1997). *Cases in leadership, ethics and organizational integrity: A strategic perspective.* Chicago, IL: Irwin.

Pellegrino, E. (1993). The metamorphosis of medical ethics: A 30 year retrospective. *Journal of the American Medical Association, 269*(9), 1158–1162.

Renz, D., & Eddy, W. (1996). Organizations, ethics and healthcare: Building an ethics infrastructure for a new era. *Bioethics Forum, 12*(2), 29–39.

Rest, J. (1986). *Moral development: Advances in research and theory.* New York: Praeger.

Rolland, P. (2009). Whistle blowing in healthcare: An organizational failure in ethics and leadership. *The Internet Journal of Law, Healthcare & Ethics, 6*(1).

Scott, R. W. (2009). *Promoting legal and ethical awareness: A primer for health professionals and patients.* St. Louis, MO: Mosby Elsevier.

Silva, M. (1990). *Ethical decision-making in nursing administration.* Norwalk, CT: Appleton & Lange.

Taft, S., Hawn, K., Barber, J., & Bidwell, J. (1999). Fulcrum for the future: The creation of a values driven culture. *Health Care Management Review, 7*(2), 387–397.

Chapter 14

End-of-Life Care: An Introduction to Hospice and Palliative Care

Alice McDonnell, DrPH, MPA, RN, and William F. Miller, MHA

LEARNING OBJECTIVES

1. To identify the demographics of 'Older America' and it's implication in end-of-life care
2. To understand the meaning of hospice care
3. To understand the meaning of palliative care
4. To identify the financial/economic aspects of hospice and palliative care
5. To discuss history and concepts of hospice and palliative care
6. To discuss the concept of 'total pain' and its relationship to expert pain and symptom alleviation
7. To review the concept of bereavement services
8. To identify adjuncts to enhance the current concept of end-of-life care

KEY TERMS

Bereavement: The grief suffered following loss by death

Grief: A person's reaction or response to a major loss, most often as an unhappy and painful emotion; anticipatory or preparatory grief is the grief the dying person or family experiences when preparing for death

Hospice Care: A program of care for patients facing an incurable disease in which curative care is abandoned and the patient's quality of life and the family's grief and support are paramount

Palliative Care: Treatment that enhances comfort and improves the quality of an individual's life by providing relief from distressing symptoms and easing of pain

Quality of Life: Describes the general well-being of an individual—unfortunately, no universally agreed upon definition exists; however, some key components are economic, cultural, and spiritual values; the Centers for Disease Control and Prevention (CDC) has developed the health-related quality of life index, which incorporates those aspects of life that affect physical or mental health

Total Pain: A holistic approach to care that incorporates the physical, psychological, social, emotional, and spiritual elements of pain, which utilizes a team-based methodology to provide care

INTRODUCTION

Sensationalized media bombards us with articles and stories of people living longer. One could find links to millions of websites that discuss everything imaginable about the topic of increased life expectancy. Topics range from "average human lifespan" to "historical life expectancies," with volumes of statistics related to the subject.

It is now common place to tune into a news show and see a report highlighting an individual who turned 90 or even 100 years of age or older. As a society, we are obsessed with the topic of doing whatever it takes to preserve our health and live longer. We spend billions of dollars on drugs to eradicate or limit the effect of diseases and to find new ways of "hunting down" what ails us. We spend countless hours of research and development time to create safer products that prevent or limit accidents or the bodily harm that may result if they do occur.

However, one constant still remains. Even though it may be delayed due to technological breakthroughs and the development of any number of life-enhancing products, death is still the final destination for our physical bodies. This idea is summarized by the following, which was overheard by the author while walking through a hospital emergency department some years ago: "We only have a finite number of hours and miles our bodies will last. For some it is longer than others and in better condition, but ultimately the body will give up in the end."

Technology makes it possible to extend lives; unfortunately, as the population ages, the likelihood of serious illness or chronic disease increases. The elimination or containment of a disease that may have taken thousands or tens of thousands of lives at an early age 100, 50, or 25 years ago increases the potential for other long-term diseases (Hallenbeck, 2003). The woman who may have died from pneumonia at age 30 could now become afflicted with cardiovascular disease at age 70.

Another, nonmedicinal, example is the fundamental change of attitude toward automobile safety. Due to improvements in safety features and the increased use of seatbelts, the number of traffic-related fatalities continue to decrease annually (National Highway Traffic Safety Administration [NHTSA], 2011). Those individuals who might otherwise have been killed in an automobile accident are now aging and have an increased susceptibility to serious illness or disease.

The combination of an increase in technology and the Baby Boom between 1946 and 1964 presents the United States with "a demographic shift unprecedented in human history" (Meier, 2010, p. 5). The first Baby Boomers turned 65 in January 2011, and the final group of Baby Boomers will reach that age in 2029. Current projections estimate the population aged 65 or older to more than double to 88 million in 2050 (Artnak, McGraw, & Stanley, 2011; Vincent & Velkoff, 2010). This leads one to ask—is society equipped to handle the issues that come with an aging population?

The leading causes of death are no longer acute illnesses such as malaria, pneumonia, small pox, and tuberculosis. Chronic degenerative disease such as cancer, heart disease, mental illnesses, stroke, and pulmonary disease are the leading causes of death in the United States (Bodenheimer, Chen, & Bennett, 2009; Meier, 2010). A person may live with these chronic diseases for years as they take a financial, emotional, social, and spiritual toll on the patient, family, and community.

Due to the duration of care, the cost of treatment of chronic disease far exceeds that of acute, life-saving treatments. Seventy-six percent of Medicare dollars are spent on patients with five or more chronic diseases (Swartz, 2010). According to Yong, Saunders, and Olsen (2010), 12% of the population uses more than 90% of the total long-term care days in the United States. The cost of treating chronic illness accounts for more than 75% of the total healthcare spending in the United States (Artnak et al., 2011; Bodenheimer et al., 2009).

These figures show the present burden associated with providing care to those afflicted with chronic disease. The future does not look any better. In 2005, 133 million Americans were living with at least one chronic disease. This number is estimated to increase to 157 million by 2020, with 81 million of that number struggling with multiple chronic diseases (Bodenheimer et al., 2009). Just what does this mean from a financial perspective? In order to provide a greater understanding of the magnitude of the financial burden, **Table 14.1** provides a summary of the current and projected cost burden associated with the seven leading chronic diseases.

Since death is ultimately unavoidable and the chance of one dying quickly from an accident or sudden illness has decreased, each individual must develop a personal acceptance of death and the dying process. Emotional, social, and spiritual conflicts arise when we, on an individual basis, are unable to "come to grips" with mortality, either our own or that of others. These conflicts begin with what Hallenbeck (2003) describes as our transition to a culture of curing.

With the advent of new technologies and our growing desire to extend life, death is viewed as a failure. We should be able to cure the sick and infirm. We believe we should never accept death as an alternative when researchers are still trying to find a cure (Callahan, 2010). However, modern medicine is not able to prevent or halt chronic disease. Artnak, McGraw, and Stanley (2011) describe this as a misunderstanding of chronic disease and the dying process. We must accept the fact that we are able to alleviate the symptoms, extend life, allow for greater comfort, and avoid excessive disability, but we are not able to cure chronic disease.

If we are unable to accept our inability to "cure," we are unable to accept that death is a reality and provide appropriate end-of-life care. Instead of embracing death and celebrating the life of the patient while the patient dies at home, which was common place many years ago, our reaction is to institutionalize and marginalize death. Field and Cassel (2010) explain that

Table 14.1 Projected Cost Burden of Leading Chronic Diseases, United States, 2003 and 2023*

Chronic Disease	2003 Cost ($)	Projected 2023 Cost ($)
Cancers	319 billion	1,106 billion
Hypertension	312 billion	927 billion
Mental disorders	217 billion	704 billion
Heart disease	169 billion	927 billion
Pulmonary diseases	139 billion	384 billion
Diabetes	132 billion	430 billion
Stroke	36 billion	98 billion

*Table arranged in descending order by 2003 cost data (includes lost productivity).

Source: Data from Bodenheimer, T., Chen, E., & Bennett, H. D. (2009). Confronting the growing burden of chronic disease: Can the U.S. healthcare workforce do the job? *Health Affairs, 28*(1), 64–74.

"death at home in the care of family has been superseded by a technological, professional, and institutional process of treatment for the dying" (p. 81). The majority of deaths previously occurred at home; however in 1987, approximately 75% of all deaths occurred in a medical institution. This is an increase of 25% from 1949 (Council on Ethical and Judicial Affairs [CEJA], 2010).

Patient and family frustration may also increase due to a lack of patient and family autonomy. Competent patients have the right to choose medically indicated treatments and refuse unwanted treatments (CEJA, 2010; Karlsson & Berggren, 2011). Problems arise when caregivers feel they know what is best for the patient, but the caregivers' ideas do not match the patient and family desires (Connor, 2009). This causes tensions to rise with all parties involved. This problem could further escalate when a patient is unable to be cured and is not capable of making decisions on his or her own behalf. Family members and caregivers may not always agree as to what constitutes appropriate care.

The legal and ethical implications associated with end-of-life care cause further conflict for the patient, family, and community. While preparing for the death of a loved one, family members have to face a number of legal and ethical decisions. An example of these is when a family member assumes power of attorney and healthcare proxy for the dying patient and must honor the wishes of a dying parent, sibling, or child.

Even when the patient's wishes have been committed to writing in the form of an advance directive, the decisions are difficult to make—especially when the patient's wishes are contrary to those of the power of attorney or other family members. These decisions are more difficult when the patient's wishes have not been committed to writing. Many times a dying patient may express his or her wishes to a loved one, but those wishes are never formalized into a legal document.

More detailed examples of the legal and ethical implications present in end-of-life care have been decided in the courts in recent history. High profile cases such as those of Karen Ann Quinlan, Nancy Cruzan, and Terri Schiavo are all examples of the issues surrounding a patient's right to die and the withdrawal of life support (CEJA, 2010; McGowan, 2011). When highly contested topics that span multiple ethical boundaries, such as physician-assisted suicide and euthanasia (these concepts differ on the level of physician involvement) are considered, the implications become even more clouded. While multiple texts and articles have been written detailing various perspectives on these legal and ethical implications, they are only briefly presented in this chapter in order to exemplify the complexities inherent in providing end-of-life care.

The issues presented thus far are best summarized by Petasnick, a leading healthcare executive. In 2009, Medicare paid $50 billion for medical care for individuals within the last 2 months of their lives. Twenty-five percent of all Medicare dollars were spent on only 5% of Medicare patients—those in the final stages of life (CBSNews, 2010; Petasnick, 2011). Petasnick also referenced articles printed in *The New Republic* and in *Frontiers of Health Services Management* that express the opinion that this increased spending does not produce an extension of life or improved outcomes for patients, their families, or society.

Petasnick expresses this point of view in the context of his wife's 9-year battle with breast cancer, during which she was provided with "everything modern medicine could provide" (p. 369). He talked about his family having to decide when to stop the various treatments and allow his wife to die a good death, which he suggests would be defined as "including being treated as an individual, with dignity and respect; receiving appropriate pain and symptom management; and having comfortable and familiar surroundings and the company of close family and friends" (pp. 371–372). He concludes by stating that his wife dying "peacefully at home" (p. 372) is not the norm. His wife was spared the discomfort and suffering so often associated with our longing for "victory" over these debilitating illnesses.

In the early 1970s, hospice care was introduced to the United States, and combined with the growth of palliative care, has evolved into a potential solution for these escalating problems. How did these concepts develop into what they are today, and how do they assist those suffering with debilitating chronic disease? The remainder of this chapter addresses these and other questions. The chapter is divided into three sections:

- History and concepts of hospice and palliative care
- Effectiveness of hospice and palliative care
- Alternate programs and enhancements to end-of-life care

HISTORY AND CONCEPTS OF HOSPICE AND PALLIATIVE CARE

The origins of providing separate care to the sick and dying could be traced back to the time of the Crusades (4th through 11th century). Incurable patients were shunned by formal caregivers and were not allowed in places of healing. The presence of death and dying was harmful to those who were trying to heal (Connor, 2009).

At this time in history, hospices were places of rest for weary travelers. They would provide care and refreshment for those traveling through the

Holy Land. The role of these hospices expanded to include care for the sick and dying. Not unlike today, care for the sick and dying was misunderstood, but these institutions held fast to their convictions and provided care to those others would not.

The Knights Hospitallers of St. John of Jerusalem was one such organization. Following their capture of Rhodes (an island in Greece) in the 14th century, they established a hospice there that provided care for travelers, the sick, and the dying. It was in this hospital that the sick and dying were treated as royalty and lived out the remainder of their lives.

The tradition that began in the 14th century evolved into the concept of the modern hospice movement with the assistance and guidance of Dame Cicely Saunders in London. She was trained as a physician, but started her career as a nurse, and then as a social worker. Saunders established St. Christopher's Hospice in 1967, where she developed a center for the care of those who were dying.

Saunders, with the assistance of Florence Wald, Dean of the Yale School of Nursing, helped spread the hospice movement to the United States. In 1963, Saunders lectured to medical students, nurses, social workers, and chaplains at Yale University. She was added to the faculty of Yale's School of Nursing for the spring 1965 semester. The relationship between Saunders and Wald continued, and in 1968, Wald took a sabbatical from Yale and worked at St. Christopher's in order to learn more about the organization and Saunders's concept of care.

Shortly after Wald's work in London, *On Death and Dying* (Kübler-Ross, 1969) was published. This groundbreaking book introduced the five stages of grief typically experienced by the dying person. Kübler-Ross used the book to emphasize and advocate for the use of home care, patient choice, and the patient's right to die with dignity.

The first incorporated hospice in the United States, Hospice Inc., was founded by Florence Wald in New Haven, Connecticut in 1971, and expanded to include home care in 1973. Throughout the remainder of the 1970s, the momentum grew and hospices were formed throughout the country and developed new models of care. A national organization soon became necessary in order to provide educational opportunities and support. This prompted the creation of the National Hospice Organization (which later became the National Hospice and Palliative Care Organization) in 1978 (Connor, 2009; National Hospice and Palliative Care Organization [NHPCO], 2010).

The introduction of the Medicare Hospice Benefit in 1983 shaped hospice care into what we know today. This provision in the Tax Equity and Fiscal Responsibility Act was the first to provide funding for "end-of-life" care. In addition, it forced a change in mindset toward chronic illness and mandated family support and bereavement services. By virtue of a number of additional changes in legislative and administrative requirements, hospice services have become an integral part of the continuum of healthcare services. Some examples of the changes that helped propel hospice care to the forefront are as follows:

- Reimbursement was increased, which compelled more hospices to become Medicare-certified.
- The hospice benefit was included in the veteran's benefit package.
- The Joint Commission initiated hospice accreditation.
- Hospice was included as a guaranteed benefit in President Clinton's healthcare reform proposal.

Though similar in spirit to the original hospices that provided assistance to travelers in the Holy Land, the hospice movement has evolved into a program designed to provide support to patients and families. The goal of the modern hospice movement is to assist patients and families to accept and embrace death with dignity while allowing all to fully participate in care when curative treatments are no longer effective and quality of life becomes paramount. It now services approximately 1.4 million people from programs based in home health agencies, free-standing independent organizations, skilled nursing facilities, and hospitals throughout the United States (Barr & Breindel, 2011; Bonebrake, Culver, Call, & Ward-Smith, 2010; Connor, 2009).

Most government and private insurance payors provide a hospice benefit and follow the Medicare guidelines for eligibility. Specific coverage guidelines may be present within each payor. However, a universal set of eligibility guidelines are shared across all hospice programs (see **Figure 14.1**).

A limitation does exist within hospice care. As the popularity for hospice care grew, so did the necessity for a program that covered patients with life-threatening conditions who needed similar services but were still seeking

---

✓ An expected lifespan of 6 months or less based on normal disease progression

✓ A life-limiting condition must exist and the patient (and/or family) must agree

✓ Curative focus is no longer desired

✓ Documentation of disease progression (general and disease-specific guidelines exist)

Figure 14.1 Hospice Eligibility Guidelines

curative treatment, did not have a specified prognosis, or were hesitant to accept the inevitability of death. These patients and their families were left to suffer as quality of life diminished and treatments were accompanied by debilitating adverse effects (Bonebrake et al., 2010; Connor, 2009). The palliative care movement bridged this gap created by hospice care.

Hospice and palliative care both offer compassionate care, and palliative care is routinely included as part of a hospice program; yet, as Connor (2009) explains, "all hospice care is palliative; however, not all palliative care is hospice care" (p. 6). These programs are distinctly different based on eligibility for care. To be eligible for hospice care, the patient must meet the specific guidelines presented in Figure 14.1. Eligibility for palliative care is not as restrictive. A patient's condition need not be terminal, and the patient may still be seeking treatment options.

The only eligibility requirement for palliative care is a desire to achieve symptom control and pain management. Palliative care seeks to use the most appropriate modern medicine to relieve suffering and enhance quality of life without regard to prognosis, while taking great care not to create additional hardship (see **Figure 14.2**). For many patients, palliative care is offered earlier in the disease lifecycle and transitions to hospice care as the patient's health deteriorates (Artnak et al., 2011; Bonebrake et al., 2010; NHPCO, 2011).

While various hospice programs have developed unique delivery methods, programs throughout the United States have adopted a number of necessary attributes that are shared by all. One must be careful to note that these are not accreditation standards or government licensure guidelines. These are the elements of hospice care that distinguish the concept from any other healthcare program (see **Figure 14.3**).

Palliative care programs share most of these same elements. One service that is offered in palliative care that is not included in hospice care is the

---

Considered to be the model for quality, compassionate care for people facing a life-limiting illness or injury, hospice and palliative care involve a team-oriented approach to expert medical care, pain management, and emotional and spiritual support expressly tailored to the patient's needs and wishes. Support is provided to the patient's loved ones as well. At the center of hospice and palliative care is the belief that each of us has the right to die pain free and with dignity, and that our families will receive the necessary support to allow us to do so.

Figure 14.2 Definition of Hospice and Palliative Care

Source: Used with permission from National Hospice and Palliative Care Organization [NHPCO]. (2011). *What is hospice and palliative care?* Retrieved January 5, 2012, from http://www.nhpco.org/i4a/pages/index.cfm?pageid=3285.

Hospice services are:

✓ Provided to the patient and family
✓ Provided around the clock
✓ Provided in a variety of settings
✓ Provided by an interdisciplinary team
✓ Designed to provide symptom management utilizing a holistic approach
✓ Designed to provide emotional, social, and psychological support
✓ Designed to prepare the patient and family to accept death
✓ Designed to provide bereavement support following death
✓ Provided by a large number of volunteers

Figure 14.3 Elements of Hospice Care

addition of assistance with navigating the sometimes confusing world of treatment options. For example, the palliative care team would assist the patient and family in understanding the various treatment options and side effects of cancer care. This example also highlights the difference between hospice and palliative care in that hospice patients do not need this service, since they have opted to forego curative care and bypass these types of treatments.

First and foremost, hospice care is designed to provide services to the patient and family.[1] Since the primary caregiver is generally a family member who is an integral member of the care team, patient and family are treated as a unit with specific roles and goals. In many cases (especially as the patient nears death), family members are often in greater need of assistance. It is important to note that the term *family* is not limited to relatives of the patient; it includes close friends and others who have a loving, caring relationship with the patient. Many times relatives are accompanied by close friends throughout this process, or in some cases, no family is present and only friends attend the patient.

The need for hospice services is not limited to weekdays between the hours of 8:00 a.m. and 4:00 p.m. Services are available to support the patient and family on an "on-call" basis until the patient is closer to death. As the patient nears death, around-the-clock services are provided. In addition, if

---

1. While the differences between hospice and palliative care have been explained, due to the similarity of the two programs, the term *hospice* will be used throughout the rest of this chapter to denote both hospice and palliative care unless otherwise noted.

the patient's needs escalate to a point where care is unable to be provided in the home or the family needs a respite from providing care, discreet inpatient hospice units or specified beds in other settings, such as a nursing home, are available.

Care is provided by an interdisciplinary team directed by the patient's attending physician. Even though the attending physician must direct the care, no one team member has a greater influence than any of the others, and each team member has an important role in the care provided. Everyone is equal, the responsibility of care is shared by all, and the care provided by one role may overlap with another. Examples of some team members are as follows:

- *Attending physician.* The attending physician must determine condition and prognosis, refer to hospice care, order all care, and is responsible for verifying disease progression.
- *Hospice medical director.* The hospice medical director oversees the care provided by the hospice organization and assists the attending physician.
- *Nurses.* Nurses are the "heart and soul" of hospice and palliative care. They carry out treatment orders, perform case management, educate the patient and family, order supplies and durable medical equipment, and they are on call 24 hours per day, 7 days per week.
- *Social workers.* Social workers provide the emotional, social, and psychological support for the patient and family. They are advocates and counselors for both the patient and family.
- *Home health aides.* Home health aides are the "hands" of the organization. They are the physical support for the primary caregiver, as they provide the personal care for the patient. Depending on the model of care, home health aides may also provide housekeeping chores and errands.
- *Chaplains.* Chaplains are the spiritual center of the hospice care team. They provide the spiritual guidance for the patient as they try to "make peace" with their faith and turn to a higher power for assistance in this time of need. Chaplains are also very important for the family. They play a vital role in assisting the family to accept the pending death of a loved one and help the family find the faith-based answer to the overwhelming question of "Why is father (mother, spouse, child, etc.) suffering?" The medical reasons for the suffering are known—the chaplains assist with finding the intangible reasons. Chaplains also provide bereavement services post death. (Bereavement services are presented in greater detail later in this chapter.)

· *Therapists.* Depending on the diagnosis and needs of the patient, various types of therapists may be utilized. The primary type of therapy called upon is physical therapy, but one may also call upon occupational, speech, or respiratory therapy. A growing trend is the use of massage therapists for pain reduction in palliative care (Connor, 2009).

· *Administrative team.* The "behind-the-scenes" workers of the organization are the administrative team. They ensure delivery of supplies and equipment, schedule and coordinate personnel, maintain medical records, bill for care provided, plus any number of other support tasks that assist the clinical team in maintaining quality care.

At the core of hospice care is symptom management. All one needs to do is review each team member's role to understand that the symptoms being addressed are not limited to the physical results of the disease. Hospice care is designed to treat the whole person in order to provide him or her with a "good death." Field and Cassel (2010) provided a definition of good death that emphasizes the importance of symptomatic relief when they stated a good death is "one that is free from avoidable distress and suffering for patients, families, and caregivers; in general accord with patient's and families' wishes; and reasonably consistent with clinical, cultural, and ethical standards" (p. 82).

It is the goal and the responsibility of the hospice team to provide each patient a good death by offering support and treatment to ease the patient's body, mind, and soul. This multidisciplinary, holistic approach is referred to as the "total pain" concept of care. The idea of total pain embraces the physical, emotional, social, and spiritual elements of care (Clark, 1999; Connor, 2009).

The key component to whole-person care is physical care. If the physical symptoms are not relieved, the emotional, social, and spiritual elements are unable to be addressed properly (Mount, 2010). The terminal illness process may be accompanied by any number of physical symptoms (some examples are pain, nausea, vomiting, dyspnea, diarrhea, constipation, and confusion), which may be caused by the disease itself, the body's reaction to the disease, or the body's reaction to those measures used to try to control the disease or specific symptoms (Connor, 2009; Hallenbeck, 2003). Those measures used to control one symptom may cause another (sometimes more debilitating) symptom. It is vital for the hospice care team to provide symptom relief in a manner that does not create new distress (Hallenbeck, 2003).

Even though the list of possible symptoms is long, the most important aspect of symptom control is pain management (Connor, 2009).[2] However, expert pain management is an inexact science. Pain could be classified as either one of two types: acute or chronic. It is important to determine which type of pain the patient is experiencing, since that will affect the pain management and overall treatment process. Foley (2010) describes acute pain as being "generally associated with subjective and objective physical signs. . . . which serve as objective evidence to the physician" (p. 253). Chronic pain is pain that lasts longer than 6 months, lacks objective well defined signs, and leads to marked changes in personality, lifestyle, and functional ability (Connor, 2009; Foley, 2010; Hallenbeck, 2003). For many patients with chronic or serious illness, acute pain was the key to proper illness diagnosis, while chronic pain is the hallmark of the disease that affects the emotional, social, and spiritual elements of the patient's life (Foley, 2010; Hallenbeck, 2003). Various approaches to pain management exist depending on the type, severity, and cause of the pain (Foley, 2010). However, for the purpose of this chapter, a cursory overview of chronic pain will be provided. Due to its effect on the patient's physical and mental well-being, the severity of chronic pain is often difficult to determine by both caregivers and family. Hallenbeck (2003) describes this problem as being "'color-blind' to chronic pain" (p. 38). Many times caregivers will use numeric or visual scales, or nonverbal cues to assess pain and establish a pain management goal, since the only person who can accurately describe the pain or provide feedback (nonverbal included) is the patient (Connor, 2009; Hallenbeck, 2003).

Alternate, nonmedication methods of pain relief (radiation therapy, chemotherapy, nerve blocks, and physical, occupational, and massage therapy) may be useful in some circumstances (Connor, 2009; Hallenbeck, 2003). When medication pain relief is the solution, two classes of analgesics are most often utilized. For mild to moderate pain relief, nonsteroidal anti-inflammatory drugs (NSAIDs) are usually the medication of choice. This class of drug is chosen because it provides analgesic effects with a low potential for addiction. The anti-fever and anti-inflammatory effects are added bonuses. They do, however, have adverse gastrointestinal and renal effects after consistent, prolonged use.

For the relief of moderate to severe pain, a stronger class of drug is preferred. Due to the resultant decreased perception of pain and the increased

---

2. A thorough examination of pain management and appropriate intervention is beyond the scope of this chapter. A number of references exist to provide further details.

pain tolerance, opioids become the medication of choice, despite the potentially extreme adverse effects and presumed potential for addiction. With proper management, the effects of opioid use for pain relief do not mirror the effects obtained by addicts, and these drugs should be used when appropriate (Foley, 2010; Hallenbeck, 2003).

Once the physical distress is relieved, the patient's psychosocial and spiritual suffering may be addressed. Just as pain management is an inexact science, so to is providing care for the nonphysical aspects of the whole person. Each patient is truly unique, has different needs, and responds differently to care; therefore, caregivers must treat each patient differently.

Connor (2009) stresses the importance of providing care for both the psychological and spiritual needs of the patient. He states that at the time in which a person recognizes death is imminent, he or she enters "an arena where psychology and religion overlap" (p. 55). A person's emotional reaction to death is shaped by spiritual beliefs, and one's spiritual beliefs are influenced by individual psychological well-being (Connor, 2009; Karlsson & Berggren, 2011). Caregivers must be able and willing to treat (from both the psychological and spiritual perspectives) the emotional stress of the patient as manifested in a variety of ways. The three most common expressions of emotional stress for the dying patient are depression, anxiety, and grief (Hallenbeck, 2003).

Hallenbeck (2003) cautions against making quick diagnoses or jumping to conclusions about the mental state of patients relative to depression. The symptoms normally utilized to diagnose depression (e.g., weight loss and social withdrawal) could be the result of the disease, pain, grief, or a longing for resolution to open issues. In addition, patients may not be able to accurately describe their current mental state. Hallenbeck states that anxiety in those who are dying appears the same as in those patients who are not dying. From the caregiver perspective, it is difficult to understand the cause of the anxiety. It is important to determine the cause before attempting treatment, as the anxiety could worsen if not treated properly.

When we discuss grief associated with death, we normally assume the grief is limited to the family, not the patient. This would be an incorrect assumption. Even though grief is common among the family, the dying patient must also deal with grief. The patient grieves the loss of one's own life, autonomy, close relationships, the joy of childhood, and more. It is normal for the patient to experience grief for the loss of any number of items in his or her life (Connor, 2009; Mount, 2010). This grief is referred to as anticipatory or preparatory grief, since it is the grief the patient must endure while he or she prepares for death. It is important for the caregiver to address these feelings of grief in the patient in order to prevent the grief from leading to forms of emotional distress (Hallenbeck, 2003).

A number of resources exist that address any number of elements of physical, emotional, and spiritual distress suffered by the dying patient; however, do we understand what patients actually desire during their final days of life? We attempt to define a good death, but does our belief match that of the patient? Due to their physical state, many patients are unable to express their desires. Karlsson and Berggren (2011) used a phenomeno- logical study to determine the needs of the dying patient by interviewing those closest to the patient—nurses. They interviewed homecare nurses in order to obtain nurses' perspectives on "what are the significant factors that contribute to the dying person experiencing good end-of-life care in their own home" (p. 375).

The results were aggregated and grouped into three themes or significant factors: safety, autonomy, and integrity. A feeling of safety was bolstered by the patient's spiritual faith and the presence of family who desired to remain with the patient through the ordeal. Another popular response re- garding safety was the assistance, support, and freedom to participate that the family was given by the knowledgeable professional caregivers. The final dominant sub-theme supporting the feeling of safety was the relief of pain and other symptoms.

Supporting the theme of autonomy was the patient's desire and ability to be cared for at home. This allowed the patient to set small goals, such as experiencing a loved one's birthday or celebrating the next anniversary or holiday. It was supported by the family's courage and desire to be active par- ticipants in providing the care most desired by the patient, while working closely with the nurses in developing common goals. Collaboration between the patient, the family, and the caregivers was important to providing the patient a sense of autonomy.

Two sub-themes supported the integrity factor. The findings revealed the family's need to be treated with respect by the entire homecare team. In addition, it was important that the family and caregivers maintained a mutual trust and confidence.

When these three factors were combined, they formed Karlsson and Berggren's (2011) idea of a dignified death in the home, from which they developed the model presented in **Figure 14.4**. If one were to closely exam- ine the two definitions of a good death previously used in this chapter, one would be able to divide the components of each into one of the three factors presented by Karlsson and Berggren, and it is the caregivers' (hospice team) responsibility to maintain the dignified environment.

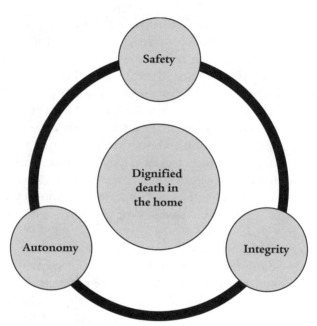

Figure 14.4 The Significant Factors That Contribute to Dignified End-of-Life Care in the Patient's Own Home

Source: Reproduced from Karlsson, C., & Berggren, I. (2011). Dignified end-of-life care in the patients' own homes. *Nursing Ethics, 18*(3), 374–385.

Now that we have examined the care provided to the patient, we will turn our attention to another vital component of hospice care—support for the family (NHPCO, 2011). As presented earlier, the family may be in greater need of assistance than the patient, especially as the patient nears death. Family members (especially the primary caregiver) may suffer emotional problems as they attempt to "come to grips" with the patient's plight, ensure their loved one does not needlessly suffer, prepare themselves for the patient's departure, and maintain their daily lives after the patient has passed (Artnak et al., 2011; Connor, 2009; Hallenbeck, 2003; Mount, 2010).

The hospice team must play multiple roles as they service the family, as well as the patient. They must be an informational resource, a guide, an assistant, an empathetic ear, and sometimes a director. Each family dynamic is different, which forces the hospice team to be prepared for anything.

Mount (2010) explains that it is extremely important that the hospice team be united and work toward the common, realistic goals established with the patient and family. This provides a roadmap for all involved to follow, especially if family members try to calm their personal issues by deviating from the plan. These goals also provide a "measuring stick" by which success could be measured as the hospice team assists the family through this emotionally trying time.

What happens when the patient dies? Does the care team move on to their next assignment and forget the family? No, hospice services provide family bereavement support for a minimum of a year following the patient's death—but why and what services are offered?

Everyone (including those in the same family) grieves differently, and how they cope will have a profound effect on their physical and mental health (Hallenbeck, 2003). Some may believe that they do not need bereavement support. Others may need a small amount of assistance in order to accept what has happened and move forward. Others may be suffering complicated bereavement and require intervention (Connor, 2009; Hallenbeck, 2003; Mount, 2010).

Connor (2009) outlines five components of bereavement services that provide counseling, education, and support to families following the death of a loved one:

1. Clinical staff members attend the funeral and visit with the family to give their condolences and say "goodbye" to the patient.
2. A staff member or volunteer contacts the family on a regular basis in the year following the death.
3. The family is provided with educational material covering such topics as common reactions, self-esteem, next steps, and coping with holidays.
4. Staff or volunteers visit or call based on need. If a family does not require special needs, the contact is usually after the first month, and then every 3 months after. If additional assistance is required, contact is provided more frequently and referrals are made to mental health professionals as needed.
5. Support groups are held and everyone is invited. The topics of the support groups vary, and the hospice team assists the family in identifying which may be appropriate.

By utilizing bereavement services, families are better prepared to handle the death of a loved one (Connor, 2009); however, everyone experiences grief at one time or another and in different ways (Hallenbeck, 2003). In order to assist more than just the families of those who have died, many hospice programs provide support to the community as well. An example of a community-oriented benefit is providing an annual memorial service for all patients who have passed while on the sponsoring program's service. The memorial service is open to all who wish to attend.

Mount (2010) provides an example of the importance of providing follow-up bereavement services. He describes a visit made to a family whose mother passed away a year prior on the service for whom he worked. The bereavement follow-up services had ended, and his visit was actually to perform research. However, what he found were three siblings who were moving toward what he termed "a pathologic grief reaction" (p. 307). Could the mental state of these siblings have been prevented with additional, more detailed follow up?

The interdisciplinary team is not the only group that assists patients and families receiving hospice and palliative care services. The system would not function without the dedicated group of volunteers that assists the hospice team. In fact, some resources consider these volunteers to be part of the care team.

These volunteers are similar to the Knights Hospitallers from the time of the Crusades. They give of themselves and dedicate their time and efforts to assist the dying patients and their families. Usually these volunteers have experienced loss and are able to understand the stressors the patients and families are experiencing. It is out of their own concern for others that they receive training and spend countless hours supporting those receiving hospice and palliative care.

EFFECTIVENESS OF HOSPICE AND PALLIATIVE CARE

Most nonhospital-based hospice programs are not good at capturing the data needed in order to provide research information. Many struggle to meet the federal reporting guidelines, let alone capturing and using data for research purposes. The primary reason for this lack of data is that most hospice programs are underfunded and are unable to afford the necessary personnel and equipment (Connor, 2009). Hospital-based programs have the advantage of being able to utilize the hospital systems and personnel. As hospice programs, they may be underfunded, but they are able to access hospital resources.

Connor (2009) blames the lack of data on the industry's inability to come to a consensus on the effectiveness of hospice and palliative care programs. Some efforts are being made by outside organizations, and the majority of these studies use cost as the primary measure. If one takes a moment to apply logic and reason to the hospice industry, one would surmise that since hospice and palliative care programs are designed to enhance the quality of life by not subjecting the patient to needless tests, these programs should be more cost effective than standard care.

Morrison et al. (2010) examined hospital cost data to compare costs of those receiving palliative care with the costs of those receiving usual care. For those patients with a palliative care consult who were discharged alive, a direct cost savings of $1,700 per admission was found. For those patients with a palliative care consult who died in the hospital, a direct cost savings of $5,000 per admission was found. The majority of the savings occurred due to a decreased use of the intensive care unit (ICU), pharmacy, and laboratory services. These services were not used since palliative care shifts care management away from the usual care pathways.

Connor (2009) references a 1995 study commissioned by the NHPCO that found a cost savings of $2,700 among Medicare beneficiaries diagnosed with cancer who were referred to hospice services. He cautions that the study only reviewed the costs associated with cancer patients. Connor also references a 2007 study by Taylor, Ostermann, Van Houtren, Tulsky, and Steinhauser that discovered savings of $2,300 among Medicare patients who utilized hospice services.

Progress continues to be made to find an elusive universal measure other than cost. Attempts have been made to develop testing models based on an overall quality management measure, outcomes measurements, quality of life measures, and quality improvement programs. Besides an objective review of cost or outcomes, the industry is unable to capture accurate data. The other potential measures rely on subjective data and are difficult to capture. The research is dependent on feedback from the patients, who are unlikely to be able to provide information as they near death, or from the family post-death.

Casarett et al. (2010) attempted to determine whether palliative consultations improved patient- and family-focused outcomes in patients near the end of life. The authors of the study relayed three results: (1) palliative consultations had an effect on the family's perception of care, (2) the consultations may not improve all outcomes, and (3) evidence exists that early exposure to palliative care is beneficial. Further research is needed to provide greater detail for each of these outcomes.

Meier (2010) references the National Quality Forum's recommendation of six quality components when developing a healthcare quality measure. The measurement tool should review if the care received is patient-centered, beneficial, safe, efficient, timely, and equitable. Per Meier, hospice care meets three of the six criteria. She references a study by Teno et al. in which they surveyed survivors of patients in hospitals, nursing homes, and home care with and without hospice care. They found that those survivors of patients who were serviced by hospice care in any of these settings were less likely to report the following:

- Inadequate help for the patient's emotional distress
- Inadequate help for the patient's pain
- Inadequate family information
- Patient was not treated with respect

The results provide evidence that hospice care is patient-centered and beneficial.

Hospice care is also efficient. It lowers cost by decreasing overall length of stay, decreasing ICU days, and decreasing the use of costly diagnostic and therapeutic intervention (Meier, 2010). These ideas parallel the results of the Morrison et al. (2010) study discussed earlier.

However, hospice care does not meet two of the National Quality Forum criteria: timeliness and equity. The industry must do a better job of community and physician education in order to demystify the services so that they are offered earlier in the dying process. Unfortunately, services are offered in the last week or last 24 hours of a patient's life. The industry must also examine the inequitable delivery of services. As described by Meier (2010), hospice care is unevenly distributed by geography, race, and ethnicity.

ALTERNATE PROGRAMS AND ENHANCEMENTS TO END-OF-LIFE CARE

While hospice and palliative care have evolved since the 1960s and have offered a solution to the current and future problems with chronic disease, additional services are necessary and other areas of end-of-life care could be enhanced. We must avoid marginalizing a growing group of patients and families. A number of patients are not eligible or ready for hospice services and do not meet or are not sure if they meet criteria for palliative care. A solution for this growing issue is a free, volunteer-supported service that enhances the communication and care between the patient and the healthcare system. The program provides an environment that supports the patient and family by matching volunteers trained to identify the changing needs of the patient (Hospice of the Sacred Heart, n.d.).

As discussed earlier, end-of-life care is wrought with a number of legal and ethical implications. Petasnick (2011) offers insight into some increasingly popular programs that may assist in resolving some of these legal and ethical problems. The majority of these problems are related to a patient's right to choose. A program started by the state of Oregon has begun to spread to other states and select municipalities. The program is the Physician Orders for Life-Sustaining Treatment (POLST) paradigm, and it is designed to effectively ensure that a patient's end-of-life wishes are communicated and honored. The Illinois State Medical Society has developed a program encouraging all adults to begin planning for their future healthcare needs now. The Wisconsin Medical Society is providing a similar program that provides educational materials that cover advance care planning and standards for power of attorney for health care.

Internationally, the United Kingdom Department of Health Services developed their End-of-Life Care Strategy in 2008. This is a national initiative aimed at caregiver education. It provides universal care pathways, materials for changing the perception of end-of-life care, and clarification of patient and caregiver needs.

SUMMARY

A combination of increased technology and a rapidly aging population linked with our overwhelming desire to control disease has produced a "perfect storm" of current and future problems within the United States. The cost and legal and ethical obligations that come with caring for those members of our society stricken with chronic or serious illness continue to escalate. Society must find a way to control these issues before it is too late.

The usage of hospice and palliative care programs has emerged as a potential solution. These programs are able to efficiently provide patient-centered and beneficial care to those patients who have replaced curative treatments with quality end-of-life care. We need to continue to expand the use of these and other programs so each patient who needs care or assistance has his or her needs met in a timely and equitable manner.

Discussion Questions

1. What are the differences between hospice and palliative care?
2. How will the aging of the U.S. population affect the incidence and treatment of chronic disease and the consumption of healthcare services in the future?
3. Why are bereavement services such a vital component of hospice services?
4. Why is it important to understand the concept of total pain as it relates to hospice and palliative care?
5. How does the utilization of an interdisciplinary team (including the use of volunteers) bolster the effects of hospice and palliative care?

References

Artnak, K. E., McGraw, R. M., & Stanley, V. F. (2011). Health care accessibility for chronic illness management and end-of-life care: A view from rural America. *Journal of Law, Medicine, & Ethics, 39*(2), 140–155.

Barr, K. W., & Breindel, C. L. (2011). Ambulatory care. In L. F. Wolper (Ed.), *Health care administration: Managing organized delivery systems* (pp. 433–457, 5th ed.). Sudbury, MA: Jones & Bartlett Learning.

Bodenheimer, T., Chen, E., & Bennett, H. D. (2009). Confronting the growing burden of chronic disease: Can the U.S. healthcare workforce do the job? *Health Affairs, 28*(1), 64–74.

Bonebrake, D., Culver, C., Call, K., & Ward-Smith, P. (2010). Clinically differentiating palliative care and hospice. *Clinical Journal of Oncology Nursing, 14*(3), 273–275.

Callahan, D. (2010). Death: The distinguished thing. In D. E. Meier, S. L. Isaacs, & R. G. Hughes (Eds.), *Palliative care: Transforming the care of serious illness* (pp. 153–158). San Francisco, CA: Jossey-Bass.

Casarett, D., Pickard, A., Bailey, A., Ritchie, C., Furman, C., Rosenfeld, K., et al. (2010). Do palliative consultations improve patient outcomes? In D. E. Meier, S. L. Isaacs, & R. G. Hughes (Eds.), *Palliative care: Transforming the care of serious illness* (pp. 370–381). San Francisco, CA: Jossey-Bass.

CBSNews. (2010, December 3). The cost of dying. Retrieved March 26, 2012, from http://www.cbsnews.com/2100-18560_162-5711689.html.

Clark, D. (1999). "Total pain": Disciplinary power and the body in the work of Cicely Saunders, 1958–1967. *Social Science and Medicine, 49*(6), 727–736.

Connor, S. R. (2009). *Hospice and palliative care: The essential guide* (2nd ed.). New York: Routledge.

Council on Ethical and Judicial Affairs (CEJA), American Medical Association. (2010). Decisions near the end of life. In D. E. Meier, S. L. Isaacs, & R. G. Hughes (Eds.), *Palliative care: Transforming the care of serious illness* (pp. 93–105). San Francisco, CA: Jossey-Bass.

Field, M. J., & Cassel, C. K. (2010). Approaching death: Improving care at the end of life. In D. E. Meier, S. L. Isaacs, & R. G. Hughes (Eds.), *Palliative care: Transforming the care of serious illness* (pp. 79–91). San Francisco, CA: Jossey-Bass.

Foley, K. M. (2010). The treatment of cancer pain. In D. E. Meier, S. L. Isaacs, & R. G. Hughes (Eds.), *Palliative care: Transforming the care of serious illness* (pp. 79–91). San Francisco, CA: Jossey-Bass.

Hallenbeck, J. L. (2003). *Palliative care perspectives.* New York: Oxford University Press.

Hospice of the Sacred Heart. (n.d.). *On the right PATH for patients with a serious illness.* Wilkes-Barre, PA: Author.

Karlsson, C., & Berggren, I. (2011). Dignified end-of-life care in the patients' own homes. *Nursing Ethics, 18*(3), 374–385.

Kübler-Ross, E. (1969). *On death and dying.* New York: Touchstone.

McGowan, C. M. (2011). Legal aspects of end-of-life care. *Critical Care Nurse, 31*(5), 64–69.

Meier, D. E. (2010). The development, status, and future of palliative care. In D. E. Meier, S. L. Isaacs, & R. G. Hughes (Eds.), *Palliative care: Transforming the care of serious illness* (pp. 4–76). San Francisco, CA: Jossey-Bass.

Morrison, R. S., Penrod, J. D., Cassel, J. B., Caust-Ellenbogen, M., Litke, A., Spragens, L., & Meier, D. E. (2010). Cost savings associated with U.S. hospital palliative care consultation programs. In D. E. Meier, S. L. Isaacs, & R. G. Hughes (Eds.), *Palliative care: Transforming the care of serious illness* (pp. 370–381). San Francisco, CA: Jossey-Bass.

Mount, B. M. (2010). Challenges in palliative care: Four clinical areas that comfort and challenge hospice practitioners. In D. E. Meier, S. L. Isaacs, & R. G. Hughes (Eds.), *Palliative care: Transforming the care of serious illness* (pp. 297–310) San Francisco, CA: Jossey-Bass.

National Highway Traffic Safety Administration (NHTSA). (2011). *Fatality analysis reporting system (FARS) summary data.* Retrieved January 3, 2012, from http://www-fars.nhtsa.dot.gov/Main/index.aspx.

National Hospice and Palliative Care Organization (NHPCO). (2010). *History of hospice care.* Retrieved January 5, 2012, from http://www.nhpco.org/i4a/pages/index.cfm?pageid=3285.

National Hospice and Palliative Care Organization. (2011). *What is hospice and palliative care?* Retrieved January 5, 2012, from http://www.nhpco.org/i4a/pages/index.cfm?pageid=4648&openpage=4648.

Petasnick, W. D. (2011). End-of-life care: The time for a meaningful discussion is now. *Journal of Healthcare Management, 56*(6), 369–372.

Swartz, K. (2010, January 22). Projected costs of chronic diseases. *Health Care Cost Monitor,* 1–2. Retrieved March 26, 2012, from http://healthcarecostmonitor.thehastingscenter.org/kimberlyswartz/projected-costs-of-chronic-diseases/.

Vincent, G. K., & Velkoff, V. A. (2010). U.S. Census Bureau, U.S. Department of Commerce. *The next four decades—The older population in the United States: 2010–2050* (P25-1138). Retrieved March 26, 2012, from http://www.census.gov/prod/2010pubs/p25-1138.pdf.

Yong, P. L., Saunders, R. S., & Olsen, L. A. (Eds.). (2010). *The healthcare imperative: Lowering costs and improving outcomes: Workshop series summary.* Washington, DC: National Academies Press.

Part III

INTERDISCIPLINARY CASE STUDIES

Chapter **15**

Case Studies

Karen E. Arscott, DO, MSc, AOBNMM

INTRODUCTION

The basic desire of anyone involved in health care is to give patients the absolute best care possible. This care should be effective, efficient, and should not "break the bank," so to speak. In this day and age of multiple healthcare disciplines, there exists a great deal of overlap. So many providers can improve the living condition of a patient that often many different consultations are requested for the same individual. This can result in one provider assuming another provider is handling something, and important aspects of care fall through the cracks, or several practitioners order and follow the same issues, duplicating efforts. Other times the opposite situation occurs, where so much is needed that the person in charge of a patient's care does not know where to begin, and so no one is consulted. Neither of these scenarios is ideal for anyone involved. It has become apparent that in order to give a patient the best possible care, there must be interprofessional education, and thus interprofessional collegiality.

Interprofessional education (IPE) has become very popular in the United States (it has been relatively common in Canada for several years). IPE is an important subject for our healthcare system, because it provides a "win-win" situation. The patient receives the best possible care, and, because everyone involved is educated about the other healthcare disciplines involved in the patient's care, it is streamlined and cost is reduced.

This chapter is designed to pull a range of information together by presenting five possible patient cases. Following the cases are descriptions of how each discipline might work with the patient (and family) in the case. The patient case should be discussed in a group setting, taking into consideration the various healthcare disciplines available. The group discussions should take into consideration the possibility that all of the disciplines represented in this section may not be available in all locales, and also that other healthcare resources not discussed in this chapter may be available. Bearing in mind the availability of care, each group in this discussion should tailor the discussion to meet the standards for its own arena. This chapter can assist the student in seeing the practical uses of each healthcare discipline. Additionally, it will be obvious that there is a great deal of overlap between the various disciplines, and so excellent care for a patient can be provided adequately by fewer individuals, thus reducing cost. Each case can be changed slightly to alter what care is necessary; suggestions for changes in the case are made at the end of each discipline discussion. Remember that changing the basic case will more than likely change the recommendations by the healthcare providers. Each group should try to create a treatment plan using the ideas of the various disciplines in a variety of combinations to achieve the best care with the fewest healthcare providers. This chapter can be used in a game-like setting, with groups competing to create the best possible care and utilizing the fewest providers. Obviously, the group with the greatest coverage of care using the fewest providers wins—as does the patient in the real world.

Case 1: Home to Acute Care and Short-Term Care—Returning Home

P.O. is a 75-year-old female individual with Parkinson's disease and osteoporosis. She resides with her husband in a home adapted to her physical needs with respect to her limited ambulation ability. P.O. is cognitively fine, with an educational level of post-graduate degree. She experiences some depression related to decreased functioning, but she has had previous episodes of depression prior to onset of Parkinson's (7 years since first diagnoses, Parkinson's is currently stable). She has become more isolated and hesitant to socialize because of mobility concerns and some feelings of embarrassment over her condition. She is also concerned about her husband and his lack of activities on his own. P.O. has a history of back pain due to disc problems and osteoporotic fractures. She used to receive steroid injections, but now is on arthritis-strength acetaminophen to help manage back pain.

Currently, P.O. is returning home after shoulder replacement surgery and 2 weeks of rehabilitation in a residential rehab setting. The shoulder surgery was required because of a fall that resulted in multiple shoulder fractures.

P.O.'s husband is very anxious about P.O. falling and causing more surgical problems, and so has discouraged her from walking. As a result of her husband's legitimate fears, she is mainly restricted to a wheel chair and is increasingly weak and limited in her ability to stand or move herself from one location to another. Due to medication related to Parkinson's, P.O. at times experiences low blood pressure. Her doctor has suggested that she drink more fluids and increase salt intake, but she's hesitant to do that because it means she'll need more frequent trips to the restroom that require her husband's presence and assistance. Her husband is 80 years old and insists that he can maintain care for her at home, yet he must do a lot of lifting to help her in and out of chairs, the bed, the bathroom, and so on. P.O.'s husband assists with all her activities of daily living (ADLs), such as helping her get bathed and dressed.

The couple had been to short-term physical therapy and received short-term occupational therapy in the home to help adapt the home and give suggestions in terms of techniques and exercises. Their home has been adapted, but follow through with exercises to strengthen P.O.'s muscles has been limited. The couple is resistant to going to Parkinson's support group meetings, because seeing other people who may be worse will make them feel more despair over P.O.'s future. Their income is limited to social security funds. There is some family support available; however, the couple's two children are grown and still fully employed. Daily activity for P.O. usually consists of watching news programs on television, time with her husband and dog, some errands, and weekly gatherings with family that may include recreational activities, such as card and other table games, and dining out.

Discussion Question

1. What can you offer this patient and this couple?

Healthcare Administration Gerontologist

One of the first thoughts is whether the couple qualifies for medical assistance. If the skilled home health visits are no longer available, waiver programs are available where various services can be brought into the home for the patient and her husband. Also, there may be relief for the husband from the area agency on aging.

Possible programs available would be transportation to senior centers by county agencies. At the senior centers, the couple or the wife alone could receive meals and take part in activities such as art, chorus, cultural activities, cards, and bingo all at nominal costs. Meals on Wheels is an additional possible service program.

With an evaluation by a social worker, a referral for adult day care might be able to be obtained. At adult day care, the patient could receive therapy and socialization. While the patient is in adult day care, the husband could be involved in his own activities. In the case where one spouse is still employed, this would allow that spouse to continue working while the patient is well cared for and receiving companionship outside of the home.

If indicated, a coordinated care retirement community (CCRC) could be taken into consideration. This would include independent homes, assisted living homes, and skilled nursing or hospice facilities as the patient's needs change.

Financial Expert

The first thought in this case is the assumption that the patient is on Medicare. If the patient was hospitalized for less than 3 days, the patient may not fit rehabilitation criteria. This must be taken into consideration when reviewing options. If the patient was hospitalized for longer than 3 days, then she may qualify for either skilled or rehab services. The difference between these two services is as follows:

- *Skilled services*—less than 3 hours per day; therapy is less intense; goal is to go home or go to rehabilitation facility
- *Rehabilitation services*—3 hours per day of therapy; and is considered intense care

An important point to remember is that in rehabilitation facilities, the pharmacy benefit for Medicare may not be recognized and any pharmacy charges may become out-of-pocket expenses. The first 20 days of care, Medicare, plus a supplemental plan, will pay almost 100% of costs. After the first 20 days of care, Medicare, plus the supplemental insurance, will split the cost with the patient. After 20 additional days, insurance will pay 80%, and the patient will assume responsibility for 20%. Pharmacy costs could be very detrimental to the finances of a patient and spouse. Care must be taken to prescribe medication on the formulary if at all possible.

Gerontology Nurse

The discussion for this area is centered on visiting nurse involvement. In-home nursing services are not a viable option, because the patient is not housebound.

A managed healthcare center, which may be affiliated with an established healthcare organization, would afford this patient the opportunity for a holistic health assessment and recommended nursing services. Graduate students in advanced practice nursing programs may be able to offer services free of charge as part of their curriculum/practicum requirements.

Additionally, if this patient and family are eligible for Medicare/Medicaid assistance, enrollment in an adult day care center would afford nursing assessments and interventions at that location. There are various model programs available around the country.

Access to a support group for Parkinson's disease, along with psychological support, could assist P.O. and her husband to come to terms with her unfortunate condition.

Although it would be a difficult decision to make, the patient and her husband could consider moving to a continuous-care community (CCC). In this setting, the nursing services provided would match her physiologic, as well as psychosocial needs.

Many CCCs employ geriatric nurse practitioners who would be able to provide advanced-practice skills in the care of this patient and her husband.

Social Worker

The gerontological social worker would first and foremost carryout a biopsychosocial assessment. There are two parts to this assessment. The first step in an assessment such as is required for this couple would be a strengths assessment. This assessment would give the social worker an idea of the strengths of the patient and spouse. In addition to the strengths assessment, the social worker would be very interested in the couple's needs assessment. Does the couple even know what they need? The social worker would attempt to help the couple understand their needs.

The strengths assessment would involve a thorough investigation into the availability of support for the couple. In particular, it would look into who is available; how much time does someone have to give the couple; and what funds are available. The search would include family, both close and distant; social networks, such as Lion's Club, Knights of Columbus, and Freemasons; and spiritual support such as the church family. Can any of these people or organizations provide meals, transportation, or even company?

The social worker would look into what types of public transportation services are available for this couple. This can vary greatly depending upon the location of the couple. Some areas have an extensive public transportation system, and others are very lacking. The social worker in the area would know what is available.

Housekeeping needs are an area that the social worker can discuss with the couple. This can be a sensitive area, as this may be a point that the couple feels is personal and a sign of losing independence. This can be especially true of a woman who has cared for the home all her adult life and now finds herself unable to carry out simple chores. The social worker would assist the couple in completing the forms necessary for a referral to the area agency on aging.

The social worker would know about the availability of Meals on Wheels. This could help greatly with the nutrition needs of this couple.

A social work referral would absolutely be required for this case. The social worker has the tools to assist this couple in almost every facet of their lives. It is important to note that someone needs to recognize the need and request the referral.

Registered Dietitian

The request for the dietitian can be made in the acute care facility, the short-term care facility, or after the patient returns home. Once consulted, the dietitian would carry out the following comprehensive nutritional assessment:

- Food/nutrition-related history:
  - Find out usual intake, preferred foods/fluids, eating ability, food preparation ability, and the patient's dental condition
  - Anthropometric data—height/weight, usual body weight, and recent weight trends
  - Medical data—retrieve medical history from patient and family, as well as the patient's medical chart
  - Nutrition-focused physical findings—such as condition of skin, hair, eyes, and nails
  - Patient's general history
- Calculate nutrient needs based on the information obtained in the food/nutrition-related history. Must account for 1-day caloric needs related to Parkinson's Disease; increased calcium/vitamin D needs related to osteoporosis; increased fluid needs related to low blood pressure; and increased protein needs to promote continued healing and to prevent pressure sores from developing.
- Make appropriate referrals, if applicable, to such disciplines as occupational therapy, physical therapy, or speech-language pathology.
- Interventions:
  - Educate the patient and her husband in the importance of a balanced diet and of meeting the nutritional needs based on overall medical/physical condition.
  - Educate the patient and her husband on what a balanced diet is and which food/fluid choices contain calcium, vitamin D, and protein.

- Provide educational materials on the MyPlate, on nutrition, and on osteoporosis.
- Suggest the patient and husband speak with her primary care physician (PCP) about incorporating a multivitamin with minerals and a vitamin D supplement into daily regimen of medications. (The registered dietitian will contact the PCP to make these suggestions.)
- Communicate with a social worker about the need for Meals on Wheels or other meal-providing organization.

Psychologist

The first thought is to explore ways for the patient to become more self-sufficient. It appears the patient is allowing her health to deteriorate out of fear for her husband's health. This acceptance of self-decline may be multifactorial. If the husband's health diminishes, the patient herself will find herself without a caregiver. This fear may be adding to the other fear of watching her husband diminish in ability before her own eyes. The psychologist would investigate this point.

The psychologist would encourage the patient to follow the medical instructions. The patient needs to understand the danger in allowing herself to become dehydrated. She also needs to be encouraged to do the exercises as prescribed.

The couple's children need to be addressed and advised of their parents' needs. Encourage the children to visit more frequently. When the children visit, the couple should take advantage of this time to do what otherwise cannot be accomplished. For example, the time when the children visit can be used either as an opportunity to get both parents out of the house, or it can be used to give respite to the husband.

The psychologist would speak frankly with the couple and explain that what is happening is a natural process. The patient's disabilities are naturally occurring, and she should not be embarrassed by her lack of ability or loss of what once was. The use of humor can work wonders in a setting such as this one. Of course, all of this depends on the couple's acceptance of the ideas of the psychologist.

Oral Historian

An oral historian could enhance this couple's life by asking the right questions. Assisting the patient to regain some of her intellectual faculties would assist in her overall well-being. Perhaps through questioning and encouragement, the oral historian could persuade the woman patient to write her autobiography. This exercise would be good for recall and would allow the patient to reconsider her life and the impact she has had in various areas. Creating an autobiography may help the patient to escape her current situation, at least in her own thoughts.

Art Therapist

To begin, the art therapist would meet with the husband and wife in the home setting and assess the patient's and husband's psychosocial experiences, and address their perceptions of physical limitations, personal needs, and therapeutic goals. Given that the relationship between the husband and wife is a significant part of the dynamics that impact treatment engagement, the husband–wife relationship would need to be addressed during the initial interview and treatment-planning session. Since the couple has some mistrust of healthcare providers, the early emphasis would be on building a trusting, supportive relationship with the clients. Initial goals may emphasize building quality of life, while in a later phase of therapy when the therapeutic relationship is more strongly formed, issues related to grief and loss related to diminished function, and/or fears regarding the health limitations of both. Development of a life-book where images and stories are combined to review life accomplishments and provide a legacy to family may be considered.

When art tasks are offered, attention would be paid to the wife's capabilities and artistic interests and preferences. Tasks would be designed to be manageable and less dependent on fine motor control. Collage boxes with pre-cut images of different types (people, places, pets, things) may be provided so that images can be selected versus drawn. Selecting images, adhering images to paper, and discussing the meaning of the images would be emphasized. Material adaptations would be made as necessary to help build the wife's sense of mastery and to diminish despair in terms of her physical limitations. Soft, nonmessy clay, such as Model Magic, may be used to stimulate and exercise the client's hands, as she would create three-dimensional symbols related to therapeutic topics.

Given the couple's isolation, the art therapist may invite extended family participation in the art-based projects to motivate increased engagement with the parents and to foster acknowledgment and appreciation of parent accomplishments and contributions.

If home-based art therapy treatment is successful in increasing creative activity and engagement, and in increasing the valuing of such engagement, the art therapist may refer the couple to community-based art or art therapy activities to increase their socialization opportunities.

Funding for art therapy may be an issue, and the couple's family may need to assist financially to support home-based art therapy treatment. An art therapist may work for a home health agency or may be working as an independent practitioner with a related mental health license. Depending on the state, the referral source, personal insurance resources, and the license of the art therapist, art therapy may or may not be covered.

Music Therapist

The music therapist would complete an intake assessment at the first encounter. This assessment would involve a thorough history and any important background information. Also included in this assessment would be the patient's strengths and what style of music the patient prefers. The music therapist would speak with the physical therapist and the occupational therapist to determine if the patient has any limitations. After the music therapist has completed the assessment, he or she would create a plan for the patient (and family).

Some of the music strategies for this case might include using music that is strongly motivating to achieve the following:

- Improve socialization skills by including family members in singing songs or working with various rhythms. This exercise can be conducted once a week. The patient and family/friends would make music together in an informal manner.
- The use of scarves waved to music may be used to assist with strengthening muscles and improving general joint movement. This can be useful in patients who are limited in their ability to sing.
- The music therapist would help the patient with visual associations with respect to music and perhaps relate these to spiritual aspects of life.
- The music therapist may introduce the idea of dance. A short dance may be suggested, implementing elastic bands and capitalizing on rhythm and movement with familiar songs from the patient's youth.
- The music therapist may recommend the patient dance with her husband. This activity may improve intimacy, communication, and openness through dance.
- Perhaps the patient and her husband can play different instruments to create music.
- The use of music and imagery is often used to identify and help the patient express various difficult-to-talk-about emotions.

One of the goals of music therapy is to increase joy in the patient's life. Other goals include the transfer of skills for self-care and improved spiritual life. Ultimately, the music therapist would help the patient achieve best function in the following areas: cognitive, physical, spiritual, psychosocial, and personal (relationships).

Discussion Questions

1. How would the answers change if the patient lived alone?
2. How would the answers change if the spouse was equally compromised?
3. How would the answers change if one of the children agreed to take the parents into their home?

Case 2: Home to Acute Care and Then to Long-Term Care

A.C. is an 80-year-old woman with a significant history of atherosclerosis, repair of a thoracic aorta aneurysm dissection 5 years ago, smoking history of 120 pack years (quit with thoracic surgery), chronic obstructive pulmonary disease (COPD), and mental confusion. A.C. lives alone in a single-level apartment; a neighbor friend checks in on her daily.

Over the past year, A.C. has been found more and more disheveled by her friends, and her apartment is disorganized. She is on a calcium channel blocker and a diuretic for her hypertension. She does not receive any meals on a regular basis and her diet is in question. Her son and daughter-in-law do not live in the area, and A.C. is adamant about not leaving her home area.

One week ago, her friend found her in her home with a fever, cough, and increased mental confusion. She was taken to the hospital and diagnosed as having pneumonia. A.C. was treated and is now ready for discharge. Physically, she is weakened and requires assistance to ambulate, and she is confused with respect to place and time. A.C. knows who she is and wants to go home. Her son is requesting she be transferred to a nursing home and has already had her apartment emptied and prepared for new occupants.

Discussion Question

1. What can you offer this patient?

Healthcare Administration Gerontologist

The main focus would be for patient safety and an increased social community, such as in an assisted living facility with a special area for patients with dementia—an Alzheimer's unit or a specialized Alzheimer's facility.

An additional goal would be for the patient to have regular therapy to avoid physical deterioration.

Finance Expert

The financial aspect would involve whether the patient qualifies for nursing home placement based on state and federal qualifications.

Gerontology Nurse

Working with A.C. in a mutual interaction model, the need for assistance should be stressed. Given her immediate physical status, independent living, without the oversight of support services, would be detrimental to her quality of life and overall prognosis. With her admission to an assisted living or other skilled facility, A.C. would receive a holistic nursing assessment and an appropriate plan of care would be formulated.

Perhaps a continuous-care community would meet her immediate needs. Should her physical and cognitive statuses improve, she may be able to regain some degree of independence.

Social Worker

In this case, the social worker would speak to the son and then explain the situation to the patient. The social worker would act as a liaison between the patient and her son. An attempt would be made to acquire some of the patient's property from the apartment prior to it being emptied.

The social worker would talk to the patient about involving spiritual support. It would be important for the social worker to listen to the patient and her friends in an attempt to keep the patient connected to her support network.

Registered Dietitian

In this case, the consult for the dietitian would most likely occur at the long-term care facility. The registered dietitian at that facility would complete the following comprehensive nutritional assessment:

- Food/nutrition related history:
  - Find out usual intake, preferred foods/fluids, eating ability, food preparation ability, and the patient's dental condition
  - Anthropometric data—height/weight, usual body weight, and recent weight trends
  - Medical data—retrieve medical history from patient and family, as well as the patient's medical chart (including all labs, tests, history and physical exams [H&Ps], and discharge summary)
  - Nutrition-focused physical findings—such as condition of skin, hair, eyes, and nails
  - Patient's general history
- Calculate nutrient needs based on the information obtained in the food/nutrition-related history. Must account for 1-day increased caloric needs related to COPD; increased potassium needs related to diuretic; and increased protein needs to promote healing and to prevent pressure sores from developing.
- Make appropriate referrals, if applicable, to such disciplines as occupational therapy, physical therapy, or speech-language pathology.
- Spend extra one-on-one time discussing food/fluid preferences to encourage patient's feelings of independence and empowerment.
- Spend extra one-on-one time discussing dining location to encourage relationship-building interactions with others that may be going through the same transition issues.

The registered dietitian would recognize that having a routine of balanced meals served at the same time on a daily basis will enhance the patient's nutritional status and may even have a positive influence on overall medical and cognitive status.

- Interventions:
  - Honor patient's food/fluid and dining location preferences.
  - Encourage patient to communicate her preferences freely.
  - Adjust menus to include potassium-containing foods/fluids and monitor electrolytes.
  - Adjust menus to include increased calorie/protein items to aid in recovery back to baseline.
  - Educate patient on the importance of consuming as much of all foods/fluids offered to her as she can.
  - Recommend a multivitamin daily.

Psychologist

The psychologist would try to encourage the son to bring articles from the patient's home for her room in the nursing home. The psychologist would ask the patient how the nursing home could be made to feel like home. The psychologist would encourage the nursing staff to constantly ask questions and then supply the answers as a way to give the patient retraining with positive reinforcement. For example, staff could ask the patient, "Where is the dining room?" and before the patient answers, give the correct answer, such as, "That is correct; it is right down the hall and to the left." Help the patient feel like she is answering correctly using behavior modification training.

Oral Historian

Place the patient in a group to be interviewed. Perhaps include the patient's friends in the group. Ask the patient what kind of room she would like to live in while in the nursing home. The oral historian would ask questions in an attempt to help the patient think about her life. Working on an autobiography would help stimulate her thought processes.

Taking part in an informal project would help inspire her memory, through being asked questions like: "What would you do on a day like this?" "Where did you go?" "What kind of food did you eat?" "Who would you go with?"

The historian might get the patient involved in a community activity with her friends.

Art Therapist

The art therapist would try to schedule a meeting with the patient and the son to obtain more detailed information and history related to family relationships, personal history, functioning levels, and therapeutic goals. Given the strained relationship between patient and son, it would be important for the art therapist to explore the patient's and son's motivation levels for change and treatment engagement. If there is motivation for the patient and son to work on their relationship, art therapy tasks would be designed to foster communication. Simple art tasks, such as use of abstract symbols or lines to communicate, may be used to decrease anxiety regarding art production. Initial artworks could be exchanged and added to by the other party and exchanged again for further artistic work. The art therapist would observe how both parties would approach the art tasks, listen to what they have to say about symbols, and shape further interventions based on those observations.

If the son was not willing to be engaged in treatment, the focus of treatment would need to shift to the patient's adjustment to her new environment. Knowledge of the patient's strengths and accomplishments in life, and experiences with creativity would be utilized in treatment plan formulation. It is likely that the first steps in treatment would be to empower the patient and to support a sense of mastery in at least one area. For example, the art therapist may assist the patient in personalizing her room. Depending on the patient's willingness and ability to engage, the art therapist may act as the patient's "hands," and the patient would act as director of activity. The art therapist may work with the client to display personal objects or help her to create or select new imagery for her room. Art reproductions that relate to a person's generation, area of origin, or interests often stimulate memories and pleasurable responses. Providing the patient with options may provide some counterbalance to the patient's feeling of powerlessness over her choice of residence. When the therapeutic relationship has been established, creative projects to build mastery and/or life-book development to help the patient reflect on and celebrate memories and accomplishments could be approached. If the center provided group art therapy options, the patient may be encouraged to participate in those opportunities to increase socialization and improve quality of life.

Music Therapist

The music therapist would complete an intake assessment at the first encounter. This assessment would involve a thorough history and any important background information. Also included in this assessment would be any of the patient's strengths and what style of music the patient prefers. The music therapist would speak with the physical therapist and the occupational therapist to determine if the patient has any limitations. After the music therapist has completed the assessment, he or she would create a plan for the patient (and family).

Emphasis would be placed on, "Home is where the heart is!" and perhaps singing the Beatle's song "Let It Be" for spiritual support. The music therapist would emphasize breath control through singing using vocal exercises. The melodies used and the timbre (quality of the sound of the instrument) are very important. The therapist could have the patient strum an autoharp or play a kazoo. The therapist would conduct various rhythmic activities to help organize and energize the patient.

A great deal of time would be spent reminiscing with the patient. The therapist would use music to both help the patient deal with losses and also to assist in reality orientation. Perhaps the therapist would involve the patient in song writing to deal with losses. Ultimately, the music therapist would help ease some of the pain the patient is feeling, bring some joy back into her life, and help her express herself in a different manner.

Discussion Questions

1. How would the answers change if the patient still had an apartment?
2. What if the patient had a sibling or another child who was very caring and attentive and willing to bring this patient into his or her home?

Case 3: Home to Acute Care and Then to Short-Term Care

C.C. is an 82-year-old man with a history of hypertension and intermittent atrial fibrillation who lives alone in a small, ranch-style home. He is in remarkably good health and is very active with volunteering and swim exercise class. He has three children, including two daughters who live locally and are very attentive to him. Over the past 2 months, he has noticed a lack of appetite, change in bowel habits, and generalized fatigue. He did not mention the symptoms to his doctor or daughters due to a pending vacation with family. Upon return from his vacation, he told his daughters and his doctor that he was passing blood in his stool, had loose watery stools, and lower abdominal pain for a few weeks. He was hospitalized to work up his abdominal complaints while reversing the warfarin he was on for the intermittent atrial fibrillation. His colonoscopy showed a large sigmoid colon mass. He was scheduled for sigmoid resection surgery, which was carried out using laparoscopic technique. His postop course was complicated by several episodes of atrial fibrillation and a postop ileus. He was ready for discharge on postop day 8. After several days and weeks of poor oral intake, major surgery, and general deconditioning, he was unable to ambulate without assistance. Although his daughters wished to care for him at home, it was determined that he required around-the-clock attention until his strength returned. It was agreed that he should be transferred to a transitional care setting to return him to a self-care state. C.C. is in agreement with this suggestion as long as it will not be for too long.

Discussion Question

1. What can you offer this patient in a short-term care facility, and how would you prepare him for return to his home alone?

Healthcare Administration Gerontologist

The healthcare administrator would request an evaluation by a gerontological social worker—perhaps through the area agency on aging. This could potentially lead to the medical model adult day care. At adult day care, therapy would be provided, along with a sense of community. At adult day care, the patient would receive meals. Or, if adult day care is not possible, the area agency on aging could refer the patient to the area Meals on Wheels and/or transportation services to an area senior center.

This may be a time to mention the coordinated care retirement community to the patient and family. Even if the patient is not ready at this time, the time may arise when it would be a beneficial option for the patient.

Finance Expert

The point to keep in mind from this discipline is that the patient needs 3 days as an inpatient in an acute care facility to qualify for continued inpatient care at either a skilled nursing facility or a rehabilitation facility. The differences between a skilled care facility and a rehabilitation facility are:

- *Skilled nursing facility*—less than 3 hours/day of therapy, less intense; goal is to move on to rehabilitation facility when stronger or to go home if possible
- *Rehabilitation facility*—3 hours/day of therapy, very intense; goal is to go home after therapy is complete

Social Worker

The social worker would begin with a biopsychosocial assessment. The social worker would complete the forms for inpatient occupational therapy (OT) and physical therapy (PT).

The social worker would need to carry out another assessment and plan for home care when the patient is ready to return home. This assessment would require a strengths assessment first. This assessment would give the social worker an idea of the strengths of the patient and children. In addition to the strengths assessment, the social worker would be very interested in the family's needs assessment. Does the family even know what they need? The social worker would attempt to help the family understand their needs.

The strengths assessment would involve a thorough investigation into the availability of support for the patient. In particular, it would look into who is available; how much time does someone have to give the patient;

and what funds are available. The search would include family, both close and distant; social networks, such as Lion's Club, Knights of Columbus, or Freemasons; and spiritual support, such as the church family. Can any of these people or organizations provide meals, transportation, or even company?

The social worker would look into what types of public transportation services are available for this patient. This can vary greatly depending upon the location of the patient. Some areas have an extensive public transportation system, and others are very lacking. The social worker in the area would know what is available.

Housekeeping needs are an area that the social worker can discuss with the patient and family. This can be a sensitive area, as this may be a point that the patient feels is personal and a sign of losing independence. However, it is important that the home be kept clean and safe. The social worker would assist the patient in completing the forms necessary for a referral to the area agency on aging.

The social worker would know about the availability of Meals on Wheels. This could help greatly with the nutrition needs of this patient as he recovers.

A social work referral would be absolutely required for this case. The social worker has the tools to assist this patient in almost every facet of his life. It is important to note that someone needs to recognize the need and request the referral.

Registered Dietitian

The registered dietitian may be consulted in either the acute care facility or the short-term care facility. Upon consult request, the registered dietitian at that facility would complete the following comprehensive nutritional assessment:

- Food/nutrition-related history:
  - Find out usual intake, preferred foods/fluids, eating ability, food preparation ability, and the patient's dental condition
  - Anthropometric data—height/weight, usual body weight, and recent weight trends
  - Medical data—retrieve medical history from patient and family, as well as the patient's medical chart (including all labs, tests, H&Ps, and discharge summary)
  - Nutrition-focused physical findings—such as condition of skin, hair, eyes, and nails
  - Patient's general history

- Calculate nutrient needs based on the information obtained in the food/nutrition-related history. Must account for 1-day increased caloric needs and protein needs related to healing/recovery, and increased vitamin/mineral needs related to healing and recovery.
- Make appropriate referrals, if applicable, to such disciplines as occupational therapy, physical therapy, or speech-language pathology.
- Interventions:
  - Focus on regenerating nutritional status during stay in short-term care facility while providing education in preparation for return to home.
  - Honor patient's food/fluid preferences and dining locations.
  - Encourage patient to communicate preferences freely.
  - Adjust menus to include increased calories and increased protein to promote healing.
  - If oral intake of this menu plan is not adequate to meet the increased needs related to recovery, recommend an oral nutritional supplementation.
  - Educate patient and patient's daughters at every opportunity about the importance of achieving and maintaining nutritional status.
  - Offer verbal guidance and written educational materials on how to achieve adequate nutritional status.
  - Educate patient and patient's daughters on what to do if appetite does not return after return to home. Educate them about high calorie/high protein food/fluid choices as well as supplemental choices.
  - Referral to the local Meals on Wheels "fast track" program or other organized meal-delivery organization.

Psychologist

There is no obvious need for a clinical psychologist in this case. This patient is highly motivated and appears to have an adequate support system in place.

Oral Historian

The oral historian would focus on giving the patient a sense of community. What does he like to do? The oral historian may even consider suggesting doing some type of volunteer work while in the short-term care facility. The patient could be of great service reading to others in the facility.

While recuperating, the patient could begin to work on his autobiography.

Art Therapist

Although this patient will go to live at home after his rehabilitation care is complete, the art therapist would begin therapy in the inpatient setting. An initial assessment interview would be completed so that creative and expressive interests could be explored and established. Important questions to be asked would be:

- What resources are available at home?
- What do different things at home mean to the patient?
- Are there community center/senior center art services in his area?
- What level of motivation does the client have regarding attending and participating in community-based programs?
- If the patient is involved in a church or other place of worship, are there creative and social outlets available there?
- Is there a creative way the patient can give back to the community? Developmentally, it is important for the patient to find value for himself in the community.
- Can the patient find an opportunity for an intergenerational creative activity?

The time at the rehabilitation facility would be utilized to identify goals and resources that would support a high quality of life, including a feeling of integrity and a sense that he is a resource of creativity and wisdom for others. If time was available, the art therapist may spend some time reacquainting the patient with materials/crafts he has used in the past or to provide exposure to new creative and expressive options. Availability of art therapy services in the community depend on the art therapy resources available in those community settings.

Music Therapist

The music therapist would complete an intake assessment at the first encounter, probably during the short-term care stay. This assessment would involve a thorough history and any important background information. Also included in this assessment would be any of the patient's strengths and what style of music the patient prefers. The music therapist would speak with the physical therapist and the occupational therapist to determine if the patient has any limitations. After the music therapist has completed the assessment, he or she would create a plan for the patient (and family).

Some of the music strategies for this case might include using music that is strongly motivating to achieve the following:

- Improve socialization skills by including family members in singing songs or working with various rhythms. This exercise can be conducted once a week. The patient and family/friends can make music together in an informal manner. Include any children in the family. This can include group music therapy in the short-term care facility.
- The use of scarves waved to music may be used to assist with strengthening muscles and improving general joint movement. This can be useful in patients who are limited in their ability to sing.
- The music therapist would help the patient with visual associations with respect to music and perhaps relate these to spiritual aspects of life.
- Using music, the therapist can help the patient with relaxation/anxiety management skills.
- Improve verbal skills and interaction with family and friends. The music therapist will assist the patient with expressing feelings using music, either with singing or with the use of instruments or scarves.
- The music therapist may introduce the idea of dance. A short dance may be suggested, implementing elastic bands and capitalizing on rhythm and movement with familiar songs from the patient's youth.
- The music therapist may recommend the patient dance with his daughters. This activity may improve communication and openness through dance.
- Perhaps the patient and his daughters can play different instruments to create music.
- The use of music and imagery is often used to identify and help the patient express various difficult-to-talk-about emotions.
- Encourage the patient to attend concerts.
- Use music and reminiscing life-review songs to relax and lower blood pressure.
- One of the goals for the music therapist is to help with the patient's transition to home. Music and movement can assist in the rehabilitation of this patient.

Gerontology Nurse

Short-term medical care is definitely the right choice for C.C. at this time. Nursing oversight around the clock will be integral to his successful recovery.

Nursing assessment will identify immediate physiological needs and constant monitoring will ensure continued improvement. Subtle changes in the patient's condition will be identified and addressed early.

Discussion Question

1. How would the answers change if this patient had no family support?

Case 4: End-of-Life Care (A)

E.A. is a 76-year-old male. He has a past medical history significant for cerebrovascular disease. Three years ago, he suffered a mild cerebrovascular accident (stroke), which left him with mildly impaired cognition. Over the past 3 years, he and his wife have been able to continue to travel and enjoy their life together. His health is excellent, with only hypertension (well controlled on medication) and hypothyroidism (also controlled with medication). The extended family includes a daughter, a son, a daughter-in-law, and three grandchildren. All children and grandchildren are local and are available to help E.A. and his wife.

E. A. and his wife have long-term care insurance and living wills. E.A. has made it clear to all that he does not wish to be kept alive artificially, and his wife not only agrees, but feels the same. They are a spiritual couple and attend church regularly.

Four days ago, E.A. suffered a massive cerebral infarction. He is in the intensive care unit (ICU) in a coma. On physical exam, he appears to have lost the use of the right side of his body and his gag reflex. He is breathing on his own at this time. A decision about his care needs to be made, as the hospital is in need of the ICU bed if the decision is that he is not going to be resuscitated as per his living will.

Discussion Question

1. What are the options at this point?

Healthcare Administration Gerontologist

The main focus would be for patient comfort and family support.

Finance Expert

The financial aspect would involve whether the patient qualifies for hospice care based on state and federal qualifications.

Gerontology Nurse

With his admission to an inpatient hospice center, E.A. would receive a holistic nursing assessment and an appropriate plan of care would be formulated. This plan would include care for the family and their emotional needs as well.

Social Worker

In this case, the social worker would speak to the family and then, if appropriate, explain the situation to the patient. The social worker would act as a liaison between the patient, his family, and the hospice agency. An attempt would be made to acquire some of the patient's important possessions from home and have them brought to the hospice room to give it a sense of home. The social worker would talk to the patient and family about involving spiritual support.

Registered Dietitian

In this case, the consult for the dietitian would most likely occur at the hospice facility. The registered dietitian at that facility would complete the following comprehensive nutritional assessment:

- Food/nutrition-related history:
  - Find out usual intake, preferred foods/fluids, eating ability, food preparation ability, and the patient's dental condition
  - Anthropometric data—height/weight, usual body weight, and recent weight trends
  - Medical data—retrieve medical history from patient and family, as well as the patient's medical chart (including all labs, tests, H&Ps, and discharge summary)
  - Nutrition-focused physical findings—such as condition of skin, hair, eyes, and nails
  - Patient's general history
- Calculate nutrient needs based on the information obtained in the food/nutrition-related history.
- Spend extra one-on-one time discussing food/fluid preferences.

The registered dietitian would recognize that having a routine of balanced meals served at the same time on a daily basis will enhance the patient's nutritional status and may even have a positive influence on overall medical and cognitive status.

· Interventions:
  - Honor patient's food/fluid preferences.
  - Encourage patient to communicate his preferences freely.
  - Educate patient on the importance of consuming as much of all foods/fluids offered to him as he can.

Psychologist

The psychologist would try to encourage the family to bring articles from the patient's home for his room in the hospice center. Ask the patient and/ or family how the nursing home could be made to feel like home.

Oral Historian

The oral historian would ask questions in an attempt to help the patient think about his life. Working on an autobiography can help stimulate his thought processes. If the patient is unable to respond, the family can work on an autobiography in the patient's room with the patient participating as much as possible.

A suggestion may be made for the family to bring in one of the patient's old address books. The family can go through it while discussing different people in the patient's life. Perhaps the family can document thoughts that E.A. has about different persons who have touched his life.

Art Therapist

The art therapist would try to schedule a meeting with the patient and the family to obtain more detailed information and history related to family relationships, personal history, and functioning levels. Simple art tasks, such as use of abstract symbols or lines to communicate may be used to decrease anxiety regarding art production. Initial artworks could be exchanged and added to by the other party, and exchanged again for further artistic work. The art therapist would observe how both parties would approach the art tasks, as well as listen to what they have to say about the symbols, and shape further interventions based on those observations.

The art therapist may assist the patient in personalizing his room. Depending on the patient's willingness and ability to engage, the art therapist may act as the patient's "hands," and the patient would act as director of activity. The art therapist may work with the patient to display personal objects or help him to create or select new imagery for his room. Art reproductions that relate to person's generation, area of origin, or interests often stimulate memories and pleasurable responses. Providing the patient with options may provide some counterbalance to the patient's feeling of powerlessness. When the therapeutic relationship has been established, creative projects to build mastery and/or life-book development to help the patient reflect on and celebrate memories and accomplishments could be approached.

The art therapist may discuss the concept of creating hand casts of the patient. This sculpture may help with closure for both the family and the patient. It is said that the family members are bidding farewell to one loved one, and the dying patient is saying goodbye to many loved ones. Hand casting is a way of leaving a piece of oneself behind with the understanding that one is not going to be forgotten. The sculpture may include the patient's hands alone or intertwined with a family member's hands.

Music Therapist

The music therapist would complete an intake assessment at the first encounter. This assessment would involve a thorough history and any important background information. Also included in this assessment would be any of the patient's strengths and what style of music the patient prefers. After the music therapist has completed the assessment, he or she would create a plan for the patient (and family).

Emphasis would be placed on, "Home is where the heart is!" and perhaps singing the Beatle's song "Let It Be" for spiritual support. The music therapist would emphasize breath control through singing using vocal exercises. The melodies used and the timbre (quality of the sound of the instrument) are very important. The patient might strum an autoharp or play a kazoo. The therapist would conduct various rhythmic activities to help organize and energize the patient.

A great deal of time would be spent reminiscing with the patient. The therapist would use music to help the patient deal with losses and also to assist in reality orientation. Perhaps the therapist would involve the patient in song writing to deal with losses. Ultimately, the music therapist would help ease some of the pain the patient is feeling, bring some joy back into his life, and help him express himself in a different manner. The therapist would also support the family and include them in all areas of music therapy.

Note

It should be noted that all of the answers are subject to change based on the ability of the patient to participate and the desire of the family to participate. All caregivers would be very aware of what is best for the patient and the family during this time of transition.

Case 5: End-of-Life Care (B)

R.S. is a 74-year-old female with a long-standing history of idiopathic cardiomyopathy. She has had a general decline in her cardiac health over the past 15 years, with a relatively rapid decline over the past 3 months. Ten days ago she developed her usual/intermittent pulmonary edema and was brought to the hospital via ambulance for intravenous diuresis and oxygen. Since this has happened frequently in the past and has always resolved with relatively little treatment, she was treated in the emergency room and admitted to the ICU. She was given medicine to help her heart beat stronger and other medicine to help remove the build-up of fluid. After 48 hours, R.S. had improved and was moved to the telemetry floor. An attempt was made to wean her off of the medicine that helped her heart beat better. The weaning of medicine failed due to probable worsening of the heart muscle. Every time the medicine was reduced, her heart went into failure and she was so weakened that she could not get out of the bed.

R.S. has a husband, two daughters, and a son. Her family is supportive, and although they are not ready to lose her, they want to do what is best for their wife and mother. A meeting was held with the cardiologist, and it was decided that the time had come to stop the heart medicine and allow R.S. to pass.

Discussion Question

1. What are the options now?

Healthcare Administration Gerontologist

The main focus would be for patient comfort and family support. The patient and family would need to discuss whether she should go into an inpatient hospice or receive outpatient hospice care.

Finance Expert

The financial aspect would involve whether the patient qualifies for inpatient or outpatient hospice care based on insurance and state and federal qualifications.

Gerontology Nurse

With her admission to an inpatient hospice center or upon transfer home and acceptance into an outpatient hospice program, R.S. would receive a holistic nursing assessment and an appropriate plan of care would be formulated. This plan would include care for the family and their emotional needs as well.

Social Worker

In this case, the social worker would speak to the family and the patient to help determine their wishes. The social worker would act as a liaison between the patient, her family, and the hospice agency. An attempt would be made to acquire some of the patient's important possessions from home and have them brought to the hospice room to give it a sense of home—if inpatient care was deemed necessary. If outpatient hospice care was determined to be in everyone's best interests, the social worker would coordinate the care, not just care for the patient, but also care for the family. The spouse may need services (e.g, hot meals delivered) in addition to the patient.

The social worker would talk to the patient and family about involving spiritual support and make whatever arrangements are necessary.

Registered Dietitian

In this case, the consult for the dietitian would most likely occur at the hospice facility, if inpatient services are chosen, or either prior to discharge or in the patient's home if outpatient hospice care is the final decision. The registered dietitian would complete the following comprehensive nutritional assessment:

- Food/nutrition-related history:
  - Find out usual intake, preferred foods/fluids, eating ability, food preparation ability, and the patient's dental condition
  - Anthropometric data—height/weight, usual body weight, and recent weight trends
  - Medical data—retrieve medical history from patient and family as well as the patient's medical chart (including all labs, tests, H&Ps, and discharge summary)
  - Nutrition-focused physical findings—such as condition of skin, hair, eyes, and nails
  - Patient's general history

- Calculate nutrient needs based on the information obtained in the food/nutrition-related history.
- Spend extra one-on-one time discussing food/fluid preferences.

The registered dietitian would recognize that having a routine of balanced meals served at the same time on a daily basis will enhance the patient's nutritional status and may even have a positive influence on overall medical and cognitive status.

- Interventions:
  - Honor patient's food/fluid preferences.
  - Encourage patient to communicate her preferences freely.
  - Educate patient on the importance of consuming as much of all foods/fluids offered to her as she can.

Psychologist

The psychologist would try to encourage the family to bring articles from the patient's home to her room in the hospice center. Ask the patient and/or family how the hospice room could be made to feel like home. If outpatient hospice care was decided, the psychologist would work with the patient and the family to reach a point of comfort and acceptance. The psychologist would encourage family interaction around comfortable situations.

Oral Historian

The oral historian would ask questions in an attempt to help the patient think about her life. Work on an autobiography would help stimulate her thought processes. If the patient is unable to respond, the family can work on an autobiography in the patient's room with the patient participating as much as possible.

A suggestion may be made for the family to use one of the patient's old address books as a memory stimulus. The family can go through it while discussing different people in the patient's life. Perhaps the family can document thoughts that R.S. has about different persons who have touched her life.

Art Therapist

The art therapist would schedule a meeting with the patient and the family to obtain more detailed information and history related to family relationships, personal history, and functioning levels. Simple art tasks, such as use of abstract symbols or lines to communicate, may be used to decrease anxiety regarding art production. Initial artworks could be exchanged and added to by the other party and exchanged again for further artistic work. The art therapist would observe how both parties would approach the art tasks, as well as listen to what they have to say about symbols and shape further interventions based on those observations.

The art therapist may assist the patient in personalizing her room. Depending on the willingness of the patient and her ability to engage, the art therapist may act as the patient's "hands," and the patient would act as director of activity. The art therapist may work with the client to display personal objects or help her to create or select new imagery for her room. Art reproductions that relate to a person's generation, area of origin, or interests often stimulate memories and pleasurable responses. Providing the patient with options may provide some counterbalance to the patient's feeling of powerlessness. When the therapeutic relationship has been established, creative projects to build mastery and/or life-book development to help the patient reflect on and celebrate memories and accomplishments could be approached.

The art therapist may discuss the concept of creating hand casts of the patient. This sculpture may help with closure for both the family and the patient. It is said that the family members are bidding farewell to one loved one, and the dying patient is saying goodbye to many loved ones. Hand casting is a way of leaving a piece of oneself behind with the understanding that one is not going to be forgotten. The sculpture may include the patient's hands alone or intertwined with a family member's hands.

Music Therapist

The music therapist would complete an intake assessment at the first encounter. This assessment would involve a thorough history and any important background information. Also included in this assessment would be any of the patient's strengths and what style of music the patient prefers. After the music therapist has completed the assessment, he or she would create a plan for the patient (and family).

Emphasis would be placed on, "Home is where the heart is!" and perhaps singing the Beatle's song "Let It Be" for spiritual support. The music therapist would emphasize breath control through singing using vocal exercises. The melodies used and the timbre (quality of the sound of the instrument) are very important. The patient might strum an autoharp or play a kazoo. The therapist would conduct various rhythmic activities to help organize and energize the patient.

A great deal of time would be spent reminiscing with the patient. The therapist would use music to help the patient deal with losses and also to assist in reality orientation. Perhaps the therapist would involve the patient and family in song writing to deal with losses. Ultimately, the music therapist would help ease some of the pain the patient is feeling, bring some joy back into her life, and help her express herself in a different manner. The therapist would also support the family and include them in all areas of music therapy.

Note

It should be noted that all of the answers are subject to change based on the ability of the patient to participate and the desire of the family to participate. All caregivers would be very aware of what is best for the patient and the family during this time of transition.

SUMMARY

In 2010, the World Health Organization (WHO) created a document entitled *Framework for Action on Interprofessional Education & Collaborative Practice* (Health Professions Network Nursing and Midwifery Office within the Department of Human Resources for Health, 2010). The first Key Message within this document states, "The World Health Organization (WHO) and its partners recognize interprofessional collaboration in education and practice as an innovative strategy that will play an important role in mitigating the global health workforce crisis."

It is now upon the leaders of health care to take this approach and make it happen in the real healthcare world.

REFERENCE

Health Professions Network Nursing and Midwifery Office within the Department of Human Resources for Health. (2010). *Framework for action on interprofessional education & collaborative practice*. Geneva, Switzerland: World Health Organization. Retrieved March 26, 2012, from http://whqlibdoc.who.int/hq/2010/WHO_HRH_HPN_10.3_eng.pdf.

Index